Daisy
Princess of Pless
1873 - 1943

Daisy Princess of Pless

Charcoal drawing by John Singer Sargent, 1912

Daisy
Princess of Pless
1873 - 1943

A Discovery

W. John Koch

National Library of Canada Cataloguing in Publication Data

Koch, W. John.
   Daisy Princess of Pless

    Includes bibliographical references and index.
    ISBN 0-9731579-0-9

    1. Pless. Daisy, Fürstin von, 1873-1943

    2. Princesses – Germany – Biography.

    I. Title.

D413.P55K62 2002a   943.09'092   C2002-905018-9

First Printing in April 2002

Copyright © 2002 W. John Koch

Published by:

BW   BOOKS by W. JOHN KOCH
JK   Publishing

Cover design by Art Design Printing Inc.
Printed and bound in Canada by Art Design Printing Inc.

Cover (front): *Princess Daisy of Pless*, painted by A. Galli in Fürstenstein, June, 1914; (back): Castle Fürstenstein in the 1990s, Daisy of Pless with her three sons at *Ma Fantaisie*, Fürstenstein, 1914.

Contents

PLEASE NOTE
the following important changes
effective August 7, 2002:

ISBN 0-9731579-0-9
Copyright© 2002 W. John Koch

Published by:
BOOKS by W. JOHN KOCH
Publishing
11666 - 72 Avenue
Edmonton, AB T6G 0C1, Canada

Telephone: (780) 436 0581
Fax: (780) 436 0581
E-mail: wjohnkoch@shaw.ca
URL: http://members.shaw.ca/wjohnkoch

FOR MY WIFE MARIA

Whoever has lived long enough,
has experienced something of everything,
and of everything the opposite.

Charles Talleyrand
(1754 - 1838)

About the Author

John Koch was born in the German province of Silesia and spent his childhood only a half hour's streetcar ride from Castle Fürstenstein, the residence of Daisy of Pless for most of her married life.

Following World War II, John studied history at the University of Würzburg before emigrating to Canada in 1954. After graduating from the University of British Columbia with a Master's degree in social work in 1960, he worked in the social welfare and health care field in British Columbia, Saskatchewan and, from 1964 to 1987, in Alberta. Since retiring, John has devoted his time to writing.

John published articles in professional journals in Canada, the United States, and in Poland. He is the author of an illustrated volume about *Schloss Fürstenstein* (since 1945 Zamek Książ). He also published the German version of the biography of Daisy Princess of Pless, *Daisy von Pless, Fürstliche Rebellin*. Both books were published in Germany in 1989 and 1990.

In 1995, John and his wife Maria completed *To the Town that Bears Your Name*, a previously unpublished story by the German-Canadian pioneer and financier Martin Nordegg, written for his daughter in 1912. Translated from German by Maria with a brief biography written by John, this book was published by Brightest Pebble Publishing Co. in 1995. It was followed by the German edition, *Zur Stadt, die Deinen Namen trägt*, in 1996. In 1997, Brightest Pebble published John's biography of Martin Nordegg, *Martin Nordegg, the Uncommon Immigrant*.

Daisy Princess of Pless Pless, A Discovery offers the English version of John's earlier biography *Daisy von Pless, Fürstliche Rebellin*. It is not a translation of the German version, but an adaptation designed for the English-speaking reader.

Silesia before and after World War I

Until the end of World War I, the entire Pless estate in Lower Silesia (Waldenburg) and Upper Silesia (Pless) was located in Germany.

Following the Upper Silesian Plebiscite of 1921, parts of Upper Silesia (shaded) including the major part of the Pless estate in the district of Pless and Rybnik were ceded to Poland.

After World War II, all of Silesia (except the district of Görlitz west of the river Neisse) became part of Poland.

Foreword

One late evening in October 1975 I jumped on the Greyhound bus in my Canadian hometown, Edmonton, in Alberta. I needed a break from my job. I had decided to drift across the western United States on a Greyhound. During the long hours of travel, I observed the changing country; I closed my eyes to think, and to sleep; and I read Barbara Tuchman's fascinating World War I story *The Zimmermann Telegram*.[1]

Scanning the index, my eyes stopped at the name of Daisy of Pless. This was the legendary princess who had lived in the magnificent Castle Fürstenstein[2] on the outskirts of Waldenburg, my birthplace in Silesia, in Germany.[3] Many years ago, my parents had taken me to this fabulous castle with its famous terraces high on a rocky ridge above a deep gorge, but I had never seen Princess Daisy. My mother, who had done some charitable work as a teenager during World War I, had been introduced to the Princess. My first schoolteacher told many stories about the Princess's beauty and how much she had done for the poor and the working people. On the streets and in the courtyards of the miners flats, where I used to play with other boys, I heard their mothers talk about *Our Daisy*.

We moved away from Waldenburg in 1936. In 1943 I was drafted into the army, and I did not return to Silesia after I escaped from a French prisoner of war camp in spring of 1946. A few months later, I found my mother in a remote village near Bremen, where she had been moved to, when the German population of Silesia was transferred to West Germany and the province had become part of the reborn Poland. I never thought about Daisy Pless anymore; not as a student in Bavaria; not after I emigrated to Canada in 1954. Now, however, in a Greyhound

---

1   Barbara W. Tuchman. *The Zimmermann Telegram*
2   Since 1945 Zamek Książ in Poland.
3   Since 1945 Wałbrzych in Poland.

rolling through the bare wheatfields of Eastern Washington with Barbara Tuchman's book in my hands, I became intrigued with Daisy Pless once more. I had not known that Daisy had published her memoirs from which Barbara Tuchmann had taken a few quotes.

Without a destination in mind, I let the Greyhound carry me across the country, eventually ending up in San Francisco. I stayed a few days to explore the city and its buildings. In the public library I was astonished to find a copy of Daisy's memoirs *Princess Daisy of Pless by Herself*,[4] a heavy tome of 529 pages. I hardly dared ask, but I did in the end; and such were the times, that the library staff let me take the book home to Canada with the promise that I would return it by mail, once I had read it. I also found out that Daisy Pless had published two more volumes of her diaries,[5] which I found in the public library in Vancouver, British Columbia a week later. Here again, I was granted permission to take the two books home. For starters, I photocopied all the books – something still permissible in 1975.

Later on, I managed to find the second and third volumes through book search businesses in New York and even discovered another edition of the diaries[6] in London. Only the first edition of the first volume, the most important one, well annotated with numerous footnotes, which I had discovered in San Francisco, remained unavailable. However, I seemed to have plenty of material for the article I intended to write about the social reform work of the Princess of Pless for a professional journal here in North America. I went to work, and read all three volumes from beginning to end!

Before I had finished reading the first volume of the diaries, I decided that rather than an article, I should write the biography of Princess Daisy of Pless. I began my research.

Up to that time, I had written a number of articles, but never a complete book. I had never done such intensive research; I had never realized what an adventure research for a biography could be. Daisy of Pless had died in 1943 at the age of seventy. Thirty-five years later, most of those who really knew her were no longer living. Against my expectations, but with increasing expertise in locating people whose current whereabouts were totally obscure, I found the two surviving sons of Daisy, the older in London, the younger in Spain. I put an ad into the

---

4   Princess Daisy of Pless. Daisy Princess of Pless by Herself. London: John Murray, 1929.

5   Princess Daisy of Pless. *Better Left Unsaid*. New York: Dutton, 1931. Princess Daisy of Pless. *What I Left Unsaid*. London: Cassell, 1936.

6   *The Private Diaries of Daisy Princess of Pless - 1873 - 1914*. Edited by D. Chapman-Huston. London: John Murray, 1950.

little monthly for the former citizens of Waldenburg. The first reply came from the nephew of Daisy's cousin Ena FitzPatrick; he lived, of all places, in Calgary, a city only three hours away from Edmonton. Soon, over a hundred old Fürstensteiners got in touch with me. They all helped enormously, as did many public and private archives in several countries. A look at the *Acknowledgements* will tell the reader how far I spread the net to discover the reminiscences, written, verbal and pictorial, about Daisy and her times.

Among the resource persons was Seymour Leslie in Ireland, cousin of Winston Churchill and uncle-by-marriage of Daisy's brother George. He opened the door to a publisher in London for me; but this gentleman insisted on a sensationalist Daisy Pless biography, which I was not prepared to deliver. Another publisher understood my aim to create an image of Daisy that was more than that of a beautiful princess. My confidence was strengthened when a descendant of the Scottish historian George Trevelyan became my editor. I was happy, but a year later, I lost my publisher. After his death, his son changed the entire publishing program and my manuscript about Daisy was one of the victims.

I turned my attention to Germany. There were still numerous smaller publishers of high reputation in that country. What I did not realize was that many of them were constantly absorbed by larger houses, that in turn amalgamated with other major houses. One of the largest publishers at that time asked for my visit. I remember the excitement when I made the appointment and my astonishment when I was specifically told not to park in front of his building and enter only through the back door in the courtyard. When I had done so, I found out that the bailiff had just left through the front door.

One day I received a letter from a gentleman in London who wrote that he had spent his childhood next to Daisy's Castle Fürstenstein. His father had been the chef and photographer there and he had thousands of photographs his father had taken during two decades. This was one of the contacts that developed into a friendship out of my research activities; it also helped me to write my first book, an illustrated book about Fürstenstein.[7] One day I was called to the largest publishing house in Munich. I was wondering why, as I had never contacted this publisher before. As it turned out, this firm had absorbed a number of smaller publishers, and among the material they "inherited" was a copy of my first English version of *Daisy of Pless*. The chief editor liked the Daisy Pless

---

7   W. John Koch. *Schloss Fürstenstein: Erinnerungen an einen schlesischen Adelssitz* – Eine Bilddokumentation. Würzburg: Bergstadtverlag Johann Gottlieb Korn, 1989.

biography, and within one day, I signed the contract that led to the publication of the German version of this biography in 1990.[8]

Actually, I had just returned from Poland, where I had obtained a great deal of documentation without which Daisy's biography would have remained rather incomplete; especially the last chapter would have been impossible to write without the material I had brought back from Castle Pless[9] in Upper Silesia. I had, of course known all along about this rich source in the archives in Pless, but these were still Communist times, and repeated attempts to receive permission for access had been denied by the central office of the National Archives in Warsaw.

In January 1988, I began my preparations for one last assault on the archives of Castle Pless. I had several friends in Poland who all helped me with letters of support and more direct interventions. They included Mr. Ryszard Wasita, publisher of one of the foremost Polish periodicals for which I had written several articles; Dr. Alfons Szyperski, local historian of the town of my birth located next to Castle Fürstenstein; Mag. Sylwia Kawwa, director of Castle Fürstenstein; and Mag. Mieczysław Karczewski, the Deputy Minister of Social Welfare for Poland.

Dr. Janusz Ziembiński, director of Castle Pless was another of my allies. He had told me to come to Pless immediately, although I had failed to even get a hearing in Warsaw. He also told me to send my friend, the Deputy Minister of Social Welfare, to the National Archives in Warsaw at precisely 11 A.M. the next morning and be prepared to speak for me. In Pless at 11 o'clock the next morning, I sat next to the director of Castle Pless and witnessed the endless, at times furious debate, he had over the telephone with his boss at the National Archives in Warsaw. After one hour, he hung up and said to me with a broad smile, "now we can get started" and introduced me to the archivist Dr. Janusz Kruczek. With Dr. Ziembiński's help and that of my other friends, especially the forceful deputy minister, my assault on the National Archives in Warsaw had succeeded!

Daisy von Pless - Fürstliche Rebellin received very positive reviews in Germany. I was ready to proceed with the English version, but two other book projects and the production of a video, all here in Canada, occupied my time for the next eight years. I had almost forgotten about the plan of an "English Daisy," but after the experiences of writing two other books and co-producing a video, and now having the time to devote to this English edition, I dug out the original, unpublished English and the

---

8   W. John Koch. *Daisy von Pless: Fürstliche Rebellin.* Frankfurt/M - Berlin, 1990.

9   Since 1945 Zamek Pszczyna.

later published German versions and set out to create a somewhat different Daisy biography, written with the English reader in mind. This book is not a translation of the German biography into English, although I have kept much of the original structure, which did not present a strictly chronological story of Daisy's life. There were valid reasons for this approach.

The many roles Daisy fulfilled, the distinct goals she set for herself, and the many different activities she pursued, did not occur one after the other. In this biography, I therefore divided Daisy's life by the roles and pursuits she chose, rather than by the chronology of events. Although unusual, this seemed the logical way to put Daisy of Pless and her complex personality into clear profile. The large number of excerpts from Daisy's diaries is intended to serve the same purpose. This approach, which includes a good deal of seemingly minor detail, was purposely chosen, because Daisy's humanitarian projects and political activities were even in her lifetime largely unknown, often disregarded, or even declared as lies, and today, they are almost totally forgotten.

Contrary to her image during her lifetime and afterwards in literature, Daisy was more than just one of the most beautiful women of Europe during the Edwardian era. She had a rich life and, even though she lived as a married woman in an extremely traditional milieu, her personal life and her decisions cannot be called conventional. Daisy had her ideals and goals, but her life did not follow a straight line. She was the happy, carefree young Englishwoman; she was the beautiful rich princess and the wife of one of the wealthiest heirs in Imperial Germany; and she was the glamorous hostess of Castle Fürstenstein, which under her reign became the preferred rendezvous of Europe's royalty and high aristocracy. Enduring an unhappy marriage, she turned her energy and talents to humanitarian pursuits and became a social reformer; she fought for peace by entering the sphere of international politics; King Edward VII was her fatherly friend; the German Emperor Wilhelm II was also her friend. During World War I, which Daisy spent in Germany, she worked as a nurse in hospitals and on hospital trains; as a divorced woman, she published her memoirs that were widely read in England, the United States, and in the German-speaking countries on the Continent. Enormous suffering became part of her life; since the birth of her third son, Daisy was not well, and after 1920, she became increasingly incapacitated and finally totally dependent on the care of others.

She counted as one of England's most beautiful Edwardian women, but circumstances forced her to spend the two world wars in "enemy territory." She never became a good German or was accepted as such, no matter how hard she tried.

This biography of Princess Daisy of Pless is based on a critical review of her published and unpublished diaries and a thorough research of public and private sources, a surprising number of which have survived the catastrophic events of two world wars, especially World War II and its aftermath, which changed the political map of the eastern half of Germany where Daisy Pless spent the greater part of her life. The documentary material for the biography was much enriched through private written and verbal reminiscences of family members, of friends, and of a number of Daisy's contemporaries and their descendants and, last not least, my knowledge of the places and locations where Daisy of Pless evolved into the socially and politically progressive personality who, as a member of her class and especially as a woman, was far ahead of her times.

I chose *Princess Daisy of Pless - A Discovery* as the title for this biography. The quest and search for source material that led me through several countries was an experience of discovery in itself. So was writing Daisy's biography which became another process of discovery, now primarily of her personality and character. May the reader also enter a road of discovery after opening this book.

W. John Koch
March 2002
Edmonton, Alberta, Canada

* * * * * *

Addenda

Emperors, Kings, Princes, etc.

Even though I was born a citizen of a republic, I grew up with a great deal of respect for the monarchy and its institutions. Naturally, I have capitalized Emperor, King, Prince, Princess, etc. all my life, when only writing about "the King" when I spoke of King Edward VII, or "the Emperor" when referring to Emperor Wilhelm II and, of course "the Princess" when I devoted an entire book to Daisy Princess of Pless. I found it most difficult to follow the modern dictum of using lowercase in such instances and, in the end, I chose to remain with the traditional spelling. Of course, the modern spelling was capably explained to me by my editor, but this was one of the very few instances where I did not follow her advice.

Footnotes

This book includes many footnotes with references to the sources of quotations. The majority of these refer to the various volumes of the diaries of Daisy of Pless. In order to avoid unnecessary clutter and repetition, the following abbreviations are used:

DPH: *Daisy of Pless by Herself*
BLU: *Better Left Unsaid*
WLU: *What I Left Unsaid*
DPP: *The Private Diaries of Daisy Princess of Pless*
DUD: *Unpublished Diaries of Daisy of Pless*

Acknowledgements

When I began my research for this biography, I knew very little about Daisy of Pless. I had heard that she had been very famous in her time; but when I was in my teens, there were only stories of the type fairytales are made of, and anecdotes, some charming, some nasty, that were left of the memory of Princess Daisy of Pless. In the course of my research, I gathered many facts and stories about people, places, and events. Above all I realized that much of the era, which had only ended a dozen years before I entered this world, had rapidly faded into history; and this was especially true of the world of royalty and aristocracy, although the world of the common man had also changed a great deal. No wonder that Daisy of Pless seemed forgotten for all the time to come.

I had hoped to discover the true Daisy of Pless and her world and understand why both had so utterly and quickly disappeared. When I completed this biography, I felt that I understood this past world so much better. As with any author writing a biography, my subject Daisy of Pless and her world came nearer and nearer out of the past as did many other people of relevance. For that I have to thank a great many people in several countries who helped me so much during the years of my research..

First of all, I wish to express my deep gratitude to the late Hans Heinrich XVII Count of Hochberg and Fourth Prince of Pless, who gave me many hours of his time offering me advice, encouragement, and after having read the first English version of this biography very shortly before his death, his approval. After his death, his wife Mrs. Mary Pless, now Lady Mary Ashtown continued to assist me on numerous occasions, often with material of critical importance; I thank her very much for that.

An often delightful, very productive correspondence stretching over several years, and a couple of meetings with Alexander, Count of Hochberg and Fifth Prince of Pless were extremely helpful; his last letter to me arrived days before his death. I also wish to thank the current head of the House of Hochberg, Bolko Graf von Hochberg and Sixth Prince of Pless in Munich, and other members of the House of Hochberg.

The following persons[10] contributed with their personal reminiscences, photographs, letters, and documents. To all of them, I express my appreciation.

CANADA: E. R. FitzPatrick; Jean Wessel.

IRELAND: Anita Leslie; Seymour Leslie; Lady Ursula Vernon.

FRANCE: Ena FitzPatrick; Margrit Willi.

GERMANY: Luise Adler; Martha Babel; Emma Berger; Gertrud Bilkowski; Frieda Bonke; Ehrengard, Baronin von Brockdorff; Helga Buss; Dr. George Cord; Ilse, Freifrau von Dobeneck; Irene Ecklebe; Johanna Fengler; Erna Franz; Artur Gläser; Gisela Graff-Höffgen; Walter Grehl; Margarete Hach; Annemarie Hanke; Edmund, Fürst Hatzfeldt; Margot Hielscher; Erhard Hötzel; Erich Hobusch; Walter Irrgang; Käthe Karuga; Jutta Klinggräf; Lieselotte Klose; Margarete Kobelt; Walter Koschnitz; Gerhard Kubatz; Alois Lindenau; Karl, Fürst zu Löwenstein-Wertheim-Rosenberg; Margarete Menzel; Tatiana, Fürstin von Metternich-Winneburg; Renate Müller; Dr. Hans Müller-Arends; Carl Päschke; Walter Päschke; Dr. Hermann Peters; Dr. Anton Ritthaler; Ina Rost; Nikolaus, Fürst zu Salm-Salm; Franziska Schal; Heinrich Scholz; Professor Dr. Eberhard G. Schulz; Charlotte Schulzik; Maria von Stumm; Professor Dr. Anneliese Thimme; Renate, Gräfin von Waldersee; Paul Joseph, Graf Wolff-Metternich; Lucia Zimmermann; Dorothea Zivier.

ITALY: Alphons, Fürst Clary Aldringen; Dr. Leonore, Gräfin von Lichnowsky.

POLAND: Mieczysław Karczewski; Sylwia Kawwa; Dr. Janusz Kruczek; Barbara Steckiewicz; Doris Stempowska; Dr. Alfons Szyperski; Ryszard Wasita; Dr. Janusz Ziembiński; Maria Ziembiński.

SWITZERLAND: Dr. Golo Mann.

UNITED KINGDOM: Doreen Batten; Keith Butcher; Joseph Crowther; D. Evans; Douglas FitzPatrick; Lady Mary Grosvenor; Louis C. Hardouin; R.J. Harford; Trevor Hughes; James Ludovici; Sir Robin Mackworth-Young; Gerhard Majewski; Eileen Quelch; Geoffrey Rhoden; Gerald Sanders; A. Warburton; Myfanwy Wood.

USA: Judy Kochaver; Professor Kris Szymborski; Professor Wacław Jędrzejewicz; Professor Ernst Scheyer; Professor Harry Young; Ann Zitzloff.

I also wish to thank the following archives and their staff for their assistance with document searches:

10 Some of those I am indebted to, are no longer among us.

AUSTRIA: Österreichisches Kriegsarchiv, Wien.

CZECH REPUBLIC: Narodny Archiv, Opava/Troppau.

GERMANY: Bundesarchiv Koblenz; Bundesarchiv-Militärarchiv Freiburg; Fürstlich Hohenzollerisches Haus- und Domänenarchiv, Sigmaringen; Herder Institut, Marburg; Kurhessische Hausstiftung, Kronberg; Patenschaftswerk Waldenburg, Dortmund; Stiftung Kulturwerk Schlesien, Würzburg; Stiftung Preussischer Kulturbesitz, Berlin; *Waldenburger Heimatbote*, Verlag Helmut Schal, Norden; Zentrales Staatsarchiv, Merseburg.

POLAND: Archiwum Państwowe, Naczelna Dyrekcja, Warszawa (National Archives of Poland, Warsaw) and their branches in Wrocław/Breslau, Katowice, and Pszcyna/Pless.

SWITZERLAND: Archives of the League of Nations, Geneva; *Neue Zürcher Zeitung*, Zürich.

UNITED KINGDOM: British Library, London; British Museum, London; Milford Historical Society, Milford; National Register of Archives, London; Public Record Office, London; Royal Archives, Windsor; *The Times*, London.

Special words of thanks and sincere appreciation go to my editor Nancy Mackenzie. What good fortune I had to find someone with so much expertise, interest in the topic, inventiveness when it came to finding alternatives, and promptness. I thank Nancy very much for all her effort and giving me such a good experience of having a great editor.

My publisher Herbert Ratsch, President of Brightest Pebble Publishing, Ltd. deserves a big "thank you" for taking on the venture of publishing a book that might not "flood the market." I am grateful to him for the past, present, and future interest and the always enjoyable co-operation he has given me.

Finally, there is my wonderful wife Maria who worked faithfully side-by-side with me for many months. She has made many suggestions, often of crucial importance; she talked with me about *Daisy* almost every day; and with her enthusiasm for Daisy Pless, Maria certainly helped me to keep going. She made sure that there were never any "low days;" with Maria at my side, work on this project was exciting and great fun from the first to the last day.

Should I have overlooked a contributor or helper, I do ask for forgiveness.

* * * * * *

Introduction

A Distant Land

A thick haze hangs heavily over the gently rolling pastures; it transforms the light of this sunny day to a yellowish, dirty tint. A smell of sulphur reminds one of the industrial plants which surround the nearby city of Waldenburg in Lower Silesia[1] with its grimy suburbs and their smoke-belching coal mines from which a subdued, subterranean rumble emanates.

* * *

The narrow cobblestone road enters the dense forest barrier that separates the populous countryside from the monumental castle that is visible in the distance only by its heavy-set, octagonal tower. A majestic sandstone portal crowned with the coat-of-arms of the castle's owners, the Counts of Hochberg and Princes of Pless, opens its wrought-iron gates to admit the visitor to the deserted park, where rare exotic trees rise out of a sea of rhododendrons, and baroque statues smile mysteriously under a mantle of green moss alongside the avenue of tall linden trees. Abruptly, the avenue turns near a steep precipice where the faint sound of rushing water betrays the hidden creek far below. Across the deep, thickly wooded gorge rises the huge castle, remote and seemingly inaccessible on its gigantic rock.

This is Fürstenstein,[2] the *Rock of Princes*, situated on the outer hills of the Sudeten Mountains, where the castle looks across the Silesian lowlands. For thirty years, it was home to Daisy of Pless, before its fame

---

1   Since 1945 Wałbrzych in Dolny Śląsk.
2   Since 1945 Zamek Książ in Poland.

and glamour came to an end forever. For its former inhabitants – masters and servants – and the people who used to call Waldenburg their home, Castle Fürstenstein remains forever inseparable from the memory of Daisy Pless.

Faithful to its name, the Fürstenstein carried, since the early Middle Ages, a nearly invincible castle on its narrow crest that is surrounded by a deep gorge on three sides, and a valley on the fourth, and so was protected from marauders and hostile armies until the Thirty Years War, when Fürstenstein lost its raison d'être as a strategic stronghold and protector of the land. Soon after the war, the changing tastes and the renewed wealth of its owners, the *Reichsgrafen von Hochberg* [the Counts of Hochberg] transformed the fortified castle into Silesia's greatest palace. Decades of further construction during the nineteenth and twentieth centuries gradually encased the medieval core of the castle and changed the remnants of its obsolete fortifications into its famous terraced gardens.

Despite its splendour, Fürstenstein retains an air of distance and seclusion to this day. Encircled by the multi-tiered terraces that rise steeply above the deep gorge, the castle remains accessible only through the narrow portal of its gatehouse, through which, in 1892, the newlywed Daisy entered her new home.

It was a home in a faraway land, a part of Imperial Germany that was *terra incognita* for the educated and well-travelled Europeans. Even among Germans in the Western half of the country, Silesia was perceived as a remote, backward province and, if not politically, then certainly culturally, relegated beyond the boundaries of what one could properly call Central Europe. Polish was still spoken in most of Upper Silesia, and the inhabitants of Lower Silesia would be infuriated to no end when visitors and tourists from the western and southern provinces of Germany arrived with German-Polish dictionaries in their pockets.

In 1292, the Polish Duke Bolko I of Schweidnitz-Jauer acquired the already fortified Fürstenstein as a stronghold and protector of the trade routes between Silesia and Bohemia. Duke Bolko belonged to the dynasty of the Piasts, the rulers of the Kingdom of Poland, who opened their western lands to German settlers. The first were monks who arrived early in the thirteenth century and were soon followed by peasants, artisans, and merchants.

In 1509, the Hochbergs acquired Fürstenstein. In 1702, Count Konrad Ernst Maximilian von Hochberg began the construction of a huge baroque wing at Fürstenstein, and created the first terraces and formal gardens. As owners of three towns, a score of villages, vast agricultural lands, forests, and the first producing coal mines of Lower Silesia, the Hochbergs were now considered rich. Their wealth became legendary, after Hans Heinrich X succeeded in 1847 to the somewhat obscure Principality of Pless,[3] which was located in the farthest southeast corner of Germany, but contained one-fifth of Upper Silesia's immense mineral resources.

In 1891, Daisy Cornwallis-West married the heir to this fabulous fortune, rumored to exceed the wealth of Emperor Wilhelm II. The emperor became a close friend of Daisy Pless and her husband, and a frequent visitor to their castles Pless and Fürstenstein, where the family, whose eldest member also carried the title of Prince of Pless celebrated the fourth centenary of Hochberg reign in 1909. In contrast, the Cornwallis-Wests could not be considered wealthy by any means. Until her marriage, Daisy's allowance never exceeded fifteen pounds per year. But to the Prince of Pless, economic matters were of no importance. Instead, he had questioned the Cornwallis-Wests about their lineage and insisted they produce their pedigree, which found his ready approval.

Among her forefathers, Daisy counted the Earl de la Warr, governor of Virginia who had given the neighbouring territory, the later state of Delaware, its name. Another ancestor took the crown from King Philip of France during the Battle of Crécy in 1346. Not by lineage, but through "guardianship," Admiral Sir William Cornwallis had become Daisy's ancestor; he had acquired Newlands in Hampshire across from the Isle of Wight, Daisy's second childhood home.

Although both, the Cornwallis-West and the Hochberg families shared a strong pride in their illustrious ancestry, they had little in common otherwise. Socially, they moved in very different circles, subscribing to values which belonged to distinctly different eras. Daisy's mother belonged to the upper ranks of the Edwardian society, which had already begun to throw off the shackles of Victorian traditions. The family of the Prince of Pless, on the other hand, remained firmly rooted in the Prussian traditions of frugality, modesty and morality.

Not only geographically was Fürstenstein located in a distant land, it was utterly foreign and incomprehensible to the young, inexperienced Daisy. To her, the traditions and customs that governed the lives of her husband and his family seemed the extreme opposites of the milieu of her childhood and young womanhood in England.

Daisy experienced a delayed identity crisis, which was sparked by the values of the society of which she became part as a young woman married to a foreigner. Daisy rebelled against the values of her husband's family and their country in an initially unrestrained way, but later she

---

3   Since 1945 Pszczyna in Poland.

responded with more caution, intelligence and thoughtfulness. Her reactions were as much based on an often obsessive comparison between the countries of her birth and her marriage, as on the example given by her mother who was notorious for her independent thought and her easy disregard, even of Edwardian society's benign conventions.

Compared to the women of Prussia's aristocracy, the women of Edwardian England enjoyed a far greater degree of personal and intellectual freedom. In the case of the Cornwallis-West family, the women even enjoyed a decisive measure of authority and autonomy. Daisy's emerging self-image and her expectations on life and her environment were to a considerable degree shaped by the example of her grandmother Lady Olivia FitzPatrick, and especially her own mother; both women were of exceptionally strong character. Daisy's father, and even more so her brother George, were distinguished by a passive, obliging nature.

Daisy's strong ties to the country of her birth, and her rejection of Prussian traditions, comprised the two poles between which Daisy's restless life took its course. A study of her character and of the development of her personality cannot avoid the speculation of whether ultimately Daisy's life was symbolic for the failed symbiosis of the character of the two nations of England and Germany at a very troubled, unsettled time in their history, or whether Daisy Pless simply remained an outsider throughout her life, a rebel in the vanguard of her class and of womanhood.

The history and the character of Castle Fürstenstein and its environs deeply affected Daisy's life, her views of mankind and human nature. It determined the aims and goals Daisy set for herself as the Princess of Pless. The understanding of this ambiguous milieu, where the supreme luxury of Fürstenstein persisted in closest proximity to an utterly impoverished working class is essential for the appreciation of Daisy's personality and her development, which caused so much controversy and hostility among her contemporaries and their descendants.

* * * * * *

1 | *Setting the Stage*

T he ancient castle, restored in the romantic mood of the nineteenth century, stands like a gentle guardian over the little town of Ruthin. At Castle Ruthin, Mary Theresa Olivia Cornwallis-West – called Daisy since early childhood – was born on the 28 June, 1873.

*   *   *

Built in the fourteenth century as a bastion against hostile neighbours from the North, Ruthin was repeatedly besieged during the Civil War. Eventually, the castle was so thoroughly devastated by Cromwell's soldiers that no one tried to live among its crumbling, fire-blackened walls, until the castle came into the possession of the Myddleton family from nearby Chirk.

In 1798, Maria Myddleton, owner of the castle, married Frederick West, third son of the eighth Baron West and second Earl de la Warr. Enthusiastically, the citizens of Ruthin observed the rebuilding of the old castle, little knowing that only forty years later the restored building would be torn down again.

In 1837, Frederick and Maria's only son, Frederick Richard West, married Theresa Whitby, the adopted daughter of Admiral Sir William Cornwallis. On June 28, 1873, Frederick Richard and Theresa would become Daisy's paternal grandparents.

The generous dowry, that Theresa Whitby brought into her marriage permitted her husband to build an almost new Castle Ruthin. What had been restored by his father from medieval ruins, was dismantled again and, in its place, Frederick West erected a rather grand building of red sandstone in the popular Tudor style. Only a few of the ancient walls, bastions, and vaulted passageways survived, enough though to kindle the fantasy of the three Cornwallis-West children a generation later. Daisy remembered "how we loved playing hide and seek in the dungeons and old ruins, which seemed designed as if by a fairy king for our play-ground."[1]

Daisy belonged to the fortunate generation born to the landed gentry at a time when the British Empire was approaching its final zenith of power, wealth, and glory. Daisy's parents, Colonel William Cornwallis-West, and his wife Mary Adelaide Thomasina Eupatoria FitzPatrick, daughter of Thomas, second Marquess of Headfort, called Patsy by her family and her Edwardian friends, were not particularly wealthy. Indeed, shortly after Daisy's birth, one of the recurrent agricultural crises temporarily forced the Cornwallis-Wests to vacate Castle Ruthin and rent out its estate. Only after an absence of five years was the family able to escape their crowded townhouse in London and return to their beloved Ruthin.

The Cornwallis-Wests knew how to live comfortably in Ruthin on the rent derived from the lands worked by their tenants. The life of the family revolved around castle and estate, or the town house during the London Season. For years, the Cornwallis-Wests had never enough money for travel, the increasingly popular pastime of Victorian aristocracy. But theirs was still a uniquely English way of life of which the large retinue of loyal servants receiving incredibly low wages was an indispensable part. Surrounded by rural poverty, but conscious of their ancestry and the responsibility for their tenants, the Cornwallis-West family lived in comparative wealth with an almost total absence of guilt about their inherited wealth and privilege. As yet, no one among the poor and rural labourers questioned the right of the rich to be rich.

Being rich did not necessarily manifest itself in an ostentatious way of life in full public view. In this regard, some of the British were rather more circumspect than their wealthy cousins on the Continent. Indeed, with some notable exceptions, like much of the rural gentry of the British Isles, the Cornwallis-Wests lived a comparatively simple, almost pastoral life. Predictable, unhurried, and uncomplicated, life was filled with many pleasant daily activities and diversions, which only the British countryside with its large estates, mostly well-tended for generations, could provide: dogs and horses; fishing, hunting, and shooting parties; gardening, and walks and drives through meadows and forests, and frequent visits to neighbours for tea, games, and conversation. Few of these pleasures were imported from the Continent or from London which, of course, was attractive enough to induce the gentry away from their idyllic country

---

1   DPH, p. 33.

life for part of the year to attend the Season. This particular way of life, in its positive as well as in its negative attributes, determined the typically Victorian childhood shared by Daisy, her brother George, and her sister Shelagh.

* * *

So much has been written about Victorian life that it is hard to banish the image of red-cheeked upper-class children roaming happily in seemingly perfect freedom in dog-carts and on ponies through the verdant countryside. Nurses, governesses, butlers, cooks, and gardeners are an indispensable part of this image. It usually included the care and companionship, that one would normally expect from the parents, provided by the servants to the children of their masters. These relationships often constituted a vital source of human warmth, support, and guidance, and permitted upper-class children considerable insight into the mentality and sentiment of different classes.

The experience of such early dependence of Victorian children on servants for their emotional survival was often remembered for a lifetime. Severely neglected as a child by his parents, the fifty year-old George Cornwallis-West, burst into tears when told that old Bolton, the former butler at Ruthin, had died. Upon Mrs. Cornwallis-West's death, her maid Dolly Crowther immediately transferred her allegiance to become Daisy's faithful companion to her last day.

Such fidelity and lifelong devotion had their roots in the unique nature of the early relationships between young masters and mistresses and the servants of the Victorian household who, often without authority or formal preparation for such a role, filled a painful void in the lives of many Victorian children who were hungry for the love and attention of their parents. As Daisy's brother George states poignantly, if somewhat cynically

> Children in my early age were looked upon partly as a nuisance and partly as a kind of animate toy, to be shown, if they were sufficiently attractive, to callers. We were always brought down after lunch, but were never expected to utter, and were consequently abominably shy.[2]

George Cornwallis-West, who never conquered his shyness in his later life – although he always succeeded in hiding it behind the façade of his celebrated charm – found it impossible to ever forgive his parents for treating him during his childhood "like a piece of property" abandoned

---

2 George Cornwallis-West, *Edwardian Hey-Days* (London, 1930), p. 5.

to the care of the servants. George's later resentment was directed against the declining standards of family life and the thoughtless upbringing of children that also astonished Princess Catherine Radziwill. She was an ardent traveller, observer, and commentator of English and Continental society. Although their fervent admirer in many respects, the Princess severely criticized the British upper classes in her memoirs for

> the absence of home life which we have been taught to think of as the exclusive property of the English nation. It has been destroyed by the mania for constant travelling, and a general sense of restlessness which has taken hold of society in general. London has become a vast inn. There is no other country, which has such charming and cozy country houses, as they exist in England; yet they are seldom inhabited. We imagined the English home as something sweet and solemn, where the mistress gathered the children around her. ... All this has ceased to exist. Children are confined to their nursery and scarcely ever see their parents, who in autumn are always rushing about between London and their country houses. ... There is no steadiness and scarcely any seriousness.[3]

What shocked the Princess Radziwill most was the retreat of Victorian morals, which were increasingly displaced by the obsessive pursuit of pleasure by the frivolous Edwardian circles, who counted Mrs. Cornwallis-West among their prominent members.

Among the landed gentry, many maintained a consistent, sincere interest in the welfare of the poor on their estates. What seemed incomprehensible for the Countess Radziwill[4] and visitors from abroad, however, was the peculiar dichotomy in the perceptions and feelings of these same adults who could demonstrate such genuine awareness of the suffering of the poor and even of the animals, while remaining so curiously insensitive to the needs of their own children.

Unfortunately, many upper-class parents persisted in the firm belief that in addition to the specific duties the servants were hired for, much of the upbringing of the children could also be left to them without great

---

3   Princess Catherine Radziwill, *Memories of Forty Years* (New York, London, 1915), pp. 42 ff.

4   Born a Countess Rzewuska, Catherine was orphaned early. A brief marriage to one of the Princes Radziwill gave her admittance to court in St. Petersburg, Berlin, and London, after she had published a newspaper in South Africa with the help of Cecil Rhodes. Her diaries were widely read. In the 1920s, Catherine Radziwill disappeared in the United States. In 1930, a distant relative discovered "a dignified little lady" by the name of Catherine Kolb, formerly the Countess Radziwill, who was giving classes in etiquette to the sales personnel of New York's fashionable stores. Catherine died in New York in 1941.

risk to their offspring. But too often, they did *not* know – or cared to know – how competent, reliable, and suitable those were to whom they entrusted the education and well-being of their children. They paid even less attention to the lower servants, although cooks, butlers, and maids often provided more affection to the children than governesses and tutors who, after all, had to attain certain educational objectives and were likely to be less concerned with the emotional well-being of their charges. Children who were not blessed with an assertive nature or did not possess a good measure of self-confidence and self-reliance, often had to endure a painful, lonely, and confusing childhood, feeling forgotten and be-trayed by their parents.

* * *

The three Cornwallis-West children were raised in exactly such a house-hold. Later in life, they had most disparate memories of their early years. At first sight, the relationships between parents and children seemed easy-going and generous. Each member of the family had his or her pet name. Father was called *Poppets*; mother was *Patsy*; everybody referred to Daisy as *Dany*; George was called *Buzzie*; and Shelagh *Biddy* (scarcely ever used were her Christian names Constance Edwina). Early in life, the three children displayed significant differences in character and tem-perament, which foreshadowed their distinct development into adult-hood and explains the conflicting recollections of their youth.

Neither George nor Shelagh, the youngest of the three children, possessed the extraordinary spontaneity, gregariousness, and resilient nature of Daisy. George's childhood was overshadowed by a succession of bitter experiences. He was unloved and severely punished by his mother and ignored by his father; easily overlooked by the servants; and, as the only upper-class child in the local school, bullied by his classmates [his parents did not find it necessary to have their only son educated by a tutor]. He never successfully asserted himself against his two sisters.

Shelagh, in contrast, enjoyed the companionship, protection and guidance of her older sister. But, as Daisy observed, "although of stronger will and deeper nature, she did not get on with people at first as easily."[5]

Daisy alone attained very early in her life a sense of self-confidence and self-worth. Adored by everyone for her beauty, sweet charm, wistful-ness, and the manifestations of a bright, intelligent mind, Daisy was never in doubt that she was well-liked by all. Her spontaneity, trusting nature,

---

5   DPH, p. 32.

and self-assuredness made her the darling of her parents, the servants, and visitors. In their eyes, Daisy could never do wrong, and mischief or mistakes were always quickly forgiven and forgotten. Unlike George or Shelagh, Daisy knew how to take possession of the love and attention of adults; she blossomed in the same environment that was hell for George, and lonesome for Shelagh. Daisy was the only one of the three Cornwallis-West children, who was able to look back on a blissful childhood.

Daisy cherished the admiration of her mother, who for her part forever delighted in discovering new traits of her own beauty and temperament in her favourite daughter. Contrary to George, Daisy did not silently crave the love and attention of her mother, she just seemed to realize how little genuine love and affection her egocentric mother was capable of giving to her children. Everything points to the quite superficial nature of this seemingly loving mother-daughter relationship, where admiration and tolerance were mutual. Her early grasp of the peculiarities of human nature, and the acceptance of its limitations probably saved Daisy from the experience of disappointment and rejection, which her brother could not overcome in a lifetime. Daisy never demanded much of Mrs. Cornwallis-West, but

> contentedly worshipped from a distance my lovely mother who could not be bothered with young children and nurseries, but wanted to live her own free, vital existence.[6]

Called *the beautiful Irish savage* by her mother-in-law, Patsy was barely seventeen years old when she entered married life. Her temperament and unrestrained conduct displeased her future parents-in-law so much that they refused to attend the wedding ceremony. Within four years, Patsy Cornwallis-West was the mother of three children whom she quickly turned over to nurses. By her twenty-first birthday, she was free to give in to her unquenchable thirst for fun and the excitement of sometimes risqué experiences. Mrs. Cornwallis-West became one of the first *professional beauties*[7] who, in the words of another professional beauty, Lady Randolph Churchill, "could hold her own with the best of them."[8] She was also daring and reckless, and her seductive charm soon became notorious. The reminiscences of the Edwardians abound with

---

6   DPH, p. 34.

7   A term used for some beautiful ladies of London Society whose printed portraits were sold in large numbers in ordinary stores.

8   Mrs. George Cornwallis-West (Lady Randolph Churchill), *The Reminiscences of Lady Randolph Churchill* (New York, 1909), p. 215.

stories about her attraction to the opposite sex and the schemes Mrs. Cornwallis-West employed in engaging the attention of good-looking, famous males. Her beauty and forthrightness were not lost on the Prince of Wales, who was her visitor for quite some time. George refers in his writings to the persistent escapades and flings of his mother as "antics," while Daisy admits in her diaries that Mrs. Cornwallis-West led

> a life of audacity and freedom which, in the society in which she was born, aroused gossip and even criticism. ... [Her husband] simply worshipped her and let her do exactly what she liked – perhaps too much so; he was intensely proud of her and in his eyes she could do no wrong.[9]

In her diaries, Daisy related with considerable tolerance some of her mother's numerous pursuits of males of every class. More amused than critical, she writes about her brother's unexpectedly early birth, which happened within moments of a wild chase with a garden hose with which the pregnant Mrs. Cornwallis-West pursued the gardener at Ruthin. Mrs. Cornwallis-West barely managed to reach a small sofa in the garden room before giving birth to her only son.

Nothing could shake the loyalty and admiration of the people at Ruthin for Mrs. Cornwallis-West who, between amorous episodes and ambitious social schemes, never failed to remember her obligations to the poor and to the old. When Colonel Cornwallis-West presented his young wife to the townspeople of Ruthin and to the tenants of his estate in November 1872, he promised that

> the sunshine of her face will often gladden the cottage door, and I will undertake to say that the social duties she owes to other classes of society will not be omitted. ... The possession of property, rank or station in this life is attended by grave responsibilities.[10]

The son of the local physician, whose father had looked after Mrs. Cornwallis-West and her family and most of the people in town and on the estate, told the author that

> the Wests were held in high esteem by all Ruthin people – Mrs. West especially – for her kindness to the poor, and indeed, in those times the 'poor' were with us. It is not surprising that the Princess [Daisy] took after her in this respect.[11]

---

9   DPH, p. 46.

10   Eileen Quelch, *Perfect Darling, The Life and Times of George Cornwallis-West* (London, 1972), p. 20.

11   courtesy Mr. R.J. Harford, Ruthin

"That she was a good wife and mother one could hardly claim,"[12] Daisy had to admit, but on her visits to the poor at the side of her mother, the young Daisy observed a different Mrs. Cornwallis-West, an example of committed humanitarianism and an inspiration which Daisy was to follow later in her life. Mrs. Cornwallis-West did not act like *Lady Bountiful*, entering the homes of the poor with her arms laden full with charitable gifts. Rather, she transcended the barriers of class, because she knew how to talk to the common people in their own language and, in contrast to her pursuits in high society, she put a practical mind to work in easing the burden of their hard lives.

What crucial influence Daisy's early experiences had for the later development of her realistic appreciation of the lot of the poor and the working classes, her compassionate love for the common people, and the determination and dedication with which she pursued her humanitarian goals later in her life, was never better explained than by her contemporary, the social reformer and politician Margot Asquith:

> If you are not bred in the country, you may admire the views, enjoy the walks and love the holidays; but you are not in touch with the men who are part of the soil, and I have watched with pity the unemotional scrutiny that betrays those who only know the country from the outside. Early contact with the people of one's own class in life sharpens the intellect but does not develop the emotions in the same way as the daily contact with the poor cottage people.[13]

Next to the strong-willed Mrs. Cornwallis-West, the personality of her husband paled in comparison. It was indeed one of the fortunate facts in Patsy's life that she was blessed with an incredibly understanding husband whose generosity and forgiveness seemed boundless. The Colonel has been described by all who knew him as an extremely kind and gentle person who was thoroughly content with the simple pleasures of country-living, and the pursuit of his interests in painting and music.

* * *

Colonel William Cornwallis-West was born in the year 1835 in Florence, the temporary home of his parents, who were enthusiastic lovers of Italian art. Following the years at Eton and the completion of his studies in jurisprudence, the young William Cornwallis-West returned to Italy where he became quite a passionate amateur painter, garnering a repu-

---

12 DPH, p. 41.

13 from Anita Leslie, *Edwardians in Love* (London, 1972), p. 258.

tation as an accomplished copier of classical paintings. But in 1868, the early death of his brother forced his return to Ruthin, where the administration of the family estate fell to him. As a married man, he remained devoted to his art and rarely left Ruthin without his easel and paints. At the Cornwallis-West residence at Forty-nine Eaton Place in London, he preferred to spend his time in his studio on the top floor of the coach-house. He was glad to escape, whenever possible, the dinners and balls Mrs. Cornwallis-West was never reluctant to attend without the company of her husband.

Mrs. Cornwallis-West's political ambitions for her husband were never fulfilled. Although he served for eight years as Member of Parliament for the Western Division of Denbighshire, the Colonel never attained political prominence. He simply did not share the political and social aspirations of his wife. Patsy's frequent escapades and her disregard of any discretion caused much embarrassment for the Colonel, who could not entirely escape public ridicule because of his unwillingness to restrain his wife's often reckless conduct. Only his closest friends knew how much the Colonel adored his wife.

For Daisy, the Colonel remained

> dear old Poppets ... not only the finest specimen of the older type of English gentleman, but a real friend and comrade.[14]

George agreed that his father was "an exceptionally kind man,"[15] but tactfully avoided raising the question of why his father had failed so utterly in comprehending his son's loneliness and fear of his mother, and why he had never protected him from his mother's wrath.

* * *

For the Cornwallis-West children, life was hardest during the London Season, remembered by George and, as much by Daisy, with horror. As nearly all other houses in fashionable Belgravia, Forty-nine Eaton Place, the townhouse of the Cornwallis-Wests, had not been built with the needs of children in mind. Forty-nine Eaton Place was not a cheerful house. Narrow-chested and five stories high, the house accommodated kitchen and pantries on the basement level, parlour, dining room, and library on the first and second stories, followed by the private rooms of the parents

---

14 DPH, p. 34.

15 See Eileen Quelch, op. cit., p. 31.

and, higher up, by the children's nursery and, finally, by the sleeping quarters of the servants.

Like most Victorian townhouses, Forty-nine Eaton Place had a dark, somber interior. The typical design of the house – narrow and deep – the heavy drapery over doors and windows, left little window space towards the street and towards the back, which could admit light during the day. George remembered the heavy furniture, the dark wallpaper of the rooms, and the dim light of the open, spluttering gas flames that often had to be kept on all day, especially during the bleak winter with its frequent heavy fog.

For fresh air and for their playtime, the children had to be taken by their nurse to the private gardens in the centre of Eaton Square. But even there, running around and any exuberant behaviour were severely controlled by the strict Mrs. Haig. Even by Victorian standards, Nurse Haig was an extremely cold person with an almost sadistic nature. Practically for the entire day, from morning to night, Daisy, George, and Shelagh were at the mercy of Mrs. Haig. It was Mrs. Haig alone who fed, clothed, and washed them and put them to bed without a reassuring word or a smile. During the day, this dreadful woman seemed to delight in mercilessly punishing the children for the slightest misdemeanours and threatening them with immediate dire consequences to be followed by even worse punishment in their afterlife.

Daisy, who hated Mrs. Haig with all her heart, was ingenious enough to scheme little strategies of revenge. Somehow she knew how to humour Mrs. Haig and escape her harsh regime. Shelagh seemed to grow increasingly subdued which totally escaped the attention of her parents, as she had always been a quiet child. But George, paralyzed in his fear of Mrs. Haig, became so frightened and nervous, that the parents decided to consult their physician. It required the patient questioning of Dr. Ticket to discover the cause for George's poor health and his increasing emotional instability. Upon Dr. Ticket's urgent advice, Nurse Haig was dismissed immediately. For once, but not for long, the parents seemed truly alarmed and concerned with the welfare of their children. They sent for Mrs. Evans, a warm, big-hearted woman from Ruthin to make up for everything the children had been deprived of under Mrs. Haig's irresponsible regime. Daisy, George, and Shelagh blossomed under Mrs. Evans' loving care. This seemed sufficient reassurance for the parents to again devote themselves wholeheartedly to their own interests and pleasures.

Nothing had changed in the nature of the relationship between the children and their parents, especially the amount of time the parents would spend with their children. Only rarely were Daisy, George, and Shelagh admitted to the parlour. Their brief appearances occurred when Mrs. Cornwallis-West entertained her lady-friends such as the Countess

Dudley, Mrs. Wheeler, or the famous Mrs. Lilly Langtry, who was a friend of the Prince of Wales and neighbour of the Cornwallis-Wests. The ladies hardly took any notice of the children who were only too glad to escape from the parlour. Once outside the parlour doors, the children would break out into loud laughter about the latest fashions worn by the ladies, and exclaim about the ladies' enormous bustles, feather boas, and huge hats, that were often crowned by what looked to the children like complete birds.

With much greater anticipation, however, the children awaited the visits of the Prince of Wales and Lord Beresford. Unlike the ladies, the gentlemen visitors at least shook hands with the children, although this consisted of offering them their index finger only, as was the custom at that time. Both men always had time for a few games or jokes. The Prince of Wales never failed to produce little gifts from his pockets, a gold coin or a little brooch or a pin for Daisy and Shelagh, or a small toy for George. Naturally, the parents basked in the attention the children received from the visitors. In contrast to their usual habits, on such occasions they lavished expressions of delight and pride on their offspring. These were precious, only too rare, moments in the children's lives. As soon as the visitors had left, Colonel Cornwallis-West withdrew to his studio, where he liked to spend long hours entertaining the painters Whistler, Millais, and other artist friends, while his wife devoted herself to her own diversions.

Only during her daily outing in Hyde Park were the children indispensable for Mrs. Cornwallis-West. For their drives along Rotten Row, where the critical eyes of gentlemen on horseback scanned the endless row of the ladies in their carriages, it was the custom for the ladies to be accompanied by their youngest daughters, who served as an additional adornment of their mother's beauty. As Max Beerbohm[16] pointedly observed, "the modish appanage of Beauty in her barouche was not a spaniel now, but a little child." When Countess Dudley traded her young daughter for her little son, the other ladies followed suit immediately. Mrs.Cornwallis-West took George, whom she detested and always considered an embarrassment, out of hiding. Finally, it was George's turn to be shown in public, but only as the silent adornment of his mother's beauty.

When the family returned to Ruthin, George stood in the centre of attention again and received a rousing welcome from the townsfolk who presented the nine-year-old George, the *Mab y Castell* – the heir to the

---

16   Max Beerbohm (1872-1956), English essayist, critic, and caricaturist.

castle – with a pony. This cheerful entrance to Ruthin was followed by the darkest and unhappiest years in George's life.

* * *

After the five confining years in the London townhouse, even Daisy, the oldest of the three children, had only the dimmest memories of her birthplace. Daisy gazed in amazement at Castle Ruthin, and walked through its large gate like a fairy princess taking possession of her palace. She had finally returned to this romantic building, where the old halls and stairways left no limits for fantasy and play. Daisy remembered whole suites of mysterious rooms, dusty and unused for years, dark passages that seemed to lead nowhere and a real dungeon with a pillar in its centre, which stimulated the children's imagination to all sorts of games. Even Mrs. Evans willingly took part in the make-believe.

Enjoying their newly-discovered freedom, the children also eagerly explored the near countryside and were soon seen galloping across the estate on their ponies followed by the eyes of the curious tenants. Feudal customs were still very much alive around Ruthin, and men would doff their caps when passed by the Cornwallis-West children, and women would curtsy. It was Daisy, rather than the awkward George or the reserved Shelagh, who broke down all barriers between masters and tenants and freely invited herself, her brother, and her sister into the cottages for tea. People at Ruthin remember that the Cornwallis-West children were forever hungry for treats.

As with other Victorian children, food played an important part in their lives. George wrote many years later that

> it was unheard of for children to be allowed the same food as grown-ups. The only meal had in the dining-room was luncheon, when special but entirely unappetising food was prepared for us. I remember my feelings at seeing and smelling the delicious-looking food offered to the more mature humans.[17]

Daisy, of course, could not care less about such matters – "her head was always in the clouds anyway."[18] What an easy lot Daisy had early on in her life! Her loving relationship with her father always seemed to include a measure of camaraderie, which is already evident in one of her first letters, written at the age of seven, and addressed to her father at his hunting lodge in the Welsh mountains:

---

17 See George Cornwallis-West, op. cit., p. 5.

18 See Eileen Quelch, op. cit., p. 31.

My Dear Old Poppets,

I am thinking how dreadful it must be in the wild mountains among the Welsh people and I think I must write you a little note to comfort you. I am taught that there are no roses without thorns, but I am sure the thorns of getting into Parliament are very prickly. ... It is very hot to-day at Ruthin. ... Take care of your little self, dear old Dads, and come home soon to your little chickens who send you a lot of big kisses and hugs.

Your loving little daughter, Daisy.[19]

Daisy continued her happy existence in Ruthin, until Newlands Manor fell to the Cornwallis-Wests after the death of Daisy's grandmother in 1886. The manor house, described by Daisy as an unfortunate mixture of "Churchwarden Gothic and bad Strawberry Hill,"[20] was by itself a not very inviting building. It lacked the grandeur of Castle Ruthin. Newlands derived its charm not from its odd-looking manor house, but from its nearness to the sea. The mild, humid climate blessed the park and the adjoining New Forest with a lush, almost Southern vegetation. Most of the walls of the drab manor house were covered with a rich growth of creepers that gave it more of a romantic character than its architect had probably intended. The vast park of Newlands almost reached to the sea, petering out into a few small groups of lonely wind-swept pine trees before reaching the Channel.

Along the sea ran the High Road, from which a narrow road branched off to wind its way through dense vegetation, crossing a small creek on a delicate wrought-iron bridge, and finally widening into the circular driveway in front of Newlands Manor.

Immediately after the arrival of the family at Newlands, Mrs. Cornwallis-West surrendered to her passion for gardening and re-designed the terraces on the west and southside of the manor. She added bosquettes, fountains, and statues in a sea of roses. Daisy would later recreate this design around her teahouse in far away Germany to ease her homesickness for her "beloved Newlands." Towards the lake, Mrs. Cornwallis-West had a long avenue laid out and designed for a unique tradition. The close proximity to the Isle of Wight, just across the Solent, quickly made Newlands the favourite stop over for the guests of the annual Regatta at Cowes and also for many of Queen Victoria's visitors at Osborne House. Those guests considered of sufficiently high rank were asked by Mrs. Cornwallis-West to plant a small tree along the new avenue, and thanks to the benign climate, the social prominence of

---

19 DPH, p. 34.
20 DPH, p. 36.

Newlands' new owners and, last not least, the traffic to Cowes and Osborne House, an avenue of stately trees soon reached the lake and continued alongside its shore. Mrs. Cornwallis-West had small cast iron plaques affixed to the foot of each tree to commemorate those who had visited Newlands over the years. Among the illustrious guests were the Prince of Wales, Kaiser Wilhelm II, Leopold King of the Belgians, and the Maharaja of Cooch-Behar who, at his first encounter with Daisy, took little notice of the fourteen-year-old Cornwallis-West daughter, but later would fall deeply in love with her.

Daisy was ready to become enchanted by the beauty of Newlands and its romantic mood. Deep in the park, she discovered hidden benches and overgrown pavilions where she spent hours writing poetry and "trying my talents at a romantic novel"[21] or thinking about the guests in the house. Daisy's beauty and charm began to invite noticeable attention. The Prince of Wales, who used to call the Cornwallis-West children *my own Wild West show*,[22] treated Daisy like a young lady now. This was also the time of Daisy's first love, to the young George Cooper, in those days a frequent guest of the family.

Unfortunately, since George Cooper was not the son of wealthy parents, Mrs. Cornwallis-West resolutely put a stop to Daisy's first relationship with a man. Not recognizing the depth of Daisy's first love, and without regard for her daughter's feelings, she forced Daisy to turn over to Bolton, the butler, the modest brooch George had given her, and asked Bolton to return the gift to George Cooper. For once, Daisy did not understand her mother and she felt suddenly treated like a small child. Daisy reacted with tears when she was told by her mother that an accompanying note to George would be entirely inappropriate. Soon after, the family travelled abroad for the first time. Overwhelmed by her impressions of France and Italy, Daisy's love for George Cooper appeared to quickly fade away. Only later did it become evident that this brief, but deep relationship had been a key experience, which would remain with Daisy all her life. Her first love would always remain the norm for all future relationships with the opposite sex. With rare exceptions, these would again and again end in disappointment.

* * *

---

21   DPH, p. 46.
22   DPH, p. 32.

Leaving George Cornwallis-West at school in Farnborough, the family spent the winter of 1889 in Florence, where the Colonel immersed himself in his love for painting while Daisy received singing lessons from the director of the Florence Opera. Impressed with her promising voice and her expressive personality, the director offered free lessons, provided Daisy would seriously study French and Italian, the absolute prerequisite for an opera singer. Her ambition fueled by the romantic notion of singing on the great stages of Europe, the sixteen-year-old girl accepted the director's offer with great enthusiasm. But the road to an operatic career was cut short when Daisy contracted typhoid fever after drinking tap water. She had hoped to save on the indispensable bottled water and help her father put money aside for the "considerable expenses" of her future musical education. The family hurriedly departed for Paris, where Daisy needed several weeks to recuperate. She then continued her singing lessons, this time at even greater expense to her father, with the famous Polish tenor Jean de Reszke.

In spring 1890, the family returned to England. Daisy eagerly looked forward to more voice training, which her mother had promised her, as Jean de Reszke had impressed on Mrs. Cornwallis-West that her daughter had true potential to become an opera singer. Mrs. Cornwallis-West had no intention to keep her word. She would not hear of such an unconventional career for her daughter, which would only interfere with her secret plans to soon marry Daisy to a man who must not only be rich, but must also belong to the highest ranks of society.

By this time, Daisy was almost ready to *come out*. Mrs. Cornwallis-West pursued her ambitious plans for her daughter's future relentlessly. She refused to listen to her husband's suggestion to at least send Daisy for a year to Mrs. Woolf's finishing school, something she considered impractical and a waste of time. With the smattering of French, the limited exposure to literature, geography, and history – all received quite haphazardly from her female tutor, Daisy should be adequately prepared for life. After all, Mrs. Cornwallis-West maintained, she herself had managed very well with even less knowledge and education. It had never bothered her that even her English spelling still gave her some difficulties. Later, it became evident that her daughter Daisy also could never quite come to terms with her spelling in her diaries and her letters, which was often in conflict with the considerable substance of Daisy's writings. Daisy's poor spelling was a natural consequence of the pitiful education she had received from her tutor, a well-meaning woman who occupied a fairly low position in the hierarchy of the household in Newlands and who had forever pleaded in vain for Mrs. Cornwallis-West's support to keep Daisy with her books.

In some respects, though, growing up with such casual parental supervision did have some distinct advantages for the daughters of late Victorian households. While their formal education compared rather unfavourably with the intensive schooling provided to upper-class girls in Germany, Austria, and France, who were taught by carefully chosen tutors and exclusive finishing schools, what English girls did receive at that time was an education for life. Especially for the daughters of the house, who were not forced to leave their family as early as their brothers, the omnipresence of servants in these large households constituted a continuous challenge to observe and study human nature, to listen, to discriminate human reactions, all the time relating to a variety of adults from differing backgrounds and classes. Even though the servants were regarded as socially inferior, they were nevertheless adults and often exercised a fair degree of authority *in loco parentis*. Despite the delegation of a considerable part of parental authority to the servants, Victorian girls, at least psychologically, were largely left to their own devices. Naturally, many of them developed a sense of self-reliance at a young age, and some of them learned to early understand the intricacies of human nature and, barely approaching maturity, knew how to judge the character of the adults around them with amazing accuracy.

This might explain why in social, political and intellectual matters, British women of the Edwardian era generally achieved greater prominence than their sisters on the Continent, where one searches in vain for a Margot Asquith, a Daisy Warwick, or an Emmeline Pankhurst. On the British Isles, of course, society was more accepting of women and their individuality, or what men might have benevolently looked upon as their idiosyncrasies. The British tradition of tolerance never excluded the mavericks from society for very long, if at all. Daisy Warwick, whose passionate dedication to social reform culminated in a political career as, of all things, a socialist, and Jenny Churchill, who unabashedly promoted the careers of her husband and her son, and many others in their time, were the great, if sometimes eccentric, sometimes capricious ladies of the late Victorian years and the Edwardian era who, unlike most gentlewomen on the Continent, attained respect and prominence in their own right by refusing to remain in the shadows of their husbands.

By all accounts, Daisy Cornwallis-West seemed predestined to play such a role in the country of her birth, but fate and the plans of her ambitious mother determined otherwise.

* * * * * *

2 *The Young Princess*

T he coronet rests slightly askew on the young woman's head. Her hands rigidly grip the armrests of the ornate chair. Its richly carved Gothic rosettes seem to provide a frame for the anxiety on her exhausted flushed face. Her eyes express apprehension, and the slightly parted lips seem to plead for reassurance about a bewildering present and an uncertain future.

* * *

This is what impressed the author in Daisy's wedding portrait, which was intended to present the bride, her radiant beauty accentuated by the veil of delicate Brussels lace, the rich brocade gown, and its long train that flows around her feet in one elegant sweep. Instead, the picture reveals Daisy's helplessness and her fearful premonitions which filled her troubled mind on the day of her wedding, December 8, 1891.

In the early hours of her wedding day, Daisy was unable to hold back her tears. Turning her back on the precious bridal gown that had been laid out for her, she put on a short walking frock. Wearing her "oldest shoes, a funny little turban hat and soiled gloves,"[1] Daisy grabbed the keys for the private park in the centre of Eaton Square and slipped unnoticed out of the house.

Daisy paced back and forth from one end of the long, narrow park to the other. If only the inner turmoil and the ambivalent feelings, which had gripped her during a sleepless night, were as orderly as this pretty garden. She almost wished that her husband-to-be would see her in this

---

1 DPH, p. 48.

agitated state – surely, he would refuse to marry someone who "looked such a fright"[2] on her wedding day!

* * *

When the family arrived in London before the onset of the social season, Daisy's mother replaced all the dresses Daisy had brought from New-lands. Mrs. Cornwallis-West intended to follow a firm plan for her daughter to come out early. Under her mother's guiding hand, Daisy was magically transformed from the carefree girl who had grown up happily in the freedom of the country to an elegant young society woman in a rapid series of bewildering events. Mrs. Cornwallis-West succeeded in making her beautiful daughter the talk of London society.

The balls and dinners attended in the presence of her parents helped Daisy become conscious of the impression she created at social affairs; she gained much assurance and began to feel superior to more than one of the young men she was introduced to. Well aware of the ultimate purpose of the social encounters her mother continuously arranged, Daisy still had fun. Never at a loss for words, Daisy raised warm, fatherly feelings among the older gentlemen, while the young men on the dance floor often resorted to silly gossip or risqué talk when they were unable to match Daisy's witty conversation. But everywhere hovered the watchful Mrs. Cornwallis-West. She screened all the young suitors and gave those she selected as a potential match for her daughter every encouragement to ask Daisy for another dance before the evening was over.

No question, Daisy did savour her popularity among the young set and her little triumphs on the dance-floor, even though she could never forget that the purpose of all this fun was Mrs. Cornwallis-West's strategy to display her eligible daughter as often as possible in the hope to marry her off before next year's Season. Like other girls her age, Daisy realized that the choice of a husband for her would be entirely in her parents' hands. In the 1890s, her brother George commented, it was still the prevailing practice that

> a girl went through a process of receiving strong recommendations as to the desirability of a certain suitor, combined with a discreet but complete schedule of the advantages obtained by such a marriage; and as she was accustomed to discipline and had not been encouraged to think for herself, the marriage ... usually took place.[3]

---

2   DPH, p. 48.

3   See George Cornwallis-West, op. cit., p. 36.

This was precisely what happened to Daisy Cornwallis-West!

In April 1891, Hans Heinrich of Pless, the oldest son of the reigning Prince of Pless, appeared in London Society. For the diplomatic corps, his appointment as secretary to the Imperial German Embassy had been an event of minor significance. Although a member of one of Prussia's most respected families, as an individual, the Prince did not create a strong impression. His extremely reserved manner was intensified by the way he spoke English somewhat haltingly and his slightly limited vocabulary. The German chancellor Prince von Bülow, a close friend of the Prince's father, thought Hans Heinrich XV "unimportant and obsessed with trivialities."[4] This opinion was not shared by the ladies of London's Society who were looking for the perfect match for their daughters.

At the age of thirty years, the Prince was considered a most eligible bachelor. The fame of his father's fabulous wealth quickly reached Mrs. Cornwallis-West's ears. After she discovered that the Prince was not only heir to an immense fortune, but was also listed in the *Gotha* – the peerage of Germany's aristocracy – as belonging to the old, highly regarded family of the *Reichsgrafen von Hochberg und Freiherren von Fürstenstein*,[5] she made up her mind to pursue the Prince for her daughter Daisy. Just as with her choice of the Duke of Westminster as husband for her other daughter Shelagh a few years later, Mrs. Cornwallis-West dreamt of the considerable financial benefits Daisy's marriage to the Prince of Pless would entail not only for her daughter, but for herself and her husband as well.

First mentioned in Silesian records during the thirteenth century, the Hochbergs acquired Castle Fürstenstein and its lands in the year 1509. Their estates included extensive agricultural lands, forests, and coal mines. In 1847, the Principality of Pless, which dates back to the times of the Polish Piast princes, fell, through inheritance, to Heinrich X of Hochberg. One year later, the reigning member of the family and his eldest son were raised to the rank of *Fürst von Pless*[6] by the King of Prussia.

Located in the extreme southeast corner of Prussia, the Principality of Pless seemed obscure and remote from the rest of Germany. Earlier in the nineteenth century, its populace, mainly of Polish origin, had suffered enormously under starvation and repeated epidemics of typhoid fever. When Daisy's future father-in-law, Prince Hans Heinrich XI,

---

4   Fürst Bernhard von Bülow, *Denkwürdigkeiten* (Berlin, 1930-33), p. 426.

5   The Counts of Hochberg and Barons of Fürstenstein.

6   The Prince of Pless

began his long reign in the year 1855, he found entire villages depopulated, and bands of homeless children roaming through the country. The Prince opened orphanages and had vast areas of marginal lands drained and distributed to the impoverished peasant population. Through the construction of attractive buildings and parks, he transformed the nondescript, backward country-town of Pless into the small, but charming capital of the Principality.

In addition to the vast forests, Hans Heinrich XI energetically developed the as-yet hardly touched mineral riches of the Principality, which were based on medieval privileges that granted the Princes of Pless rights and opportunities comparable to "the enormous land grants made to the men that built the Canadian Pacific Railway."[7]

Next to the Ruhr-Basin, Upper Silesia soon expanded into the second most important complex of mining and heavy industry in Continental Europe. Its agricultural and mineral resources and its industry were controlled by five families of Upper Silesia's aristocracy, the Hohenlohe, Schaffgotsch, Henckel-Donnersmarck, Tiele-Winckler, and the Prince of Pless. Each of these families belonged to the ten wealthiest families of Imperial Germany. Admired by some, they were generally less kindly referred to as the *Upper Silesian smoke-stack barons* [die oberschlesischen Schlotbarone]. Before the outbreak of World War I, the Prince of Pless was said to possess greater wealth than even the German Emperor. World War I would bring enormous changes to this tragic land with its mixed, predominantly Polish population

> because of the conflicting historic, geographical, political and racial struggles of which it has been an unending scene.[8]

Mrs. Cornwallis-West had done her research and prepared matters well. The events which decided Daisy's future – introduction to her husband-to-be, engagement, and wedding – followed each other at breathtaking pace.

Daisy's first encounter with Hans Heinrich at the opening ball of the Season did not raise any suspicion in her mind. She was only slightly impressed with this tall, slim, quite good-looking, but already balding man and, after only a short conversation, found him too formal and rather uninteresting. For once, Daisy, who always knew how to charm, flirt and maintain a lively conversation, was left at a loss by the Prince's

---

7   William John Rose, *The Drama of Upper Silesia* (Brattleborough, 1935), p. 40.

8   BLU, p. 20.

stiff, humorless personality. In his presence, she felt curiously inhibited and unusually passive.

Within weeks, Hans Heinrich of Pless proposed to Daisy during a masked ball at Holland House. Having her eyes on a young peer whom she adored from a distance, Daisy was completely caught off guard. With a stammered response she tried to explain to the Prince that she was far too young to be married to a man his age, that she did not feel any affection for him, and could not imagine ever falling in love with him. Besides, compared to his family, she came from a noble but poor background. What Daisy did not dare to reveal were her hurt feelings of being "second choice." Everybody in London knew that the Prince of Pless had been transferred to the German Embassy for the purpose of marrying Princess May of Teck, the later Queen Mary.

Such rumors, however, did not deter Mrs. Cornwallis-West in the least from energetically realizing her goal of marrying Daisy off during her first Season to a man of her choice. Helplessly, the distressed Daisy watched Colonel Cornwallis-West and Hans Heinrich's father disappear in the library of Forty-nine Eaton Place. Behind its closed doors, the final decision about her future was about to be made. After the Prince of Pless had left the house, the exuberant Mrs. Cornwallis-West could not restrain herself from sharing her satisfaction with Daisy about the splendid match she had arranged for her daughter. Besides, Hans Heinrich's father had also readily agreed to assume all costs for the bridal trousseau and for the wedding itself. No one paid any attention to Daisy who, deeply resented this unromantic prelude to her life as a married woman.

Hans Heinrich, in his matter-of-fact manner, tried to reassure the tearful, anxious Daisy, that love would come in time anyway. He persisted in describing the fabulous life awaiting Daisy in Germany – a glamorous world of palaces and parks, with ladies-in-waiting, and hundreds of servants, with parties and travels, and a local populace waiting enthusiastically for the young Princess from far-away England. In the end, overpowered by her mother's enthusiasm and her confused feelings about her relationship with Hans, Daisy made herself believe that she was destined for the life of a fairy-princess in a foreign land. Only later did she angrily write in retrospect, that

I did not realize it clearly at the time, but I was just being bought.[9]

The wedding ceremony, performed on December 8, 1891 in St. Margaret's church on the grounds of Westminster Abbey, was indeed

9   DPH, p. 47.

worthy of a fairy princess; it seemed to herald a brilliant future for the eighteen year-old Daisy Cornwallis-West. On the following day, the pictures of the bridal couple dominated the third page of *The Daily Graphic*. Under the heading "A Brilliant Scene," Daisy's spectacular wedding gown was described in all its detail.

> The wedding gown was of *Empire* style, being a fourreau in the richest pearl-white satin, edged with Malines tulle, caught up with garlands of orange blossoms. The train was of the richest brocade, attached to the shoulders with a silk collar. The veil was held by a magnificent diamond and pearl crown, the gift of H.S.H. the Prince of Pless, and the bride's other ornaments were a diamond cross, the gift of the Princess of Pless, and a single stone diamond necklace, the gift of the bridegroom. The bridal bouquet was composed of real orange flowers in foliage, tied with streamers to match. There were eight bridesmaids. ... The Bishop of St. Asaph performed the wedding ceremony assisted by the Archdeacon of Westminster and the family's minister from Newlands.[10]

No less impressive was the list of guests published by *The Daily Graphic*; its names elevated Daisy's wedding to an affair of the highest rank:

> Prince of Wales, the Duke and Duchess of Teck, the Prince and Princess of Saxe-Weimar, the ambassadors or highest in London accredited diplomatic representatives of Germany, Turkey, France, Russia, Italy, Portugal, Denmark, Greece, the Netherlands and the United States.[11]

Among the numerous guests, *The Daily Graphic* also mentioned Lady Randolph Churchill, wife-to-be of Daisy's brother George, and Lady Lilian Grosvenor as one of the bridesmaids and relative of the Duke of Westminster, the future husband of Daisy's sister Shelagh.

On the steps of St. Margaret's, the Prince of Wales embraced Daisy and admonished her to always be a loyal subject of her husband's country and learn its language well. Daisy and Hans Heinrich stepped into their wedding-coach, and under the loud applause of the crowd, which lustily shouted in pure Cockney "God Pless You!"[12] they left the grounds of Westminster Abbey.

The lavish reception took place at Portman Square in the house of Mrs. Cornwallis-West's friend Miss Fleetwood Wilson, the later Princess

---

10 DPH, p. 48.

11 *The Daily Graphic*, December 9, 1891. p. 8.

12 Actually, "God Bless you!" In Cockney, 'b' is often pronounced as in "p" resulting in the well-wishing of "God *Pless* You" directed at the Princer and Princess of *Pless*.

Dolgoruki. Everything went much too fast for Daisy, who as yet did not feel like the Princess of Pless and burst out laughing when one of the first guests in the receiving line addressed her as *Your Highness*. And much too soon, the end of the reception arrived. Daisy realized that for the first time in her life, she would have to leave her family. Almost with envy, Daisy spotted her sister in the crowd that had gathered in the hall to say goodbye. Shelagh had been such a serious bridesmaid, but now she looked excited and "happy like a child."

As always, when tension threatened to overwhelm her, Daisy had committed one of those sometimes impulsive, sometimes deliberate blunders, which left her either triumphant or humiliated. Before her departure on her honeymoon, Daisy had put on the elegant going-away frock ordered from Paris by Hans, back to front. Mrs. Cornwallis-West thought that hilarious, and her laughter helped Daisy cope with the tense last minutes of saying goodbye to her parents. The carriage taking Hans and Daisy to Victoria Station had not even left Portman Square when an angry Hans loudly reproached Daisy for her unforgivable faux-pas. For a fleeting moment, Daisy sensed how her youth, her ignorance, and her inexperience left her totally defenseless for life at the side of a husband who talked like a stern father, if not like a stranger to her. Later, she wrote,

> I began my life totally unprepared for any of its experiences, duties or responsibilities. Literally, I knew nothing. ... I kept pondering what 'being in love' meant. ... Without a rudder or chart, I was at the mercy of any wind that blew close enough to reach me. Either of my parents would have done anything in the world for me – except tell me the truth.[13]

The emotional stress and tension, which had not left Daisy since the morning of her wedding, became even more unbearable during her first days in Paris. Daisy, who had only fond, romantic memories of Paris and her singing lessons with the kind Jean de Reszke, had actually been excited when Hans decided on Paris as the first stop over on their honeymoon. But the kinds of theatres and nightclubs Hans took her to introduced Daisy to a world she had never even heard of. She was disgusted and revolted. Being in such places in the company of men who seemed to enjoy risqué and lascivious talk in the presence of a young woman, and who had little in common with the type of English gentleman Daisy knew and felt comfortable with, turned into a frightening experience.

---

13 DPH, p. 50.

Only when Hans, as she now called him, took her to the famous salons of Parisian fashion and, "with the keenest eye for women's clothes,"[14] helped her select a new wardrobe, did some of Daisy's self-confidence return. When her husband presented her to the German Ambassador who had been his superior, she remembered the advice of her motherly friend Lady Theresa Londonderry: "My dear, always enter a room, as if the whole place belongs to you."[15] Hans was extraordinarily pleased with her on this occasion. When Daisy witnessed the cordial welcome extended to Hans by the German Ambassador she found for the first time a reason to truly admire her husband who so obviously continued to be well-regarded at the Embassy. Hans had been forced to resign from the foreign service because the Imperial German Government did not permit junior staff in the diplomatic service to marry, a regulation Daisy did not object to considering herself fortunate to have her husband all for herself.

After Daisy's success at the German Embassy, Hans seemed to shed his pedantic, critical attitude towards her. Happily, Daisy decided that, as Hans was a far too old-fashioned name for her husband, she could call him from now on *Tommy*. Perhaps without fully realizing it, she spontaneously chose this cheerful name, because first of all, it was English and, secondly, it somehow seemed to make her so much older husband less powerful. At any rate, Hans laughingly agreed to accept his new first name and, after all the doubts that had plagued her during the past days, Daisy was all of a sudden convinced that she was falling in love with her husband and that their marriage would be a happy one. On the morning of the departure for Pless, she hastily scribbled a note to her mother. Everything was going well, she wrote; Hans was turning into the perfect husband, and everything he had promised her was beginning to come true.

Cheerful and content with herself, Daisy settled into the luxurious private compartment of the express train that would take her to distant Pless. Freed from the constant guidance and protection of her mother and feeling certain of Hans's love, Daisy felt she was finally growing wings. With delight, she discovered little towns and villages hidden in the snow of a deep winter in the romantic countryside her train was crossing at high speed. Hans proved to be a loving husband and, pleased by the interest Daisy finally displayed, did not stop describing her new homeland and their residence in Pless in every detail. In his enthusiasm, he

---

14 DPH, p. 51.

15 DPH, p. 45.

did not notice the anxious expression on Daisy's face when he explained to her that the Principality of Pless almost reached the famous *Three Emperors Corner*, where the borders of Germany, Austria-Hungary, and Russia touched each other. For a fleeting moment, Daisy registered with alarm that her long journey would almost end in the Empire of the Czar.

In the beginning, Daisy had found the German countryside quite charming and inviting, but when the train finally came to a halt at the station in Pless, she could no longer subdue the feeling of foreboding that had seized her during the final hours of the long journey when the train had travelled through a less and less populated country, and the view from the window had been obscured by endless, dark forests. At first sight, Pless looked rather shabby. It was built around a town square, which was lined by plain-looking, low two-storey houses except for one corner which was dominated by the huge Castle Pless. The vastness of the square seemed incongruous considering that Pless was only a small town of a few thousands inhabitants. It happened to be market-day, and the straw and manure-covered town square was full of carts and scruffy-looking horses tied to them. Bewildered, Daisy stared at the dark-clad peasants who silently watched her carriage, as it clattered over the wet, rough cobblestones. To Daisy, Pless looked oddly picturesque, but very, very foreign.

This perturbing first impression was extinguished after the carriage passed through the narrow entrance of the gatehouse which opened onto a snow-covered park laid-out in English style. The carriage circled around the wide lake whose icy surface glimmered like silver in the late afternoon sun. On its opposite shore, Daisy noticed the stately Castle Pless, built in the style of the French Renaissance.

The steps leading up to the terrace and the entrance of the castle were lined by the forest rangers and game-keepers of the Prince of Pless in their green uniforms, and in the Great Hall, the directors of the Pless enterprises, high government officials, and representatives of the town stood ready to greet the new Princess of Pless.[16] Behind them, Daisy noticed the large assembly of the servants including the footmen in their

---

16 Confusion may arise due to the English meaning of *Prince*, which in German serves for *Fürst* (i.e., Prince) as well as for his son (i.e., *Prinz*). Sons and daughters of Emperors, Kings, Princes, etc. are generally referred to as *Prinzen* and *Prinzessinnen*, although there are exceptions as in the case of the Fürsten von Pless (Princes of Pless) where the first-born son was given the title of *Prinz von Pless* (i.e., *Prince of Pless*), while his brothers and sisters were addressed as *Grafen/Gräfinnen von Hochberg, i.e. Counts/Countesses of Hochberg*. Under the same etiquette, Princess Daisy of Pless was *Prinzessin von Pless*, while her mother-in-law – stepmother of Hans – was called *Princess Mathilde*, but was not a *Prinzessin*, but a *Fürstin*.

old-fashioned livery, and the maids in the colourful folk-costumes of the region.

Daisy felt very uncomfortable to greet her new relations, most of whom were total strangers to her, under the eyes of the entire personnel of the house. But her self-consciousness vanished under the spontaneous embrace of her father-in-law. His gentle manner and warm smile reassured Daisy that in him she had found "a fatherly friend and protector."[17] To call him *Vater* seemed easy for her; at this hour, it was the one German word Daisy could utter without shyness and hesitation. Daisy's mother-in-law also greeted her with a quiet, friendly smile, but Daisy felt oppressed by the severe stares of the other relatives who had come to Pless to greet the young couple. Her frantic attempts to respond to the few English or French phrases they offered her as their greeting were soon drowned out by the noisy conversation among the family members. Daisy decided that she would learn to master the German language as quickly as possible.

Daisy spent an almost sleepless night. She was relieved when Hans had told her that to-day she would not be expected to join him and his parents on their customary morning ride through the park. She needed time to think and sort out her ambiguous feelings. She wanted to be by herself this first morning, but to find some privacy in this huge house proved to be impossible. The servants, who seemed to follow her everywhere, did not react to being dismissed, even though they seemed to understand Daisy's command. While the footmen carried out the etiquette of the house without the trace of a smile, the maids who stationed themselves in Daisy's apartment broke into embarrassed giggles when Daisy tried to strike up a conversation.

What started like a comedy of errors, soon became an annoying nuisance, as Daisy kept trying to escape from the presence of the ubiquitous servants.

> When I wanted to leave one room for another a bell was rung, a servant opened the door and a footman walked in front of me wherever I wished to go. And all I wanted was to steal quietly away with a tight throat.[18]

Daisy hoped that Hans, who was certainly familiar with the informality of English country life and the laughter that filled its houses, would understand her need for privacy and interpret her wishes to the servants. Rather than agreeing to speak to the servants, Hans appeared quite

---

17 DPH, p. 53.
18 DPH, p. 53.

agitated and, during the family's dinner, lectured Daisy gravely on never speaking privately even on superficial matters with the servants, who well knew their place and must never be asked to act against rules and etiquette of the house. No one around the dinner table came to the rescue of this "undisciplined" new member of the family. Only Vater placed his arm around Daisy's shoulder with the gentle command, which was to become a proverb at Pless and Fürstenstein:

Leave the child alone; she will come in front of you all in time![19]

Daisy's father-in-law had become

Vater, a faithful friend and protector. ... He understood me. ... Above all, he believed in me. ... This gave me courage and I did my utmost to please him by being tactful and learning to do things as I should.[20]

In her own mind, Daisy's rebellious spirit could hardly wait to escape from the stifling atmosphere of Castle Pless to Fürstenstein, which Vater had assigned to Hans and Daisy as their residence. In Fürstenstein, she would liberate the castle and herself from the bonds of Prussian etiquette; at Fürstenstein, she would not be under the constant scrutiny of censoring relatives and, removed from the bonds of Pless, Hans would also become a free spirit. Daisy longed for the day when she and Hans would leave the somber Pless and its oppressively over-decorated palace where

the family lived a life completely isolated from their humbler neighbours, and hardly seemed aware of the sources of their vast wealth, or the thousands of miners and others who toiled to secure it.[21]

Only Vater appeared to understand the confused feelings which Daisy revealed to the family during her first weeks in Upper Silesia. Everyone else, especially Hans, treated her as

only a girl well under twenty who should have been content to sing, dance (very occasionally), embroider, and listen to her seniors' talk, according them continuous, almost fulsome silent admiration.[22]

---

19 DPH, p. 53.

20 DPH, p. 53.

21 BLU, p. 20.

22 BLU, p. 64

Despite the immense size of the castle and its dramatic location, Fürstenstein in its romantic setting appealed to Daisy at first sight. And while in the gray of winter, the populace of Pless had barely taken any notice of her arrival, Daisy was touched to tears by the presence of thousands of jubilant people who, as Hans animatedly explained to her, had come from the neighbouring town of Freiburg, from the district capital of Waldenburg, and from all the villages once belonging to Fürstenstein to greet them on this beautiful summer day.

The next day, the *Freiburger Bote* and the *Waldenburger Wochenblatt* enthusiastically reported

The Events Celebrating the Arrival of the Prince of Pless on the 6th of July 1892.

It was a joyful day of unforgettable celebrations prepared by thousands of eager hands which had given the entire town a festive appearance. ... The streets were profusely decorated, and not one house could be found without colourful trim or without a flag on its roof. ... Garlands, freshly cut trees and one triumphal arch after the other greeted the couple with welcoming words such as *Be Welcome German Eagle with Albion's Rose!* For miles, the streets were lined with all the organizations and all the schoolchildren of the town. Everyone admired the serene wife of the Prince, a picture of youth, of a singularly graceful and utterly charming appearance. In generous words, the Princess acknowledged the extraordinary reception in her address to the representatives of the town. ... Under the enthusiastic applause of the populace, the Prince and the Princess proceeded to the village of Polsnitz, where thousands of miners, officials and farm labourers dressed in traditional Silesian costumes and carrying shiny sickles, scythes and pitchforks, formed two long lines which reached up to the entrance of the Castle on the hill. ... On its way from the railway station to the Castle, the coach of the Prince and the Princess had to be halted again and again for the numerous speeches, songs, poems and the music of brass bands and, last not least, the presentation of gifts. ... The celebrations ended late in the evening with grandiose fireworks on the hills opposite the magnificently illuminated castle.[23]

The shouts of *Hoch* by the welcoming people crowding the Palace Square wafted through the open doors of the entrance hall, where the retainers and servants, the men in their uniforms and liveries, and the women in bright Silesian costumes formed a semi-circle. There were many smiles and a sense of genuinely happy excitement and joy, because Castle Fürstenstein would finally be occupied by a senior member of the family again. For years, Hans's father had only visited Fürstenstein.

---

23 *Der Freiburger Bote*, July 7, 1892, pp. 2-3.

Although his family had lived there for almost four hundred years he had chosen Castle Pless as his permanent residence.

The wide staircase leading to the Great Ballroom on the second floor was lined with the footmen in blue frockcoats, white gaiters, white gloves, and powdered wigs, an ominous sign to Daisy. Already on the next day, she had to acknowledge her great disappointment about Fürstenstein to herself. As burdened with pomp and etiquette as Pless, perhaps even more so, the first home of her own had, despite its romantic character, very little in common with the country houses where she had grown up in England. Again, Daisy found herself surrounded by servants. Even in the evening, she had to tolerate two maids in attendance in her bedroom who were there only to open the covers of her bed. In addition

> a gorgeously dressed man with a cocked hat and a tall silver staff was always on duty outside the front door. He signalled one's approach to the servants, flourished his great stick and saluted like a regimental drum-major of the English Guards. Privately I christened him *Guy Fawkes*. ... Fürstenstein is not a really peaceful place; one cannot get on the green grass away from the servants. One is always passing a Musketeer, and the terraces are stiff, and there are always old men and women working on them, keeping them far too tidy and formal-looking.[24]

Daisy felt horrified by all this pomp and splendour, by the ubiquitous uniforms and liveries, and by the elaborate etiquette. And she was not overly surprised any longer when an uneasy Hans explained to her that she would have to learn to live in a milieu where all these men and women would always be there, day after day. In retrospect, Daisy thought Pless almost modest in its style and etiquette. All of a sudden, the first pangs of homesickness for England arose in her heart, and trivial things which normally would have merely amused her, began to grate on Daisy's nerves, like

> Uncle Bolko's revolting gargling practice, ... at the end of a meal; ... the ugly blue glass finger-bowls, ... the nasty kissing habit.

> On moon-lit nights, I used to wander on the terraces alone, and then come up the steps to hear German, and smell cigars – and the sound of the river in the valley made me think of the sea at Newlands, one wave following another for ever and ever.[25]

---

24 DPH, p. 58.
25 DPH, p. 57.

From the beginning, Hans somehow lacked the needed empathy, patience, and imagination to comprehend his wife's longing for a simpler lifestyle. It did not help that Hans's grandiose plans for a much changed Fürstenstein of the future disgusted Daisy, who only foresaw "a vulgar, nouveau riche imitation of the Imperial Court in Berlin." Her pleading not to ignore her ideas but let Fürstenstein reflect both their personalities, fell on deaf ears.

An agitated dispute about what Fürstenstein should represent ended in Daisy's first defeat. It was the start of a never-ending discord between them that frequently erupted in quarrels. Afterwards, Daisy invariably felt ashamed for being so childish and stubborn when the problems usually concerned mere trivialities such as the placing of certain pieces of furniture in certain rooms; or whether it was appropriate to plant the colourful but modest nasturtiums, *her* favourite flowers on the elegant terraces. But at the same time, Daisy could not ignore her feelings of being degraded and diminished by the power Hans exercised over her. Hans played the superior male who possessed greater knowledge and experience to the hilt.

In the meantime, Daisy valiantly struggled to regain some of her self-confidence and self-respect. She wanted to be accepted as what she was, as Princess Daisy, the Englishwoman, instead of being forced to submit to being molded in the image Hans had of her. Seeking the recognition and acceptance she failed to receive from her husband, she ignored his request not to speak more than was absolutely necessary with the servants, something he considered as "*absolut nicht fürstlich.*"[26] On her daily outings on horseback, she loved to exchange horses with the groom, enjoying not only the wild ride across the meadows on a man's saddle, but as much the thought of disobeying Hans, who would be horrified by her behaviour. There were numerous other little escapades Daisy needed to commit in order to retain a certain sense of autonomy and freedom from the control of Hans. All of a sudden, people in the villages around Fürstenstein talked about the Princess and her courage and informality. Anecdotes were passed house-to-house by the people, who began to refer affectionately to the Princess of Pless as *Our Daisy*.

One particular episode, also described in Daisy's diaries, was immediately related by the excited servants to the community and circulated widely. On her way to dinner with Hans and Vater, Daisy was observed wandering through the halls of the Castle in a robe stitched together from fodder-bags spirited from the stables to her apartments. In the

---

26 "absolutely not princely," i.e., inappropriate for a prince or a princess.

dining-salon, Daisy was received by her husband and her father-in-law, waited on by nine servants in full livery. Behind their forced smiles, the men concealed the realization that Daisy confronted them with another outburst of her rebellion against the ridiculous etiquette of Fürstenstein and the tradition-bound attitudes of her husband and his family.

Neither did the first visits on the estates of her neighbours in Lower Silesia mellow Daisy's determination to resist the oppressive atmosphere of Fürstenstein which threatened to suffocate all her joie de vivre. At first sight, Daisy liked many of the residences of the Silesian nobility. But with the pride in their traditions and their strict observance of etiquette, their owners hardly distinguished themselves from Hans. Like Hans, "they belonged to a nation which attaches absurd importance to trifles."[27]

Neither did Daisy's first visit to Breslau improve her negative mood. The huge Gothic churches built of brick darkened over the centuries to near-black, and the narrow, gloomy streets in the centre of the city all had an appearance foreign to a disappointed Daisy. She had expected Silesia's capital with its population of nearly half a million to have a certain splendour and elegance. She was horrified by the "incredibly old-fashioned and primitive" furnishings[28] of Breslau's best hotel.

All these impressions only fostered Daisy's longing for her homeland. Her constant comparing of Germany to England turned into an obsession of glorifying everything English. Daisy lost all objectivity. What had been likeable, even charming traits of naiveté and spontaneity changed to sarcastic criticism of a society and a milieu, which seemed to become more unbearably *Prussian*. Instead of a conciliatory attitude, Daisy adopted a condescending, cynical tone, which the family was no longer willing to tolerate. Nearly everyone was in an uproar about this young, immature, and tactless Englishwoman.

The family did not understand at all how desperately the lonely Daisy reacted to the overwhelming impressions of a world that she still did not comprehend and could not come to terms with, and how helplessly she tried to live up to the expectations placed on her. Eighty years later,

Daisy's oldest son Hans Heinrich (called *Hansel* by family and friends) expressed his sympathy with his mother to the author:

> When my mother was married at such a young age, she had really no idea of what the world was like. She had only spent one Season in London; she was still a child when she left England. When she arrived in Germany, she

---

27 DPH, p. 53.
28 DPH, p. 60.

had to find her way all by herself, totally inexperienced in almost everything, even in things English! Nothing in her past life had prepared her or could help her to compare different ways of life. And not even my grandfather, who really loved my mother, could comprehend the extent of the difficulties my mother had to struggle with as a young married woman.[29]

Far from Fürstenstein, at Kronberg in the Taunus Hills north of Frankfurt, the Dowager Empress Frederick was waiting to give solace to the young Princess of Pless. Her brother, the Prince of Wales, had urged the widow of Emperor Frederick to give a helping hand to Daisy. If there was anyone in Germany capable of offering compassion and, above all, advice to Daisy, it was the old Empress, Queen Victoria's daughter, who lived a lonely life at Castle Kronberg. Her own painful experiences as a young Englishwoman at Prussia's court in Berlin vividly in her mind, she wrote to Fürstenstein inviting Hans and Daisy to visit her at Friedrichshof in Kronberg.

The parallels in the lives of the two Englishwomen were striking. Both were transplanted to Germany through arranged marriages as very young, inexperienced women, although the marriage of Queen Victoria's daughter to Prince Frederick of Prussia was an exceedingly happy one. While Daisy would forever struggle for her husband's understanding and recognition of her humanitarian and political ideals and pursuits, the Crown Princess and the Crown Prince of Prussia were one at heart in their ideals and objectives for a modern Prussia and Germany, which were, as the future Empress Frederick wrote to her mother, Queen Victoria,

> "the only ones which can alone be the saving – not only of Prussia's position in Germany and Europe – but of the Prussian monarchy."[30]

Remembering her early years as the wife of the young Prince Friedrich Wilhelm of Prussia to whom she had been married in 1858, the Empress Frederick resolved to give Daisy her protection and share with the young Princess the wisdom she had gathered during thirty trying years in a country, that had never accepted or trusted her.

In contrast to Daisy, who had been tossed into a country utterly unknown to her, for young Victoria the step across the Channel had not been frightening. After all, her father, Prince Albert, was a German; many of her relatives she already knew well. They all belonged to the royal and princely houses of Germany, and she had long considered

---

29   Conversation in London, summer 1980.

30   Roger Fulford (ed.), *Dearest Mama* (London, 1968), p. 332.

them part of her own family. German language, music, and poetry were not foreign to her. German was often spoken among her own family in England. Whereas Daisy hardly knew her husband before marriage, young Vicky, proud and in high spirits, was already deeply in love with her *Fritz* when she arrived in Berlin. Outside her marriage, there were few happy memories. The huge correspondence of the Empress Frederick with her mother over a period of more than thirty years is filled with longing for England, complaints about isolation and hostility, and finally the loneliness of old age. The letters to *Dearest Mama* foreshadowed the fate of Daisy of Pless. Indeed, at times passages in Victoria's letters and in Daisy's diaries seem interchangeable in their content and even their phrasing, as if written by the same author. On May 11, 1864, Vicky writes to her beloved mother:

> I cannot do the simplest thing without it being found to be in imitation of something English and therefore anti-Prussian. ... I was never popular here.

> Oh if you knew how my love daily increases for my dear home – ('the home of the brave and free'); attached as I am to this country and anxious to serve it ... the other will ever remain the land of my heart.

> and I have so few to whom I think aloud, and from whom I need not hide feelings which are so strong which grow every day, ... and cause one to cling to all that is English.

> You cannot think how painful it is to be continually surrounded by people who consider your very existence a misfortune and your sentiments evidence of lunacy.[31]

The Empress Frederick counted the German Chancellor Prince Bismarck as her archenemy. He referred to her as

> an Englishwoman, suspected of Liberal, of free thinking and artistic tendencies, of cosmopolitan and humanitarian sentiments and the like abominations.[32]

Could the Empress Frederick have given Daisy genuine support? Long before her isolation in Kronberg, she wrote to her mother. "If I were to die today how little, how very little I should have done of what I ought to."[33]

---

31 See Roger Fulford, op. cit., passim.

32 Otto Fürst von Bismarck, *Gedanken und Erinnerungen* (Stuttgart, 1922) p. 198.

33 See Roger Fulford, op. cit., passim.

Perhaps the young Daisy gave more to the lonely, embittered Empress than she received from her. Perhaps it helped Daisy that Hans left Friedrichshof for a hunting trip soon after paying his respects to the Empress. Without him, Daisy felt relieved and at ease, although "she had been taken to Kronberg very, very terrified."[34]

The Empress opened her arms and her heart to Daisy who recognized in her "a rare tenderness ... and a loneliness in her thoughts."[35] For the first time since leaving England, Daisy felt safe to unburden her heart to someone who, she knew, would truly understand her plight.

So compassionate was the reaction of the Empress, that Daisy poured out all the feelings she had suppressed for months: her resentment of German rules and etiquette; of most of her in-laws, indeed of most of the German women she had met so far; her anger at her own husband who censored her behaviour and feelings; and finally at herself for committing so many mistakes and for making a fool of herself.

The Empress freely shared her own memories, some comforting, others rather disturbing and frightening. Daisy still tried to cling to the belief that her future would eventually become truly happy. The Empress cautioned her that her homesickness for England would never cease. Through painful trial and error, Daisy would have to find a way to survive, neither surrendering herself to the expectations of her husband and his family, nor hoping that all her German in-laws would ever respect her.

Hans had repeatedly warned Daisy about the embittered mood of the old Empress who, even Daisy had to admit, was inclined to follow more her heart than her intellect. And, despite sincerely trying to help the young Daisy, the Empress had unintentionally burdened her with her own unextinguished bitterness as well. In the end, the visit at Friedrichshof had restored some of Daisy's optimism and self-respect. On the day before her departure, Daisy entered a note of gratitude into the personal guestbook of the Empress, which she impulsively signed *Daisy of Pless*.

Hans was not amused when he returned to Kronberg from his hunting trip.

Against his will, Daisy had signed as *Daisy of Pless*, much to the dismay of Hans, who always insisted on the "appropriate" signature of *Mary Theresa von Pless*. For Daisy, this was a small triumph which she ascribed to the example of the old Empress. Later, Daisy gratefully remembered her in her diaries.

---

34 DPH, p. 62.

35 DPH, p. 62.

As long as she lived, the Empress never failed me, and one of her last acts was to charge the Emperor her son to protect and help me.[36]

Daisy could not have wished for a better preparation for her first official visit to Berlin and her presentation at Court than she had received at Kronberg. In the train that took Hans and her to the Imperial capital, Daisy concluded in a happy mood that as the young Princess of Pless, she would make the best impression at the Imperial Court.

* * * * * *

36   DPH, p. 63.

3 | *The Beginning of a Friendship*

T he rising prominence of the military and its predominance at Court confronted Daisy on the day of her presentation to the Emperor. Hans did not have a uniform to wear for court and as he did not hold either a military rank or a diplomatic position, Daisy "went in after a Countess who was a mere 'Frau' until last year."[1] Having prepared herself for a spectacular entry, Daisy felt furious and humiliated but had her "day in court", when the Emperor kissed her left, gloveless hand "with the words 'I do not kiss a hand with a glove on' and then went straight up to the other ladies and kissed their gloved right hands."[2] With a singular charming, some said daring gesture, the Emperor bestowed unexpected prominence upon the young Englishwoman. Daisy could hardly await her first ball at court!

* * *

The *Palais Pless* in Berlin's Wilhelmstrasse, designed by Destailleur, the architect of Castle Pless, seemed uncomfortable and gloomy, far too large for its purpose of providing a dignified temporary home for the family. Even Hans would invariably prefer the nearby *Hotel Kaiserhof*, because the *Palais Pless* did not even have a single modern bathroom. However, the advantage of its location in the centre of the political and social life of Berlin and close to the Tiergarten could not be overlooked.

This first visit to Berlin gave Daisy few opportunities to get to know the city. Her impressions were restricted to its centre – the Wilhelm-

---

1   DPH, p. 66.
2   DPH, p. 172.

strasse, the Tiergarten, the elegant avenue *Unter den Linden* and, at its eastern end, the Imperial Palace. All the more lasting was the effect Emperor Wilhelm and his court had on the young Princess of Pless.

Young and forceful, daring and impetuous, the Emperor seemed to embody the modern Germany storming relentlessly under his leadership towards a glorious future. For many Germans, this future had already begun; they were ready to follow their Emperor in his quest for the creation of a powerful Germany seeking, if necessary by the threat of force, her deserved *Place in the Sun*; a latecomer among the richer nations of Europe that would not dare refuse Germany her rightful place among the powerful of the world. Traditionalist in some ways and progressive in others, the dynamic, multi-faceted personality of Wilhelm II appealed to widely different segments of the population. To the military, the civil service, and to the majority of Prussia's landed aristocracy, the Emperor represented continuity of tradition. The burgeoning class of industrialists and merchants praised Wilhelm II for his interest in science and technology that helped promote the flourishing German trade and commerce throughout the world. The pomp and circumstance of Wilhelminian Germany excited the lower middle class and it also led many an artist to a sycophantic, often tasteless celebration of the Emperor and the German Empire.

There was still much poverty among the working classes and the rural proletariat. The Socialists representing a growing, political force, were deeply distrusted by the bourgeoisie and detested, if not hated, by the Emperor and the aristocracy. Young writers and poets openly expressed criticism and dissent. On the whole, however, the majority of the population seemed optimistic and content, and most parties and groups, including the Socialists, professed their loyalty to the monarchy. Strangely absent was a general awareness that most of the cherished Prussian traditions had in fact ceased to determine the course of events. As the Princess Radziwill observed,

> the general public imagined that nothing had changed; they failed to realize that after the triumphs of Sadowa and Sedan[3] neither the Emperor nor his ministers could proceed upon the same lines as before. No longer were they heads of a mid-European state; their territory was now of wider significance; their eyes were lifted towards the hills, and in the consummation of 1871 they saw the beginnings of an Empire which should be wide-spreading in territory, far-reaching in power, and knit together by a love for the father-

---

3   The decisive battles in the wars of 1866 and 1870-71.

land which should make the German Empire supreme in the councils of Europe.[4]

Denying the fact that the country was passing through a period of enormous change left the Prussian aristocracy, which had literally carried the old Prussian kingdom on its shoulders, without its former role of power and influence. As the Princess Radziwill pointed out, in the Second Reich, the aristocracy soon

> followed blindly any instructions which the *Wilhelmstrasse* chose to give. ... This group was mostly composed of large landowners and members of the highest aristocracy of the country. The Princes of Hatzfeldt, Carolath-Beuthen, Pless, and Hohenlohe, the Dukes of Ratibor and Ujest, ... all had seats in the Prussian Upper House and some were also deputies in the Reichstag; ... they largely constituted the majority upon which the Government would always rely. It was a party submissive to the rulers of the country, but not disciplined. It sedulously sought its own interests and its own advantages, and they were pecuniary.[5]

Next to its growing military strength, it was largely the unprecedented economic dynamism which gave the young Empire its new identity and the loyalty of its citizens; it provided the force that kept the country together. In his *History of Germany since 1789*, Golo Mann surveyed the country's development:

> In 1870 German industry had not yet overtaken France; better military organization, not a superior industry, gave the Germans their victory. Thereafter the curve rises noticeably more steeply; first under Bismarck, and then even more so under William II. Like a speck of grease in a plate of soup the pompous Imperial regime floated on a stream of prosperity created by others.

> Between 1848 and 1914, the population of Berlin increased tenfold, from 400.000 to 4million. [And the Second Reich] this nation state without responsible government, without internal unity, was one of the greatest centers of energy there has ever been. Its population increased annually by almost a million, its industry was surpassed only by that of America and its army was second to none.[6]

Nowhere was this new Wilhelminian Age – its material wealth, its pomp, and its poverty – more visible than in Berlin. Other German

---

4   See Catherine Radziwill, op. cit., pp. 156-57.

5   See Catherine Radziwill, op. cit., pp. 169-70.

6   Golo Mann, *The History of Germany since 1789* (London, 1968), pp. 199-200.

capitals like Munich, Dresden, and Stuttgart, although retaining their predominant role in the arts, but no longer the centers of political power they once were, changed little compared to Berlin, where the economic power of the bourgeoisie celebrated itself in the elegant districts of the Westend and the Southwest, while the northern and eastern districts of the city were dominated by huge factories of world-renown surrounded by a sea of overcrowded tenements where the working population subsisted under deplorable conditions. Between the East and the West of Berlin – remaining two worlds apart – the centre of the city accommodated the Imperial Court and the seat of the Prussian and the Imperial German governments, neither of which succeeded to form a link between the upper bourgeoisie in the Westend and the proletariat on the opposite side of Berlin.

This was not London, Daisy recognized, where ladies were allowed to appear in public in their *barouches* on their own in Hyde Park. Daisy decided to break some of Imperial Berlin's etiquette. Rather than remain confined to the Palais Pless when Hans or Vater were absent, she did manage to appear in the Tiergarten without them, offering her company to an old aunt of Hans whom she actually quite disliked. And despite Vater's protestations, "Child, that is something you cannot do in Germany,"[7] Daisy insisted on walking with her father-in-law through the Wilhelmstrasse and *Unter den Linden* without wearing the obligatory black frock long enough to sweep the pavement. Instead, Daisy chose

> a very pretty quiet gray frock. ... Vater looked at me very kindly and sadly said: 'Child, have you no black frock. ... Never mind then, come but as you are,' and we went.[8]

When, during a reception in the *Prinzessinnenpalais*, she was seen seated next to Prince Eitel Friedrich on the same sofa – the Prince had failed to sit on a separate chair at a respectable distance from her, as etiquette dictated,

> Vater explained to me, saying, 'Child, don't do that in Germany; we never let a man sit on the same sofa as a lady.'... This made me smile, but he was far too dear to me to argue with him.[9]

---

7   DPH, p. 63.

8   DPH, p. 63.

9   DPH, p. 63.

Berlin society began to murmur about the rebellious Princess of Pless and decided that her breaches of etiquette were no faux pas, and certainly not the result of her ignorance!

It is fascinating to hold Daisy's criticism up against the nearly identical impressions of the German Imperial capital and its Court, that were recorded by Lady Randolph Churchill who had stopped with her husband Lord Randolph in Berlin on their return to London from St. Petersburg, in 1888. Still under the impact of the ultra-fashionable upper society of St. Petersburg and its imposing court, "lavish in its extravagance, barbaric in its splendour," Jennie Churchill found the German Imperial Court

> unpretentious and, perhaps, a little dull, but full of traditions and etiquette. ... Signs of the all conquering and victorious army were everywhere apparent; everything military was in the ascendant.[10]

Balls at the Imperial Court hardly distinguished themselves for a relaxed, informal atmosphere. Only those who had received permission by Imperial consent were allowed to step onto the dance floor, and only after several rehearsals under the tutelage of a strict dance master who criticized every incorrect step he observed from his little balcony high above his illustrious guests. Minuets and gavottes were practiced for hours; Daisy felt she was drilled for a parade. No wonder, Jennie Churchill never forgot how during her visit in 1898 the Emperor laughingly explained to her that to his court balls "men came for discipline and women for deportment."[11] Minuets and gavottes had to be danced until His Majesty gave a signal for a waltz or a polka.

Daisy thought it ridiculous to dance to the tunes and figures of the eighteenth century vis-à-vis a partner wearing a modern German uniform. She enjoyed a small triumph when the Emperor asked her rather quickly for a second dance by beckoning to her with his index finger and then pointing to the floor, a gesture Daisy did not appreciate at all. This peculiar habit of calling someone to his side was one of the notorious, much disliked practices of the Emperor; it made the ladies blush in embarrassment, while men would gnash their teeth in anger and humiliation.

In the opinion of those present, both the second dance and the Emperor's casual request for it came unseemly early. Flattered by the Emperor's renewed attention, and feeling quite superior and proud of

---

10 See Mrs. George Cornwallis-West (Lady Randolph Churchill), op. cit., p. 234.

11 Ibid., p. 236.

her English upbringing, which never confused informality with rudeness, Daisy advised the Emperor that she would always obey his Majesty's word, but never again His Majesty's index finger! Daisy's words did not escape the horrified attention of those guests within earshot. Her frankness did not provoke the angry outburst expected from the Emperor, but only his appreciative smile.

During the following weeks, more and more stories made their rounds among the shocked society. With indignation, one noticed that during dinners at court and in the opera the Emperor would turn to the Princess of Pless again and again in animated conversation devoting far too much attention to her and rudely neglecting his other guests. During the weekly *Schleppencour* at court, which required all ladies to appear with their shoulders bare and with a long train attached to their waist, Daisy who "would not go about with shoulders like Queen Victoria's early pictures"[12] persuaded the *Mistress of the Robes* to let her wear two strips of chiffon over her shoulders. These constantly replenished stories fueled the gossip about the daring Princess of Pless, whom the Emperor seemed to forgive every new breach of etiquette with a benevolent smile. Overnight, Daisy acquired her reputation for not only being rebellious and for flaunting all rules adhered to by society, but for also getting away with her unacceptable conduct.

Vater and Hans were in a state of constant agitation about Daisy's frank approach to the Emperor, who was known to put fear into the heart of most women. They were perplexed about his easy-going, friendly reaction to Daisy. Daisy herself gave her own explanation some years later admitting that "when I first met the Emperor, I immediately liked him."[13] Within her first few weeks in Berlin, she also found him of

> great intellectual quickness and ability, highly intelligent but vain and always 'acting.'... He always *thought* he *knew*, ... [He] posed to his intimates and friends, perhaps even to himself.[14]

Instinctively, Daisy seemed to know how to approach the Emperor. She never touched his pride as a man and a monarch, setting the pattern for a relationship which would last for two decades. They would always

> exchange ideas frankly. ... Whatever the risks, I was amongst the few, the pityfully few, who were always honest and outspoken to their Sovereign. ... I

---

12 DPH, p. 65.

13 DPH, p. 67.

14 DPP, p. 293.

am vain enough to think that the Emperor liked me better and treated me with more sincerity than almost any other woman he knew. There were many reasons for this. I was English; I was different; I was never afraid of him.[15]

Except for the positive reaction of the Emperor, Daisy's first weeks in Berlin included few memorable events. She was glad to leave the Imperial capital and its society. Hans had decided to return to Silesia via Bohemia. After prosaic Berlin, Daisy was enchanted by the beauty of Dresden with its baroque architecture and its elegant riverside promenades. Called *Florence on the Elbe*, it was the first German city Daisy really liked.

Among Hans's friends in Bohemia, Daisy was delighted to finally discover the spontaneity and uncomplicated friendliness she had missed so much in Germany. With their easy-going, gracious manners, the Bohemian nobles welcomed Daisy with open arms. In Teplitz,[16] Prince Alphons Clary-Aldringen delighted Daisy with his gentle Austrian charm and his discreet admiration of her beauty. And in Castolovitz,[17] it seemed easy to make friends with *Fanny*, the intelligent, witty Countess Franziska Sternberg. Hans noticed with relief how content Daisy felt and how, for the first time, she approved of his friends without any reservations. Hans would not have failed to recognize Daisy's undertone of undiminished resentment when she commented on the differences between the Bohemian and Silesian nobles. The former securely, but not rigidly, followed their own traditions, while the latter forever looked to the court in Berlin as their model of conduct. Among the Bohemians, Daisy felt that "one can say (more or less) what one thinks and that one could never do in Court Circles in Berlin."[18]

Inspired by the impressions and memories she took back to Silesia from her weeks in Bohemia, Daisy arrived in Fürstenstein in a happy mood. In spring of 1894, her wish for a garden in the English manner finally came true when Hans called for a gardener from Newlands.

In July, Daisy started out for her first extended visit to England since her wedding. At home in Newlands, Daisy did not hold back her tears when she related her discouraging experiences in Germany. Even though there were stories of successes and triumphs to tell, unburdening her heart to her parents did not disperse her beginning doubts about her marriage and the foreboding that nothing in Germany would ever

---

15 DPH, p. 112.

16 Teplice in the Czech Republic.

17 Castolovice in the Czech Republic

18 BLU, p. 169.

replace the beauty of Newlands and the happiness of being with her own family. In these days, Daisy decided to confide her thoughts and feelings, her hopes and fears to a diary.[19]

My Diary received its first entry on August 10, 1894.

Daisy's first diary offers a captivating picture of the restless, often superficial nature of the hectic social life of the international set of which the Prince and Princess of Pless were prominent members. During the first twelve months, between the Cowes Regattas of August 1894 and 1895, Daisy reports of staying in more than fifty different locations! Still enamoured with a way of life quite new to her, she breathlessly describes her experiences, the sailing, riding, and shooting parties, the succession of dinners, balls, and excursions that followed one after another in almost monotonous continuity. Within this period of twelve months, more than one hundred famous names appear in the diary, to which Daisy soon begins to add quite witty and pertinent observations and often more or less sarcastic comments.[20]

Typical of the nature of her earliest entries, which often appear quite hurried, superficial, and not free of grammatical and spelling errors, Daisy begins *My Diary* in August 1894 on

> Friday night Aug 10th Just come back from the Osborne where the Emperor dined with the Prince of Wales, some ladies were asked afterwards. I expect Lady Londonderry and some others are tearing their false fringes off in rage at not being invited, particularly as I and Mrs. Lancelot Lowther & our two husbands sailed yesterday in the *Britannia*[21] with the Prince of Wales, & Prince George.[22] I was in the race against the *Vegilant* [Vigilant] whose owner is Mr. Gould an American. It was a beautiful races & the *Britannia* won. ...[23]
>
> At the start we nearly ran into the *Vegilant* who was bearing down so near upon us. ... Our hearts were in our mouths for about twelve seconds. We headed the *Vegilant* & when we were quite sure she had no chance to win,

---

19 See Foreword.

20 Quotations between August 10, 1894, and April 28, 1896, are excerpted from the first, unpublished volume of Daisy's diaries in their original form, including all errors in spelling. In order to convey the flavour of Daisy's writing, early entries are reproduced in their entirety, while later entries are shortened.

21 The private yacht of the Prince of Wales.

22 The later King George V.

23 DUD, passim, i.e., all quotations from hereon to p. 85. Original not consistently numbered.

we sang all the popular comic songs. But I was frightened at first as I had never been on a racing yacht before. Luckily I am a good sailor. ...

Aug 11th We have had a very nice day we lunched on the Osborne & steamed down to Newlands to stay there the night The party consists of the Prince of Wales the Duke of York Mr. Paget the Prince's equerry & Sir Charles Cust the Duke's equerry, the Honble Mr.& Mrs Lowther (she is a nice little woman of about 26) my sister, husband & self. In the evening the Pierrot band came from Cowes, & delighted the Prince who kept time to their guitars tapping his little fat feet on the ground. ['fat' crossed out; 'he has nice feet' added later]

Next day, as a consequence of this lovely party at Newlands, Daisy found herself entangled in a breach of protocol for the first, but by no means for the last time in her life.

Aug 12th I am afraid the Prince is in hot water as well as ourselves for we were invited yesterday (we got this invitation in the morning) to a tea party on the *Hoenzolen* [the *Hohenzollern*, the Imperial yacht of Emperor Wilhelm II]. We went to see the Prince to ask him what was best to do, & he said, 'I commanded you several days ago to lunch with me on the Osborne & go to Newlands, I am coming more or less as your guest as you are the daughter of the house & your husband is son-in-law you could not possibly throw me over.' I explained we could follow & be in time for dinner etc etc, but the Prince wouldn't hear of it, so he wrote a note to the Emperor which we took hoping to find him on board but as bad luck would have it he was out, so we gave the note to a gentleman in his suit [suite] who was to give it to him. They were all furious on board the *Hoenzolen,* saying that the Emperor's orders came before the Prince of Wales' etc etc. ... In my heart I agreed with all they said but couldn't get Hans to think so.

He went to Count Hatzfelt [Hatzfeldt] German Ambassador who said also we ought to go with the Prince of Wales so we went, & there will be one more black deed put down in the Emperor's book against my husband. I wonder how this Emperor business will end & what I shall write in my diary in years to come. But whether Emperor or Czar of all the world he ought to have asked the Prince before whether it would suit him to have the tea party on such, or such a day & not send an invitation to the future King of England the day *before,* as we are sure he only did so to break up the party at Newlands, as he was sure the Prince would go to the tea party instead. ... The Emperor seems to think he is a God wherever he goes to be worshipped by all the world.

We came back from Newlands today on the Osborne and had grouse for lunch. This afternoon we went to *Egypt House* which Lord & Lady Algernon Gordon Lennox have taken for the season. They gave a garden party it poured with rain so the Emperor did not come as he promised to do, He leaves Cowes tomorrow so there will be no chance of saying something about having had to go Newlands etc etc. ... We dined together at home we three, Wood & the Lowthers, Mr. Leycock came in after dinner & asked us to go to Scotland. But Hans has to go back to Germany.

This was the first time that Daisy took note of the strained relationship between the Prince of Wales and his nephew the Emperor, who, with his impetuous temperament had again angered his uncle, whether intentionally – as Daisy seemed to think – or not. Protocol, etiquette, and the strain between England and Germany began to intrude into Daisy's personal life.

Aug. 13th We were to have met Mother and Father today to settle about Scotland Hans thinks it would'nt be proper for Shelagh & I to go there together which I think nonsence as I am married & could surely chaperone her anywhere, & Mr. Leycock's married sister is to be there. ...

I & Gwen Lowther walked with the Prince to *Egypt House* where I & Prince George ... played croquet together. ... the Prince asked me to race on the *Britannia* again tomorrow.

Aug 14th Went to race on the *Britannia* but we were beaten by *Santaneta* [*Santa Anita?*], it was fearfully rough, ... we lunched on board & got back about 5.30. I was so tired and went to bed till seven, dined on the Osborne, Pierrot band came & played & sang after dinner a very happy evening, poor Prince George sniffling next to me. It is very nice chaperoning little Shelagh & I feel very proud. . . .

Aug 17th Sun. We sat in the garden in the morning ... and settled with the Prince for him and I to go to Carisbroke Castle in the afternoon. He asked who else he should take as the carriage only held two & one on the box I longed to say Prince George but did'nt like to, but to my surprise Prince George appeared in the afternoon & we took our tea & had a very pleasant afternoon. But both their royal Highnesses fell asleep driving there & it gave me the giggles & I tried not to look at the two sleeping future King's of England, Prince George teazed me all the time about the Emperor.

On August 15, Hans had returned to Fürstenstein after reluctantly giving his consent for Daisy's journey to Scotland with Shelagh. For the next few years, Shelagh would become her older sister's steady companion, her presence often, but not forever, a great comfort for Daisy. In Fürstenstein, with her cheerful nature, the eighteen-year-old *Little Shelagh* would innocently diffuse the disagreements between Hans and Daisy and help them both to bridge the beginning distance from each other, that was so painful, especially at dinner and sometimes throughout the entire day.

I hope they will leave Shelagh with us Hans loves having her & so do I & it would make and it wouldn't all the difference to me having her with me in Berlin. ... Shelagh is with me ... what a blessing that I have Shelagh at my side. ... God bless Little Shelagh.

As Daisy never confided her disappointments and her increasing doubts about her marriage to her sister, Shelagh unwittingly became the catalyst in Daisy's strained relationship with her husband. Shelagh's daily presence also helped Daisy to maintain an emotional lifeline to England.

Aug 19th Rosshire Yesterday was a lovely day and we rode ponies right over the mountains to fish in a lake I got nineteen trout with a fly & was very proud. Today it poured & we took a long walk returned 'across country' over rocks through bogs & rivers & got very wet. There are two ladies here, ... both nice countryfied short petticoated good women not very interesting, but it gives one a peaceful feeling to be with them, after these few petti-coated, jaleous, & generally immoral women of Society. ... I have never been to Scotland before & shall be miserable to leave in a day or two for Baden-Baden where I meet Hans. ... Shelagh is coming with me.

Shelagh's role as Daisy's travelling companion became almost rou-tine, especially since Hans insisted on his strange habit to follow his wife on their journeys a day later or to precede her by a day or two to their next destination or back to Silesia. Deprived of her husband's company too frequently, Daisy began to cautiously confide her thoughts and fears to her diary.

Oct 14th I dont know how to keep my diary, ... what ever I feel inclined to write, so I think I will do so, ... but ... as the years go by & I write things down, other people reading them might interpret them differently to the way I intended, & if I was not there to explain some hearts might be made unhappy, & harm done perhaps to my poor dead soul in thoughts. ...

Shelagh and I travelled from Scotland to Baden-Baden alone with the maids. ... I did not want at all to go back again to Germany so soon. ... The driver a real frank Scotsman tried to comfort us. ... the train was not in so we had milk and biscuits at the station hotel, the old lady owner asked me to write my name in the book so I wrote, it felt so funny writing 'Princess HH Pless' as when I am not with Hans & alone with my people & Shelagh & running about on Scotch hills etc it seems as if I were not married.

Baden-Baden was "on the whole quite amusing." The Prince of Wales who was on his way to take the waters at Bad Homburg, joined Hans and Daisy for a few days.

Oh! how funny the World is Dolly Furstenberg [the Princess Fürstenberg] who was always very charming to me suddenly got a little freezie, infact a lot of women were jealous simply I think because the Prince talked and walked about more with me than with them but as he knew me when I was a little child & half the other women he had never seen before I think it was quite natural.

The reactions of her hostess and the ladies of Baden-Baden society should not have surprised Daisy. At the races and at the balls, at the *Corso of the Flowers*,[24] which Hans had not cared to attend, and in the Casino, the Princess of Pless was always seen at the side of the Prince of Wales; Hans never gambled. If Daisy felt animated in the company of the Prince, others thought she was openly flattering or even "courting" him. For Daisy, these were days of pure enjoyment and light-hearted fun. On her last evening in Baden-Baden, she won a bet that "cost the Prince a dozen hats," which he would later purchase in Bad Homburg and send them to Fürstenstein with the note "We were so happy, too sad that our stay had to be so short."

It had not escaped the attention of the Prince of Wales that Daisy seemed less than happy in her marriage. Only once had she mentioned to him how difficult she found it to follow the advice he had given her on the day of her wedding "to become a good German." Wanting to help his protegée, the Prince suggested a trip to India for which he would make all necessary arrangements. Hans responded with unexpected enthusiasm for he was a passionate hunter and he welcomed the opportunity to go on a tiger hunt.

As always, Hans returned to Fürstenstein ahead of Daisy, while Daisy and Shelagh accompanied the Prince of Wales in his private railroad carriage as far as Frankfurt.

He gave us a very good dinner ... & after dinner he went to sleep in a small chair, the carriage was very shakey & his head *wabbled* so it looked exactly as if it must role off, & he looked so ugly & *drunk*, that I had to burst out laughing, I did'nt dare look at Shelagh. At Frankfort we all walked together to our train, ... we waved our heads and our handkerchiefs out of the window when the train moved on.

The restful days Daisy had looked forward to in Fürstenstein did not come about, as "the house began to smell & we found the drains were all wrong. I had always said they were as I never feel well here." The unbearable stench drove Hans and Daisy away. They decided to visit the Duke of Schleswig-Holstein, brother of the Empress, in Primkenau.

---

24   A competition of carriages richly decorated with flowers.

Duke Holstein is a great flirt *too* great a flirt to dare to flirt with besides I am such an idiot I can't flirt, I should not like a man think I cared 2d about him particularly as one can never tell if he cares for you; so he would laugh behind your back & say 'poor woman she is falling in love with me,' I cannot think how other women one sees flirting manage I wish I knew, as Hans says I may flirt, he says that I suppose because he knows I cant.

Whatever Daisy thought about her inability to flirt, she did complain to her diary about the other ladies being "fearfully jaleous," in Primkenau and on the *Albrechtsburg*[25] in Meissen, the next stop on the journey. "When a woman is really bad she is much worse than the worst man I think."

The return to Fürstenstein brought two disappointments. The sewage system was still under repair and the Emperor did not visit as expected.

The Emperor expressed with many regrets that he was too busy with the manoeuvers. ... I admire the man in the Emperor, the dozens of ideas and purposes he carries in his brain at once, but I loath his cowardly devilish character, & I am sure I shall be a German nhiylist [nihilist] soon.

The dreaded visit to Pless was preceded by a stay with the cheerful Larisch family in Solza across the border from Pless in Bohemia. "Certainly Austrians are the most charming people," Daisy observed again.

Oct 21 We arrived here 'Pless' yesterday. ... It is fearfully dull here & I always feel seedy here I am sure the drains are very bad; We stay here a whole week! ... We all went out riding this morning, Ah! the bore of having to go a 'slow little canter' pace all the time, & to take care here because it is slippery & to keep more to the right as it is a little *deep* on the left etc etc. I had a very uncomfortable saddle and a horse, ... poor beast he wanted to go for a good gallop I was told to pull gently etc etc, I think the next time. ... I will give him his head & all the rein & let him run away. ... It would be a little break in the monotony of our morning ride.

In an afterthought, as if feeling guilty about her complaining, Daisy wrote "My father-in-law is not in a very good temper but he is always a dear old man." On went the journey to more relatives, always with Shelagh!

Nov 2nd *Fürstenstein* From Pless we went to Klitschdorf to Hans' sister [Lulu von Solms-Baruth], ... a dear charming pretty woman of thirty with four children & five of her sister-in-law who are orphans. She is a pattern

---

25 A residence of the Saxonian Kings near Dresden.

'Haus Frau' & a *bonne d'enfants* to all the children, ... we came here day before yesterday & are off again tomorrow to hunt at Pardobetz.[26] Yesterday Shelagh and I went for a ride all the saddles have gone except the one I kept to take tomorrow & one man's saddle so we had to ride on that & took turns to do so; When ever we saw any one or got into a road we quick put the unwomanly leg over on the womanly side, & tryed to stick which we did, but it is rather difficult to ride 'lady ways' on a gentleman's saddle. I felt like a girl... . I have a lot of things I would like to write 'heart thinks' but perhaps it is better not to do so.

November 7th Pardubetz We have had a very nice time here, Austrians are so natural and lively taking life as it comes & making the best of it. ... Little Shelagh enjoyed her time with me, I think Count Hansi Larisch is rather in love with her, but she must marry an English man, dear little girl. ... Dear old Dads [Daisy's father] has come to another standstill with his money. ... I wish I was rich & could help them a bit, my father-in-law is very rich & he gives us Pds.5000 a year to live on & with all the travelling about, ... Hans is borrowing money, & I am sure his father will find it out. ... We leave here tonight via Dresden Hans meets us in Hanover, he went to Berlin last night. ...

For the next five months, Hans and Daisy continued their visiting tour in England. The diary reports about repeated stays in London, in Newlands, at Ruthin, and at a number of country houses including Somerly Grove, Houghton (for the New Year's Ball), Melton (meeting the Duke of Schleswig-Holstein), Warwick (for a "not very amusing" fancy ball), Shrewsbury (meeting Gordy), and Pitchley (for the famous Pitchley Hunt). The days were filled with shooting parties, balls, and dinners, with conversation, singing, and card games. In the beginning, Daisy loved it all despite the damp cool winter; she was too happy to be among her own people. But she soon found herself confronted by some unexpected, unpleasant experiences, which caused her a good deal of confusion, heartbreak, and conflict of conscience.

A play in London, while of rather second-rate quality – where the heroine who has run away from her husband falls in love with "a very wicked man," made Daisy

wonder, as I often do, why I am never to know what passion is. is there such a thing or does it only exist in books & plays or between wicked people, the fortune telling woman told me that I should be once tempted but would resist & *so I will* & be true in thought word and deed to one of the best husbands a woman could have, so help me God.

---

26 Pardubitz in Bohemia, location of the famous *Pardubitz Steeplechase*; since 1919 Pardubice in Czechoslovakia, now Czech Republic.

Three years of marriage had failed to give Daisy a much needed sense of certainty and security about her relationship with Hans. Her heart and mind were filled with doubts about herself and her expectations on her own life as a married woman. Hans was always kind to her; he adored her, but in his own way, like one adores a precious possession. He had failed to ignite the love Daisy so much longed for. Her disappointment in Hans battled with a sense of duty to never doubt that she was blessed with "the best of husbands." Ambivalence continued to fill the pages of her diary.

> November 28th Melton Hans is hunting & will I hope come back without having had a fall. ... At dinner sometimes when I am alone with Hans & we are not talking, I look at the flowers on the table & think they want refreshing & then it flashes across me that I must die I often think about it. ... shall I really see my little baby again whose brown hair I have around my neck in a locket. ... Ah!, what can the next World be like ... there is no marriage or giving in marriage.

During these months, quite a few names of certain admirers appear in the diary again and again, each man conscientiously categorized by Daisy according to age, rank, appearance, intelligence, discretion, and trustworthiness. Although not one of them was taken seriously by Daisy, who despite her constant doubts about herself as a woman, felt superior to them all, rumors and gossip spread about "the mad Princess who was seen to through [throw] a loaf of bread at somebody's head at Willi's restaurant." All of a sudden, Daisy felt almost persecuted by the society she had looked forward so much to be part of. About her stay at Castle Warwick, she wrote

> Every thing I said was turned the wrong way, ... I felt miserable, & to think that they took me for that sort of woman. I blame no man though it is the women of to day I blame. Once at lunch I felt as if I must do something or scream so I choped a spongecake that was in front of me, they made a rhyme 'Princess Pless has made a mess, What was it guess.' Lord Chesterfield was sitting there & he answered 'She ought to have said no, But I fear she's said yes.' ... When I got upstairs I howled for a minute with rage.

* * *

The cause for the sudden controversy about Daisy of Pless was *Little Gordy*,[27] first mentioned briefly in the diary on October 14, 1894 during

---

27 Likely Gordon Wood; he died in the South African War.

Daisy's stay in Scotland. In February 1895, Gordy had come to Shrews-bury.

> Gordy was there we walked lot together he showed me the town & gave me a bouquet for each ball.

Gordy seemed to follow Daisy, turning up in Ruthin, Newlands, and other places. At his departures he left Daisy as confused in her feelings as he must have been himself. Both seemed to have fallen in love without being ready to openly admit their feelings to each other or knowing how to handle their relationship in the ubiquitous presence of the other guests at the various country houses and in London. The gossip about the two young people took a vicious turn, which troubled Gordy more than Daisy. Gordy also did not fail to notice the admirers who followed Daisy everywhere. Too often, Hans was not at her side.

> Feb 22nd Friday I have had no letter from Hans since being here, But I dont mind as I know he loves me just the same dear good husband if only I could love him as he does me, perhaps I do & dont know it. ... Gordy has left this morning. ... He seems changed I cant think what it is, he is often cross to me & not with the others not a bit like he was at Culmington & Shrewsbury. The other night he glared at me about something & then when I said good-night, I said to him, 'dont look at me as if you hated me;' & he held my hand a long time & said 'you silly,' dear Gordy he is a real good man.

Daisy was very well advised to exercise discretion, even though she could not hide her happiness when being near Gordy. No wonder the gossip continued making Daisy very angry, and Gordy most uncomfortable. The necessary restraint brought discord into their relationship.

> March 8th Friday I heard in London that Gordy is called my 'aide de camp' & that our names are been spoken off together, yes I thought the gossips would leave us alone a *little* longer, Gordy is a great friend of us all; & what ever they say will not make me change towards him; I do not think he knows they are talking about us, ... but what difference will all that make in me none what ever. ... I will not go through the world as if I was afraid of it, I will snap my fingers. ... Half the wrong done in the World is done through cowardness. ... I am disgusted with the whole world. I sometimes wish I had been born a clergyman's wife with eight children & nothing to think about but bread & milk & socks.

Her mixed-up feelings were beginning to show. From Gordy, Daisy turned immediately to her married life:

> I wonder when I shall get a baby! ... I hope they will leave Shelagh with us Hans loves having her & so do I & it would make all the difference to me having her with.

Daisy desperately needs Shelagh to build a bridge between herself and Hans and keep him in good spirits. But thinking about the other man in her life, she wrote about

> Gordy's broad shoulders & red hair. ... Gordy pilots me & it makes all the difference to a woman I think to have someone follow.

This is what Daisy is longing for rather than

> Poor old Hans, who feels so weak & seedy that he has gone to London to see his doctor. He is *eneamick*, I think... I *do* wish Gordy was here & I do wish that I did not wish it, but *cant* help my thoughts, wishes & thinks, one can surely control ones *self* and *ones* actions.

On March 25, Hans joined Daisy in Somerley. Gordy was there and brother George. Daisy found it most difficult to deal with her relationships with the three men, so different in character and closeness to Daisy's heart.

> I asked Gordy what ideas he (George) had about managing his property as he will be twenty one next November, and I am so afraid he might be persuaded into doing something silly.

It is Gordy rather than Hans whom Daisy elects as her confidant. Their relationship becomes at once more beautiful and stressful, teetering on the brink of bursting into unrestrained, uncontrolled love.

> I went to sleep last night in the brougham coming home ... with Gordy this morning. Hans hasn't a penny in the bank & no money to give me either & we go on living as if we had a lot. And in a fortnight I shall leave this little house & Gordy. ... My breakfast is here I suppose I must eat & I would much rather cry, I felt like that last night good-ness why. I didn't want to come up to bed and *do my duty* I suppose, the very idea made me mad so I danced while Hans played, & I sang & looked & seemed particularly happy & I felt suffocated. George came and put me to bed and we had a nice talk, he ... has seen & knows much more than people think.

Hans still did not feel well enough to go hunting, and Count Heini Larish wanted to be Daisy's companion. A "little diamond buckle" he insisted Daisy accept, made Gordy angry and jealous.

> To-day. ... I pulled his horse's ear. ... Gordy was very angry he had never been angry with me before but I believe he pretended to be more so than he really was because he saw how miserable I was. ... I said I did not care & he said he would soon make me care etc., but diary will you believe it I wished at that moment that he had struck me with his crop or caught hold

of my arm I would not have minded if he had hurt me. Am I mad do you think. What is this feeling I have!

Daisy is playing with fire. Gordy, who had warned her in a letter of his burning love for her, appears in an even mood again, but on the day before her return to Germany, she writes

there is a hidden fire in him which if I once kindled I should be frightened of, & yet how I long for it to burn for me. I asked him why he had behaved so rudely to me & at last he told me that I was called his shadow. ... He went away on purpose so that people should not talk about me & him. ... I shall not probably see him till next August how I hate leaving here tomorrow. ... I am more miserable than any one here in Melton. ... We rang the bell at White house where Gordy is I felt to touch the bell of the house where he lives I must be mad indeed. ...

I *cryed* last night. Shelagh must stay here & take care of little mother so I must go alone to Berlin. ... Diary *do* understand me I know it is wicked but I hate to go to Germany for of course I am treated as a German & told from morning till night that I *am* a German & reminded of it in every way. & I am *not* a German & nothing & nobody will ever make anything but a thorough English-woman of me with a dash of Irish in her!

In Berlin in May 1895, Daisy rode through the Tiergarten every day and

I gallop fast & in that way let out my bottled up feelings. ... I have not felt particularly happy. ... I am wicked, unthankful, horrid I know but I feel a sort of sinking despair when I think of the future, my thoughts my very life are in England & always will be, of course I love Fürstenstein it is a lovely place but I am not quite happy there when I am alone all day I like to have some English people staying with me. I must run about & do something all day & then in the evening I feel so tired & lonely I want to cry (while Hans plays melincoly tunes on the piano).

I cant help thinking of Newlands & wishing I was there, Oh! what a blessed time it was. ... I was seventeen, ... with a sense of perfect freedom, ... and no letters this morning. ... & Gordy hasn't written in ages, 'out of sight out of mind.'

The summer of 1895 brought two more trips to England where Daisy felt everywhere pursued by aggressive admirers.

Diary I am not really wicked, I can't help it if men like me & I like them *inocently* in return. I like so many men and there is safty in numbers. ... Gordy I think of still the great draw & the good man he always is. ...This next winter I may see him, but Hans talks of going to India.

In Fürstenstein, Daisy's impatient thoughts are in England with Gordy.

Gordon [!] didn't write after all. ... I shall not write him once more, but somehow I feel hurt, thats a secret?

With Hans away in Breslau and no word from Gordy, Daisy tries again to conquer her longing for Gordy and, struggling with ambiguous feelings, fathom the causes of her unfulfilled marriage.

July 23rd Tuesday A French lady writes: 'Et pris, voiyez-vous, le marie que vous revez, vous ne trouverez pas; toutes les jeune filles le revent comme vous; aucune ne le remontre. Savez-vous pourquoi? Parce qu'il n'existe pas. ... Ce mari-la n'est pas un marie; il s'appelie L'Amant![28]

I suppose there is some truth in this, ...if you only knew the feelings I have sometimes & how wicked I am I am afraid of myself, afraid to think how I am going to manage & take care of myself. ... You are nicer than you want to be just because you see the man loves you. ... & you like him too, ... so you let yourself go a weeney bit too much & then this man he takes you all & you feel lost, & a sort of weak dispear that you dont even want to fight comes over you & then! ... Oh! diary, what shall I do, its naturel I want to know what 'love' is & yet I dont! not even the best husband a woman could have & who I love very very much has taught me.

The other night on the terrace I felt a sort of wild feeling, it was rather dark & a beautiful warm night & thousands & thousands of stars & I wanted to feel myself loved, & I wanted to love in return as a girl, ... when she is on her honeymoon & first learns what love means. ... I felt as if I wanted to be like a woman in a novel, or a woman in a picture in the moon light with her lover, but it wasn't any use, Hans wanted to finish his cigar in peace he said & not walk up & down a lot of steps, so I did not get my love, & I did not love! & my heart felt topsy turvey, & I was miserable miserable! as my conscience kept saying it isn't your husband you want on the terrace with you, it is the excitment you want, to be with some other man who you know loves you. Oh! God help me to be good. ... Hans is so indifferent I wonder sometimes does he care one little bit.

And the wish to have children remains uppermost.

---

28 "Don't you see, the husband you are dreaming about, you will never find; all the young girls have such dreams like you do; but no such husband will they ever find. Do you know why? Because such a husband does not exist. Such a partner is not a husband; such a man is called a lover!"

Just finished lunch & talked to doctor Ismer about attending Mrs. Beeney when she gets her baby in September. I wish it was me who was going to get a little baby?

Three weeks later, in England again, Daisy forgot all her doubts about her marriage in the carefree surroundings of Newlands and under the excitement of the Cowes Regatta. In Osborne, Queen Victoria wanted to know everything about her life in Germany, and in Newlands the Emperor listened graciously to Daisy's pleading to permit her husband's return into the diplomatic service. But the stay in Baden-Baden afterwards was "hardly amusing" without the presence of the Prince of Wales, and in Fürstenstein the old doubts and somber thoughts preoccupied Daisy again. Hans was travelling from auction to auction to sell some of his horses to raise much needed money.

Left behind in her grandiose, but empty palace, with much time on her hands, Daisy felt lonely, forgotten, and lost, plagued by fears and dark thoughts, which she committed to her diary in lengthy entries – over thirty pages on the following day – about Hans, in-laws in Silesia, true friends, and not so trustworthy friends in Germany and in England, about her parents, George and Shelagh, about Gordy, of course, and much about herself. She concluded with thoughts about those who were already dead:

Oct 12th Fürstenstein .ten days after my little baby was born I knew it was going to die, & once or twice (this I have told no one) as it layed in my arm I looked at it & said to myself, would I mind if it died, & I suppose I was weak, I had suffered & somehow I wasn't myself & I answered no. But when she did die Oh! my heart! my heart! I had never known such misery or dispear. One day about five o'clock I was waiting for my tea it was dusk, & I laid in bed thinking of nothing, I never felt that joy when my first baby was born as some mothers do, yet I longed for one so & I loved it so even before it was born. I remember how I used to stroke myself & smile & say 'my own little baby.'

Her feelings of despair, loss, and guilt were overpowering:

Well as I was waiting for my tea I looked up at the ceiling & there was my baby as it were painted on the ceiling, ... it only lasted a moment but then I knew that she or I would die... .Well two nights afterwards she began to cry but such strainge sharp cryes & then how I felt the perspiration come out all over my body for I knew for sure then she would die & that that cry was a convulsion. Oh! how I prayed & prayed.., and her crys seemed to pierce my whole body. ... I was always drawing pictures of babies as angels before she was born & one day I saw Mother take up the sketch book after she died & give a start & look at me, I saw afterwards that I had drawn the picture of a little dead baby with its eyes shut & its hands crossed in front...

I also feel that darling old George will die before he marries, or that if he marrys, he will have no children.

I liked Gordy much the best. ... & I used to call after him & cry Gordy come back, if only you knew you silly thing. ... everyone could see that Gordy was in love with me only he was a real good man & wouldn't show it. ... He & George Cooper are the only two amongst them all I felt I really cared for, & for whom my heart ever forced my eyes to shed a tear. ... In my bible ... I came across an old old dried white clove pink I picked in Newlands to give to George Cooper. ... I have had the lines in my hand told very often & they always say, someone was very fond of you when you were sixteen & he made a line in your heart that will always remain. I often realize now how much I really loved him & how tearful & miserable I felt when I had to get back to my German grammar (I was 17 then). He loved me too I think. ... Whether it was girls sentiment or not, I shall never forget it, it was a girl childs feeling of what a man ought to have been. ... He is dead now, died of consumption in Africa. ... my thoughts go back six years ago (can it be so long) to that same garden with you, & I smell again the same roses and the same white clover pinks. Bless them & you and the remembrance of that time.

This compulsive, almost morbid pre-occupation with the death of her baby and the tragic demise of George Cooper, the groundless fear that brother George would also face death very soon, must be regarded as manifestations of a deep depression. Daisy desperately looked forward to the forthcoming trip to India. For the first time in her married life, she and Hans would finally be alone, removed from the hustle of social life and the worries and aggravations of daily life at Fürstenstein; and, finally, Daisy would be far away from the watchful, critical eyes of Hans's family. For the first time, she would escape from all such influences on her marriage. Desperately searching for any sign whatsoever of a re-awakening love for Hans, Daisy remained plagued with wrenching ambiguity in her heart. The diaries expressed her feelings of guilt for her never-ending doubts about her husband's love for her. Years later, here or there in her diary, she would change some sentence or remark, for example what she originally had hoped to find in Hans, crossing out original entries and correcting them with remarks added in brackets, each entry betraying her deep, lasting disenchantment.

November 11th Fürstenstein 1895 We came back yesterday from Padobitz [Pardubitz] Hans came only for two nights. ... It was great fun & we [Daisy and Shelagh] danced nearly every night. ... Whoever she [Shelagh] marries, the little girl will be happy and find as good a husband as Hans [last part of sentence concerning Hans crossed out later].

In India far away, I do not want a 'comfort' [member of the family travelling along], but to be alone once with my husband we are both looking forward to it. I love all my people very very much, but after all Hans & I are never alone, quite alone, little Shelagh has been with us for months now of course I am delighted we have had such a happy time together, but now that we have a reason & chance to be alone together it would be horrid if someone came between. ...

We went for such a lovely walk together, so happy & talked of the time when please God we may have some little children. We talked of the future, of improvements and arrangements in & outside the house, & then when I stopped up a hill for breath he kissed me & called me 'his own little Dany wife.' He is so good & loves me so, I would not hurt his feelings, or do anything wrong... & I pray all day that I will make him a good wife. I love my own dear Hans [crossed out later; much later written above: 'Later I knew that Hans preferred to be with Shelagh & told her this was the reason he went to India – he could not bear go on living here'].

Before leaving for India, Daisy managed to visit England "without poor old Hans" and see Gordy. Daisy was playing with fire again, not only in her relationship with Gordy. On her own, she decided to consult a London gynecologist, much to the anger of Hans. When she was on board ship sailing for Egypt, she wrote

Dec 5th past Brindisi I was in London and in Newlands for ten days. ... Gordy took my Fairy bracelet away he said it was disgusting, ... he was furious & said rude things to me. ... I did not mind a bit what he said as the crosser he got, the more it seemed he showed he liked me. ... He send me a lovely writing desk & a green cushion to take on the journey with me. ... In London we had a private supper at Bachelor's & afterwards got the drawing room down below to ourselves. ...till one o'clock, & then Gordy drove me home in a fourwheeler, ... of course I would not have driven home so late at night with *any other* man.

I saw Dr. Croner. ... He said I am quite crooked inside & possibly could not get a baby until I was put right; I wired & wrote to Hans as I thought perhaps he wouldn't want to go to India, but rather let me go to Edinburgh as the doctor wanted me to be put straight. ... But Hans wired me to come at once. *He is very obstinate* and says the doctor is a d— liar & and — swindler, & that I am perfectly straight & he quite believes going to India now will give me a baby. I am quite certain it will *not* be so. ... I went to Pless to meet Hans & we went to Trieste."

Dec 11th Red Sea We got to Alexandria Saturday 7th (fancy I have been married four years!). ... We went to the Pyraymid. ... I climed to the top (still feel the effects of it in my bad leg).

The *Oldenburg* taking Hans and Daisy through the Red Sea and across the Indian Ocean turned out to be a slow and decrepit vessel of considerable age. In the stifling heat of the Red Sea, the cabin seemed confining for Daisy. The bed was too hard and far too short for Hans. Neither Hans nor Daisy were in a good mood. With much time for ruminating about her life, Daisy spent hours with her diary rather than with her taciturn husband. In an eighteen-page long entry, she finally gave her long bottled-up feelings free rein. With suddenly exploding resentment, she wrote

> Dec 14th/95 We have just done dinner it is blowing quite hard & yet it is very hot. Only six more days, what a delight it will be to get out of this. ... Hans has just been saying that I shall not go back to England till Cowes that means in August but it is simply nonsense as I cant go without seeing little Mussie & Dads & Biddy & them all for ten months. Oh! why cant Hans sympathize with me in the love I have for my own people & my old home. It makes me miserable when I think of it, that we have scarcely any sympathy together & different religions for I cant make up my mind to be a catholic, particularly in secret, as his father & no one would be able to know; he never reads a book, so we can never talk about a book together that we both have read. He likes risqué stories, risqué conversation etc., & I cannot get him out of this. If only he knew how I sometimes long to cry! I can stop other man, but I cannot deliberately snub my own husband. ... The greatest shield for every married woman I think ought to be her husband. ... But what happens after the girl with the pale cheeks & tearful wondering pleading eyes is joined to life to the man she scarcely knows, she in less than a week knows as much as a married woman of many years & what she does not know — her husband or someone else informs her, as a subject of amusement & laughter, she sees for the first time probably at a french theatre imorality taken off on the stage, of which she a week ago knew nothing & even now is dazed & does not understand it all (how well I remember in my honey moon in Paris going to a theatre where a Harem was acted, & asked what a 'unique' [eunuch] was I think I have spelt it wrong, I think it is ynik, I shall never forget the burst of laughter & surprise of them all & Hans, & the misery I suffered till I got home & asked Hans.) Then Hans raged when I would not let him undress me the first night but kept Ellen in the room. Then the child wife is taken to a restaurant, even not the very best; to "cafés chantant," etc & there is shown the poor woman the fruits of men's vices, she is not told it is wrong but simply something to see now that she is married, it is a natural thing in natur, you hear men & women say 'cocottes' in the same breath as they may tell you the names of their last born baby. The man is often jealous of the parents of his wife & her home, if only he would realaise what a safe guard it is for a woman, the great love of her own people and her past happy girlhoods time. Oh! men it is easy to blame the woman, ... if only you would help them & honour them how much happier your own lives would be. ... Think of your yourselves, your minds & bodies are corrupted but your wild oats have been sown & please God cut & reaped & never to be sown again. Then why not guide the mind & body of the girl

given to your care to be the mother of your children, & not even the first week you are marrried show them the seed of evil in her by showing her things & places she need not perhaps ever see, at any rate not then, & why even tell her anything of all the filth & horror that go on in life... & that seed you the husband have yourself, your very self have sown, if it brings... misery for you & her; poor woman, God help her, *she* gets *no* forgiveness for what is counted in you as naught. But help her, the woman you chose for your mate & if you see tears & weeds growing in her soul, take them out with a tender careful hand.

While Daisy later added the note "from the book of Marie Carelie" at the end of this entry, the anger poured into these lines reflected her true feelings, quite precisely expressed in the words of the French author into which Daisy indeed managed to successfully interweave her own feelings, a result of her frightful experiences as a bride on her honeymoon, and her anger at Hans – indeed even at the entire male gender of her time – for not understanding his young wife and not caring about her innocence, ignorance, and fear. It took Daisy four years to finally dare to express her hurt and anger to her diary, even though it had been her secret confidante for so much longer. Nevertheless, at the onset of the India trip, she still remained imprisoned in the role of the innocent, helpless victim. A few months later, on her return from India, a different Daisy would be confiding to her diary!

More than the heat and discomfort of sea travel must have affected Daisy. She arrived in Colombo so physically and emotionally exhausted that her immediate admission to a hospital became imperative. Only on January 13, 1896 did Hans and Daisy set out for Calcutta via Madras, Bombay, and Hyderabad. This was the itinerary the Prince of Wales had prepared for them in detail. Everywhere, the Prince and Princess of Pless were most cordially received. Daisy was intrigued by the

barbaric beauty of the art of India, but much disappointed by the social life which in comparison to England, seemed utterly boring, frozen in empty formality and devoid of imagination. Lord & Lady Wenlock's home is lovely, situated in the middle of a big park, it looks exactly like an English park. ... But – there are very few flowers!

Eager to see more of the cities and the countryside, Daisy was forever disappointed having

come to a foreign land where you naturally want to go about & see everything, ... we have left Europe about the middle of October & then we should have had more time to spend at each place.

Instead, Daisy and Hans were caught in the well-meant plans of their hosts who seemed to think that Daisy was only interested in their homes, in government buildings, and race tracks!

Lengthy stays in Bombay and in Hyderabad and endless days on trains in "terrible heat" brought Daisy close to exhaustion again. By the time, Hans and Daisy arrived in Calcutta, she wrote that "I am quite used to it now, but at first I was quite disgusted with myself." In the middle of February, Hans left for his tiger hunt. A day after his departure, the Maharaja of Cooch Behar, who had so ardently courted the fourteen-year-old Daisy in Newlands 7 years ago, arrived in Calcutta.

February 23rd Culcutta Hans left on the 16th for Hyderabad & got to Madras five days later, ... leaving me alone for six whole weeks. ... I have had two charming letters from the Maharaja I do like him very much, but I am afraid he likes me too much, he grabbed hold of my hand & kissed it before he left. ... I expect I shall go to Cooch Behar on Friday.

During her stay at the Maharaja's palace, Daisy found no time to devote herself to her diary. Why, she explained after her departure from Cooch Behar five weeks later.

Darjeeling – April 12th/96 It seems nearly impossible to begin to write again after all this time. But the last days in Cooch Behar I was nearly in bed all the time. We ... had to put off coming here for a whole week, & all because of unlucky me who fell down just the night before we ought to have started that was Friday my unlucky day. I was running from the Maharaja – we were on wheel skates – & fell flat on the marble floor on my face. He was in a terrible fright the blood poured from my face. I did not faint but kept on asking him 'what is the matter what have I done.' I walked to the washing stand in a senseless sort of way to bathe my face but I was too dazed to know what I was really doing, I know he went on his knees & put his arms around my waist, & said 'Daisy! Daisy! what have you done.' then he lifted me up & put me on a sofa. It was dreadful. ... My face, nose eyes mouth were swollen enormously, they wired to Calcutta for the very best doctor. So I layed in bed covered up with 'Aunt Theresa's lace shawl. ... One night at two o'clock I felt a hand on my forehead & there 'the Lion' stood, I did not feel frightened as I knew I looked so positively hideous; & so I quick put the veil on & then we both laughed as he said that if I was otherwise of course he wouldn't have come. He came like this three times, & then as I got better we settled that he mustn't come any more & it was so nice when he came he used to kneel down by my bed & stroke my forehead talk a bit & pray I think, & then go in about ten minutes.

We got here on Friday. ... This is certainly a lovely place we are living seven thousand feet above the sea. ... I am to see the Maharani at 1.30 it is no good I can't be natural with her, they have had a final row & both settled to go their own way. He told me yesterday that she had found out that he cared for me, of course he denied it but she wouldn't believe it, I think that was when I had the fall he showed too much what he felt, ... how the Maharani could have guessed anything, I cannot think, ... when she is there we scarcely say anything to each other, & she has never seen us alone together, or does she know that he has just kissed my forehead sometimes & whispered 'God bless you dear.' He is so unhappy... she is the most discontented woman I ever met. ... It seems so funny this sudden change in temperature. I feel like somebody else, & can scarcely talk with the Maharaja here, at Cooch Bahar he used to take me every evening in the victoria & then tell me all his troubels.

Alone in the train for Calcutta, Daisy again turned to writing poetry, just as she had done after saying good-bye to Gordy. This time, after leaving the Maharaja the first poem is intriguingly titled:

FLIRTATION
Just another phrase of mankind to explore.
Pretending for some weeks to love nothing more.
Just another subject, just to form a flirt
Just such little play games cannot really hurt.

Daisy's reminiscing about her flirt with the Maharaja quickly turns to her first true love,

GEORGE COOPER
And so you go together, laughing, loving, indifferent to the rest
Till the man, who stronger is, at last to
passion yielding, takes you to his breast.
Then you cry bitterly, Oh! God I did not mean "this ending."
But! ... this end has come with tears and there is no mending!!!

I often think I have forgotten all the years gone by
But, Ah! no my dear I have not & I do not even try.
It was a year t'is sweet to think of.
Full of love, & flowers, & Spring.
And my heart was happier then, than it ever
since has been.

I did not understand then this love of woman & man.
But I loved you in a way, that never again I can.
A girl's love full of purity, thinking this world all fair.
Thinking all life was sunshine without sorrow
or care. ...
And now you are gone forever from me.
Dead far away across the sea. ...

So these days passed on with our love to unfold
I in mad childishness growing more bold

But it could not last the truth you were told
And I to a higher bidder was sold.

Not very good poetry, and poor rhyming, no doubt, but it was Daisy's first step on a painful journey to free herself from past experiences and begin a process of self-recognition leading, for the first time in her married life, to a sense of personhood and control over her life and emotions. Soon she would meet Hans, and soon she would be a different partner in their otherwise unchanged marital relationship. Although much soul-searching and many decisions lay ahead of Daisy, a sense of detachment, of being herself rather than an helpless appendage of her husband, shines through in the first lines of her last entry during her India trip.

> Culcatta. April 21th 1896. at Mrs.Gladstone I leave for Bombay where I arrive the first I meet Hans there & start that same morning on the *Imperatrice* bound for Brindisi. All my Indian trip is over. ... I never thought when I began this book that I should finish it in India. Life is very changeful, thank goodness one does not know what will happen to one from one month to another & from this year to the next!!![29]

With these somewhat resigned words, Daisy closed the first volume of her hand-written diaries. The long absence from Europe had not brought her and Hans closer to each other. The weeks of being alone with Hans that Daisy had so much looked forward to had turned into a disheartening experience. That Hans remained completely unaware of the crisis Daisy went through in these months explains his surprising decision to go on his tiger hunt and leave his twenty-two year old wife by herself for six weeks in a country so foreign to her.

Not once did Daisy complain to her diary about the long separation from Hans and the fact that he only wrote her once in six weeks. Instead, Daisy feverishly utilized these weeks to free herself from the memories of her confusing and painful first days as a married woman, experiences she had not shared with anyone and not even confided to her diary so far. With this catharsis, Daisy removed Hans from the pedestal where her Victorian innocence and inexperience, and her romantic notions of love and marriage had placed her husband.

The struggle of freeing herself from false hopes and guilt continued after the departure from Bombay. Although it was a painful process for Daisy, it finally ended the years of tormenting self-doubts that had poisoned her married life. Daisy realized and accepted that Hans did love

---

29   DUD, passim. End of quotations from this volume.

her in his own way and that he always tried to be kind to her. She also realized she could not demand things from him that were not part of his nature. This breakthrough in understanding Hans's character as much as her own, liberated Daisy from the years of feeling guilty for not discovering enough love in her heart for her husband "who is always so good to me." She finally appreciated, how much – or how little – she must expect from Hans and, even more importantly, what she must strive for in order to give her own life sufficient meaning, as a married woman as much as a person in her own right.

Daisy decided she had to reduce her expectations on Hans. It had been in vain to discover and raise intellectual, artistic, or literary interests in him. His seeming ambitions to succeed in public or political life were also quite shallow. Only when talking about his ideas to transform Castle Fürstenstein into a magnificent residence did Hans become genuinely excited. Although Daisy would rather have Fürstenstein changed into a more modest, cozy home for Hans and herself, she consciously decided to encourage and support her husband in his plans, in order to create a common bond of interest and activity. Hans had always wished for a more glamorous social life in Fürstenstein. If he had shown any ambition, it was in regard to the future of Fürstenstein. Daisy knew that she would make Hans happy, if she supported his plans. And she knew what more she could do: she had always noticed how Hans beamed with pride and satisfaction when his wife became the centre of attention during social events. To elevate Castle Fürstenstein to an elegant rendez-vous of Europe's upper society was an ambition for which Daisy would find her husband's delighted agreement and unqualified support. However, her decision to primarily attract English society and thus transplant a small piece of her beloved homeland to Fürstenstein remained her secret for the time being.

This was the first succinct, personal role, independent from her husband, that Daisy defined for herself in her married life. No longer was she entangled in romantic hopes about her relationship with Hans. Daisy accepted that partners of such different temperament and background as she and Hans could only strive for limited fulfillment in their marriage. More mature in outlook, and self-assured, Daisy returned to Fürstenstein in July 1896. Life no longer looked so bleak. Daisy had made her plans for her future.

* * * * * *

4 | *The Glamorous Hostess*

V*ater and Mathilde expected us at the depot at Freiburg in the best of tempers, they really are charming. ... Everybody is so nice to me, I scarcely believe these are the same people.*

* * *

Daisy seemed quite unaware how easy she made it for the family to forget all the old frustrations and resentments. For the first time, she appeared really happy to be in Fürstenstein. she had finally accepted her home, although some of its character would still have to change according to her ideas. At least temporarily, she had reconciled herself to the limitations inherent in her marriage. For the first time, she felt capable – with Hans's blessing – to infuse a different life into Fürstenstein with some of her own ideas and throw off the role of the outsider in her husband's family. At last, she had taken psychological possession of Fürstenstein and her husband's family.

Of course, Daisy could not change her nature; patience had never been one of her virtues. As it turned out, the big building plans Hans had been dreaming of had to wait and only bathrooms and running water were installed. There was not enough money to keep Hans busy with Fürstenstein, and as long as Vater remained the head of the family – kind, but powerful, as was his nature – "there was simply not enough to do for Hans." Once more, Daisy tried to encourage Hans to seek entry into public service pointing to the many examples among their Silesian neighbours. Whether Daisy really helped matters by lobbying for her husband remains doubtful. Daisy was painfully aware that Hans tended to become "easily over-anxious to do everything according to etiquette; to others he often seems stand-offish, ... even brusque."[1]

In reality, Daisy knew, Hans was desperately shy. It needed her efforts to help Hans get back into public life. Always, when Daisy developed a new plan, enthusiasm and firm resolve to succeed made her set her sights too high.

Was it Daisy's ambitiousness, was it the boredom of living with Hans in Fürstenstein, that soon began to cloud her days again, or her impatience with a husband far too phlegmatic for a wife so much younger? In Pless, Daisy surprised the Emperor – not for the first time – with unexpected questions and requests. "I begged him to give Hans something to do."[2]

With the good nature he always displayed whenever Daisy asked him for a favour, the Emperor told Prince Hatzfeldt, the President, and the highest government official[3] of the Province of Silesia to occupy Hans in his administration in some fashion. Prince Hatzfeldt immediately carried out the Emperor's wishes, and within weeks, Daisy urged Prince Hatzfeldt "to be sure and say to the Emperor that Hans is working very hard in Breslau, finds it interesting, and so on."[4]

And in London, Daisy made a special visit to Prince Hatzfeldt's relative, the German Ambassador Count Hatzfeldt, urging him to somehow arrange with his superiors in Berlin a posting for Hans at the London Embassy.

Soon after, the Emperor appointed Hans to the Prussian Upper House, an empty honour, as far as Daisy was concerned, who still wanted Hans to enter a career in the foreign service. It was true that the Emperor had become genuinely fond of Hans. As an enthusiastic huntsman, Hans made a splendid companion. Unfortunately, neither the Emperor nor other influential people seemed too impressed with Hans who, Daisy sometimes wondered, perhaps suffered unfairly under the constant comparison with his distinguished father. In what became almost a conspiracy, Daisy told her mother to use every opportunity and tell the Emperor how impressed she was with her son-in-law. Patsy complied only too willingly and wrote Daisy that the Emperor had assured her in Newlands that he "was keeping an eye on Hans and the progress he was making."[5]

---

1   DPH, p. 93.

2   DPH, p. 83.

3   Oberpräsident.

4   DPH, p. 131.

5   DPH, p. 142.

It was the German Chancellor Prince von Bülow whom Daisy had singled out to arrange a diplomatic posting for her husband. Seated between the Emperor and Prince Hatzfeldt at a dinner in Breslau, Daisy attacked Prince von Bülow for not giving Hans the posting of first secretary at the Paris Embassy "which he had promised *me* for him." But in his notes, Bülow had characterized Hans "in comparison to his eminent father an unimportant man."[6]

Instead, the Emperor sent Hans as his special representative to the United States to open the German Trade Fair in New York. Hans found a positive press which reported at great length about the long hours the Prince of Pless had spent with President Theodore Roosevelt in the White House. The press clippings that she consumed with delight back home in Fürstenstein were enough for Daisy to suggest to the Emperor a diplomatic posting for Hans in Washington. However, the Emperor probably presumed that it was not the great statesman, but the passionate hunter Theodore Roosevelt had enjoyed in the Prince of Pless. In the end, it was a close friend of Hans and Daisy who brought Daisy back to reality. In an otherwise comforting letter, Prince Karl Max Lichnowsky, an experienced diplomat admonished Daisy:

> I am so sorry poor old Hans is not getting on so well as he ought to! Speaking to you as a real friend I advise you not to do anything about his diplomatic ambitions just now, nor to trouble yourself about making him work at the Foreign Office. That is by no means necessary. ... Besides, Paris is not free. ... Let me know when you come to town and we shall talk it over, but don't frighten poor Hans with the idea of having to go and work in an office![7]

Daisy gave much credence to Lichnowsky. As a close neighbour to Pless, he had known Hans well for many years. It was Lichnowsky who made Daisy resign herself to the fact that she had failed in her plans for

> Hans who somehow is never nice to, nor on good terms with, the right people; he hasn't 'a way' with him, as the Irish say. ... If Hans does not do something between now and when he is fifty he never will.[8]

Feeling "very doubtful," she still supported Hans's idea to replace Prince Hatzfeldt as President of Silesia. She was not surprised when Hans did not succeed, but did not have the heart to argue with him when he readily accepted Chancellor Bülow's explanation that he had not been

---

6   See Fürst von Bülow, op. cit., vol. 2, p. 425.

7   BLU, p. 63.

8   BLU, p. 68.

chosen for the post because he was "too Catholic and took too much the side of the Poles."[9] The chapter of Daisy's struggles to get her husband into the diplomatic service was closed forever.

If Daisy envied her Silesian neighbours at all, it was for the role they played on the highest administrative level of Prussia and the high ranks they occupied in the army. Several neighbours residing in the immediate vicinity of Fürstenstein belonged to families whose forefathers had occupied illustrious positions in the history of Prussia and of Europe. Only a few miles from Fürstenstein, the Moltkes in Kreisau and the Blüchers in Krieblowitz lived on their large estates. Other famous families belonging to this group of Silesian land-owners included the Seydlitzes, Yorcks, Gneisenaus, and the Humboldts.

Aside from their illustrious lineage, Daisy looked upon most of her neighbours as unremarkable, and "terribly Prussian," and little fun to entertain. They, in turn, had similar reservations about the Princess of Pless, who insisted on cultivating her English image. With some exceptions, notably the Hatzfeldts and the Lichnowskys, Daisy's enthusiastic efforts had little success in including her neighbours in the blossoming social life of Fürstenstein. Daisy soon concluded

> these people are afraid to see me, thinking that my house is always full of a younger and more fashionable society than they know (which is a fact).[10]

Anchored in the Prussian traditions of modesty and frugality, Silesia's nobility looked at the extravagant lifestyle and the easygoing social life fostered by Daisy in Fürstenstein with disgust. Her regime seemed to transform Fürstenstein into a foreign enclave in stolidly Prussian Silesia.

These early years of Fürstenstein's fame as the rendezvous of the international set promoted the image of Daisy of Pless as the ambitious and vain Englishwoman. It developed into a pronounced prejudice among German aristocracy, which Daisy's Austrian friend Prince Alphons Clary-Aldringen deplored:

> The pronounced prejudice among German aristocracy resulted in the deplorable consequence that neither the humanitarian and the political pursuits of the Princess of Pless nor her undoubted successes ever received the recognition they deserved; nor did the Princess find the respect and appreciation she should have been entitled to.[11]

---

9   BLU, p. 177.

10   BLU, p. 216.

11   Letter to the author.

It is unlikely that Daisy fully appreciated the rejection and jealousy that so negatively affected her image. Much of it was based on the correct impression that Fürstenstein had become an almost exclusive domain of foreign visitors. Truly, this was only logical in view of Daisy's origin, and the multitude of social relationships Hans and Daisy entertained beyond Germany's borders, especially in England, Italy, Spain, and Austria-Hungary. The majority of Fürstenstein's visitors came from these countries, first and foremost, of course, from the country of Daisy's birth. Gradually, however, Germany's upper aristocracy and members of the families reigning in German states prior to 1871 became more prominent in Fürstenstein; as were the members of the reigning houses of Spain, Greece, Romania, Bulgaria, and of the Romanow, Habsburg, and Hohenzollern families.

Among all of these was the youth, the jeunesse dorée, who gave Hans, Daisy, and Fürstenstein – with its lavish balls, elegant garden parties, and enormous shooting parties – a radiance and an aura of wealth and luxury. The neighbours were left breathless. The extraordinary pomp with which the exalted guests were received by the Prince and Princess of Pless was contemptuously called "un-Prussian extravagance."

During a visit by the author to London, Gerald Saunders, a nephew of Alexander Stewart, the headgroom at Fürstenstein who was brought over from Scotland, shared his reminiscences and photographs of unforgettable summer holidays at the Castle Fürstenstein of the early 1900s. He described how

> Whenever important guests arrived, the jubilant citizens would assemble along the streets leading through the town of Freiburg up to the Castle ... and the excitement and pleasure of seeing the details of what was a private kingdom and something that will never again be possible. To see the coaches bringing visitors from the station each drawn by six horses with three postillions and two coachmen, was a sight in itself, added to which the woodmen and gamekeepers stood along the drive with torches to add a fairylike appearance to their welcome, and on entering the castle they were greeted on the grand staircase ascending to the great marble ballroom by a sight which had to be seen to be believed of twenty-one powdered footmen on each side of the staircase.[12]

Childhood memories of former Fürstensteiners also reflect the fairy-like atmosphere that characterized the Castle and its environment especially during festivities,

---

12 Letter to the author.

when the heavenly music of the bands and the choirs wafted from the hills where they were posted, across the gorge to the Castle and how at night, the magic glow of the thousands of Benghal lights everywhere in the park and the hills added to the already overwhelming impression of the Castle splendidly illuminated with thousands of lights as well.[13]

In retrospect, this incredible pomp appears almost immoral, already anachronistic for its time. More than once, Daisy had second thoughts about the unrestrained display of wealth, especially after she became aware of the crass poverty among the working classes in nearby Waldenburg and the surrounding industrial towns and villages, home of more than 20,000 miners, of those, over 5,000 miners in the employ of her husband alone.

Interestingly, the people employed by Hans in Fürstenstein and those living in the neighbourhood of the Castle saw things differently. With great excitement and delight, they never failed to watch like participant observers all this pomp and circumstance; they did this with almost a sense of ownership, free from envy and hostility. After all, as a former inhabitant of the village of Polsnitz, who in her childhood carried a basket of fresh eggs to the castle on the hill every day, wrote the author

> hundreds of our generation, all of us poor boys and girls found employment in the huge castle and were given an inside view of this exalted society which turned out to be very helpful for us, after we entered the wider world ourselves. Besides, the luxurious life style which filled the Castle, gave thousands of tradesmen, merchants and little people a secure livelihood without want.[14]

For the English, there definitely was no other place in Germany which could match Fürstenstein's comfort and delightful informality. They came in droves, attracted by Daisy Pless – the charming, inventive hostess with her inexhaustible ideas and surprises – as much as by the stimulating company of the other guests they always expected to find there. "Masses of people" came every summer Daisy reported.

> We had paper chases, motor-trips, dances, a fancy ball, shot partridges, fished and caught crayfish, played golf and croquet – in fact all the usual things. ... [In winter] we were in a fairy paradise. ... Every little twig or blade of grass, ... covered with frozen hoar-frost, ... glistening in the winter sunshine, when the sky was often as blue as in June. The avenues that before

---

13   Margarete Kobelt.

14   Margarete Kobelt.

looked so long and gray and dismal became just fairy ways, the trees meeting in one long high arch of dazzling white, like filigree-work diamonds.

One December night ... we all went out tobogganing after dinner; a full moon, no wind, and every tree and twig covered with hoarfrost. I had Chinese lanterns hung on the trees all the way down the toboggan run, and as a surprise, had coloured Benghal lights lit at the ends of the avenues and against the sides of the hill. The whole place glowed in red and then melted away to pale blue and green; it was quite beautiful.

Really, it was a mad night; each of my five Arab ponies drew two people in a sleigh, flying over the snow. We went to the *Riesengrab* [*Giant's tomb* – a huge rock] to look at the Castle from the other side of the valley; by moonlight it looked, somehow, high, and so far away. ... Then we started off over the fields for the *Alte Burg*,[15] while the ponies kicked up the snow into our faces. As we arrived, dogs barked. We rang the bell and nobody came. Two of the men, against my wishes, burst open the gate; what I really feared was that the dogs inside might be loose and spring upon us. ... We made so much noise that the caretaker in his nightgown at last opened the window and put his head out. I told him it was only I and that he need not be afraid; he did not seem in the least surprised, brought a lamp and carried it in front of us upstairs. Then somebody else took it and we went all the way through the ghostly-looking rooms. When we came to the Chapel someone blew it out and we were left in the moonlight that shone through the windows. I was really frightened; I could not help it, so I caught hold of the largest man there and hurried out.[16]

What Daisy so aptly described not only celebrated the magic of winter at Fürstenstein, but also her companions, the pleasure-seeking, daring set of young Londoners she had transplanted to her home in Germany; Daisy felt part of them every moment!

They all came, again and again, enchanted by the alluring mixture of the harsh, but bright winter of Silesia and her hot, languid summers, and the ambience Daisy had created in Fürstenstein, so typically English with its particular diversions and pleasures, which soon even included golf.

Especially the young made Fürstenstein their playground in winter and in summer, Victoria Sackville-West, Violet Mar, daughter of the Earl of Shaftesbury, Bernie Paget, Guy Windham, Hugh Duke of Westminster and his wife, Daisy's sister Shelagh, the Duke of Alba and many others; for all of them, Daisy's Fürstenstein was paradise. Summer and fall with

---

15 *The Old Castle*; a fake ruin on a steep hill on the other side of the gorge across from Castle Fürstenstein, erected around 1800 in the romantic taste of its time.

16 BLU, pp. 76-77.

shooting parties, picnics, theatricals, and musicales, were the preferred seasons for the older generation, the Lonsdales, the Grenfells, Elchos, Gleichens, the Curzons, and others of England's great families. The Duke and Duchess of Connaught were entertained with playlets and songs performed by the *two Daisies*, Daisy of Pless and Princess Margaret of Connaught.

George and Jennie came, and Daisy opened her arms to the former Lady Randolph Churchill, who had become married to her brother in 1900. Daisy could never forget that Jennie's son Winston was the same age as his stepfather George. Intensely observing George and Jennie, Daisy concluded that

> Jennie still loves him immensely, poor dear; she is uncommonly nice and still very handsome, but of course the difference in age is sad and a terrible drawback.[17]

Among the Austrians, Hungarians, Poles and, to a lesser extent, the Germans, most mingled easily with the trendsetting visitors from Great Britain, all enjoying each other's spirited, sophisticated company. Especially popular was Betka Potocka whose home Łańcut in Galicia had become almost as popular for its social life as Fürstenstein. Like Hans and Daisy, Betka and her husband Prince Roman Potocki had opened their palace in Łańcut to the international set.[18] From Hungary, the Esterhazys, Apponyis and Hojos brought their Gipsy bands. Once, when he arrived earlier than invited, the impetuous Count Kinsky almost ran into Jennie, who had gone through a brief but passionate affair with him. Loyal friends of the Hochberg family, the Clary-Aldringens, Sternbergs, Czernins, and the Larischs from Austria, the Reuss, Salms, and Hohenlohes never missed a summer in Fürstenstein. In the presence of the alert, intensely listening Daisy, Count Wolff-Metternich, German ambassador to London, his Austrian colleague Count Mensdorff-Pouilly, and Prince Gottfried Hohenlohe-Schillingsfürst, Austrian military attaché in St. Petersburg exchanged their views about the political state of European affairs.

The Emperor and many of the German and Austrian visitors were passionate hunters, who went on to Pless for big game of elk and bison following the shooting parties in the woods around Fürstenstein. No matter how much atmosphere and etiquette had eased at Fürstenstein

---

17 DPP, p. 163.

18 Having survived two world wars without damage, Łańcut retains to this day the ambience that Fürstenstein tragically lost as a result of World War II.

under Daisy's reign, the hunting protocol at Fürstenstein and Pless remained bound to centuries-old traditions. With much amusement, Daisy's brother George recalled the strict protocol he was expected to observe during his hunting days in Silesia.

> The funniest hunts I ever attended took place at Fürstenstein. ... It was a drag hunt, or *Schleppjagd*, run by artillery officers. ... We were a party of about twenty, mostly English and Austrians, and we commandeered every one of Pless's horses – hunters and carriage horses. ... The Master, so far as his cap, tie and pink coat were concerned, was immaculately dressed, but the rest of his turn-out was a bit weird. He had large black Hessian boots with long spurs, and the buttons of his white breeches, instead of being at the knees, went the whole way up the seams of both legs. We were warned by Pless that the line would be about four miles over grass, ... and before we started we were addressed by the Master in German. He said: 'First will come the hounds, then I, and the Frau Fürstin von Pless, and then the rest of you. Anyone who rides in front of me will be fined five marks, and anyone riding in front of Her Highness one mark!'
>
> At the end of the hunt, ... the bandsman dashed into the thicket, from which he emerged carrying a sprig of young spruce. Drawing his sword, he laid it on the hilt, knelt and solemnly presented it to my sister. ... It was all serious and none of us dared to laugh. Poor Daisy! How we chaffed her afterwards. ...[19]

George, who had participated in game hunting on three continents, described in his entertaining memoirs *Edwardian Hey-Days*, never ceased to be amazed by the hunts in Fürstenstein where

> half the population of the neighbourhood was rallied as beaters walking up partridges, while at Pless, an army of beaters was employed, at least three hundred, and to every ten a *Jäger* was allotted, whose duty it was to see that his squad kept their line. We were four guns; my brother-in-law, self, and two officers from the garrison, who were not particularly good shots.

This party of four killed over eight hundred hares! George called the hunting protocol

> perfect and, ... a striking proof of German efficiency. ... In the case of big game such as dear, elk, moose, or the famous Pless bisons, ... there was something picturesquely medieval about shooting in those days. All the old customs were kept up. Every *Jäger* carried a bugle, and over each species of game after it had been laid out on the ground a different form of the *Last*

---

19   See George Cornwallis-West, op. cit., p. 197.

Post was played by the buglers. ... Even when one went out alone after roe deer, the *Jäger*, on arrival at the gate of the Castle, would stop and blow a blast announcing the death of the roe deer.[20]

The image of Fürstenstein as the playground of Europe's jeunesse dorée was tempered, however, during the Imperial Maneuvers between 1901 and 1906 that were held on the nearby former battlefield of Hohenfriedeberg. It was here that King Frederick II of Prussia won a decisive battle against the armies of Empress Maria Theresia in 1741 during the 2nd Silesian War. From the tower of Castle Fürstenstein, one could comfortably follow the movements of the troops engaged in the war games. The Imperial Maneuvers attracted emperors, kings, generals, and diplomats to Fürstenstein, often accompanied by their wives, some of whom shared a fate not unlike Daisy's. During 1905, Daisy welcomed two of the Emperor's sisters, the Duchess Sophie of Sparta [later Queen of Greece], Princess Margaret of Prussia, and Queen Victoria's other granddaughters Princess Margaret Connaught [Crown Princess of Sweden], and Marie, Crown Princess and later Queen of Romania. Daisy and Marie were especially close. No other women, born in England and transplanted to the Eastern reaches of Central Europe and beyond, suffered a fate as alike and as challenging as Daisy of Pless and Marie of Romania.

Of the two women, Daisy had no doubt drawn the better lot. Daisy lived in a highly civilized and economically advanced country; even though her marriage did not bring fulfillment, Daisy had to admit that "with all his faults and shortcomings, Hans has always been very good to me."[21]

In Bucharest, however, Marie found herself at the mercy of a suspicious, tyrannical father-in-law and an incompetent husband she did not love. The two men reigned over a backward, impoverished country, which to Marie seemed located not only at the edge of Europe, but beyond the reach of civilization.

Both Daisy and Marie did not hesitate to immediately question the customs and values of their new, uncongenial environment. Their ensuing rebellion turned their lives into unexpected, and for their time, unconventional directions. Both women sought a sense of belonging to their new country through identifying with the common people – Daisy through humanitarian, and Marie through political action. To a greater extent than Daisy, Marie succeeded thanks to her position as Crown Princess and later as Queen of Romania. With her passionate engage-

---

20   Ibid., p. 201-202.
21   BLU, p. 124.

ment, Marie decisively shaped the fate of Romania, even entering into the high politics of Europe, which Daisy could only hope to influence in an unofficial, discreet way.

Both women had a deep understanding for each other's fate. When Marie's in-laws accused her of being power-hungry, Daisy comforted her discouraged friend:

> whether galloping astride a wild horse and dressed in Romanian costume through the forests, as you did the other day in Fürstenstein, whether presenting yourself to the public and especially to your people wearing a crown and in full regalia, you eclipse all your contemporaries, ... because you have accurately gauged the somewhat primitive tastes and ideals of the Romanian people giving them exactly the sort of monarch they want and understand, you will always be loved by your people.[22]

Many years later, from the drabness of Bucharest and the wilderness of the Carpathian mountains, Marie longingly remembered her days at Fürstenstein in a letter to her friend Daisy:

> Thank you for your photograph, ... so gay, smiling, kindly, ... an incarnation of those days of peace, wealth and prosperity. There is a sort of peace in perfect attainment, particularly when one has known struggle and the uncomfortable shabbiness of things not yet well established; this faultless achievement of beauty for me was peace.[23]

The friendship between Daisy and Marie lasted until the death of the Queen of Romania in 1937. It was never affected by the failure of their plan to unite their families through the marriage of Daisy's son Alexander to Marie's daughter Crown Princess Ileana of Romania.

Friendly relations with a woman politically as engaged as Marie, or with Emperor Wilhelm II and King Edward VII, with other monarchs, statesmen, and politicians naturally stimulated Daisy's interest in European politics. Routinely, Daisy began to include in her diary comments on the political inclinations and interests, or their lack of it, of nearly all her friends and visitors. She was puzzled by the complete lack of interest in political and humanitarian issues by the Austrian Archduchesses Elizabeth, Christina, and Henrietta. She did not hide her dislike of the successor to the Habsburg throne, Archduke Ferdinand, "a powerful man,"[24] but admired his morganatic wife, the Duchess Sophie of Hohenberg:

---

22 DPH, p. 124.

23 BLU, p. 257.

24 DPP, p. 71.

I liked her very much indeed. She ... filled a very difficult position with conspicuous success, and was heart and soul devoted to her husband and her young family.[25]

After the departure of Archduke Franz Ferdinand and his wife, the Archduke's nephew, the later Emperor Karl arrived in Fürstenstein after a long journey:

I really could not sit downstairs for a whole hour now and make conversation, so I showed the Archduke to his room and said that as he had got up so early I was sure he would like a little rest. They all laughed when I came downstairs and said I had told him to go to bed like a little child. ...[26]

With disgust, Daisy compared the well-bred Austrian Archduchesses and the shy Archduke Karl with the egocentric, irresponsible and wild Grand Dukes Boris and George of Russia,

who are a law unto themselves and ... have no concern for the welfare of the Czar who often looks so ill and weak. ... One would have thought, had they been men of character, strong will, and perception, that the fiasco of the Russo-Japanese War would have served as a warning and awakened them to the dangerous position of Russia, not only abroad but at home. ... Gottfried von Hohenlohe[27] has told me everything that worries him about Russia so much.[28]

Emperor Wilhelm was always a pleasant guest in Fürstenstein and Pless. For years, Daisy observed great caution when political matters were part of their conversation. While she often did not agree with the Emperor's opinions, she did not dare jeopardize the respect he obviously had not only for her charm and beauty, but also for her intellect. The Emperor cherished *"die Gemütlichkeit of Fürstenstein* where I feel more at home than sometimes in Berlin."

In the ambience created by Daisy in Fürstenstein, the Emperor appeared far more natural and relaxed than in the highly-charged atmosphere of his Court in Berlin. His *Hofmarschall*, Count Zedlitz-Trützschler, a Silesian neighbour of Hans and Daisy, was often appalled by "the restlessness and superficiality of the Emperor... and his crude

---

25 DPP, p. 244.

26 DPH, p. 213.

27 German Ambassador to Russia.

28 DPP, p. 129.

jokes."[29] However, after a visit in Fürstenstein, he noted how relaxed and natural the Emperor was "when removed from those who know how to handle the Kaiser and flatter him."[30]

Daisy had soon discovered the shortcomings in the Emperor's character, but she never failed to pay him, as monarch and as man, her unqualified respect. She recognized his enduring qualities as well as his weaknesses.

> I had a great belief in and respect for him as a man; I had little of either for him as a Sovereign. He was surrounded by incompetent people, and for this he must before the Bar of History bear the blame. ... I am afraid the real cause is that the Emperor was never big enough to face the truth.

It is true that the Emperor always listened to me with patience and with apparent respect for my opinion. But I was never misled by this. Had I been old and plain, frumpy, tedious and dowdy like the majority of women he knew, he would have put me where, mentally, he put all women, that is, into a nursery, a kitchen or a waste-paper basket. ... He was an unfailing and loyal friend to me personally, and this I will always acknowledge most sincerely and gratefully. But he was not an unfailing and loyal friend to the best and highest that is in himself.

Because she respected the Emperor as a man and clearly perceived the conflicts within his personality, Daisy was capable to temper her judgment of him as a sovereign with understanding and sympathy:

> He never had a real chance. He served no apprenticeship... long, tedious and... invaluable ... as served by his uncle Edward VII. ... Even so, I am not quite sure that any apprenticeship, any friend or advisor, could have saved the Emperor from himself. ... Had all the circumstances been different, there was one woman who might, possibly, have helped the Emperor's fine native qualities to develop along different lines, and that was his mother, the Empress Frederick. She had vision, brains, disinterestedness. But, with her sons, she was incredibly tactless. ... I loved and admired her; but she was as stupid with her sons as my beloved parents were with me — and as I, perhaps, am with my own children.[31]

Daisy certainly did not share with the Emperor's mother her "almost incredible ignorance of the psychology of manhood."[32] If one disregards

---

29 BLU, p. 159.

30 Graf Robert Zedlitz-Trützschler, *Zwölf Jahre am deutschen Kaiserhof* (Stuttgart, 1924), p. 68.

31 DPH, pp. 256-65, passim.

32 DPH, p. 484.

for the moment Daisy's marital relationship, one must admit that she demonstrated in practically all her relationships with the opposite sex an intuition, a sophistication, and an unusually sound appreciation of the male ego. This earned her the envy of other women and never ending gossip.

Gossip blamed Daisy for the conduct of the men who seemed to fall prey to her charm. It is to the Emperor's credit that he never responded to such gossip other than by censoring the behaviour of Daisy's friends or, when it became necessary, his own sons Joachim, and Crown Prince Wilhelm. Both had fallen in love with Daisy and displayed their infatuation in a very immature fashion, which Daisy should have discouraged much earlier.

Considering the diversity in origin, age, rank, and taste among the hundreds of visitors descending on Fürstenstein every year, it is astonishing that incidents which would fuel gossip or cause the departure of certain guests from Fürstenstein remained so rare. They all came back, again and again, the young nobles from the Continent, the young Edwardians from England, and, of course, the older generation. This hectic social life was concentrated within certain weeks only during summer, fall, and winter, when Hans and Daisy were not travelling themselves. A look at Daisy's diary from 1901 and 1902 confirms Hans and Daisy's own boundless travel mania!

> In July 1901, we came back from Russia where I found St. Petersburg demoralized from top to toe, Grand Dukes, Government and all.

Within days of arriving in Fürstenstein, Hans and Daisy left for London to continue from there to Lochmore, the Scottish property of Daisy's brother-in-law, the Duke of Westminster. August was reserved for the Regatta in Cowes and a visit to Newlands.

> During September, we simply had too many visitors at Fürstenstein; we were glad to escape to Wolfsgarten, near Darmstadt, to stay with the Grand Duke and Grand Duchess of Hesse. ... Within a week, we went to Eaton[33] for the Chester Races, and the end of the month found us at Keel Hall with the Grand Duke Michael Michaelovitch and Sophy Torby. ... Our next port of call was Newlands where we found Patsy, Poppets, George, Shelagh and Bend Or.[34] ... From there we went to lovely Rufford to Lord Savile. ...We rushed home to Fürstenstein to a small party we had for Prince Albert of Schleswig-Holstein. ...

---

33 Residence of the Duke of Westminster.

34 Shelagh's husband, the Duke of Westminster.

In December we had a party at Pless. The Emperor was the chief guest and was extremely pleased because he shot two wild aurochs,[35] one with a single bullet. ... December found us in Trachenberg in Silesia with Prince Hermann and Princess Natalie Hatzfeldt.[36]

The days before Christmas had been occupied with parties for the poor people and the miners and their families who lived around Fürstenstein. On December 28, Hans and Daisy "rushed off" to Chatsworth, which had become their traditional place for celebrating New Year. Residence of the Duke and Duchess of Devonshire, the huge house was always filled with royalty and high aristocracy, "a nice mixture of people with brains," as Daisy enthusiastically reported. After 1904, when King Edward and Queen Alexandra regularly joined the Chatsworth crowd, the New Year's parties became almost legendary for their fun and their informality.

Daisy recorded in 1904 that as guests, the King and the Queen

were simplicity itself. One curtsied when saying good morning and good night, but on no other occasions. ... Queen Alexandra enjoyed Chatsworth enormously.

The Queen is charming and beautiful as always, and the King very well and in good spirits. ... Generally, to amuse the Queen, I am made to go and sing and dance. ... The Queen danced ... we each took off our shoes to see what difference it made to our height. The Queen took or rather kicked hers off, and ... I never saw her so free and cheerful – but always graceful in everything she does. ... Mr. Balfour was urbane, smiling, amused, and took a surprisingly intense interest in everything that went on. Somehow, one does not expect a great philosopher, statesman and writer to be human.[37]

Daisy called Sir Frederick Ponsonby[38] "the ideal guest." No wonder, because he was charmed by

the Princess of Pless who sang some songs and looked lovely. After each song she quickly changed her dress, beginning as a geisha and ending in white fur, short skirts, and red-brown boots, while snow fell on her.[39]

After the New Year's party, the round of visits continued. Hans and Daisy stayed at Warter Priory, with the Duke of Marlborough at Blen-

---

35 European bison.
36 DPH, p. 83.
37 DPH, pp. 125-26.
38 The King's equerry.
39 Sir Frederick Ponsonby, *Recollections of Three Reigns* (London, 1951), p. 209.

heim, with Shelagh and Bend Or at Eaton Hall and at Grosvenor House in London, and with Patsy and Poppets in Newlands. When King Edward's coronation had to be postponed because of his illness, Hans and Daisy had "some unexpected, quiet days in Fürstenstein." Early in July they returned to London to attend Shelagh's first great ball in her own home, at Grosvenor House. "Everybody was there," also Marie of Romania who dedicated two full pages of her memoirs to a celebration of the Cornwallis-West sisters:

> In this ballroom, with its beautiful pictures looking down upon us, amongst them *The Blue Boy*,[40] the very cream of London society had flocked together including some of the most beautiful women in the world. Foremost amongst these was Princess Daisy Pless, tall, magnificently English, in the splendour of her pink-and-white bloom.
>
> Gold-clad, with a high diamond tiara on her honey-coloured hair, gay, smiling, kindly disposed towards all men, she was indeed a glittering figure, a perfect incarnation of those days of peace, wealth and general prosperity. Our hostess, Daisy's sister, was her dark counterpart, she was also a tall, brilliantly effective woman, covered with jewels. ...
>
> One of the sights which has especially remained imprinted on my mind was the exquisite supper-hall, ... all in blue and decorated with silver plate and blue hydrangeas. ... Daisy and Sheila (sic), the fair and the dark, all eyes turning towards them, they so entirely fitted into the beautiful setting.[41]

July 1902 "turned out to be a terribly full season." Daisy sang at charity concerts and presided over the German stall at the Coronation Bazaar in Regent's Park organized in aid of the *Great Ormond Street Hospital for Sick Children*. In Newlands, Daisy gave a huge ball in honour of the Emperor who was attending the Cowes Regatta and invited Daisy several times to sail on the *Meteor*, his new yacht. On August 9, 1902 in the stall normally reserved for the King and the Queen in Westminster Abbey, Hans and Daisy witnessed the Coronation of King Edward VII.

> Immediately afterwards, we rushed home to a long string of parties in Fürstenstein and in Pless.[42]

This was the end of an incredible year of travelling during which Hans and Daisy had only spent twelve weeks at home in Fürstenstein!

---

40 by Gainsborough.

41 Leslie Field, *Bendor – The Golden Duke of Westminster* (London, 1983), pp. 82-83.

42 DPH, p. 89.

Such "insane rushing-about," Daisy decided, should never occur again. Aside from the annual visits to England, there would be fewer trips, but they led to more distant destinations like Egypt, where Lord Kitchener presented Daisy with the sword of the Mahdi he had captured during the Battle of Omdurman. Daisy and Hans also travelled to Italy, Spain, Austria, Hungary, Russia, and France. For winter and early spring, Hans leased a villa on a cliff above Cannes. While Daisy loved the gentle climate and the colourful vegetation of the French Riviera, she was less impressed with its society.

For Daisy, the year before, 1901, had been overshadowed by two sad events, the death of Queen Victoria and, a few months later, the death of her daughter Vicky, the Empress Frederick. Daisy wrote, "It was as if I had lost a second mother, and made me feel very lonely and defenseless in Germany."[43]

From Newlands, Daisy had sent her condolences to the Emperor, who in his acknowledgments seemed to be more pre-occupied with Daisy than with the death of his mother!

Wilhelmshöhe, August 17, 1901.
Dear Princess Daisy of Pless,

I am very much touched by your kind letter of condolence to me, on the death of my beloved mother. ... One of my last conversations on the 15th of June this year was about you. She had a great liking to you, and when I told her that I know of no woman whom I admired and loved more than you, she said I was perfectly right, that she thought you the most sweet, lovely and lovable being she had ever seen; that your arms, neck and hands were perfection and happy the man whom you possessed and who was beloved by you, and that she hoped I would always prove a friend to you and not let you be maliced or anything be said against you as long as I could put a stop to it. I thought you would like to know how dear Mama spoke of you, and it is unnecessary for me to say that I fully endorse and approve of ALL that Mama said: What a blessing indeed for a man who is worthy to be possessed by you![44]

What the Emperor tried to say in this fascinating, rather curious letter, went beyond an empty admiration of Daisy's beauty. Years later, Daisy wrote

---

43   DPH, p. 78.

44   DPH, pp. 79-80.

He promised to continue for me the care and protection his mother had always shown, and to be honest and truthful, I must say that in all the difficult years after he never once failed.[45]

There were other expressions of admiration, too many unfortunately celebrating Daisy's physical beauty only.

The Marchioness Curzon described Daisy as "a dream of beauty," she would "never see such grace, dignity and perfect carriage again."[46] The Duke of Teck declared Muriel Beckett and Daisy of Pless "the two most beautiful women in Europe."[47] While paying tribute to Daisy's intellect elsewhere in his widely read memoirs, Chancellor von Bülow devoted an entire paragraph to a most detailed description of

the Princess of Pless, one of the most stunning women I have ever met, a typical English beauty, tall, of wonderful stature, beautiful complexion, pure white skin, exquisite teeth, a ravishing beauty.[48]

No wonder, Daisy could not help

beginning to think that I really must be good to look at, as men are so attentive to me and – all the women are so nice to me.[49]

* * *

Daisy had risen to the highest ranks of Edwardian society, but she doubted very much that anybody ever cared to discover her true nature and respect what she believed in.

One of the few who did appreciate Daisy's complex character and her innermost feelings was the great painter of Edwardian society John Singer Sargent. For several generations, indeed until the very recent past, Sargent's work has failed to receive the recognition of more than an enormous accumulation of Edwardian portraits, skillfully executed, but limited to the presentation of the superficial beauty of its subjects. Not until the 1970s did a re-discovery of John Singer Sargent's unfailing ability to capture the character and feelings of his subjects reoccur in Europe and the United States.

---

45 DPH, p. 352.
46 See Eileen Quelch, op. cit., p. 86.
47 BLU, p. 165.
48 Bernhard Fürst von Bülow, *Memoirs* (London, 1931), vol. 2, p. 425.
49 BLU, p. 179.

A remarkable example is Sergeant's portrait of the 38-year-old Princess Daisy of Pless completed in Sergeant's famous studio in Chelsea's Tite Street. Sargent's portrait became the witness that Daisy of Pless had reached the zenith of her life.

With the vivacious expression in her eyes, the slightly parted lips and the barely raised chin, Daisy reaches out to the observer in a spontaneous, astonishingly immediate manner, very much as in real life – it was well-known that conversation would always cease as soon as the Princess of Pless entered a room full of people. She seemed to relate instantly to everyone present, a sense that was heightened, as soon as she approached a particular group of people.

The bare indication of the exceptionally elegant dress and the long string of the famous Pless pearls symbolize not only the exquisite taste and great wealth of the Princess of Pless, but her belonging to that part of the upper class, which in its expectations, style, and sophisticated attitudes considered itself in the vanguard of society. The delicate band of silk that Daisy wears in her hair adds a touch of the grace and charm she was much admired for. Typically, in terms of fashion, it was also ahead of its time. Most ladies still preferred huge hats and heavy robes. To be ahead of her time in attitudes and ideas was true for Daisy in more than one respect.

It is impossible for the observer to escape the impact of Daisy's beauty, of her harmonious features, her slender neck, which, slightly accentuated by Sargent, is reminiscent of a proud, graceful swan. At first sight, Daisy's physical beauty, her elegant dress, and the precious pearls seem to dominate the portrait. But soon, the observer is captivated by the indications of a strong, determined and self-assured personality, expressed in the eyes, the chin, and the backwards tilt of the head. Inescapable is also the aura of a delightful, spontaneous personality who loves life and people. Prolonged communication with Sargent's subject, though, reveals the presence of a certain somber mood, of melancholia, and resignation. In her eyes, one begins to perceive some of the sadness which Daisy knew so well to hide from her environment; a sadness she shared only with her diary and a very few of her closest friends.

"Nothing escapes him that is written in the face," wrote John Singer Sargent's biographer Martin T. Wood.[50]

Neither her prominent position in society nor the growing satisfaction Daisy found in her humanitarian work could substitute for the lack of love and fulfillment in her marriage. Only in the beginning had there

---

50 Martin T. Wood, *Sargent* (London, no year), p. 31.

been occasional moments of romantic love. They were followed by a friendly, in the end, casual liaison interspersed with frequent arguments and conflicts. There were always barriers and differences. Hans would do little to bridge the gap between the older, conservative husband, and the younger, vivacious wife. He did not realize how much Daisy hungered for his love.

> I wanted him to take me in his arms and be very dear to me, but – he was just as usual; he might never have been away at all. He found all my clothes wrong and grumbled at everything, and, as hundreds of times before, I was again disappointed. Although I realized that he ... really loves me immensely, though more as a useful friend – I know he could not do without me – it all leaves me lonely and sad and feeling old.[51]

At times, the stress in the marital relationship must have been immense, as recurring episodes of arguments and unexpected reactions demonstrate. On the way to Scotland in August 1903, Hans suddenly decided to leave the train at Crewe and go to Ostend instead. Again, torn between longing for Hans's love and anger at his rejection, resigned and cynical at the same time, Daisy was

> furious and disappointed. ... He was so like a baby and really *so sad* at the idea of being bored during a whole week in Scotland. ... After he had trumped up a beautiful excuse ... I did then believe that it was possible to laugh and cry at the same time. ... I hated to be left alone and longed for ... holding Tommy's hand and just talking 'little nothings that make a world of thought.' ... I wanted to feel he would be happy with me, ... but Hans would not stay and my soul must get used to its loneliness.[52]

Nothing changed during the following years. Bitterness and anger about Hans alternate with self-blame for being uncontrolled and "acting stupidly." Even small matters take on disproportionate significance. Discussing the furnishings of some rooms in Fürstenstein results in a big row, because Hans ridicules the "cottage arrangements" Daisy proposes.

> I nearly cried with disappointment. I know I behave like a child, and I am an idiot and everything you like – but ... I never get credit for anything, and to be told I make nothing but blunders![53]

It was inevitable that Daisy would become more critical of Hans, especially when his absences from Fürstenstein became more frequent.

---

51 BLU, p. 74.

52 BLU, p. 117.

53 BLU, p. 176.

Cynically, she observes "Hans does not seem to be able to catch a train lately ... he hates writing, although I wired to him."[54]

And years later, there would still be the same complaint "Hans hasn't written in ages although I have written to him asking if there is any particular hurry for me to return; at any rate he isn't in a hurry as he hasn't answered."

When she cannot induce Hans to say that he wants her with him, Daisy decides she must return to Fürstenstein because "I can't stay away any longer from the children."

In February 1900, Daisy had given birth to her first son Hans Heinrich, called *Hansel*, and five years later, again in February (1905), Alexander, called *Lexel*, was born. Both boys had the most exalted royal sponsors one could find in Europe. Emperor Wilhelm II and King Edward VII were Hansel's godfathers, while the Prince of Wales, the future King George V, Queen Alexandra, the Crown Prince of Prussia, and Daisy's brother George became Lexel's godparents.

Finally becoming a mother meant a great deal for Daisy, but her hope that the children would bring her closer to Hans was never fulfilled. Of course, Hans was jubilant, to have a son and heir. He jealously assured Hansel's upbringing according to the traditions of his own family, forcing Daisy to give in constantly to the precepts of her husband. Later, Daisy reproached herself for not insisting on her own concepts of bringing up little Hansel and for spending far too much time away from him in England.

Lexel was born in London and, not without triumph, Daisy noted that later in his life, her second son became "incurably English." Daisy lavished all the love she had not found and could not give in her marriage, on little Lexel, who remained her favourite son throughout her life. When it came to Lexel, Hans did not hinder Daisy in any way, even though he often considered the mother-son relationship as overly close.

There was, however, one relationship extending over many years, which was probably the deepest and most rewarding in Daisy's life, even though conscience and convention did not permit it to blossom to its ultimate fulfillment. As such, this relationship was not without its tragedy. Significantly, Daisy did not reveal anything about the man she respected and loved, a member of Austria's highest nobility.

The depth of this relationship becomes apparent in the chapter *A Perfect Friendship* in the third volume of Daisy's published diaries. It is

---

54   DPH, p. 181.

quite likely that it was her editor Major Chapman-Huston's decision, to publish Daisy's reminiscences and correspondence from this particular episode in Daisy's life. What is more than significant is that this is the only instance where Daisy's diaries report about someone *en clef*, about

> *Maxl*, a member of an Austro-Hungarian branch of an illustrious Bavarian family which had spread into Württemberg and Prussia. Down the centuries its members occupied some of the greatest places in the Holy Roman Empire, and had frequently married in Imperial and Royal Houses.[55]

Daisy and Maxl first met in Castolowitz at the home of their common friend, Fanny Sternberg. Under the impact of Daisy's disappointing marriage, their friendship developed into an idealized love relationship, which returned to a friendship, not free of melancholy, after Maxl got married in 1910. Aside from the short-lived first-love episodes with George Cooper and Gordy, Daisy's relationship with Maxl remained the sole, profound experience of genuine love in her life. While it blossomed into the romantic love Daisy had always been longing for, it was over-shadowed by the constraints Daisy felt as the married woman and the older of the two, and the constant need to observe conventions and exercise caution.

Later in life, Daisy regretted having responded to Maxl's affection far too late. The reason she gave says more about Daisy than Maxl, who was a very shy, young man at the outset of their friendship.

> Maxl was shy and reserved and (in spite of all my boasted powers of intuition) it was five years before I got to value him at something like his true worth. As a matter of fact, in those days I was far too busy with social trivialities to have time for intuitions, or indeed anything else that really mattered. Then we became friends. Maxl fell in love with me. Really in love. Now that can be either the ending or the beginning of a friendship. With Maxl it was the beginning of a friendship, fine and beautiful, that lasted as long as his life.[56]

In July 1906, "five years after I REALLY got to know Maxl," Daisy wrote in her diary:

> Our relationship is indeed a perfect example of what I have always said is possible. In spite of the man, for instance, feeling passion and wishing for more than a platonic relationship, a real, fine, close friendship is QUITE possible between two people who, even when perhaps experiencing a bodily

---

55 WLU, p. 41.

56 BLU, p. 41.

sympathy or attraction, can transmute and exalt this feeling with their thoughts, ideas, intellect and common interest in everything around them, such as politics, art, religion, literature and sport. Thus they sustain and inspire one another and hold together throughout the sundering years.

No matter how Daisy celebrated the enduring friendship, the enforced sublimation of her deep love for Maxl, which shines through her sentences, must have exacted a high price.

> Convention and prudence introduced an element of deception into a friendship that should have been 'artless as the air and candid as the sky.' I have always thought that a married woman who keeps an unmarried man tied to her is a despicable creature![57]

Maxl in turn must have suffered even more under the seemingly unrequited love. He had no choice but to accept the boundaries set by Daisy and observe the required discretion at all times. Unfortunately, none of Daisy's letters to Maxl have survived. Maxl's weekly letters do attest not only to his passionate love for Daisy, they reflect Daisy's love for Maxl.

> Schloss S ... Bohemia, Dec. 8th, '01.
> To leave you for months, ... that is *more* than *I* can bear. And that I can bear pretty much, even you must admit — for you told me enough these last days. ...
>
> Nevertheless, I am the fool who, after all that, tells you again and again: I cannot live without you; and though I am such a monster 'on whose shoulder you wouldn't even for a single moment lay your head' and 'for whom you *never* felt anything' – *though* I know all that, and heaven knows how often you have told me – I want to be and will be your friend. ... But this monster is so *full* of you, ... madly fond of *you*, of your soul, of your thoughts, of all that is in you.[58]

The theme of suffering under Daisy's unrequited love persisted throughout Maxl's letters for years:

> As often as I am in Fürstenstein I never can have you (I mean for private talks, of course), because it is always: 'Maxl, I must write letters. ... It is dangerous, Maxl, somebody might come in. ... I have *so many* letters to write.'

---

57 BLU, p. 47.

58 WLU, pp. 42-43.

And again,

I realize how little I am to you, and still I keep writing – loving – *adoring* you! It is a little sad, but, dearest, you are so much to me.[59]

Vienna, July 19th, 1906
You looked so well in Fürstenstein. ... I never felt quite well since I was ill and now I often get ... so depressed. ... Does it mean anything? ... I only know that I long for you more than ever. ... I will never do anything to spoil our friendship, as you fear; but I still think things are not exactly as you describe them. If two people are really and truly fond of each other for a long, long time, nothing that could happen really matters. ...
Good night, my precious angel – I love you. M.[60]

In this letter, Maxl's disappointment about Daisy's visit is still alive. Daisy had rushed to Vienna in order to visit Maxl in the hospital.

Every day for a week, but always chaperoned! Once I took Prince Festetics along who is already a grandfather, the other time Maxl's brother, and in the end, a priest. That should have been sufficient to protect Maxls and my reputation![61]

More than "convention and worldly prudence" compelled Daisy to follow the dictates of her conscience rather than her emotions. Daisy had found an intimate relationship without the ultimate fulfillment, a relationship which could not be sustained without constant risk and danger to herself and Maxl. Besides, she could never give what Maxl ultimately needed, a relationship that Daisy curiously calls "a married friendship," perhaps unwittingly elevating her relationship with Maxl on the same level as a marriage, minus its legal trappings!

Maxl's nature was such that it craved for a home and love and married friendship; I could give him none of these things and I always tried, as it were, to force him to seek for them.[62]

But Maxl's love and passionate feelings for Daisy remained unabated, revealed in the succession of letters addressed to "My Dear, Dear Rattie," "My Dear Old Thing," "My Dear Old Angel."
In 1908, when a young woman entered Maxl's life; Daisy was the first person to be told. Maxl confided all his hopes and plans to her.

---

59 BLU, p. 45.
60 BLU, pp. 45-47.
61 BLU, p. 50.
62 BLU, p. 47.

Berlin, January 23rd, 1908. Thursday.
MY DEAR OLD ANGEL,
you must be the first person to whom I say this – and now don't be too much surprised – that I am nearly engaged to a sister of the little Rosalie! ... I go on Sunday to their place in the Hungarian mountains, ... and there I think I will be *declaré*. ...

Good-bye, dear old angel, I know you will think of me with all possible kind and affectionate thoughts, and I feel glad for that. Always yrs., and always the same true friend, Maxl.[63]

Schloss T. ... Hungary, February 2nd, 1908.
MY DEAR OLD THING,
I must write you a few lines to thank you for your kind letter by which I was really very, very much touched. Please don't think that we shall be less friends than we have been for so many years. ... You will see what a charming and extraordinarily nice creature Gabrielle is. ...

And now good-bye, dear old friend, and be sure that I shall always be your greatest friend, and always interested in everything that concerns you. Always yrs., Maxl.[64]

This was the last letter addressing Daisy in Maxl's usual affectionate manner and using the familiar "Thou." On May 15, 1908, a letter from Wien arrived in Fürstenstein addressing Daisy as

MY DEAREST PRINCESS DAISY,
I thank you so much for your kind and nice letter. ... I am sure we shall always remain the same true friends. ... The only thing by which you can make me angry is to say that 'you have lost a friend.' You mustn't say that because it is not true. ... My wedding is fixed for the 3rd of June. ...[65]

Mähren, June 24th, 1908.
. . . Thank you very much for asking us to come to Fürstenstein now, but I am awfully sorry that we can't come; we must leave here to look for a house where we can live in the autumn and near the regiment to which I am posted. ... Always yours, my dear Princess, with my very best love, Maxl.[66]

The continued friendship Daisy had hoped for had become reality, likely at considerable emotional cost for Daisy, as the alternately protesting and re-assuring words in Maxl's letter indicate. More than that, the

---

63 BLU, pp. 48-49.
64 BLU, pp. 49-50.
65 BLU, pp. 50-51.
66 BLU, pp. 51-52.

role of being the stronger partner and advisor had changed from Daisy to Maxl. His "Dear Old Angel" had become "My Dear Princess." In July 1910, Maxl introduced his young wife to Daisy in Fürstenstein.

> After many postponements and disappointments both for Maxl's sake and the sake of her sister Rosalie, whom I loved, I was prepared to love Gabrielle. There was no need to make allowances; she was all or more than Maxl had painted. She ... liked Fürstenstein.[67]

Maxl continued to write faithfully, always respectfully addressing "My Princess Daisy." He remained the faithful friend, concerned about Daisy's health and her mood and giving her sound advice. Letters from Maxl, not quite as frequent as before, became much longer. Reports about social events, comments on politics, and at times a bit of gossip filled most of the pages in Maxl's letters to Daisy. These were matters that had been ignored as totally unimportant when their relationship had been at its height.

> Vienna, January 5th, 1911.
> MY DEAR PRINCESS DAISY,
> I was in Hungary the day before yesterday for the funeral of poor Friedrich Carl Hohenlohe... .The Prussians are so ridiculous; poor Friedrich Carl was simply a private person, ... yet all those fools were dressed up as if they were at a Court Ball. Plumes, decorations, swords, spurs, top-boots and God knows what. ... I cannot help finding this rage of dressing-up simply ridiculous.
>
> The Emperor Wilhelm, of course, adores it. I saw him this year ... at my father-in-law's, with golden spurs, yellow boots, and whole birds on his hat; in short, all the paraphernalia which you know so well and which make me think of a circus-master! Poor man, he means so awfully well; everything he does is intended for the best, and still he is so completely destitute of tact that everything turns out exactly opposite to what he intends. ...
>
> I wonder how things will go in Germany after the new elections; very badly I think, thanks to the blunders of the conservatives who ... won't make concessions, ... in order to safeguard their position.
>
> Gabrielle sends you her very best love. ... Many, many nice thoughts from your *great* and true friend who likes you very, very much. Maxl.[68]

For Christmas 1913, Maxl and his wife came to Pless. Because of a heavy cold, Gabrielle had to remain in bed. It was a memorable Christ-

---

67 BLU, p. 56.
68 BLU, pp. 58-60.

mas in several respects. It was the last Christmas before the Great War, it turned out to be the last opportunity in Daisy's and Maxl's life to spend some time together, and it was the last Christmas in her life Daisy spent in Pless.

Perhaps it was the premonition that future events in the great world as much as in Daisy's personal life would separate them forever; perhaps it was the remembrance of the deep love they had experienced for each other, that led Daisy "to give Maxl the greatest proof of greatest friendship that a woman can give, ...her trust."[69]

The next day, overwhelmed by the emotions of her last hours alone with Maxl and the bitter-sweet memories of past days together, she wrote in her diary:

> Christmas 1913, Pless.
> They all seemed happy here, and last night, just as in the old days, little Maxl came into my upstairs sitting-room and played the piano while I dressed for dinner, and we talked through the open door. ... He played all the dear, favourite tunes and songs of mine which we have known for years and as I left the room to go and dress, I leant down and kissed the top of his bald head as he played an old song called *How can you expect me to forget you* and, my dear Diary, this was the first kiss I have ever given him – and he in all the years has only once or twice just touched my hair or forehead.
>
> My eyes were full of tears – and he saw them — and tears came to his eyes also, remembering Fürstenstein as it used to be, the blue sofa I used to rest upon while he played to me the evenings before dinner, while Hans was enjoying Bridge or Patience downstairs.
>
> He took my hands and held them, and said he had no friend like me, and he was ever and always would be the same true comrade.
>
> I had him on my left-hand side at dinner and we talked – of all things in the world – politics! And then I turned often to the right and spoke with the Crown Prince Wilhelm of old times.[70]

Two days after his departure, Maxl's letter arrived in Pless, delivered by special courier. Still filled with the melancholy thoughts of having to say goodbye to Daisy after the unexpectedly fulfilling hours in Pless, Maxl realized that Daisy must feel as sad and resigned as he. Maxl knew that deep in her heart, Daisy felt lonely and abandoned.

---

69 BLU, p. 62.
70 BLU, pp. 62-63.

Once more and for the last time returning to the intimate *Thou*, Maxl encouraged Daisy with deep understanding and celebrated her courage:

> If you had only one ace in your hand the struggle would, of course, be unequal and I could well understand your discouragement; but, as it is, you hold not one, but many trump cards, so don't get nervous and play them all. Be a good diplomat and you will still do with people whatever you like. Everybody is fond of you, you know how to take people, how to talk to them, and so forth. Last, but not least, you are in a position where you can do lots of good. You hate snobbism and 'pretending' as you call it; and so do I, but one has always to play one's little part in one way or another. So play your part now as the gracious Princess; you will remain yourself – my dear old white angel – all the same! Take it as a new page in your lifebook — one has to turn pages sometimes. The first part of this book was 'Princess Daisy'; the new one will be just as attractive as the first one; you can not only *do* what you like, but you will do it *well*. So let it appear as the new book for Christmas 1913; *you and the whole world* will enjoy it![71]

* * *

AUTHOR'S NOTE: Throughout her published diaries, Daisy of Pless never failed to identify the subjects of her reports or commentaries by their proper names. Only once did she digress from this practice, and that was in the case of Maxl, Rosalie, and Gabrielle. Writing about them *en clef* must be accepted as proof of her deep love for Maxl, and the respect she had for him, his wife, and his sister-in-law.

Nevertheless, comparison of names, locations, certain events, and the dates they occurred, made the identification of the personalities Daisy protects *en clef*, possible. As a result, the author found himself confronted with the question whether to reveal the identity of the said personalities or retain the discretion exercised by Daisy of Pless.

Maxl, Gabrielle, and Rosalie belonged to the highest circles of the Habsburg monarchy. While they faithfully carried out the roles assigned to them in life, in their respective positions they were far from exercising power or influence over the events and currents of European history. Recognizing that protecting their anonymity would in no way affect the historical value of this biography, the author felt it appropriate to retain the discretion chosen by Daisy of Pless.

* * * * * *

---

71 BLU, p. 63.

5 Benefactress of the Poor

G laslough Co. Monaghan, Ireland, December 20, 1915.

Dearest Jennie,

Clare[1] is bravely facing her first Christmas without Wilfred and the children are a joy. We are determined to be happy. ... Among our friends, of course Cousin Kitty has filled us with rage & shame – telegraphing the Kaiser out of pure snobbism, but the person I am desperately sorry for is Daisy Pless – Can you imagine the misery of being an English woman cooped up in Germany during this terrible war? She had a less frivolous side – she strove to explain us to the Kaiser (who adored her, you know) and her wonderful efforts to look after poor people must have made her greatly loved. I really liked her better than Shelagh & George – that fellow such an ass to lose you – & now he suffers for it! Leonie.[2]

* * *

With the second Christmas of World War I approaching, Leonie Leslie, sister of George Cornwallis-West's first wife Jennie, remembered an almost unknown part of Daisy's life: her humanitarian work prior to the war.

The Emperor had always followed Daisy's social reform work with interest. He was one of the few who acknowledged her commitment and her successes. Chancellor von Bülow also took Daisy's work seriously and responded to her requests for financial support of her social reform projects in Silesia.

---

1   Clare Frewen née Jerome, sister of Leonie Leslie [writer of this letter], and of Jennie Churchill.

2   By permission of Seymour Leslie.

Among the German nobility, however, Daisy's humanitarian pursuits were, with a few exceptions, refused recognition. Instead, it was pointedly noticed that the Princess of Pless did not restrict herself to the traditional charitable work in her immediate environment, as it had been practiced by generations of the female members of Germany's nobility. The "progressive" tone with which the Princess of Pless justified her social engagement and her humanitarian goals were considered unseemly for a member of her class. Her concurrent political engagement was even perceived as dangerous for Germany. In the opinion of the nobility, the Princess of Pless had recklessly transgressed the boundaries she should have respected as a foreigner, as a woman, and as a member of the highest circle of Germany's aristocracy.

Daisy never succeeded in overcoming the prejudices that remained alive among her German peers. Even more than forty years after Daisy's death, a descendent of a well-known branch of Prussia's nobility, highly respected in present-day circles, could not hide her surprise when she wrote to the author in 1985:

> Most of my peers still insist on the myth that Daisy of Pless never had any social or humanitarian interests; and in obvious contrast to most other women of her class, she never bothered about caring for the well-being of the women, children and the sick living on her properties. ... If there indeed existed even a single humanitarian project, it was hers only in name, no doubt realized by competent secretaries. ... And if any documents indicate that the Princess was involved on hospital trains during the war, such activities must have served one purpose only, her need to gain more prominence socially.[3]

Opposed to this devastating judgment by so many of Germany's nobility stand the numerous faithful and loyal workers and officials formerly in the employ of the Prince of Pless, as do the positive opinions and reminiscences of many of the former residents of the city of Waldenburg and its environs. There are many who have retained a positive image of the Princess of Pless. Among them and often their descendants as well, reminiscences have remained vivid to this day about *Our Daisy* who, with her spontaneous nature and her often awkward, never fully mastered German, made it so easy for the common people to approach the great lady. Many of those who benefited from Daisy's idealism and her practical mind remember with fondness and gratitude what *Our Daisy* had achieved for the poor – young and old – and the working women. The "ordinary" people have always praised Daisy in letters and

---

3   Ehrengard Baronin von Brockdorff

countless stories passed from one generation to the next, but outside their class, the voice of the ordinary people has been rarely heard.

Because of this great divergence of opinion of what Daisy was really like, it appears necessary to place her in the centre of the environment within which she translated her idealism into practical results. Perhaps only someone who experienced this environment of poverty, deprivation and poor health (as the author did in his childhood and youth) will appreciate that Daisy can only be understood if seen in the context of the Lower Silesian Industrial Basin and its character. This necessitates a degree of branching out beyond the usual boundaries of a biography, into the political, economic, and social history of this area. These forces played such a decisive role in Daisy's life because they shaped a vital part of her personality and character.

No matter how inexperienced she appeared as the young Princess of Pless, Daisy was aware of her role within the traditional relationship between master and servant, and between owner and laborer. The role involved a responsibility that had been vividly demonstrated to Daisy in her youth by her mother. However, her childhood in remote Ruthin and pastoral Newlands had not even remotely prepared her for the confrontational relationship between the capitalistic system and the industrial proletariat.

The strikingly visible poverty and deprived living conditions of the miners and their families immediately outside the park gates of Castle Fürstenstein did not remain hidden from Daisy's observant mind for very long. However, her persistent questioning as to why her father-in-law and her husband had done so little to alleviate the worst manifestations of need never received a satisfactory explanation. The differing opinions about the obligations of the wealthy for the people in their employ and for the poor in general caused frequent arguments and painful disagreements between Daisy and Hans and even with the beloved Vater. Overwhelmed by the conditions she observed among the working and non-working poor, Daisy considered Vater's measures to improve the lot of his miners and their families as ridiculously inadequate. At times, she ignored her father-in-law's efforts altogether. In her youthful inexperience, Daisy did not realize that Hans and Vater felt her attacks were without justification. Both considered themselves socially responsible landowners who did as much or more for their agricultural workers than most of their Silesian neighbours. For "his miners," Vater had also introduced a number of measures to secure a better existence for them.

Castle Fürstenstein itself was looked upon as a model workplace with respect to the wages paid and the other multiple benefits, which included comfortable free living quarters, free heating fuel and agricultural produce, clothing, garden plots with a specified number of fruit-bearing trees, and progressive sickness and old-age insurance. No wonder that the personnel of Castle Fürstenstein, from the higher officials down to the stable boys felt privileged and proudly referred to themselves as *fürstlich,*[4] or *färschtlich* in the local dialect.

The attribute of *fürstlich* had also been adopted by the thousands of people working in the mines and other industrial enterprises of the Prince of Pless around Fürstenstein, even though they had to pay a price in the form of slightly smaller wages in exchange for improved benefits. Their pride in working for the Prince was always expressed in the local idiom in the popular, widespread saying *lieber a Biehma winger, oaber färschtlich.*[5] It was a frequently heard saying one would hear from young and old in the streets, courtyards, and schools of Waldenburg and its suburbs.

Daisy, however, soon strove beyond goals her father-in-law had set for himself. Daisy felt responsible for all the poor and the entire working class of the Lower Silesian Industrial Basin. In her thinking, planning, and actions she began to explore new directions, finding the ways and means to bring a greater measure of personal and social well-being and security to thousands of people – men, women and children – living in the region. Daisy's idealism, the mission she chose for herself, and the decisive role she had played in the lives of so many people was praised by the last German resident who remained at Fürstenstein. During one of the author's visits to the castle in 1985, this woman, who was born and raised in Fürstenstein, related how kind, generous, and fatherly Daisy's husband had been in his concern for the welfare of his employees and their families at Fürstenstein. She did not fail to mention that

> for ourselves and the other families living in Fürstenstein, it was always crystal-clear that we lived in a protected, sheltered world, removed from the stress of the everyday life on the outside – we truly lived in a paradise. We also realized only too well that the Prince, that is Daisy's husband, who never failed to be anything but understanding and kind to us, simply had no idea of the poverty and want among his miners and their families in Waldenburg, and therefore never personally concerned himself with their hard life. Only Daisy knew from personal experience how the people had to struggle to survive in their daily life. She always went among the people, while her husband simply closed his eyes refusing to look at the conditions under which his miners had to survive from day-to-day. These so-called good years, before World War I, were certainly wonderful years for us at Fürstenstein,

---

4   "Princely," or "working for the Prince."

5   "Lieber einen Groschen weniger, aber dafür für den Fürsten arbeiten," or "rather have a penny less but work for the Prince."

but for the people outside, life was unspeakably hard. And only Daisy understood that fully and tried her best to help.[6]

* * *

The depressed social conditions among the proletariat and large segments of the working population remained hidden behind the increasing prosperity of the young German Empire. The economic changes began with Chancellor Otto von Bismarck's creation of the German Empire following the Franco-Prussian War of 1870-71. The huge indemnities received from the defeated France enormously strengthened the new Empire, but it took years for Germany to adapt herself to the changed conditions, before her industry and commerce blossomed to an unprecedented degree. On the twenty-fifth anniversary of the German Empire, Wilhelm II proudly proclaimed Germany's status as a world power.

During this unique economic expansion, the demographic and social structures of the country experienced rapid, often painful changes. Existing cities expanded dramatically and new cities grew out of sleepy villages wherever new industrial complexes and factories sprang up. The rapid urbanization of the population resulting from the migration of agricultural labourers to the new centres of industry reduced the percentage of rural dwellers from seventy-five percent to twenty percent of Germany's population within a single generation. The Lower Silesian industrial basin became a prime example of this phenomenon and its disastrous consequences for the working class.

It was the dispossessed, pauperized, underpaid, and uneducated proletariat in this area to which Daisy, against the wishes of her husband and his family, passionately directed her attention. With growing self-confidence and determination, she wrote in 1902

> I am perhaps not quite an ordinary woman because I still see the need of fighting and do fight, whereas so many seem to give up the battle. ... I have a great longing to make people happy; I try to do what is right, and yet it is not with any religious motives that I dream of living with heart and hand full for the poor, the miners and the needy Socialists about here.[7]

One might question whether Daisy truly understood the nature of the German Empire and the peculiar power structure within its society. Her attitude towards the common people was articulated in ideas about promoting social change and achieving social progress. Daisy's ideas were the battle-cry against her own class and the prevailing social order.

---

6   Mrs. Doris Stempowska.

7   DPH, p. 195.

Only too soon would Daisy feel the backlash from her own class, which fearfully reacted to the growing politically organized presence of the working class in trade unions and in the Social Democratic Party. In the eyes of the aristocracy and the bourgeoisie, the millions streaming from the rural areas to the growing cities did indeed seem to constitute a new, potentially dangerous power.

The self-confident German Empire represented itself through its nobility, the officers corps, the land-owners (who mostly were members of the aristocracy), the bourgeoisie, and the civil servants. From a certain level upwards, the higher-ranking positions in the army and the country's administration were almost exclusively occupied by members of aristocracy. The bourgeoisie proudly maintained its dominant role in industry and commerce. The ranks of the working class never identified with the power and the glory of the Empire and its progress.

Indeed, aristocracy and bourgeoisie reacted with hostility especially to the Social Democratic Party that eventually reached a membership of four and a half million (prior to World War I the party garnered 35% of all votes). No wonder, the middle and upper classes perceived the labour unions and the Social Democrats as a constant threat to the security of the state, even a danger to the personal safety of the upper class individual and his hard-earned prosperity.

The millions streaming into the cities and expanding industrial regions seemed an anonymous mass of millions of *Reds*, all of them enemies of the state. No longer did it seem possible to throw bridges across the chasm between the poor and the wealthy. The rich felt threatened and the poor resented the continuing class distinctions, which to them seemed designed to maintain the power of the wealthy and the separation of the dispossessed from the more fortunate classes. Fear of *die Roten*, the *Reds,* and their revolutionary aims remained all-pervasive in the consciousness of the upper classes and even the petty bourgeoisie.

Daisy did not hide her sympathy for the "poor socialists" or for the Social Democratic Party, which fought for the interests of the impoverished proletariat in the Waldenburg Industrial Basin. Much later when, in spite of the excesses and failings of the Russian Revolution, a socialist system was still considered worth striving for in many circles, Daisy found it necessary to revise her opinion. She had become sceptical of the freedom and the benefits socialism promised the individual who was without means and property. Her comments are remarkable in light of the various routes socialism has taken in the past eighty years – ranging from benevolent state control to the darkest, bloodiest totalitarianism. In 1925. Daisy wrote with surprising insight:

Were Socialism ... established as long as capitalism, it would have developed far more numerous and intolerable evils than the existing system has, ... because Socialism is based on strictly disciplined organization and, although individuals may often be harsh and overbearing, organizations and systems *always* are.[8]

* * *

There were voices of reason, but the Kaiser's was not one of them. As early as 1906, Chancellor von Bülow was warned by a friend.

If the Kaiser goes on being so overbearing and particularly so indiscreet, this palace [the Imperial Palace in Berlin] will sooner or later be menaced or even stormed by the masses.[9]

And in the same year, the leader of the Prussian Conservatives said to a left-wing deputy

... the future belongs to you. ... The masses are going to make themselves felt and rob us aristocrats of our influence. ... We will never surrender voluntarily.[10]

Nobody mustered the courage to confront the Emperor for his thoughtless attitude towards the German working class. Following the bloody clashes between workers and police in the streets of Berlin during the franchise demonstrations in January 1908, Count Zedlitz-Trützschler, Court Marshal of the Emperor, confided his concerns to his diary:

When we were talking about the thirty people who had been injured, the Emperor said: 'I am very pleased at the attitude of the police, but the next time they will have to set about them with the sharp edge of the sword and not with the flat.'[11]

The incredible shortsightedness of the Emperor did not permit him to appreciate the outstanding qualities of the leader of the Social Democratic Party who, in the Emperor's eyes was his enemy. In reality this man, August Bebel, wanted justice for the German worker, but faithful to crown and country, he was not a revolutionary.

---

8 DPH, p. 138.
9 See Bülow, op. cit., vol 2, p. 314.
10 Arthur Graf von Posadowski-Wehner.
11 See Robert Count Zedlitz-Trützschler, op. cit., p. 214.

It was not possible to listen with indifference to Bebel when he was speaking of the miseries of suffering humanity, and one had the intuition that he was telling the truth, and not trying to rouse the pity of his audience. ... When he was appealing to the feelings of justice and humanity of the German people, and imploring it not to follow some of its children to be made outlaws on account of their political opinions, one could not help thinking of those prophets of ... the Bible. ... Bebel was essentially an idealist, and this constituted perhaps his greatest strength. ... He was a demagogue, but he was also a man of order who detested anarchy and repudiated its doctrine. In his opinion, liberty stood above everything else, except the German Fatherland.[12]

This striking characterization of a man venerated by his followers as a democrat and human being is found in the memoirs of the Princess Catherine Radziwill, who received so little deserved credit for her sharp mind and astute observations.

* * *

In contrast to Princess Radziwill, who never in her life had come face-to-face with the destitute life of the proletariat, Daisy could not ignore the immense differences between rich and poor, between privilege and the absence of it. The beauty and pomp of Castle Fürstenstein, and – less than a ten minute coach-ride away – the gray desolation of the ugliness of the highly industrialized Waldenburg, symbolized the economic and social dichotomy of her time. Fürstenstein was located at the edge of the Lower Silesian Industrial Basin, while Castle Pless touched the industrial region of Upper Silesia. Both of the large properties guaranteed the Prince of Pless his immense wealth, and yet were counted as the economically and socially most depressed regions of Imperial Germany.

For generations, the industrialized districts of Lower Silesia were also areas of recurrent social tension and unrest. When the wave of Europe's industrialization reached Silesia, the introduction of mechanical looms began in Waldenburg in 1810. Weaving as a cottage industry, the centuries-old livelihood for thousands of families, disappeared rapidly. Even though dozens of newly erected mills soon sprang up in the long-established weavers villages, they could not provide enough work for the former cottage weavers. Those who were fortunate to find employment in the mills, worked for starvation wages. In 1844, joined by the unemployed, the underpaid weavers rose in the bloody revolts which are immortalized in Gerhart Hauptmann's drama *The Weavers*.

---

12   See Catherine Radziwill, op. cit., pp. 174-75.

Four years later, in the wake of the German Revolution of 1848, the coal miners of Waldenburg congregated at the gates of Castle Fürstenstein with their demands for better wages. At this time, it was still sufficient for Hans Heinrich X to offer food and drink and promises in order to encourage his miners to return peacefully to their places of work. Rather than being recognized as the vanguard of social unrest, this event was quickly turned into an amusing anecdote popular around Waldenburg.

Five years later, the unchanged working conditions, pitiful wages, and destitute living conditions led to the first large-scale miners' strike in Germany. Of the 7,000 miners employed in the district, 5,000 began a well-organized strike that could only be broken, when Waldenburg was occupied by Prussian troops. The strike failed, but left a legacy of bitterness and a hatred of the propertied class.

It was no accident that Waldenburg became the scene of this first miners' strike in Germany. Although of high metallurgical quality, the Lower Silesian coal could only be recovered under unusually precarious circumstances due to the prevailing geological conditions. Further to the high cost of production, the distance from major markets added to the costs of transportation. Altogether, the competition with other mining areas such as the Ruhr Basin and even Great Britain made the recovery and sale of coal increasingly difficult at a time when industry and commerce in most parts of the Empire flourished beyond expectations. As a sad consequence, the wages paid to the miners of all companies around Waldenburg, including those working for the Prince of Pless, remained the lowest in the entire country. Part-time employment was introduced for miners, and unemployment became chronic.

These were conditions for which Hans Heinrich XI of Pless and the other mine-owners around Waldenburg could not be held responsible. Nevertheless, the working population around Waldenburg soon developed all the traits of the industrial proletariat that subsisted under living and working conditions that were considered to be the worst excesses of capitalism in Germany. A once pastoral countryside with idyllic villages of picturesque farmhouses on steep hillsides had been transformed to smoky, gray, desolate urban settlements with endless rows of ugly, overcrowded tenement houses stretching for mile after mile through the long, narrow valleys.

From the Franco-Prussian War into the early twentieth century, the entire area was caught up in a wild, uncontrolled construction boom designed to house the enormous number of people arriving from rural areas who were in search of work. Only Waldenburg had some zoning laws; the former farming villages surrounding the city had none. Thousands of four and five storey tenement houses of primitive quality were erected rapidly, placed haphazardly on the outskirts of Waldenburg and all over the valleys around, with no regard for human needs. Outside town limits, for decades, there was no water- or sewage system.

These miners' tenements were of depressing ugliness. Their roofs were invariably covered by cheap tar paper rather than by the otherwise predominant red clay tiles that used to brighten the appearance of towns and villages. The static strength of these buildings was so poor that they had to be literally held together by long iron rods embedded in their walls. These rods protruded in all their ugly significance on the outside where they were covered by huge round iron plates. The large iron nuts placed over these plates had to be regularly tightened in order to prevent the building's collapse.

These horrible tenement houses usually accommodated up to three or four dozen families. Even though most miners had many children, rarely would a family's home consist of more than the standard flat of kitchen and one room, often indeed of one single room only. It was common for several children to share one bed. While father or adult sons were at work, it was equally common to rent out their bed for a few pennies to so-called *sleepers*, young bachelor miners off-shift, who could not afford their own accommodation. For each two stories, there was one water-tap on the landing between the stories and sometimes even a toilet. Usually, however, the toilets were found in the courtyard.

Tension and frustrations ran high under such overcrowded, un-healthy conditions. They were in part responsible for the miners' habits of stopping at the local pub on their way home from shift. Small, dark, and poorly furnished pubs could be found everywhere in large numbers. Open from early in the morning to late at night, the always busy pubs were the bane of the miners' wives, who needed every penny of their husbands' wages. Especially after shift-change, the crowds of miners with a bottle of beer or a glass of cheap brandy in their hands, often overflowed onto the street. On paydays, the wives gathered at the mine gate in order to catch their husbands, before they could turn their hard-earned wages into alcoholic spirits.

The consequences of widespread alcoholism exacerbated the al-ready poor health of the population. After less than thirty years of work underground, most miners were placed as *invalids* in poorly remuner-ated retirement, while their wives had to improve the wretchedly low family income through long hours of housecleaning or poorly paid factory work. Housing, nutrition, and hygiene remained on the lowest possible level. Tuberculosis was rampant and typhoid epidemics recur-rent. Until the second decade of the twentieth century, the area was plagued with the highest newborn and infant mortality rate in Germany. George Cornwallis-West recalls one of the hikes he took in 1906 from

Fürstenstein to a woodman's hut where his party was prevented from enjoying the planned lunch, because "two people had been lying in this hut, dead from cholera."[13]

Related by George to the other guests present for the Imperial Maneuvers, this story caused "much embarrassment" and earned a denial from his brother-in-law Hans that this discovery was symptomatic of the conditions in the entire area.

Another phenomenon of capitalistic development was the sudden emergence of a new class of nouveaux riches, that grew out of the formerly poor population of farmers who had sold their mineral rights to the expanding mining companies for huge sums of money. Risen overnight from *Dreckpauern*[14] to the detested newly rich *Kuxbarone*,[15] these families used their sudden financial windfall to build, without discretion or shame, their mansions. Formal gardens surrounding the mansions separated the *Kuxbarone* from the wretched tenement houses of the miners. This unrestrained display of wealth and an ostentatious lifestyle provoked great bitterness and hostility among the dispossessed proletariat, that barely subsisted from one payday to the next. The *Kuxbarone* were only one new strata in a social pyramid that also included the greatly expanded classes of the manufacturers, merchants, and civil servants – all of them formerly of insignificant numbers.

Manufacturers and storekeepers were generally well-liked by the workers, especially since they gave work to their wives. But there was still another class the miners confronted with unabated mistrust, hatred, and eventually, with open conflict. These were the lower and middle-level officials of the mining companies, who in slavish loyalty to their employers, relentlessly carried out their cruel regime of controlling and harassing the miners under their supervision, often at the worksite deep underground. Too often, the foremen and immediate superiors exploited their power of hiring and firing by passing out demerits and penalties, and would even hold back part of the hard-earned wages. Under such constant threats and pressures, even the miners of the Pless enterprises tended to forget that the Prince of Pless was by far not the worst of the employers in the mines around Waldenburg. The Prince's supervisors and foremen had the reputation of spying on the miners and their political opinions and activities. All political comment, discovery of membership in the Social Democratic Party, or the call for organizing a

---

13 See George Cornwallis-West, op. cit., p. 255.

14 Dirt farmers.

15 Mineral rights barons.

trade union were promptly reported to the administration for punishment. Often, this meant immediate dismissal.

In 1911, the accumulated anger and hatred among the miners exploded into a battle-cry published in the form of a pamphlet directed at the *Reichstag*:[16]

SETTLING OUR ACCOUNTS WITH THE ADMINISTRATION OF THE PRINCE OF PLESS IN LOWER SILESIA

prepared for the enlightenment of the Deputies in the Reichstag and the Prussian Legislature, for the Civil Service and for All Concerned Citizens and Workers[17]

The continuing harassment and oppression was demonstrated in over thirty pages of cases that included the names of the miners and supervisors. It is likely, however, that these involved cases had never been brought to the attention of the Prince of Pless. Pointing to the increasing migration of Waldenburg miners to the better-paid employment in the Ruhr basin, the pamphlet closed with a challenge to the administration:

> The miners union of the Pless mines will not die a slow death by the hands of the administration. ... We will not hesitate to boycott the mines of the Prince of Pless and, if necessary, will do our utmost to assist the miners in maintaining their human dignity by supporting their migration to other mining districts. ... The miners employed by the Prince of Pless have nothing to lose but their chains and ... labour relations which are the worst in the German mining industry. ... So far, we have carefully refrained from playing with fire, but if we are forced to do so, we are convinced that the miners will be the last ones to have their fingers burned.[18]

When Daisy read this pamphlet, she was sad, but not surprised. For more than ten years, she had tried her best, eventually with obvious success; but the dimensions of need, the all-pervasive poverty remained overwhelming. As she did in Ruthin years ago at the side of her mother, Daisy first began to visit the poor around Fürstenstein trying her best "to give with full hands." But the extent of the existing need soon exhausted her resources, even though her efforts did not reach beyond the immediate neighbourhood of Fürstenstein. Daisy quickly became aware of the tens of thousands of people in Waldenburg and the surrounding miners' villages who did not need a bit of charity, but someone who would with

---

16 Lower House of the German Parliament.

17 Hausmann & Co., Bochum, 1911.

18 Ibid.

energy and resources purposefully attack the underlying causes of the desperate social conditions out of which the persistent misery in their personal lives evolved.

The path that led Daisy from being the benevolent mistress of the castle to the courageous, imaginative, and vigorous social reformer was hard and lonely. Little understanding and support was forthcoming from Hans. He reacted to Daisy's humanitarian ideals and her involvement in social and political issues with disbelief, and irritation that easily turned into open anger. Early on, he was appalled by Daisy's wish "to go among the common people.., something which absolutely was not *comme il faut!*"[19]

The beloved Vater, who was adored by the poor people for his generous nature, failed to comprehend why Daisy insisted on devoting her energies to social problems which, in his opinion, had been resolved long ago.

Indeed, as an employer, the *Old Duke* deserved unqualified recognition. The protective and supportive social measures he had introduced for the personnel employed in his enterprises were outstanding for their time. As early as 1879, he had ordered the creation of the *Pension Fund of the Prince of Pless* for his officials. Within a few years, the benefits of the pension fund were made available to all the workers in his employ as well. The generous provisions included retirement pensions for officials, and workers, and their widows; protection in case of illness, accident, and premature disability. Improved during succeeding years, this progressive system protected the miners and others working for the Prince of Pless until World War II. A claim approved in 1943 that granted pension benefits to a prematurely disabled driver working for the coal mines in Waldenburg was still based on the pension statutes of 1879 that had been introduced by the *Old Duke*.

With pride, Daisy's son, Hansel explained to the author how the pension system introduced in 1879 by his grandfather Hans Heinrich XV for his employees had been one of the forerunners and primary models of Bismarck's social legislation begun in the 1880s. In more detail, the social welfare measures of the Prince of Pless were presented in the booklet titled

INSTITUTIONS FOR PROMOTING THE WELFARE OF THE
WORKMEN ON THE FÜRSTENSTEIN MINES
His Serene Highness the Prince of Pless
WALDENBURG Silesia Germany[20]

---

19 BLU, p. 61.

20 German Title: Arbeiter-Fürsorge auf den Fürstensteiner Gruben Sr.Durchlaucht des Fürsten von Pless, Waldenburg in Schlesien (Waldenburg, 1904), passim.

Printed in English and German with a colourful cover and many illustrations, this booklet was specifically prepared for the display of the German mining industry in the German Pavilion of the 1904 World's Fair in St. Louis. To this day, it remains a remarkable document significant for the history of social welfare in Europe.

The pamphlet opens with a description of the German statutory social insurance measures of which the Prince of Pless assumed half of the cost, as well as measures provided by the Prince of Pless to promote health and hygiene (including treatments in health resorts).

Under the title of *The Voluntary Social Welfare Programs of the Prince of Pless*, measures designed to improve the quality of life for the Pless miners and their families focus on the housing program. Three thousand of the five thousand Pless miners were married. Of these, eighteen percent lived in "miners colonies" built and maintained by the Pless administration. The Pless housing estates were far superior to the prevailing standard. For many years they remained the envy of miners working for other companies. They had a pleasing exterior and were surrounded by green space that included playgrounds for children and benches for the old invalids and a garden plot for each family.

Complementing these benefits was the large *Department Store of the Prince of Pless,* which offered a wide range of food products, clothing, linen, furniture, and other goods at sharply reduced prices. Annual profits of the department store were distributed to the miners, who received an average of nine percent of the sum the family had spent during the preceding year.

Further welfare measures described in the booklet demonstrated the combination of socially progressive ideas and practical thinking. Quite unique was the practice of paying a subsidy to those families where the bread-winner was absent and unable to earn a wage during the compulsory annual military exercises. Special funds were given to the families during severe crises such as accidents or death of the bread-winner. For the generally undereducated apprentices, who entered the mines at the age of fourteen, special *Fortbildungsschulen*[21] offered six hours of schooling each week in German, arithmetic, drafting, history, and geography. Attached to these schools were libraries. For the daughters of the miners, in turn, special schools teaching cooking and other homemaking skills offered full-day courses lasting three months, free of cost. Several health clinics operated by Protestant nursing sisters for the care of the sick were funded by the Prince of Pless.

---

21 Continuing education schools.

Truly impressive were the two *Casinos*, social centres comparable to private clubs, providing a healthier and more dignified environment for the miners than the infamous pubs.

By 1904, the year of the St. Louis World's Fair, the capital costs for these facilities designed "to ease the hard lot of the miner as much as possible and brighten his hours of rest and leisure," had reached the sum of 3 million Marks; annual operating expenses were reported in the booklet as 563,000 Marks.

Of all the generous social welfare measures implemented by the Prince of Pless, the large-scale housing program for his miners was quite outstanding for its time. The thousands of miners working for other companies, however, were not so fortunate. Conditions that still existed twenty-five years later, ten years after World War I, shocked the German President Paul von Hindenburg during a special visit to the city on September 19, 1928. He was visibly shaken by the living circumstances he was shown. At the reception concluding his visit to Waldenburg held in the City Hall, Hindenburg summarized his impressions in a speech ending with the following words:

> More than anything, I have been most painfully distressed by the living conditions of the working population, especially their substandard, terribly overcrowded housing. From the bottom of my heart I wish that fruitful co-operation between employers and employees will promote badly needed improvements. I in turn promise to do my utmost to give all the help possible within the restraints of my position. ... And now that my official functions have ended, I must tell you again how shocked I still am after what I have seen and heard to-day. Help must be brought to these people, conditions must not be permitted to go on as they are.[22]

Waldenburg again came into focus a year later through the medium of the social documentary *Hunger in Waldenburg*,[23] one of the first films of its kind. The film's graphic evidence of the misery and the deplorable, social problems extant in the Waldenburg Industrial Basin, showed conditions that were nonexistent to such a degree anywhere else in Germany.

Between 1925 and 1933, the Social Democratic city council built a number of well-equipped schools of outstanding architecture that earned the otherwise rather non-descript Waldenburg the reputation of "the city of beautiful schools." But still, during the author's school years

---

22 Neues Tageblatt, September 19, 1928.

23 *Hunger in Waldenburg, Ein Film des Volksfilmverbandes,* producer Leo Lania (Berlin, 1929).

in Waldenburg, conditions were far below the standards of the country in general. Attending elementary school between 1931 and 1935, the author shared a classroom with more than sixty students each year. Although a well-nourished child from a fairly well-to-do family, the author was asked by his teacher to participate in the daily *Quäkerspeisung*[24] consisting of a glass of milk and a roll, for the sake of discretion and as a gesture of solidarity with the other students in the class who almost without exception came from poor households. The general state of health of the students was pitiful. Each year, there was at least one death among the author's classmates. The author also remembers the high percentage of disabled or physically handicapped children and how visits to the homes of his classmates established that most of them still lived in the old, run-down, two-room flats that had been erected before World War I.

For the children of the working class, the hope of eventually escaping this dreadful poverty was practically non-existent. By 1936 parents of children attending high school still had to pay a monthly fee of 20 Marks, a sum unattainable for working class families. The author was the only one of his class of sixty students to transfer from elementary school to high school in 1935. There, he found forty classmates at the entry level, only a minute representation of the children of a district with a population of 175,000.

* * *

This incidental forward glance to the years after Daisy's social reform engagement was provided to the reader in order to demonstrate the dimensions of the chronic poverty and the widespread destitution among the working class that confronted a helpless Daisy during her early years in Fürstenstein. No matter how much the needs of the poor challenged her and troubled her conscience, Daisy initially lacked the courage and self-confidence to respond to them. It seemed easier to devote her energies to projects in her familiar England where she found support and recognition that was not forthcoming from her husband.

It is understandable, therefore, that during the first ten years of her marriage, Daisy primarily participated in humanitarian activities in the country of her birth. In England, her experience was crucial for her future mission as social reformer and politically engaged woman. The

---

24 Popular among the elementary school children the "Quaker Feeding" maintained by the United States Society of Friends, the Quakers, under the impression of the documentary *Hunger in Waldenburg* was outlawed by the Hitler authorities immediately after January 30, 1933.

roots of Daisy's social and political awareness and her passionate striving for peace and understanding between the people of England and Germany can be traced to these years. These were the years when Daisy first experienced a conflict between her idealism and belief in the inherent goodness of people and the ugly reality of the growing prejudice and hostility between the country of her birth and the country of her marriage.

In 1897, on the occasion of Queen Victoria's Golden Jubilee, Daisy participated in the fundraising for the *Institution of Jubilee Nurses* aimed "at all English women married to Germans or any Germans in England."[25]

This first engagement ended in deep disappointment and an early appreciation of latent distrust between English and German people. Although Daisy was proud in her success of having reached thousands of potential donors in Germany and in England through appeals published in newspapers in both countries and through more than a thousand letters written with the assistance of her secretary Freytag, the results of her campaign were discouraging. The Bavarian *Order of St. Theresa* which she received in recognition of her efforts, was small comfort, as four hundred of the English women married in Germany did not respond at all, and some "had even written to say that her husbands will not allow them to send anything."[26]

In England, even the active support of her friend, the German Ambassador Count Hatzfeldt had little effect. Daisy was left with the conclusion that "the feeling between Germany and England can really be called nothing less, I think, than hatred."[27]

During King Edward's coronation in 1901, Daisy presided over the German stall at the Coronation Bazaar in Regent Park in aid of the *Great Ormond Street Hospital for Sick Children*. She also raised funds through "musicales and theatricals" for the *Canning Street Childrens Hospital*. This was the first time she had presented her talent to the public, and she did raise funds, but after these events, Daisy reeled under the hostile reactions to the first campaign she conducted on her own. Mindful of the tensions growing as a result of the Boer War, she decided

> to do my own small part, to do what I could to make harmony out of discord and smooth over as far as one individual could, the jealousies and suspicions aroused in Germany by the South African War. ... If the Boers were German-Dutch and their conquerors English, at least they were equal in

---

25 BLU, p. 53.

26 BLU, p. 54.

27 Ibid.

honour and heroism in their soldiers graves! ... efforts would not only comfort individuals, but perhaps do something to heal the wounds of war.[28]

Daisy's "small part" was to organize a Guild of Women who would be responsible for the graves of the soldiers from both sides who had lost their lives during the South African War. At this, she was not very successful. German sympathies had been clearly with the Boers. In his notorious telegram to President Krüger, Emperor Wilhelm II praised the Boers for their courage and fortitude, after they had repelled the British troops in the Transvaal in 1896. Daisy's only success, then, was in raising controversy in Germany, which for the first time, caused the public to question the loyalty of the Princess of Pless to the country of her marriage.

These early controversial experiences of standing quite alone in the public limelight, as a woman appealing to the heart and conscience of the peoples from two nations, fostered a growing sense of self-assurance and autonomy in Daisy. This happened at a time when hopes unfulfilled in her marriage had created a vacuum, a sense of emptiness, and lack of purpose, which drove Daisy even harder to help "with heart and hands full for the poor, the miners and the needy Socialists about here."[29]

She also realized that the path of the active humanitarian would be a very lonely one. Hans would neither develop much interest in her humanitarian strivings nor actively support her. "On such matters I can never talk to him. ... He never reads; he does not even allow himself to think!"[30]

And even Vater observed that "Hans always says Nein!"[31] After ten years of marriage, Daisy confesses in resignation

> a spirit of sadness, with many illusions gone, most of my ideals broken (for I have begun to believe that nothing really exists except one's own imagination). ... most of the gold has rubbed off the dazzling frames that held but phantom pictures. ... Hans always says that I am all that he wants. ... Such a declaration should be sufficient to satisfy the desire of any good and modest woman, but ... possibly I am neither good nor modest.[32]

There was only one way to proceed. Daisy gives her declaration to the diary:

---

28 DPH, pp. 76-77.

29 DPP, p. 61.

30 DPP, p. 150.

31 DPP, p. 118.

32 DPP, p. 61.

Perhaps it is best in the circumstances that ... I go among the working people; before ... I was always told it was not 'princely' to do so. ... But I want to get to the heart of the people and understand them and, now in sheer desperation, I have broken bounds. I order my carriage and go where I choose: almshouses, hospitals, homes for the old people, everywhere. In time, my personal interest in my poorer neighbours will be acceptable and, I hope, helpful.[33]

Determined to go her own way, with or without the permission and support of her husband, Daisy cautiously began to widen the circle of her volunteer activities. Stories and anecdotes passed from her generation to the next ones tell how quickly Daisy conquered the hearts of the people. Survivors of these early days remember how the young beautiful English princess immediately became popular among the common people with her spontaneity, her warm, radiant smile, and her fearless attempts to speak with them in their own language. Encounters between Daisy's haphazard, limited German, about which she could laugh as much as the people, and the strong dialect of the locals, unintelligible even to Germans from other parts of the country, caused numerous comical and hilarious misunderstandings that quickly became popular local anecdotes, and only increased the people's fondness of their princess. It did not take long for Daisy to break down all barriers, always helping the ordinary people to easily overcome their initial shyness:

The people around here ... forget I am the Princess of Pless, and talk to me as a fellow mortal.[34]

The admiration of the people became boundless. New stories about the princess turned up regularly. Hans, when he became aware of them, was rarely pleased. One especially popular story of how his wife had tried to acquire some of the more explicit expressions of the local dialect, simply infuriated Hans:

Riding through open country near Fürstenstein, Daisy had her carriage stopped when she noticed a farmer lying under his wagon trying, with loud cussing, to fix a broken wheel. Daisy hurried across the muddy field and pulled the angry farmer from under his wagon with the words, "Father, you are trying too hard, you need help." Daisy dragged the loudly protesting man to her carriage where the poor fellow, mud-encrusted boots, dirty work clothes and all, had to sit next to the beautiful princess in her elegant carriage. On the way back to his village, Daisy

---

33 BLU, p. 151.
34 BLU, p. 62.

embarrassed the poor man no end, when she insisted that he explain the meaning of the strong words he had just used. The story of this unusual carriage ride that had been witnessed by the astonished villagers as it finally ended in the farmer's own yard, spread with all its details like wildfire. No matter how Hans felt about such escapades, episodes like this one helped Daisy to introduce herself to the people in the image she was striving for.

> I want the agents, labourers, miners, woodcutters, poor people, old men and women, and even children, to realise that I, Hans and the staff at Fürstenstein are here to advise and help.[35]

The fervent wish to help would not be enough in itself. Of equal importance was the way in which such help would be offered and provided. At this time, concepts and principles of providing social support were rarely articulated or consciously practiced. The conservative attitudes of Daisy's in-laws and their traditional ways of providing help became a true challenge for Daisy. She had to formulate her own ideas about the causes of the problems that needed to be alleviated and the means to reach the goals of her humanitarian objectives. What set Daisy immediately apart from her in-laws and even from her beloved Vater, though, was her decision to help all people in need and not only those in the employ of her father-in-law. Such novel views about one's responsibilities for all one's fellow human beings could only be perceived by Vater and Hans as a sabotage of their own humanitarian endeavours, and yet another manifestation of Daisy's rebellious nature.

The success of Daisy's early, comparably small social projects immediately demonstrated that she had chosen the right path for their realization. So much needed to be done, but Daisy never turned into what Samuel Coleridge so aptly characterized as women who stormed at the poor with "a fierce and terrible benevolence."

* * * * * *

---

35 DPH, p. 195.

6 | *The Social Reformer*

I know, my greatest fault is that I cannot wait, I always want everything done right at once. ... But nobody should any longer imagine I am only a pretty woman and think ... some extravagant compliment ... is all I want. From now onward I intend to show them that I expect something quite different – and I will get it some day![1]

Daisy of Pless

* * *

That day would arrive sooner than Daisy expected.

Daisy's social projects did not originate in profound empathy alone. Hopes and ideas that developed into ultimately successful projects were based on intense observations of the people within their own immediate and more distant environment and were put through careful, unimpassioned analysis. For a deeper appreciation of Daisy's chosen mission as social reformer, it is worthwhile to follow the history of her humanitarian work with the critical eyes of the modern-day social scientist.

Charity was ultimately of no lasting benefit to the impoverished and the working poor, unless it respected their dignity under all circumstances. How important it was to preserve the dignity of even the poorest people, Daisy had already learned as a child from her mother. It was this attitude that helped Daisy find such quick acceptance among the common people around Fürstenstein and Waldenburg, and from then on guided all her humanitarian activities.

---

1   DPP, p. 78.

On December 20, 1901, Daisy had returned from Waldenburg in a state of shock and anger. With intense shame, she had witnessed the annual distribution of Christmas gifts to the poor people. It had been an incredibly thoughtless, disorganized affair; the old people

> were kept standing for over three hours, and they had walked all the way there, and had to walk back, and were given nothing to eat or drink! I was furious. ...[2]

Determined that she would never permit such a heartless event, Daisy reported at Christmas 1902 that "everything is done my way, as generally happens in the end."[3] People were no longer called to a local inn and just given their present; for the first time, they were invited to come to Castle Fürstenstein:

> In the salons next to the Great Ballroom, gifts had been laid out on long tables and tea and cakes were ready for 2500 people, among them 700 children. I had persuaded Hans to accompany me, for the first time in his life! ... The clergyman said a few words, some Christmas songs were sung, and then I walked around and gave each person a shawl, petticoat, stockings or something. They all kissed my hand and blessed me. ... if only I had more money I would do lots more.[4]

And in Pless, a few days later, Daisy received Vater's permission to invite the poor to the Castle for the first time.

> The big salon looked lovely put up for the fête for three hundred children on the last day, with three big Christmas trees in the windows. ... never in the past at Pless or Fürstenstein had they had such a Christmas. ... I shook hands with four thousand people in seven days.[5]

To the local people, Daisy was a fairy princess, and Hans was also very pleased and accepted in good humour his wife's reminder that "I know I really am quite sensible at times!"[6]

The happy sense of fulfillment did not last much beyond Christmas. During gray, desolate winter days, a rarity at Fürstenstein, a lonely, depressed Daisy brooded about her fate. There were few visitors and hardly anybody, least of all Hans, with whom she could share her impa-

---

2   BLU, pp. 77-78.
3   BLU, p. 78.
4   BLU, p. 77.
5   BLU, p. 78.
6   BLU, p. 79.

tience to do things in ways she considered useful. She wished Hans would sense how she was changing.

* * *

For Daisy, these weeks of seeming idleness and frustration also brought days of relentless stock-taking, unsparing self-examination, and decision-making; they were days of crucial importance. When spring arrived, Daisy had decided to what problems and needs she would devote her energy and what directions she would take to be successful in helping the people around Waldenburg.

Daisy had taken the vital step from being the benefactress of the poor to the social reformer. From now on, she would no longer restrict her role to only helping the individual poor, the old, and sick; she would also analyze and improve their environment, which affected the health, well-being, and the quality of life of the individual as well as of entire communities. Understanding the nature of this environment, she would search for the causes of the problems that so visibly plagued the area. Full of ideas and enthusiasm, Daisy would try to ameliorate or even solve the problems she had recognized through her own initiative and effort. She planned to appeal to those whom she considered responsible for the existence of the problems in the first place. In 1903, she wrote:

> I have been trying to think out some way of raising money to have the river around Waldenburg cleansed . ...[7]

Daisy referred to a creek that ran through the length of Waldenburg and the villages to the north. Called *Laisebach* in its upper reaches, it was hardly wider than eight metres. Ironically, in its lower region it carried the name *Hellebach* [clear brook], although it received over its length of less than 25 kilometres not only the entire industrial effluent of the area, but also the human wastes of almost 100,000 people. Its once romantic banks were now lined by ugly, overcrowded tenement houses, while the trout that the kings and princes visiting Fürstenstein had loved to catch had disappeared long ago.

This horrible creek, in reality an open sewage canal, had become a sluggish, pitch-black body of water that exuded an evil smell forever penetrating the adjoining villages; it often rose even to the terraces of Castle Fürstenstein from the deep gorge through which the *Hellebach* wound its way.

---

7   BLU, p. 64.

Daisy decided to identify the source of the horrid smells emanating from the *Hellebach*. She not only discovered dozens of mines and factories discharging their wastes into the creek. In the overpopulated villages, which stretched for miles along the *Laisebach* and *Hellebach*, she was also horrified to discover hundreds of outhouses adjacent to the river bank, and immediately next to them, only metres from the polluted creek, wells from which the people obtained their drinking water.

Daisy's impassioned appeal to the local administration resulted merely in an "official inspection made locally." The inspection confirmed the unhealthy conditions as causes of the recurrent epidemics of cholera and typhoid that regularly took many lives. Daisy turned to the provincial government in Breslau, the Prussian government in Berlin, and even to the Kaiser to describe the conditions around Waldenburg in vivid terms

> where thousands of people still lived in hovels with no 'conveniences' of any kind, forced into the horrid custom of placing 'cabinets' – mere shelters – upon the banks of streams and rivers, thus polluting the washing and even the drinking water.[8]

Nothing changed except that Daisy

> did all I could to make myself disagreeable to the local authorities and ... [the Kaiser] blamed the conditions I described to him, on Vater's coal, ... although I made it clear to him that this was not the chief fault.[9]

Daisy realized her own observations and recommendations would be useless without additional scientific evidence. As a first step, she obtained the expertise of a famous bacteriologist from the university in Breslau, who established a bacterial count of the *Laisebach* that far exceeded that of the *Kanaljauche*[10] of the provincial capital, a city of 500,000 people. Continuing on her path from fact-finding to solution, Daisy engaged experts from her own country. Under the direction of Dr. Greene, this group completed a detailed design for a large project that included a separate sewage system; the closing of all wells near the river and their replacement by running drinking water to every house in the district; the covering of the polluted river in populated areas; a large sewage cleaning plant; and a cost estimate of the project. With pride, Daisy presented the findings and recommendations as *The Report of the Greene Commission* to the Prussian government in Berlin.

---

8   DPH, p. 106.

9   DPH, p. 97.

10 Raw sewage.

During these busy months, Daisy had learned to proceed carefully and logically, exercise patience, and wait for the right opportunity to promote her cause. Unexpectedly, the glamorous Kiel Regatta of 1903 gave Daisy the long-sought opportunity to find the Kaiser's undivided attention, and present her urgent concerns to a member of his government. During a dinner on board the *North Star*, the private yacht of Cornelius Vanderbilt, Daisy shocked Chancellor von Bülow, who had just complained to the daughter of the Duke of Westminster that "Daisy never looks at me ... is she not beautiful and dangerous? I love her. ..."[11]

Instead of falling for this rather bold compliment, Daisy responded by giving Bülow, the Kaiser, and the other dinner guests an impassioned account of the deplorable health conditions in Waldenburg and what she thought the government ought to do about them immediately. The sad and, for some guests quite unappetizing topic did indeed touch Bülow's heart. He quickly responded to the additional documentation Daisy had included in a letter written to the German Chancellor before her departure for Kiel. From his holidays at the North Sea, Bülow sent a reply to Daisy that concluded with an expression of respect remarkably different from the crude flattery Daisy had tolerated on board the *North Star*.

Dear Princess,
Norderney, 9 August 1903

I have read with great interest your detailed letter, so charming in spite of its sad contents, which forms a valuable completion of the intelligence received from you at Kiel, and dealing with the horrid state of affairs in the towns situated near Fürstenstein. Your suggestion that part of the sum to be granted for the flooded territory of the Province of Silesia should be utilized to effect changes in the bad conditions which you so kindly exposed, can unfortunately not be carried out, because the money is intended to benefit only those who have suffered from the flood. But I will gladly see to it that an official inspection is made locally and I hope that we shall succeed in doing justice to your meritorious suggestions which are proof of your humane sentiments... I am,
Your sincerely devoted, Bülow.[12]

More than one year passed, until a jubilant Daisy, in Newlands in March 1905, read a letter to her mother in which the Emperor advised

---

11 DPP, p. 98.
12 DPH, pp. 97-98.

her "that all necessary funds will be granted for the project you so valiantly promoted."[13]

With triumph and pride, but also with a dash of bitterness, Daisy stated to her mother:

> When I make up my mind to get a thing, I generally succeed. Were I a great statesman or businessman this would be called tenacity; as I am a woman it is only called stubbornness.[14]

Daisy needed to resort to much more stubbornness, as the funds the Kaiser had promised did not come forth. At a special meeting with the Prussian finance minister Freiherr von Rheinbaben in Berlin,

> we got along beautifully, ...but he let me go with the excuse that if one place gets help all Germany will come forward and expect it, and some parts of East Prussia are even worse off than we are.[15]

Two weeks later, Daisy returned to Berlin with the suggestion that the parties affected by its future benefits share the costs of the project. To Daisy's surprise, Rheinbaben promised to divert moneys from the special funds dedicated for Silesia, provided Daisy could confirm the commitment of contributions by the parties she had named. Buoyed by her success, Daisy hurried directly from Berlin to Pless where she succeeded in persuading her father-in-law to assume one fifth of the cost of the project.

Having succeeded in Berlin and in Pless – never again would Daisy achieve such support from Vater or from Hans to such extent – Daisy did not find it too difficult to commit the local governments in and around Waldenburg to financially participate in the project. Nobody could deny the benefits of the project for the entire population of the district.

Without realizing it, Daisy applied practices in promoting social reform measures that became accepted practice only much later. Addressing herself to government and industry she successfully identified the problems and those who carried a legal and moral responsibility for their solution; presented the plan and its costs; and lobbied for support and a cost-sharing scheme. There is no question that Daisy's beauty and her social skills as much as her intelligence were also part of the success of her project of "cleaning the rivers."

---

13 DPH, p. 106.

14 DPH, pp. 106-07.

15 BLU, p. 168.

In 1907, *Der Verband für die Kanalisation des Laisebachgebiets in Schlesien*[16] *started* construction. The last phase of this huge project was completed in 1912. It is not without significance that a year before, in 1911, the village of Altwasser in the most densely populated part of the industrial district experienced the last outbreak of typhoid in its history. Daisy's first major project of improving the health and quality of life of the people had come to fruition. Few of those who benefited from this example of social and public health reform realized the decisive role the Princess of Pless had played in this project. In the meantime, Daisy had already turned her attention to other projects.

* * *

Had she not persisted in visiting the worker families in their homes and their children in the schools, Daisy would not have become aware of the poor health of so many children; she was especially troubled by the high proportion of visibly disabled, "crippled children." What future opportunities did these children have? As she had been told, less than two percent of all school children in the town of Waldenburg continued their education beyond the age of fourteen in the local high school, while half of the children entered into an apprenticeship at that age. The rest depended on unskilled labour in mines and factories. No wonder Daisy could not see anything but a hopeless future for children stricken with a physical handicap. Hardly anybody seemed as concerned as Daisy and, as usual, Hans thought that her easily excitable nature was again exaggerating the extent of the actual problem. Daisy began to look for a kindred soul.

Few of the directors of the Pless administration Daisy had met during the annual receptions in Fürstenstein had impressed Daisy except for one man. Director Schulte became her resourceful ally, if only after much caution, because "such things were usually handled by His Highness, the Prince, himself."[17] But soon, "with a compassionate heart and cool intellect," Schulte energetically approached the task Daisy had given him of assessing the need for a special school for crippled children.[18] It quickly became clear to Daisy that in temperament and in work habits, her idealistic, impatient nature, and Schulte's experienced and methodical personality complemented each other very well. Always responding to Daisy's new ideas and integrating them into his proposal Schulte

---

16   The Association for the Canalization of the Laisebachdistrikt in Silesia.

17   BLU, p. 145.

18   Fortunately, the term "crippled children/adults" denoting individuals with a physical handicap or disability has fallen into disfavour. As such terminology was in use in Daisy's time, however, the term "crippled" has been retained with all respect.

completed a research study with recommendations that went far beyond Daisy's original plan. On July 29, 1905, Schulte presented his far-reaching report

THE POSSIBLE CREATION OF A CRIPPLE SCHOOL OR OTHER CHARITABLE INSTITUTION
prepared for Her Highness the Princess of Pless
submitted with the expressions of deepest reverence by
Your Highness' most devoted servant Schulte.[19]

As if to demonstrate his objective nature, Schulte opened his report by emphasizing the sad facts that

> crippled children enjoy no legal protection whatsoever. There exists not one piece of legislation in the country obliging the State to provide appropriate educational and training facilities to such children. The few charitable organizations devoted to crippled children lack the funds to develop and maintain admittedly expensive training facilities. ... Besides, in Waldenburg no attempt has yet been made to statistically establish the number of children excluded from the existing educational facilities and from apprenticeships because of their disabling conditions.[20]

As a first step, Schulte painstakingly developed a registry of crippled children and their specific disabilities in a scientific manner. Within the boundaries of the town of Waldenburg, Schulte identified 162 children who were unable to attend regular school classes because of their handicaps. He agreed with Daisy's strong conviction that such children must not be sent to residential schools, something which nearly all parents objected to. Besides, after years of being educated and housed in a residential institution, such children would hardly be capable of re-integrating themselves into their own families.

Instead of a residential school, Schulte recommended the opening of a full-day school for crippled children, differing from the normal half-day schools attended by all children. Education and training of crippled children would naturally proceed at a slower pace and, further, the subjects and activities offered in such a specialized school would have to exceed in number and intensity those one would find in classrooms designed for healthy children. From the outset, educational programs

---

19 Die eventuelle Einrichtung einer Krüppelschule oder einer anderen Wohltätigkeitsanstalt erstellt für Ihre Durchlauchtigste Prinzessin! Gnädigste Prinzessin und Frau, überreicht mit dem Ausdruck tiefster Ehrfurcht von Euer Durchlaucht untertänigstem (sig.)Schulte. Waldenburg, 1905.

20 Ibid., pp. 1-2.

and training activities for crippled children must include reading, writing, arithmetic, and other subjects; but, just as much, practical preparations in skills for yet-to-be-identified work opportunities on the regular labour market which would permit as many crippled children as possible to eventually earn their living side by side with non-disabled workers because

> to enable the disabled child to eventually fend for oneself successfully must be the undisputed goal of any program for crippled children.[21]

In order to succeed, it would be absolutely essential for crippled children to enter into a specialized education program at the age of six. Under all circumstances, one must prevent their starting in a regular school setting, only to be removed from there because of their failure and then – too late – be transferred to the cripple school. Even a specialized program geared to their needs would in many cases no longer be successful with children who had already experienced failure and rejection in a primary school environment. As a consequence, it would be of greatest importance to identify all crippled children in the town of Waldenburg and its immediate environs at the earliest opportunity possible in order to ensure their placement in a specialized school at the age of six.

Naturally, it would be very expensive to operate such a school. It would require specially trained personnel and many other resources including ongoing medical supervision and care that was essential for assisting each child to reach an optimum state of health and ability. Therefore, admitting requirements would need to be carefully developed and rigidly adhered to, because

> unfortunately, it cannot be denied that the otherwise so beneficial social legislation (accident and disability insurance for workers) has brought about unintended side-effects, for instance the tendency of some people to capitalize on even small handicaps and skillfully exploiting them for some financial gain.[22]

Daisy and Schulte agreed that children of the planned school must have hope for a reasonably rewarding life of self-support. Besides, the high cost of their education, training, and preparation for life must be justified by their outcome. Daisy and Schulte were determined not to release children into the notorious sweatshops for the disabled where they would face a dreary future of manufacturing brushes, baskets, and artificial flowers. Together, they visited factory after factory and made

---

21 Ibid., op. cit., p. 3.
22 Ibid., op. cit., p. 5.

unexpected discoveries. Waldenburg was the home of three large widely-known china manufactures. Among the potential opportunities in their plants, Daisy and Schulte identified the painting of china by hand with the help of stencils, a type of routine work for which many disabled people were found to be better suited than persons without a handicap. Finally, Daisy looked for a trained nurse to be responsible for the ongoing and preventive health care of the children in the cripple school. A local orthopedic specialist for children, well-known throughout Lower Silesia, agreed to accept responsibility for medical care and physical rehabilitation of the children.

While elsewhere, large, expensive residential institutions for disabled children were still being built, Daisy and Schulte had already recognized the distinct disadvantages of institutionalizing children to the detriment of family cohesion. Again, Daisy – with the resourceful, faithful Schulte at her side – moved in the avant-garde applying concepts that only much later became generally accepted. Joining education, occupational training, and specialized medical care – the entire program directed towards the eventual integration of crippled children into the community – combined already at this early age the major concepts of modern-day rehabilitation!

In 1907, the *Waldenburger Krüppelschule*[23] was opened, for once with much support from Hans. For the next ten years, Daisy would unfailingly contribute to the financial support of the school in various ways. Among the particularly successful fundraising strategies were her song recitals, given in the theater in Bad Salzbrunn[24] during the summer season and, during the winter, in Waldenburg and Breslau. The first concert in Bad Salzbrunn was Daisy's "moment suprême."[25] She raised 1,900 Marks for her school. Unsuccessful was her plan of recording her songs on phonograph disks designated for the support of the School for Crippled Children, and carrying her signature, to be sold in music stores and at the end of her concerts. Daisy's idea proved to be ahead of its time, technically difficult, and too expensive for its charitable purpose. But Hans kept his promise to give adequate financial support to the school, which remained in operation until 1933.

* * *

---

23 *The Waldenburg School for Cripples*, a horrid name for a school that achieved a great deal.

24 An elegant spa near Fürstenstein, property of the Prince of Pless until 1931; since 1945 Szczawno Zdrój.

25 DPH, p. 129.

Schulte's efforts to determine the incidence of crippled children in Waldenburg had an additional, unexpected outcome of far-reaching consequences. In vain, Schulte had searched for relevant statistics. What he discovered instead were meticulously collected morbidity data on the widespread infant mortality in the district of Waldenburg. The numbers established an infant mortality rate that was one of the highest in Germany. Alarmed, he advised Daisy of

> this most frightful picture; and equally frightening is the fact that these appalling, easily accessible statistics have been totally ignored by the government!

> During the past ten years, data from the major industrial towns and villages where 75 % of our miners are living, indicate an average infant mortality rate (i.e., infants up to six months old) of 45.5 %.

> In some villages, e.g. Altwasser, conditions are particularly bad; in one specific year, the infant mortality in Altwasser reached the unbelievable rate of 75.98%; i.e., more than three quarters of all newborns died before reaching the age of six months or, in other words, less than one quarter of all children born in Altwasser[26] survived beyond the first six months of their lives. ... In most cases, Intestinal Catarrh (Enteritis) is reported as cause of death.[27]

When Schulte readily blamed the mothers for the death of their infants, Daisy strongly disagreed with him. During her visits in the industrial districts, she had noticed in what pitiful state of exhaustion most mothers returned from ten hours of daily factory work; often far too exhausted, she thought, to nurse their newborns. In her diary she wrote about the vicious circle ruling the lives of mothers and their babies she had observed herself. After the birth of a child, most women could not afford to stay home for any length of time, as the family's survival literally depended on the extra income of the mother from factory work. Besides, the women were always afraid to lose their jobs during their absence before and after giving birth. Without fail, such desperate circumstances would drive the young mothers back to factory work as quickly as possible. Constantly over-demanded, they were not only incapable of nursing a healthy infant; often, especially if their baby had died, they entered too quickly into the next pregnancy, still in a state of exhaustion and poor health; and again the next newborn was weak and,

---

26 One of the major industrial settlements, formerly a well-known spa, popular throughout Germany and Eastern Europe, until its springs suddenly dried up in 1876.

27 See Schulte, op. cit., p. 12.

being deprived of the care of a well-rested healthy mother, faced early death or a deficient early childhood. In the age of women's liberation, it seems absolutely ironic that Daisy became a social reformer in her time, when she searched for ways to liberate the working class women from the burden of being forced to go to work.

With great empathy for the women and young mothers, Daisy asked Schulte to revise his opinion and conduct further research.

> We must recognize and accept that after the long hours of often hard factory work, most women are far too exhausted to be capable of nursing their babies. Furthermore, the town of Waldenburg and its surrounding district does not have any organized distribution system for milk and, besides, the milk is often of poor quality and, out of ignorance, given by the young mothers to their babies without being boiled![28]

As always, Schulte searched the literature for useful ideas and discovered the system of *Gouttes de Lait* which, together with the *Consultations des Nourrissons*,[29] had been introduced for working mothers in the coal-mining districts of Northern France. In his report on the *Gouttes de Lait* Schulte implored Daisy to realize that her goals should be determined by the question

> how to, within the financial means available to Her Highness, create those charitable services which reach the greatest number of people with the highest benefits possible. ... The distressing infant mortality rate in our district described in my earlier report, is crying for a solution! The institution of the *Gouttes de Lait* described above would certainly go far in reducing the unacceptable mortality of newborns in our district. A solution to this particular problem would not require more than one tenth of the cost required for the crippled children's school, but the benefits which cannot be measured in numbers, would be much, much greater[30]

Under no circumstances was Daisy willing to abandon her project of the *Krüppelschule*. Instead, with immediate enthusiasm, she accepted the challenge Schulte[31] had thrown out to her. Within one year, Daisy established a number of *milk depots* throughout the entire district where mothers received free pasteurized milk for their babies. The Catholic and

---

28 Ibid, p. 14.

29 Ibid, p. 15.

30 Ibid, p. 16.

31 Schulte, who later became director of all Pless mines, never received public recognition for his pioneering research. He was honoured for his administrative performance, though, when one of the Pless mines in Waldenburg was named after him.

Protestant churches, which Daisy had persuaded to accept responsibility for operating the new *milk depots*, also accepted her request to participate in the operation of *mother and baby clinics* modelled after the French *Consultations des Nourrissons*. The churches became part of Daisy's strategy of effectively supporting young women and helping them to become "better mothers."[32]

* * *

1907 was not only a year of triumphs. Vater had become gravely ill while staying with the King of Saxony on the Albrechtsburg above Meissen on the Elbe River, a few miles downstream from Dresden. On August 14, 1907, the *Old Duke* died before Hans was able to reach Meissen. Never would Daisy forget the lonely, sleepless night. While she was anxiously waiting for the dreaded telegram from the Albrechtsburg, like a bad omen

> a dear old bell, that hung in the Gateway Tower at Fürstenstein and rang every night at ten o'clock, fell the night Vater died.

> Dear Vater! It is quite extraordinary what he has done for the property which he held for fifty years. ... He was truth itself, honest and noble, lovable because he was always so kind, so appreciative of anything that he felt was right and in anybody who he felt was trying to be and do good; I am thankful indeed that he has left everything in such perfect order, and thought of every one. ...[33]

> Well – somehow I can't realize it all . ... I only hope that whatever Hans does will be right and whichever way he thinks I could be of use, I shall help him with all my heart, poor old boy. I think he felt his father's death very much as he really loved and respected him, and I feel sure intends to do all as well and rightly as possible. But it is difficult I think to find one's absolute self-confidence at once, and later on when one knows the map of all the business and how all its machinery is worked the self-confidence *must* be there, otherwise the *Verwaltung*[34] will laugh and do whatever it likes, and we shall find ourselves ruled by our own *employees*! The way a big property like this is managed abroad no one in England has the smallest idea. The people getting wages from Hans are if anything over nine thousand souls; there are over five thousand miners alone.[35]

---

32 Schulte, op. cit., p. 17.

33 DPH, p. 137.

34 The Administration.

35 DPH, p. 136.

In her heart, Daisy hoped that Hans, free from his responsibility to his father, would be more generous in his support of her charitable projects, but fundamentally, Hans never changed. At times disinterested, at other times critical or tending to ridicule, his attitude soon led to open conflict. Daisy did have more than one reason to worry about even the immediate future. It became clear that Hans had his own agenda for spending vast sums of money on projects that were far from Daisy's heart. Daisy missed Vater more from day to day. He had always supported her humanitarian work, even though he did not always agree with her. Vater had respected her for wanting the best for people; she had often felt closer to him than to her husband. Now, with Vater gone, the last restraining influence over Hans was gone. Immediately he began to realize his long-cherished dream of spending enormous sums on re-building and enlarging Castle Fürstenstein into one of the grandest and most palatial houses in Europe.

Within months of Vater's death, the famous architect Ritter von Walcher arrived from Vienna with a team of architects. The project of changing Fürstenstein, which had proceeded on a very modest scale prior to Vater's death, immediately reached a gigantic scale of construction that would continue irrespective of war and revolution into the early 1920s. The Castle was enlarged by an entire wing, its exterior appearance altered, and its interior expanded to more than 600 rooms. The medieval West façade was soon hidden behind a ten story high addition designed to accommodate the Imperial apartments and the never completed *Emperor's Hall*. Many kinds of art treasures, several dozen of Renaissance fireplaces and doorways, were imported from Italy; expansive terraces rising dramatically above the Fürstenstein Gorge were built on several levels along the south and west front of the Castle; their formal gardens were adorned with a surfeit of statues, Italian fountains, and cascades. One terrace accommodated twenty-seven fountains.

Hans had fallen victim to a building mania, which horrified Daisy. She also very much resented that Hans never consulted her about the planting of the terraces, the choice of tapestries in the salons, or the furniture. Daisy wished for a home-like ambience. Hans was aiming for a palatial residence worthy of receiving emperors and kings. For the planned *Three Emperors Maneuvers* Hans had ordered that all doorways leading to the great ballroom, the salons, and the Imperial apartments must be wide enough to permit the passage of the Emperors of Germany, Austria, and Russia side-by-side in order to avoid any complications in protocol and etiquette. This idea Daisy found utterly ridiculous.

I really should have enjoyed seeing the three emperors under the same roof, had Hans Heinrich ever succeeded in getting them there. I will swear that the nearest they would ever have got to each other would have been when they passed side by side through a doorway at a formal moment. The temperamental, personal, dynastic and political differences between them were unbridgeable. Franz Joseph, cool, reserved, thinking and feeling entirely in terms of the eighteenth century; Wilhelm, effusive, voluble, always striving for effect; Nicholas, saying nothing, doing nothing, feeling everything![36]

Increasingly worried about the enormous sums Hans was spending on his building projects – he never had any money available to assist her humanitarian projects – Daisy "went through the books behind his back" scanning the daily newspapers for the fluctuations of the price of coal, the major source of income of the family.

> In Berlin, I spoke with Hans quite seriously about our financial situation; the enormous administration employing far too many people, and how in relation to our properties our income was ridiculously small. ... Hans seemed to be very understanding, we both remained calm and for once, this time he did not get annoyed at all.[37]

Daisy still failed utterly to help Hans comprehend the poor impression his pompous rebuilding of Fürstenstein caused in Silesia, especially in Waldenburg. The luxurious castle, the huge stud farm, and the numerous building projects in Bad Salzbrunn were unworthy of a noble family; they were simply nouveau riche and certainly indicated that Hans was in no way "socially conscious." He ignored the unsatisfactory living standard of the general population and the low wages paid to those whose labour made Hans's building mania possible in the first place.

Hans was far too obsessed with his building plans. He grew to live apart from the administration and became isolated from the employees of his industrial enterprises. As a consequence, he failed to exert sufficient influence on the attitudes of the directors of the Pless enterprises towards the thousands of his employees, especially the miners. Daisy's constant complaints that she and Hans, as much as the administration, must demonstrate a more socially enlightened attitude towards their employees fell on deaf ears. It was time again for Daisy to proceed on her own.

Conditions had been bad for years, although Vater had done much for his miners. The *Old Duke* had had the respect of the miners, because he had lived in relatively modest, unpretentious circumstances. Now,

36 WLU, p. 158.
37 BLU, p. 257.

Hans was creating a different Fürstenstein, where enormous wealth was unabashedly displayed in luxurious buildings, and in a lifestyle that only seemed to encourage the Pless directors and officials to identify themselves more than ever with this new way of life, and show even less concern for the working people under their control. Daisy became more and more impatient and critical of her husband's top administrators.

In order to accommodate Fürstenstein's guests during the rebuilding period, a large hotel, at the time of its opening the most luxurious in all of Germany, had been built in nearby Bad Salzbrunn. Again, Daisy found much to criticize having in vain suggested that the hotel

> ought to have been built more of wood and tiles with nice Heidelberg balconies ... instead of Louis Quinze decorations.[38]

Surprisingly, Hans agreed to let Daisy be responsible for the interior decoration of the new *Grand Hotel*, later to be called *Schlesischer Hof*. He was enchanted with Daisy's ideas for the 180 guest rooms, the large central hall, the dining room, the music salon and the lounges. This pleasant task enjoyed so much by Daisy took an unexpected turn towards open conflict, however, when Daisy discovered that Mr. Keindorff, the General Director of the Pless enterprises, had ordered rugs, linen, china, and other items for the hotel through the *Fürstliches Warenhaus*[39]

> I spoke with Keindorff, our General Director here, the architect, and Herr von Pohl. I am going to do the whole thing myself, including linen, silver and china, as I feel I can do it cheaper than they would with their enormous ideas, and Hans is pleased to let me do it, and seems quite proud of me.
>
> He agreed with me afterwards and was surprised at the way I took the proposal to order carpets, for instance, at our own *Warenhaus* in Waldenburg. Keindorff said we would get them twenty or nineteen per cent cheaper. Then I boiled over and said if we did things like that, of course the town of Waldenburg would be (as they are) against us. Vater had built the store to do good for our miners and workpeople by enabling them to buy at cost price. The question had already been raised in the papers about the Fürst von Pless's *dry goods store*, and Hans had told the Emperor (in fact written to say) that he did not built it, but that Vater did to benefit the miners and workpeople only, and we gained nothing by it. But of course if we did what the General Director and the others suggested, it would be contrary to what I considered to be right. Keindorff was much surprised and shut up.

---

38 BLU, p. 250.

39 A large, well-appointed company store for the Pless miners.

Daisy had won, but she was under no illusion that she had reached the social consciences either of Hans or Keindorff. Her own conscience and political instincts would soon be proven right.[40] And Daisy continued in her diary:

> We had another talk about expenses. The money for this hotel is being borrowed, over a million marks at four and a half per cent. ... The whole thing is an absurd mistake. ... I feel there must come a financial crash if we go on wasting money like this, and I almost enjoyed the idea as I walked with Hansel yesterday thinking what a relief it would be not to have so many parties; a small stable and nice simple liveries with no silver braid; no gala liveries for the servants in the house; fewer servants outside, no *Garde Förster*, and so on.
>
> I drove a little way to the station with Hans to-day, and I hated the dressed-up grooms, very expensive black horses simply for station work, and a *Jäger* behind with plumed hat. I felt like a nouveau riche. ...
>
> Diary dear, don't you understand, it is wrong to advertise one's riches and power in the faces of those who have not got either. To do things in a quite dignified way is quite another thing.[41]

* * *

There came a period in Daisy's life when her dedication to the improvement of the quality of life of others was not only blessed with success but, finally, with the triumphant experience of proceeding entirely on her own; without the interference of her husband and his administrators. Once more, Daisy devoted herself to a project of social reform, before World War I would lead her to different tasks.

This time, Daisy devoted her energies to an industry away from Waldenburg. This last project brought Daisy perhaps the greatest fulfillment in her life; it was exclusively devoted to the welfare of women of all ages, by rehabilitating and revitalizing the long-suffering, depressed industry of the Silesian lacemakers around Hirschberg.

The Silesian lace industry was concentrated 50 kilometres west of Waldenburg on the slopes and in the valleys of the Giant Mountains, which were frequented, because of their rugged beauty and the romantic charm of their valleys, by well-to-do tourists. The lace industry had been born during the severe economic crisis which followed the Silesian Wars

---

40 Almost to the day nine years later, when the German Empire collapsed under the onslaught of the November Revolution of 1918, the miners stormed through the streets of Waldenburg with the cry "Hängt den Keindorff!" [Let's hang Keindorff!]

41 BLU, p. 257.

between 1740 and 1763. When Silesia became part of the Kingdom of Prussia after the Seven Years War, Frederick II of Prussia tried to find ways to alleviate the terrible poverty among the population. Their livelihood was endangered because all economic ties between Silesia and her former motherland Austria had been severed. One of the projects of Frederick II was the Silesian lace industry, but before the young industry could gain profitable markets, the Napoleonic Wars brought its development to a standstill. When around 1810 mechanical weaving looms were introduced in Silesia, most of the lacemakers entered the new mills as weavers and abandoned their lacemaking skills. In the 1830s, a series of economic crises nearly destroyed Silesia's mills. Lack of work of any kind, repeated crop failures, and typhoid epidemics were of such dimensions that the Prussian government could no longer cope with the misery. It legalized begging on certain days of the month declared by royal proclamation as *Royal Begging Days*.

Finally, the Prussian government decided to revive the lace production based on the cottage system. In the year 1855, the government offered incentives and subsidies to businessmen willing to organize the lace making industry, which unfortunately but not surprisingly attracted men who secured large profits for themselves while paying mere subsistence wages to the lace makers. The fate of the lace makers was forgotten. Interest and demand temporarily revived when the German Empress ordered a much admired bridal veil for her sister in 1889. But the lace makers had lost much of their skills and their inventiveness.

The system of government-subsidized middlemen never worked to the benefit of the lace makers. The middlemen soon earned the reputation of exploiters. The wages they paid for lace soon sank to an absolute minimum. Nobody was concerned with the training of young lace makers. As a result, the quality of Silesian lace sank to such a low level that only a small portion could be sold. In 1906, two ladies belonging to the upper middle class tried to revive the Silesian lace industry around Hirschberg. Despite their dedication and their artistic expertise, they could not liberate the lace makers from their dependence on middlemen who mercilessly dictated prices and controlled market conditions.

Nevertheless, some exquisite lace was still produced and more than once had Daisy admired samples of the beautiful Silesian lace at court balls in Berlin or during visits with her Silesian neighbours. Not until she visited the home of a lace maker during an excursion to the Giant Mountains in the spring of 1908 did Daisy become aware of the desperate situation of the lace makers.

On June 1, 1908, at the end of her stay at Cap Martin, Daisy addressed her concerns about the Silesian lace makers to the German

Empress. In a long letter, she passionately described their plight and asked the Empress for her protection:

> they mostly work in their own homes and the middle-men who purchase their lace underpay and sweat them frightfully.[42]

Daisy's attempt to break the dependence of the lace makers on the middlemen – a necessary first step in her plan to improve the situation of the lace makers – would cause much resistance. Daisy begged the Empress to

> give me her practical support in breaking down the frantic opposition I was sure to arouse. Every one, I realize, will be against me and will make endless difficulties.[43]

At the end of July, Daisy visited the Empress at Castle Wilhelmshöhe near Kassel to talk about the lace makers once more. The Empress was enchanted with little Hansel and little Lexel, but

> she never made a single proposal, only 'it interests me very much and I shall be very much obliged if something could be done to help the poor people.' For a woman in that position I never met anyone so devoid of individual thought.[44]

Early 1909, Daisy assumed the protectorate of the *Deutscher Verein für Schlesische Spitzenkunst*[45] – for the first few months jointly with the Crown Princess Cäcilie of Prussia. Realizing that little support would be forthcoming from the Empress, Daisy decided to open her own lace school in the hopes that her products would give the industry new prestige and pride, both of which she found sadly lacking. This was also the beginning of her collaboration with Mrs. Bardt and the Baroness von Dobeneck, the two ladies who had founded the *Schools for Artistic Lace Making* in 1906. The co-operation was not free of conflict between Daisy's high-flying social and commercial goals, and the ladies Bardt and von Dobeneck's emphasis on raising the quality of lace through training. Daisy purchased their lace schools in 1911 and retained the two women as teachers. From then on, Daisy rapidly expanded her lace schools, now named *Lace Schools of the Princess of Pless*. Daisy's philosophy was stated in the schools' pamphlet:

---

42 DPH, p. 155.

43 DPH, p. 160.

44 Ibid.

45 Gisela Graff-Höfgen, Schlesische Spitzen (München, 1974), p. 60.

The Lace Schools of the Princess of Pless are a charitable institution for the benefit of the Silesian cottage lace industry for the purpose of providing all local lace makers with excellent designs and returning all profits made to them.[46]

Much work and many decisions, some of them requiring a great deal of political courage, remained. Daisy felt quite correctly that not only the quality of Silesian lace, but also its variety of design badly needed improvement. Used for decades, all designs seemed rather old-fashioned and not overly attractive. Above all, however, Daisy was determined to bring an end to the long-established system that she described as "pure exploitation," namely the practice of encouraging the lace makers to utilize well-known Brussels lace designs for their products and sell the lace through middlemen to dealers in Belgium, who marketed the lace there as "genuine Brussels lace." When Daisy attempted to purchase one of the major lace enterprises near Hirschberg in order to reach her goal of controlling the production and sale of Silesian lace locally, she provoked an angry, hostile reaction in commercial circles in Silesia, which soon reached the Court in Berlin. In a letter of eight pages addressed to the Countess Brockdorff, Oberhofmeisterin[47] at the Imperial Court in Berlin, Daisy defended herself and begged the Countess Brockdorff to explain her aims, her work, and the actual situation to the Empress. The letter represents also the most encompassing statement of Daisy's objectives:

Fürstenstein Bez. Breslau June 14th, 1912
My Dear Countess Brockdorff.
Please forgive me bothering you – but, I would be so pleased and thankful if you would give me your advice, and kindly ask *Her Majesty* what *She would also advise me what to do. I have now 14 lace schools* and they all want to have more and the clergymen encourage it, so every month I have to open more schools.

Frau Metzner asked me two years ago to buy her school, but I could not afford it ... but now I am going to. ... She is not doing it because she is unhappy – nor is Frau Hopper either as (*please understand*) I do not spoil the market as some people say in Berlin – all my lace is sold at the same price as Frau Hopper & the same price as Frau Metzner sold hers. The only *difference* will be that any benefit we hope to make will be used to *benefit the workers* – for instance when they are ill – to give them presents when they marry; & *prizes to encourage them to work* – it will also give work to the married women in their own homes, so that they can remain with their children –

---

46   Ibid., p. 42.
47   Mistress of the Robes

& the young girls will not be so anxious to go to the factorys where their daily wage is much *lower* than what I pay.

Please, dearest Countess tell me what you think – and *what Her Majesty thinks* – if the Empress will so kindly give an opinion. ...

I am coming to Berlin on the 23rd to see a heart specialist for my dear little baby – & also for myself – as my veins are giving me much trouble. ...[48]

Daisy had obviously entered a territory – free enterprise – barred to women of the nobility. This was the major complaint that had reached the court. However, the undeniable success of her lace schools, and the unqualified praise of Daisy's humanitarian approach by the Lutheran clergy were much listened to at court in Berlin, and had much diminished the earlier caution of the Empress. To Daisy's delight, the Empress spontaneously offered her protection and sponsorship for an exhibition of Silesian lace, which Daisy opened at the posh *Hotel Esplanade* at the Potsdamer Platz in Berlin. The press in attendance reported with surprise that for the first time, the Empress had lifted the protocol that forbade the Imperial Princesses to enter the premises of a commercial establishment. Daisy, by the way, had been astute enough to set the date for the opening of her exhibition two days prior to the Emperor's birthday. Many of the foreign dignitaries coming to Berlin for the occasion did not fail to attend Daisy's exhibition.

All of a sudden, Silesian lace became the rage among the public. Daisy had purchased the *Silesian Lace Factory* of Mrs. Metzner, and had begun negotiations with lace makers in Italy and on the Azores in the hopes of bringing to Silesia new teachers, to broaden the range of the designs of her products.

What Daisy had intentionally failed to mention in her letter to Countess Brockdorff was the next stage of her project, now of a strictly commercial nature: After gaining control of the production, she was ready to enter the retail market. Consciously using the fame of her name and her personality, Daisy opened her first retail outlet of *The Lace Schools of the Princess of Pless*, an elegant store in the center of Hirschberg across from the best hotel frequented by wealthy tourists. This venture came about following the advice Daisy had sought from Count Karl Pückler, Councillor at the German Embassy in London, when she was searching for new ways to raise the profitability of her lace school enterprises. As Gisela Graff-Höfgen, author of *Schlesische Spitzen*[49] reported in her well-

48   Courtesy Bundearchiv Koblenz.
49   See Graff-Höfgen, op. cit., p. 45.

researched book, Daisy opened her stores, all under the name *Spitzen-Schulen der Fürstin von Pless*[50] in quick succession in such attractive resorts as Warmbrunn, Schreiberhau, Wiesbaden, and Nauheim, and in the cities of Berlin, Munich, Hannover, Hamburg, and Königsberg.

If one follows Daisy's extraordinary accomplishment, one cannot help but identify some specific factors that contributed to Daisy's personal triumph as much as to the remarkable success of her lace schools.

First of all, nobody interfered with Daisy's ambitions and plans as had invariably happened in all of her previous social reform projects. Away from Fürstenstein and Waldenburg, Daisy did not have to endure the disinterest and negativism of her husband and the confrontations with his administrators. The large project of the canalization of the river in Waldenburg and the other projects Daisy had realized in the area had certainly carried attributes of a social defense against misery and threatening social unrest. Daisy's lace schools around Hirschberg, however, became a genuine example of progressive social reform, originating in deep convictions and based on a sound educational approach aimed at betterment of women's lives; self-determination for the individual; and fruitful collaboration by all involved. The women joined Daisy's lace schools in large numbers not only for the better wages. Pride also became part of working for the *Lace Schools of the Princess of Pless*. Nowhere did this pride find a more striking expression than in the tiny Pless crowns with which the lace makers began one day to initial their products. And nothing pleased a grateful Daisy more than this spontaneously started custom.

It had been Daisy's specific aim to terminate the exploitation of the lace makers and the unscrupulous capitalistic profit system that had determined the fate of the Silesian lace industry for decades. Under Daisy's leadership, the Silesian lace schools did indeed move away from their capitalistic ways and acquired instead a co-operative character based on the precepts of socialism. Finally, one cannot fail to recognize that in this last of her social reform projects, Daisy exclusively dedicated her efforts to the welfare and security of women. While in Waldenburg she was unable to reach her aim – the liberation of the young married women and mothers from the hardships and tribulations of factory work – her achievement in changing and improving the lives of the Silesian lace makers around Hirschberg became an unqualified success. It is not insignificant that all those Daisy had engaged in working towards the realization of her dream were women!

---

50 Lace Schools of the Princess of Pless

Did Daisy feel like the pioneer, who helped an entire group of women hitherto poor, suppressed, and powerless, reach a never hoped for level of personal security and unexpected, successful participation in shaping their livelihood? Did Daisy see herself as a pioneer in the budding movement towards social progress that liberated women from economic dependence?

Daisy gave one answer in a letter addressed to the Empress at the height of her success. Proudly, Daisy reported to the Empress:

> Many people saw failure in my undertaking – but it seems to have rushed into success in a short time. And the people are so happy and satisfied.[51]

* * * * * *

---

51 June 14, 1912

7 | Advocate for Peace

O n July 7, 1892, the Freiburger Bote *enthusiastically reported the spectacular arrival of the young Princess of Pless at her new residence Castle Fürstenstein. On the same pages, the thrice-weekly newspaper commemorated the Battle of Sadowa,[1] one of Chancellor Bismarck's final links in his strategy of excluding the House of Habsburg from his creation of a unified, powerful Germany under the leadership of Prussia's King Wilhelm of Hohenzollern[2]*

* * *

Pursuing his policy of *Blood and Iron,* Bismarck relentlessly attacked all those forces he considered inimical to his goal of shaping the young German Empire into a politically and economically powerful European force under the determined leadership of Prussia. He decided to create a Germany whose stability, peace and security must never be disturbed, neither by internal nor by external forces. Without mercy, he attacked all those he considered disloyal to the Prussian Crown: the Catholic Church and its political wing the Centrist Party, the trade unions, and the Social Democratic Party. Equally suspect in Bismarck's eyes were the progressive liberal forces in the country, who impatiently looked forward to the reign of the Crown Prince, the later Emperor Frederick III with

---

1   In Germany usually referred to as Königgrätz.

2   Five years after Prussia's victory over Austria at Sadowa on July 3, 1866, the armies of the German Federation, under Prussia's leadership destroyed the Second Empire of Napoleon III during the Franco-Prussian War of 1870-71; on January 18, 1871, the King of Prussia was proclaimed as Wilhelm I the first Emperor of the new German Empire. Bismarck's strategy had successfully relegated Emperor Franz Joseph I and the Austro-Hungarian Empire to the periphery of central and western Europe.

whom – and more so with his wife, Queen Victoria's daughter "Vicky" – Bismarck maintained a strained relationship characterized by mistrust and suspicion. Only the tragically brief reign of Frederick III, who died ninety-nine days after ascending the throne, prevented a dramatic confrontation between the progressive monarch and his conservative chancellor.

Frederick's successor Wilhelm II, Germany's last emperor, soon felt strong enough to dismiss the aging chancellor. Bismarck grudgingly retreated to his estate in the woods near Hamburg, but he maintained his popularity with much of the Prussian aristocracy, the conservative small landowners, and even with a considerable segment of the common people.

Bismarck enjoyed receiving large and small delegations of well-wishers almost every day. Political pronouncements he made to his visitors were always promptly reported in the press, such as the one Hans discovered in the *Freiburger Bote* next to the story of Daisy's glamorous reception in Fürstenstein.

> After being treated to a morning song by a visiting male quartet, Prince Bismarck had invited the four vocalists to join him at the breakfast table. When one of the gentlemen recalled the anniversary of the Battle of Königgrätz, Prince Bismarck observed animatedly that 'we will never experience another Königgrätz, but we must expect a second Sedan as a certainty.'"[3]

It is unlikely that Hans translated Bismarck's ominous statement for Daisy, who had never heard of the battles of Königgrätz[4] or Sedan,[5] which had sealed the fate of the Second French Empire and made Emperor Napoleon III the King of Prussia's prisoner of war.[6] During these early months of her marriage, Daisy's mind and heart were preoccupied with the search for romantic love. The entire world still looked beautiful and peaceful to her.

Soon, Daisy became conscious of social tensions and injustices in Germany and England. She found herself confronted with the rising tensions between the country of her birth and the country of her marriage, which no longer enjoyed the celebrated relationship between "two

---

3   Freiburger Bote, July 7, 1892.

4   The decisive battle in the War of 1866 between Prussia and Austria.

5   The decisive battle in the Franco-Prussian War of 1870-71.

6   After surrendering during the Battle of Sedan, Napoleon III was held prisoner at Castle Wilhelmshöhe in Kassel; he later went into exile in England.

cousins." Even before the end of Queen Victoria's long reign, Daisy noted with alarm the deteriorating relationship between England and Germany for which she readily blamed Emperor Wilhelm II and his advisers.

* * *

In comparison to the dynamic, impatient German Empire, Austria-Hungary seemed an island of peace with its charming, if in some respects old-fashioned way of life. For Daisy, visits to Bohemia, so close to Fürstenstein and to Pless, became sojourns into an uncomplicated, amiable, and chivalrous world. No matter how anachronistic its atmosphere, Daisy much preferred the Imperial Court of Vienna to the court of Wilhelm II in Berlin. Not until the Great War did Daisy realize that behind a deceptive façade, the Habsburg monarchy constituted a complex conglomerate beset by political, social, and ethnic problems because of the presence of so many restless nationalities striving with increasing impatience for autonomy and independence. The third largest nation in Europe, Austria-Hungary had been destined by Bismarck to become Germany's major ally, after he had masterfully succeeded in healing the wounds of the Austro-Prussian War of 1866.

In her fondness for Bohemia, the most beautiful of the Habsburg crown lands, Daisy was not alone. Indeed, for their Sunday excursions and for their holidays, Silesians rich and poor flocked across the border to enjoy Bohemia's hospitality, good food, and its famous beer, and the charming music played in simple country inns and on the elegant promenades of the great spas of Karlsbad, Marienbad, and Franzensbad.[7] The poorer people stopped in the villages just across the border, which on Sundays were filled with the uniquely gentle sound of Bohemian brass bands. Perhaps unconsciously, these visitors from German Silesia yearned for the friendly and easy-going Bohemian mood. Bohemia seemed pervaded by an atmosphere of gentle, unpretentious joie de vivre. This satisfied a deep nostalgia for an easier way of life Germans could no longer find in their own assertive, hard-working country.

The cities and towns of Bohemia exuded a certain, unique charm. A few hundred years of Habsburg rule had adorned them with beautiful palaces, grandiose churches, and monasteries. The prosperous bourgeoisie of modern times had proudly added imposing city halls, schools, and other public buildings. Nearly every city had a grand, elegant theatre, an impressive post office, and an often monumental railway station. The numerous parks were adorned with monuments and fountains.

---

7   Karlovy Vary, Mariánske Lázne, and Frantiskovy Lázni in the Czech Republic.

Underneath all this beauty and charm, noticed but ignored by many of the German citizens of the Habsburg monarchy, was the threat posed by the rising nationalism and intransigence of the Czechs and other ethnic minorities, which soon would imperil the survival of Austria-Hungary. Still, to the outsider, Austria-Hungary remained quite an idyllic country whose political activities seemed to affect the balance of power in Europe much less than the increasingly strident expressions of power emanating from Berlin.

Being fond of Bohemia and impressed with the Imperial splendour of Vienna, it is perhaps understandable that the young Daisy was oblivious to the political and social manifestations that threatened the Habsburg Empire. During her first audience at the Palace of Schönbrunn, Daisy compared the fatherly, gentle personality of the old Emperor Franz Joseph, who seemed so much to represent the past, with the strident Emperor Wilhelm II in Berlin, who constantly kept Europe in suspense with his threatening, often thoughtless pronouncements. Although she believed in Emperor Wilhelm's best intentions when he liked to present himself to the world as *the Emperor of Peace*, Daisy also observed his striving for fame and success. As she came to know him better, she noted strong traits of vanity and impetuousness, that often drove her to despair, despite the strong sympathy she always felt for Wilhelm II.

Similar concerns were expressed by Daisy's Silesian neighbour Count Robert Zedlitz-Trützschler, Lord Chamberlain of the Court in Berlin:

> Sometimes I cannot help thinking that the Empress Frederick was not wrong when she said at the time of her serious differences with her son: 'Pray do not believe for a moment that my son does anything for any other reason but vanity!' A calm observer can naturally see many others, but no doubt this motive of vanity is immensely important.[8]

Among the numerous critical voices, there were those who with sympathy and sometimes compassion "firmly believed that the Emperor wanted to be remembered as the Peace Emperor."[9] But

> The Kaiser never grew up, and never learned from his own mistakes; but his desire for the maintenance of peace was absolutely sincere. He was a stage hero, not a warrior. His real responsibility is to be found in the pretentious and menacing utterances, public and private, which caused the world to believe that he aimed at conquest. The deepest tragedy of the *Peace*

---

8 See Count Robert Zedlitz-Trützschler, op. cit., p. 123.

9 Ibid., p. 223.

Kaiser in shining armour is that he would never understand his own share in producing the situation which led to war.[10]

Across the English Channel, the image of the Emperor began to darken. Sir Frederick Ponsonby, King Edward's equerry, having observed the Emperor on many occasions and under differing circumstances concluded that

... the Emperor was the creation of the Germans themselves. They wanted a sabre-rattling autocrat with theatrical ways, attempting to dominate Europe, sending telegrams and making bombastic speeches, and he did his best to supply them with the superman they required.[11]

King Edward VII called his nephew Wilhelm II "the most brilliant failure in history."

Daisy's pronouncement on the Emperor's character was less sharp than Ponsonby's and not as unforgiving as King Edward's, but with fairness acknowledged the Emperor as a child of the Germany of his time:

There is a never-ceasing internal conflict in the Kaiser's mind; on the one hand his splendid gifts, his delight in ceaseless activity, his eagerness to look forward and to strive, like a true son of our times, for the good of his country and its development; on the other, his impulse to gather all the threads into his own hands and to rule as an absolute monarch. It must be everybody's hope that both the power of circumstances and the true nature of the Emperor will make for the victory of liberal ideas. Whatever the end may be, it is on this that the fate of the German people will very largely depend.[12]

What Daisy appeared to grasp more than some of her contemporaries could was the effect of the role Germany wanted all of a sudden to assume in the concert of the nations of Europe. As with any young nation, the new German Empire passed through a dynamic phase of expansionism at a period when most other European nations wanted to enjoy a sense of peace and equilibrium. These nations were acutely disturbed by the newly felt presence of this powerful nation in their midst. Germany also happened to be the most populous country of the Continent, aside from Czarist Russia which, after all, was located more or less at the fringe of Central Europe.

* * *

10 Comment by Otto Hamann, head of the press office of the Foregin Ministry of the Weimar Republic.

11 See Sir Frederick Ponsonby, op. cit., p. 259.

12 BLU, p. 287.

After many trials and mistakes, Daisy had gradually learned how to master her life in Germany. She had earned a measure of acceptance and respect from her in-laws. Yet even after years of living in Germany, Daisy did not lose the sense of being different. It did help her to realize that this sense was not rooted in the idiosyncrasies of her personality alone; what did not help was the constant experience of being made to feel different as an Englishwoman living among Germans. She felt more knowledgeable than most people in her environment because of her regular visits to her homeland, and the frequent encounters with King Edward and Emperor Wilhelm, and their ministers. Political discussions in both countries, at times as passive listener, at other times as active participant or partner, provided Daisy with remarkable insights into the character of political decision-makers and the increasingly worrisome political currents of her time. As in social and humanitarian matters, Daisy soon felt challenged to do something for the relationship between England and Germany. No doubt, her decision to become actively involved in political matters was also rooted in a painful sense of being threatened in her identity, part of which was the hard-to-maintain dual loyalty to both the land of her birth and to the homeland of her husband, and her boys.

Political developments placing England and Germany at opposite sides never seemed to come to an end; these events would never let Daisy feel confident about a secure future for herself in Germany. It began with the Boer War, which pitted even the ordinary people of both countries against each other. The rising feelings quickly affected Daisy and brought her at odds with husband and in-laws, who naturally supported the Boers in South Africa.

It was the Morocco crisis which truly alarmed Daisy. On March 31, 1905, the German Emperor had visited the City of Tangiers which, together with most of North Africa, had for decades been considered by France a part of her sphere of influence. The population of Tangiers had received the Emperor with flowers and garlands and this intensified the feeling of the French government of again being provoked by Germany. As a solution to the growing crisis between the two countries, a conference was convened in Algeciras where Germany found itself opposite a solid front of European nations. England, Russia, and Italy all condemned the German actions of the spring of 1905. This political defeat had tremendous internal repercussions in Germany. In the Reichstag, the leader of the Social Democrats, August Bebel, condemned with great passion Germany's foreign policy as a danger to international peace. However, popular opinion did not side with Bebel, and the conservative press angrily attacked England for her alleged desertion of Germany at Algeciras.

146

Three weeks after the Algeciras conference, Daisy returned from Newlands to Fürstenstein, not yet knowing how best to hide her feelings and endure the hostility expressed by Hans and his family against England. On the train to Silesia, she wrote in her diary:

> No one who has not been through it can realize what it is to leave one's own country. Even for the sake of husband and children it is impossible to forget. One can only try not to feel too much; and at all events one can and must learn not to show one's feelings. ... Our two countries are of the same race, yet absolutely different in every way.

> And I stand away – apart from it all, apart from them, and have to make and live my own life which I honestly do with the greatest interest and much love. ... My soul – what I cling to – is the little island called England ... the sentiment born in my childhood dreams and romances, it is all I have left buried there, and whose grave I stand over now when I go back home. ... And in passing by I have to try and pick up my stick of courage and go forward in a land across the sea, and think of my sons who will wear Prussian uniforms.[13]

Returning to Germany felt more and more like an ominous obligation, while the once happy expectation of returning to the cherished homeland became more and more clouded with the apprehension of having to face the increasing reserve towards everything German. Every meeting with King Edward or Emperor Wilhelm re-enforced Daisy's fear of the terrible day when her dual loyalties were bound to be put to the crucial test. Conscious of the deep rift between the two monarchs, Daisy tried to do justice to both their complex personalities. As much as she worried about the impetuous nature of the Emperor, she did not believe him to be war-like. But she also worried about King Edward's dislike of his nephew who was "half-English anyway, and ... always wants to be first!"

With sympathy, she recorded a private hour after a day of hunting in Pless, when the Emperor confided "with tears in his eyes" his bitter disappointment about England and her King:

> To the Emperor it is a bitter disappointment to be misjudged and to be disliked and he always wants to be first. He is apt to rise to a pitch of excitement so difficult for his ministers to control, that they do not tell him everything for fear of what he might do.

> A nephew on one throne, the uncle on the other; both countries believing themselves to be right and both sides sincerely believing that each wishes to dominate the other in the eyes of the world. I am sincerely sorry for both.

---

13 BLU, p. 266.

> The King simply dislikes the Emperor. I am sure he has no real and dangerous intentions towards Germany; but he just shows his teeth when a German approaches him. There are great mistakes on both sides![14]

Spurred in part by the deteriorating relationship between Germany and England, and in part by the increasingly more frequent confrontations between German and English views in her environment, Daisy decided to go beyond meetings with the King and the Emperor "in private." By 1906, she began to utilize every possible opportunity "to bring the great ones of the earth" together. There were opportunities enough, in Berlin and London and, of course, in Fürstenstein and Pless.

Such an opportunity offered itself in September 1906 during the Imperial Maneuvers held on the fields of nearby Hohenfriedeberg when Fürstenstein had been chosen as residence for the Emperor and his illustrious guests. The Emperor spent his evenings in the entertaining company of the Duke of Connaught, the future queens of Romania and Greece, and the charming Counts Esterhazy and Apponyi, who had brought their gypsy bands from Hungary for the great Manoeuver Ball. After dinners and dancing, Daisy did not fail to arrange informal get-togethers with the Emperor, especially for the members of the delegation from England, which included Sir Lawrence Oliphant, Sir Ian Hamilton, and the generals Brooke and Lambton. Above all, Daisy devoted special attention to Winston Churchill. She fervently hoped that the Emperor would listen to the fearless and articulate Winston who

> was so intensely alive and individual, and in this age of stereotyped personalities that is much, ... but sometimes I am awfully sorry for him, he is like a race horse wanting to start at once – he has so much impetuousness ... and much personal magnetism. ... He may someday be Prime Minister and why not, he has energy and brains![15]

Whether the emperor paid attention to Winston or not, Daisy had been right in her judgement of the future prime minister. Winston Churchill would remain an intense observer of Germany, fascinated by what he witnessed on the old battlefield of Hohenfriedeberg and, three years later, near Würzburg in Bavaria in 1909:

> How magnificent was the spectacle of the German military and Imperial splendour. ... The maneuvers, however, for all their impressive scale and mechanism revealed many questionable features to an instructed eye.

---

14 BLU, p. 286.

15 DPH, p. 73.

Würzburg showed a great change in German military tactics ... in modern-
izing the infantry formations and adapting them to actual war conditions.
The absurdities of the Silesian maneuvers were not repeated. ... They were,
I believe, substantially the formations with which the German army five
years later entered the Great War and ... proved to be superior in efficiency
to those of their French opponents.[16]

With little pleasure, Daisy joined the Imperial party which moved
from Fürstenstein to Pless for the annual hunt. She noticed that the
war-like talk among the guests that "there must be war soon!" did not
cease, even though the maneuvers were over. Daisy could barely wait to
escape from the inimical atmosphere of Pless to London where the
German Ambassador Count Paul Wolff-Metternich had prepared an
apartment in the German Embassy that would serve for several years as
the London home of Hans and Daisy.

Daisy could not wish for a more favourable stage for her political
objectives than the Imperial German Embassy in London! Count Wolff-
Metternich was "the perfect old dear," although King Edward described
the ambassador as "DD – a dull dog;" he avoided the German Ambassador whenever possible, as he found his company utterly boring, which
was not surprising, as politically, Metternich had rarely anything of
importance to say and seemed to be largely ignored by his superiors in
Berlin. Among London society, "Old Metternich" was reputed to have
quite a soporific effect on people. Awkward in his manners, "he was a
typical old bachelor, with a crooked jaw and hard of hearing, fortunately,
so what people say about him does not ever reach him."[17]

In reality, the gentle Metternich was deeply devoted to Daisy and
always grateful if he could take her to the theatre, watch her try on hats
or, once in a while, entertain her at a private dinner. For Daisy, Metternich became the perfect, safe companion, an old bachelor of distinguished lineage with the reputation of never having demonstrated any
interest in women. Even though she very soon realized that Metternich
had hopelessly fallen in love with her, Daisy saw no need to terminate
the relationship; Metternich asked for very little and could always be
easily satisfied with a small favour.

Daisy was genuinely fond of Metternich, but she also had her own
agenda; how many opportunities did this hardly stimulating relationship
with the German Ambassador promise? What better invitation could

---

16   Winston Churchill, *Amid These Storms – Thoughts and Adventures* (New York, 1932), pp.
     75-82 passim.

17   DPH, p. 139.

Metternich offer to Daisy than "Yes, if you were always with me I might be able to do something, for I have no ambitions, but you have."[18] Daisy took this as an open invitation to assist Metternich in his ambassadorial functions; it meant nothing else than "that he wants me to help him — if only I could be in London more often!" Immediately, Daisy persuaded Metternich to give a grand ball; it would be the first since he arrived in London as Germany's ambassador. Almost overnight, the role Daisy had so long wished for, had practically fallen in her lap; a role in which London society readily accepted her. With pride and satisfaction, Daisy reported to her diary in July 1906 that

> at the Court the other evening I represented Germany; the Ambassadors and Ambassadresses, Ministers and their wives went in according to the printed programme. I was surprised that I was given such a position but there is no German Ambassadress. ... I sat on the Diplomatic bench and watched all the people pass the Throne.[19]

And soon after about the first ball at the German Embassy:

> ... beautiful women, plenty of men, a fine house, a good floor, lovely flowers, perfect music, perfect food and wine, a good hostess and good luck ... a sprinkling of Dowagers, Diplomats and Royalty. ... I had wonderful flowers everywhere. The great terrace overlooking St. James's Park was fragrant with them and all went well. Metternich was delighted and, better still, had the pleasure afterwards of paying the bills – of which there were plenty![20]

Did Daisy's account, entered into her diary when her emotions ran high after the success of the ball, indeed "her ball," betray a bit of selfishness, of exploiting the good-natured, passive Metternich for her own goals of using the German Embassy not as the social — which she did not need by any means — but the political stage for herself? If this was her intention, her hopes were only in part realized. While in political circles her role at the side of Metternich noticeably furthered her image as the politically interested and informed woman, she never succeeded in motivating Metternich to cultivate the contacts with diplomats and politicians she had established for him during the social affairs she arranged at the German Embassy.

In her love for England and "what is good and strong in the German character," she felt a strong kinship with Metternich. She was often

---

18 DPP, p. 120.

19 DPP, p. 153.

20 DPH, p. 120.

angered, though, by his lethargy and apparent lack of competence. Furiously, she wrote:

> He is never there I don't believe he ever reads the paper; he takes quite a sleepy view of everything – and things seem to me to be looking bad. ... Only last night the King had talked to me after dinner. ... Here and in Germany, they say it is impossible to find out what his Majesty really feels. ... But it was not difficult for me to find out![21]

Metternich, however, could not be moved to report Daisy's observations to Berlin. In exasperation, she called him "so weird; ... but then he can also be really very nice when he likes to be, and is really fond of me."[22] The fondness was mutual and the memory of "the happy days in London" would survive, even "after the world got upside down."[23] Likely, Metternich never became aware of his most important contribution to Daisy's life; without realizing it, he had provided Daisy with the setting from which, in her own way, she could begin to influence the political relationships between England and Germany. Daisy probably never assured him of her gratitude for that.

* * *

Hans, if at all, did not give Daisy more than faint praise for her success as hostess of the German Embassy. Daisy, however, did not give up hope and wrote in somewhat good humour:

> I am nothing if not persistent and ... I had worn down his resistance a bit. He never at any time encouraged or supported my various activities; at best he just tolerated them. Poor dear, to have really understood me, he would have ... to be 'made over.'... I understood him and his standpoint well enough, but I just wasn't going to 'stay put!'[24]

Poor Daisy! Would she ever win Hans over? After Vater's death, there was even less reason for Daisy to remain even a little optimistic.

Hans fell into his mania of rebuilding Fürstenstein; in front of Daisy, her home was changed almost beyond recognition and lost all its old-fashioned, romantic charm. Alarmed about the vast sums of money being spent on this enormous project and disgusted with the different

---

21 DPH, p. 202.

22 Ibid.

23 DPH, p. 434.

24 BLU, p. 74.

character her home received against her will and wishes, Daisy pleaded with Hans to no avail. The never-ending arguments continued.

Finally, hoping to direct Daisy's mind away from his project, Hans offered to build Daisy a little teahouse in the woods. There, she could give free rein to her own ideas. Daisy picked a site at a little trout stream in the valley of the Schwarzer Graben.[25] According to her wishes, a dam was built at the end of the valley to create a small lake. Daisy's imagination knew no bounds. Everything she had missed in Fürstenstein was to come to life in this quiet, romantic valley. Thousands of rhododendron and azaleas were to be planted along the hillsides and the meadows above the valley. An intimate garden, in part a copy of the terraces leading off Newlands Manor, was to surround her cozy little cottage. With its thatched roof, it would always remind her of her beloved England. For once, Daisy thought she could realize one of her dreams. For her, the tea house in the Schwarzer Graben would be *Ma Fantaisie,* where she would spend her happiest hours with her children.

A few years would pass before her dream came true. Hans was continually worried about raising enough money, as his building plans quickly exceeded their projected costs. He would not listen to Daisy's pleading to reduce the scope of the project or temporarily stop part of the construction. Instead, he surprised her with his decision to complete the huge new stud farm at an accelerated pace. At any rate, there would be no money at this time to complete Daisy's dream, her little tea house in the Schwarzer Graben. Daisy would even have to let some of her own servants go, as money was needed to pay the wages of the English personnel for the stud farm.

To Daisy's dismay, Hans refused, for the first time, to pay the travel costs for Mr. and Mrs. Cornwallis-West's annual visit to Fürstenstein. When they did get to Fürstenstein, a furious Daisy took her parents to the impressive three-story villa that had just been completed for the English head groom Alexander Stewart, pointing

> to the expensive oak for the stairs and banisters, the big marble tiles for the kitchen floor and the larder. ... It is absurd the amount of money spent ... on a house for a servant! And nothing happened in the Schwarzer Graben – it is really shameful the time they have taken![26]

For once, Daisy did not stand alone. The entire family was in uproar about Hans's "building mania," especially Daisy's brother-in-law Fritz

---

25   Black Creek.
26   BLU, p. 251.

Hochberg who, ironically, was also rebuilding his manor house in Halbau according to his own exquisite, expensive taste. Old, gentle Uncle Bolko complained loudly about the financial risk Hans exposed the family fortune to, on which every single member in the family depended. Only Hans's sister Lulu von Solms-Baruth seemed calm and helped Daisy with her realistic, down-to-earth view. Hans's ambitious building was "only vanity, ... really *you* never can want all those rooms to live in. Perhaps once or twice a year, *he* will fill them with guests."[27]

* * *

From now on, Hans and Daisy agreed to disagree about the re-building of Fürstenstein. Except for some of their social obligations and their two sons, there remained little that the two had in common. In political matters, however, Daisy remained steadfastly at her husband's side. More than once, Hans found himself in difficulties in Berlin for his sympathies for the Poles. It was well-known that Hans had, in keeping with family tradition, given Hansel and Lexel Polish nannies; that Hansel's education in foreign languages not only included English and French, but Polish as well; and that Lexel, still too young for formal education, already conversed with his mother mainly in English.

As heir, Hansel was prepared for his future duties at an early age; mastering the Polish language was a natural part of his education, as except for the upper administrators, practically all people in the employ of Hans in Upper Silesia were of Polish origin. This was a fact never understood in Berlin, even though during the federal elections in 1907, five of Upper Silesia's electoral districts had fallen to Polish candidates.

The reputation of being a "Polonophile" created particular problems for Hans in spring of 1908 when the *Polish Expropriation Bill* was brought before the Prussian Upper House. Daisy deplored that "this in many cases meant people being forced to give up their ancestral homes, often the very land containing the graves of their fathers. And all just because they were Poles."[28] With unexpected courage, Hans attacked the Bill, which was to provide for the legal expropriation of lands in Polish hands that were located in the provinces of Posen and Westpreussen. Members of the oldest Polish aristocracy had owned these estates for hundreds of years. For once, Daisy was proud of Hans. She remembered the heated arguments Hans had with Berlin over the telephone, and the hurried ride to the train station at the Riviera to get Hans to Berlin where

27 BLU, pp. 287-88.
28 DPH, p. 150.

his vote against the Bill could be crucial. Upon returning to her villa, Daisy tried to reach the Emperor via his sister Princess Charlotte, whom "I told exactly what Hans and I thought of the wicked Polish Expropriation Bill."[29]

Passed on September 27, 1908, the Polish Expropriation Bill was fortunately never executed. For Hans, however, because he had spoken against its intent so strongly, there were repercussions. Daisy wrote,

> we were always sympathetic towards the Polish people and their aspirations. Indeed my husband's pro-Polish activities were not always acceptable to the Emperor, and were sometimes used by ill-disposed persons to try and do us both harm.[30]

Even as late as January 1911, reports about Hans were directed to the Emperor "for talking Polish in Pless, but the Emperor was very nice about it, although Hans had to see two ministers on the subject. ..."[31]

It said much about their relationship, that Hans and Daisy seemed closest whenever there were political battles to be fought on matters on which they agreed. This was particularly true of their passionate loyalty to the predominantly Polish population in and around Pless; in matters concerning the "Polish question," they saw eye to eye; there were no arguments between them, and Daisy felt unconditionally close to Hans. Unfortunately, such experiences, so positive for both, did not last very long, and Hans soon seemed to forget them. His feelings for Daisy seemed to be as fleeting and superficial as his interests in her humanitarian and political pursuits.

Left alone in her hotel room in Breslau by Hans who had just departed for a shooting party with the Sternbergs in Castolowitz, Daisy contemplated the lot of married women of her class in deep pessimism:

> We are *all* to be pitied; so many of us try our best, and our best is so *feeble*, and it is such a *waste of time*. Compared with what we could do with our lives if circumstances allowed it; every woman with a husband, children and house is tied. Such a woman has to live according to the position she is almost *paid* to fill. And if the situation happens not to suit her she cannot give notice and change it!
>
> If the woman is content to appear nice to herself in the glass, and makes friends of (mostly) fools, have furs and diamonds, and forget her *soul*, she may be happy, but *not* otherwise![32]

---

29 Ibid.

30 DPH, p. 151.

31 DPH, p. 147.

32 WLU, p. 34.

This was the outcry of a woman who felt suppressed, who at the zenith of her life saw her ideals and talents wither under the conventions and restrictions of her time and her class. Brooding over her diary, she could hardly face the next day when, as always, she would be received at the railway station in Freiburg and taken to a home she no longer loved

> by the hated dress-up grooms, very expensive black horses simply for station work, and a Jäger behind with plumed hat. I will feel like a nouveau riche again. ... I look at Fürstenstein with a restless eye now, feeling that so many walls are to be pulled down, so much dust raised and disorder made. I shall know no peace there for many years.[33]

The pulling down, the dust, the chaos at Fürstenstein seemed symbolic of Daisy's shattered hopes and the direction her life and her marriage were taking. What little she tried to preserve of what Hans and she had in common seemed to slide through her fingers. The mood at Fürstenstein was disagreeable nearly every day, and even while away from home, at places of cherished memories, where once Hans and Daisy had been happy, tension was their constant companion.

During November 1908, Daisy spent a few contented weeks in Wiesbaden at the home of her friend *Mossy*, Princess Margaret of Hessen, a sister of the Emperor. Refreshed and in control of her feelings, Daisy had been eagerly waiting for Hans for days, but

> Hans arrived this morning to see me but only for the day. ... Perhaps he would have stayed longer if I had asked him, but I saw he would have been sorry to miss his hunting at Pardubitz. ... I cried myself (but not to sleep) last night thinking of all that 'might have been.'[34]

It was December 8, her wedding anniversary, but Daisy kept a stiff upper lip, hiding her growing disappointment and anger about Hans and her marriage from everyone. Only in her diary Daisy left her feelings and her sarcasm free rein: "At Cowes, the darling was cross at everything, furious, ... but I only smiled and was patient." There were no traces in her diary of her mounting concern about Hans's more and more frequent trips to Vienna. Daisy was too discouraged and too tired, but also fearful of a confrontation with Hans on such a threatening matter.

On November 13, 1909, Daisy's worst suspicions were confirmed. In terse words, she recorded on the following day:

---

33 DPH, p. 186.
34 BLU, p. 237.

I have had two surprises yesterday, one happy, one not. By order of Hans all letters were now sorted in the Secretariat, placed in large yellow sealed envelopes and sent direct to his sitting room and mine, and the rooms of our guests. One therefore opens them without looking at the addresses. Amongst others was one looking like a bill marked 'Urgent.' I opened it without thinking and found it was for Hans. ... Perhaps the day had been too full of sunshine. ... If ever I had to find out he really wanted to marry someone else I would separate from him at once, and never believe anything again.[35]

This fateful letter[36] destroyed Daisy's last illusions and all hopes. But it was not so much convention and financial dependence on Hans than love for her children that kept Daisy from leaving Hans, or at least confronting him about his unfaithfulness. More than ever did she miss the advice and consolation of her father-in-law. Should she approach King Edward who "since I was a little girl loved me like an uncle?"

But the King was far away and in poor health. Since his last visit to Berlin when the King had suffered "an attack" in her presence, Daisy worried about him. She saw more reason to be apprehensive about his health than did those in his immediate environment.

In retrospect, Daisy considered the King's state visit to Berlin "in spite of the sumptuous preparations" a political failure and an unnecessary risk to his endangered health. Besides,

My opinion is that all such visits, indeed all intercourse between the King and the Emperor, however outwardly friendly, had negative results because the King thoroughly distrusted his nephew.[37]

Perhaps there was, in addition, an inherent antipathy. King Edward, naturally genial, human and unassuming, hated the Emperor's pose and swagger, which, by the way, was largely assumed. When the Emperor unbent he could be most human and interesting.

In public he is ... impossible, he has no manners; he cannot choose his friends. In little ways that perhaps don't even count – and yet farthings go to making pounds – he is bourgeois, and loud, and yet he sometimes has the charm of youth. But these traits, however unimportant, are exactly those apt to drive the King to despair.[38]

---

35 BLU, p. 252.

36 Neither content of the letter nor identity of its writer are revealed in the diaries. Daisy's entry points to a relationship of Hans, of which Daisy had previously been unaware.

37 DPH, p. 173.

38 DPP, p. 206.

The visit of King Edward and Queen Alexandra to Berlin in February 1909 turned into a string of unfortunate events; for Daisy, it fit perfectly into other events which made 1909 "such a horrid year." The Queen loudly complained to Daisy about "being dragged to Germany totally against her will." Ironically, Daisy, with her own ambiguity about Germany, found herself "explaining the Emperor and Germany" to Queen Alexandra, who had never forgiven Prussia for her attack on her homeland Denmark in 1864. Thus, the Queen helped little to brighten the mood of the King who had accepted the Emperor's invitation with so much reluctance.

Although in diplomatic circles no one expected any positive results, the royal visit still caused a good deal of diplomatic activity behind the scenes. Sir Edward Grey did not "expect much good of it."[39] But he did share his concerns about the unresolved naval question with Count Wolff-Metternich, who immediately sent a cable to Admiral Tirpitz imploring him to give Chancellor von Bülow free reign in any negotiations. As usual, no one in Berlin paid any attention to Wolff-Metternich.

Quite typical for February, the weather was raw and windy in Berlin; the ninth was a particularly chilly and damp day, which aggravated the King's chronic bronchial catarrh and made him dislike Berlin even more. Right from the start there were many unexpected difficulties, which seemed unexplainable considering the well-known German efficiency.

> At the entry into the city, the horses failed. They were all performing poorly, and the carriage of the Empress and the Queen proceeded so slowly that at times the police and the public had to assist by pushing it; and then, there were moments when the horses reared and refused to move forward. The Empress and the Queen were obviously very frightened and eventually changed to the empty carriage which had followed them.[40]

This happened in the view of tens of thousands of onlookers lining the profusely decorated *Unter den Linden* from the Brandenburg Gate to the Imperial Castle. On the first evening, during a glamorous command performance at the Royal Opera, the King, who hated opera and was very bored, fell asleep. The following days presented a rapid succession of receptions and dinners, culminating in a grand ball at the Imperial Castle. All events had been personally planned by the Emperor, who went out of his way not only to impress, but truly please his uncle. But for the King, who looked more tired and uncomfortable from day to day, there

---

39   DPH, p. 173.
40   See Count Robert Zedlitz-Trützschler, op. cit., p. 256.

was far too much pomp and etiquette. He could not be his true self; the numerous official functions left him too exhausted for the political discussions with his nephew "en privat," Daisy had hoped for.

She termed the visit a wasted opportunity, because normally,

> the King's great flair for foreign affairs arose from the fact that for thirty years he had watched the eddies of international politics from a position of great eminence divorced from direct responsibility. A gregarious nature, he went everywhere, saw everyone, and listened. The European Press, and even the British and foreign statesmen and diplomats, saw in his Continental visits nothing but social jaunts, whereas they were, behind the façade of amusement, serious missions.[41]

Only the last day gave the King an opportunity to be himself. At the reception by the City of Berlin Count Zedlitz-Trützschler watched the King laboriously ascending the stairs to the Great Hall inside the City Hall and noticed that "the King of England is so stout he completely loses his breath when he has to climb upstairs," but the King appeared animated and jovial when the Lord Mayor presented the council members and the delegations from Berlin's trade and commerce, from the arts and sciences to him.

> The whole building was crammed with people, and the Burgomaster made a long speech and presented an album in a case. The King replied in German, and there was breathless silence. At the conclusion of his speech he received enthusiastic applause.[42]

An equally enthusiastic public surrounded the City Hall by the thousands. From the balcony, the King addressed the loudly cheering crowd with a few words, again in German. These were probably the happiest hours the King spent in Berlin. He departed from City Hall in a noticeably cheerful mood, but Count Zedlitz-Trützschler could not help worrying, because again, "the other day, the King fell asleep during dinner in the Castle; ... he eats, drinks and smokes in colossal amounts."[43]

The royal visit ended on an alarming note when the King experienced a serious, never fully explained attack during a luncheon at the British Embassy. Interpreted variously as a coughing spell, a fainting spell resulting from the overly heavy schedule, or at worst an attack of asthma, this frightening episode which occurred shortly after lunch, was per-

---

41 DPH, p. 180.

42 See Sir Frederick Ponsonby, op. cit., p. 257.

43 Count Zedlitz-Trützschler, op. cit., p. 259.

ceived by Ponsonby "like the forerunner of disaster." Bülow, who was present when the King addressed the assembled guests, could not help but feel that he "was listening to a dying man, for the King seemed exhausted and was very short of breath."[44]

The most frightened guest was Daisy, who had been asked by the exhausted King to accompany him to an adjoining room.

> The King and I talked together for an hour, I think because he didn't feel well, so he didn't have to make forced conversation. He was furious at all of the Princesses not being asked for dinner last night and hoped I would tell the Emperor, which of course I shall. We sat on a rather low sofa and he would smoke although he coughs badly. Suddenly he coughed and fell back against the back of the sofa and his cigar dropped out of his fingers, his eyes stared, he became pale, and he could not breathe. I thought: 'My God, he is dying; oh! why not in his own country.' I tried to undo the collar of his uniform (which was too tight), then the Queen rushed up and we both tried, at last he came to and undid it himself.[45]

Sir James Reid, the King's personal physician, who was called to the embassy, diagnosed the attack as a mere coughing spell. Daisy, who had seen the King "near death," was panic-stricken. During the next twenty-four hours, until the royal couple's departure, she caused a storm of indignation. Violating etiquette and medical protocol, she attempted to get the kind of help, which in her opinion would protect the King from further attacks such as she had witnessed in the British Embassy. Still deeply upset by the experience of holding the King's life in her hands, if only for a brief minute, she refused to accept Sir James Reid's professional opinion that the King would very soon enjoy the best of health again. During the next few days, Berlin was full of rumors that the Princess of Pless had tried to force the services of a man of dubious medical qualifications on the King. According to Daisy,

> I persuaded him to see the Doctor I have had here each day, and who made me inhale this morning with a special machine; it did me good, so the King saw him to-night. And he told me later it had done him good too and that he is seeing him again to-morrow. Please God, this dear, kind, able Monarch is not in for a serious illness![46]

This episode found its way into historical literature in various interpretations; with one notable exception they were all quite malicious,

---

44 DPH, pp. 176-77.
45 See Bernhard Fürst von Bülow, op. cit., vol. 2, p. 246.
46 DPP, p. 211.

lacking all compassion for Daisy's understandably upset state of mind. Embellished and falsified, they describe in great detail how Daisy

> near one of the many Pless properties[47]... her elegant, figure swathed in furs, was observed standing alone on the platform, the radiant expression on her face changing to one of bewilderment and then of dismay as the train slid slowly past.[48]

Various accounts located this scene to different railway stations that ranged from the Berlin suburb of Spandau to a station near the Dutch border 400 kilometres to the west. Where Daisy actually did wait for the King's train was never established; it was no doubt at one of the stations on the outskirts of the city, quite likely Spandau. Whatever annoyance the King, who was known to ignore his endangered health completely, might have felt after Daisy's unwanted intervention, it is inconceivable that with the respect and affection he had always shown for her, he would have amused himself watching Daisy standing alone in deep disappointment on the lonely, wind-swept platform.

Sir Frederick Ponsonby's is the only eyewitness account. Although differing from Daisy's report, it appears to be the most objective account of the affair:

> The day before we left Berlin I received a letter from the Princess of Pless begging me to tell the King of a wonderful throat doctor and adding that if His Majesty would see him, she would arrange matters. This was a medical question and I gave it to Sir James Reid who naturally consulted the Emperor's physician. The Emperor was apparently told about this letter and said if the man (the doctor) came to the Castle, he would have him forcibly ejected.
>
> I therefore wrote and told the Princess Daisy that the King would not wish to see him. My letter crossed with another from her saying that if the train could stop at the station just outside Berlin, she would have the man there ready. When, however, she received my letter, she wrote to Charlie Hardinge and invoked his assistance. He was under the impression that this was quite a new request and asked the King whether he would see the man, but the request was refused. So the train never stopped, and I saw the Princess Daisy of Pless and a man, standing disconsolately on the platform of the station she had named, as we glided past.[49]

---

47 There were none for hundreds of miles around.

48 Gordon Brooke-Shepherd, Uncle of Europe – *The Social and Diplomatic Life of Edward VII.* (London, 1975), p. 346-47.

49 See Sir Frederick Ponsonby, op. cit., p. 258.

Obviously, Ponsonby had decided to keep the contents of Daisy's letter from the King. It is also entirely possible that in his memoirs, Ponsonby had left out an essential part of the episode – that the King might actually have seen Daisy's doctor – simply to not expose any possible breaches of protocol and to avoid any renewed gossip. The reminiscences of the third party, the King himself, remain in accordance with his orders, inaccessible to the public.

In the end, one cannot deny that Daisy acted as a woman filled with empathy for the King. There was certainly no motive to gain publicity, as Daisy tried her utmost to reach her objective in secret. Sadly, Daisy's fear for his well-being would be proven right only too soon!

> The seizure or whatever it was, that King Edward had while he was in Berlin caused me and others a great deal of uneasiness. I had known him for years and realized that his life was not a good one.
>
> His Majesty perhaps smoked too much, and did too much; moreover, the political situation at home and abroad worried him a great deal. Those who knew only the gay, social figure, or the kindly factual sovereign, were unaware of how seriously he took to his kingly position and responsibilities. The situation in Ireland too, a country for which he had sincere affection, was very perplexing.[50]

This had been King Edward's last visit to Germany, and after the many stays in Baden-Baden, Homburg, and the castles of his German relatives, this stay in Berlin had been the least pleasant of all.

The busy schedule to which the King returned immediately after his Berlin visit fostered the illusion that everything was well again. Although the King never betrayed a lack of energy while in public, he tired more easily. The general political situation worried him greatly.

In the King's opinion, much would depend on Germany during the coming years. The messages from London which reached him in Biarritz in March 1909 were not reassuring. In deep resignation the tired King wrote to Charles Hardinge:

> It is sad to see the difficulties I have to contend with. It is strange that ever since my visit to Berlin, the German Government have done nothing but thwart and annoy us in every way ... but Grey has worked with the greatest caution and determination. If we can only ensure peace, it is worth giving way, as long as we can do so with honour and dignity. ... Unless the military party in Vienna is too strong, I hope that war with Serbia may yet be avoided.

---

50 DPP, p. 215.

... We may safely look upon Germany as our bitterest foe, as she hardly attempts to conceal it.[51]

The King's rising animosity against everything German was only nurtured by the shrill editorials and the sarcastic, tactless cartoons of the King that filled the pages of German newspapers. Neither did the English press fail to retaliate in ridiculing the German Emperor. Daisy was shocked by the King's extremely angry reaction when she raised the German question during a visit to Windsor Castle in June 1909. Resigned to the fact that the German government and the German public would not modify their anti-British attitude, she decided that only direct, unreserved communication between the King and the Emperor might have a chance to save the deteriorating relationship between their two countries. Perhaps the Emperor could be flattered into making concessions to his uncle; perhaps the King could be persuaded to see his nephew once more – but only in private, Daisy decided.

> I left England with the strong conviction that ... I ought to try and do something practical to relieve the growing tension between England and Germany. It seemed to me that if I could take a nice message from the nephew to the uncle it might be helpful.[52]

With a frankness which she was certain the Emperor would accept, because it came from her, Daisy composed a long passionate letter to him:

> Sire,
> I write this letter to give utterance to thoughts which keep me awake at night. When I was in England last, I said to Mr. Balfour: 'Tell me honestly, is there a treaty between England and France that is known as the *Entente Cordiale*?' He answered that it could not be called a treaty; there was nothing on paper, nothing signed. I lamented this incomprehensible feeling of distrust between England and Germany. He said:
>
> 'Do believe me, I think of it from morning till night. I would do anything to find a real reason, but whatever England does Germany attributes it to enmity in one form or another.'
>
> Oh Sire! I have lived in Germany all these years, and I am English born; I know the faults of both countries and I hear far more than many people, even diplomats. ... In Germany people talk openly before me and to me, for they know I love the country and my boys are German and will serve in

---

51   Philip Magnus, *King Edward the Seventh* (London, 1964), p. 419.
52   DPH, p. 184

Your Majesty's army. In England they speak to me as they would not speak before Count Metternich or any German, as they think of me as English.

How *can* one country truly know what another country thinks and believes? How are Emperors and Kings to hear the truth? They scarcely ever do. The people to whom they talk listen to every word they say and answer nothing, and go home and tell their wife and children: 'The Emperor said this and that,' and are delighted.

The fact is, English people are too conceited; Germans too touchy. What care and tact I have to use continually! If I say something or judge something, they at once think I am measuring by English standards, when I was simply judging by my own brain and not thinking of England.

I enclose a copy of a letter of a friend of ours who was in Fürstenstein this summer, and which has appeared in most of the English papers. Sire, there was a time not so long ago, when no Englishman would go to France, when France was England's bitter enemy; during that period an Englishman would have been glad even to possess an old glove of Your Majesty's, and this attitude will come again. In families the nearer the relationship the more frequent the quarrels; so it is now between Germany and England. Born an Englishwoman and as one who mixes with many different classes of people in that country, I beg Your Majesty, to know and believe that Germany is looked up to in many ways. I also beg Your Majesty not to be too proud when the time comes to put out your hand to my land and say, let us be friends and when we do knock up against each other on the high seas of commerce, let there be no bruises.

King Edward is more of a King than anyone in England ever anticipated. Now that his diplomacy has been so successful the whole country adores him; indeed, the feeling of loyalty in England is extraordinary. I often see the King and never in all those years has His Majesty ever said one hard word against anything German; in fact he advised me to learn the language well, to get to know the people, to take interest in the country, and so on. And he meant it; one must not forget that he is more than half a German, and in all differences between the countries he has thought: 'The German Emperor is my nephew,' and this fact has given him often a pride which Your Majesty cannot understand and probably will not believe; he has had Your Majesty in his heart and I know this. The same blood flows in the two countries; it cannot and must not surge up in enmity.

I shall see the King in England very soon. Cannot I bring one word of peace? Not to put in the papers, nothing to be delivered officially just a word of friendship.

English people *en gros* are a good sorts, and forget easily. They are not revengeful, they do not turn round now on Germany and jeer at any defeat in Africa. It is such a happy island and so prosperous. They are not always thinking of and criticizing their next-door neighbour, and if once Germany and she should shake hands there would be a great wave of joy over England and a burst of hurrahs, and Your Majesty's reputation would be held by the people even higher than it used to be, while the word I have so often heard would be repeated: 'My God, the Emperor is a grand man.'

Oh Sire, forgive me: Your devoted subject

DAISY OF PLESS.[53]

Daisy actually offered to assume a role typical for the personal diplomacy of later times, especially during the Cold War, when neutral, often politically unimportant personalities who were free from political obligations to either side, tried to or were used to explain in discreet private ways the positions, aspirations, and fears to the two opponents. They also hoped to become ambassadors of good will and reconciliation. Taking on such a role, Daisy was ready to pave the way for the Emperor, in confidence, discreetly, and without risk.

Taking advantage of every opportunity Daisy did not shy away from also challenging King Edward. Interestingly, the King asked her point blank at Windsor Castle whether she would not ever be afraid of him. He immediately reassured her "no, no, for that I am far too much an old friend of yours." If this had been meant as a good-natured warning, Daisy did not allow herself to be intimidated, neither by the King nor by the Emperor. Full of triumph, she wrote:

November 30, 1909. Pless.
'I could say so much and I will say it,' are, I see, my last words. Well, I did say it! And on the very first night as the Emperor sat by me at dinner. He began: 'A nice state your country is in! What are they doing there?' and that sort of talk. We discussed this atrocious 'Socialist' government;[54] then the Navy; I told him that in almost every way England wished to copy Germany, her Army, Navy, Old Age Pensions, factory, mining and labour legislation, Insurance, and so on. ... I pointed out that it was natural for a great country like England, which up to now had always been first, to be annoyed at suddenly finding another country excelling her in almost all things. ... The agitation in England against Germany was largely a ruse of those who desired to see more men become soldiers and sailors. And then I discussed the idea of a shipbuilding agreement, and the English fear of invasion. ... He said that the idea of invading England was the absolute greatest rot; what would Germany do with England; what would she want it for? Besides, it would be perfectly impossible. The wisest and the best thing England could

---

53 DPH, pp. 184-86.

54 Mr. Asquith's government, April, 1908-1915.

do would be to make a treaty with Germany. Then I said: 'Your Majesty, that's all very well, but you surely can't make a treaty about nothing.' He said: 'My dear child, it could be done.'[55]

"A quiet serious talk" with Metternich two weeks later, was to no avail. The ambassador was as disinterested as always. Daisy found a more attentive listener at her sister Shelagh's home Eaton Hall:

> The King talked to me after dinner last night. Here, and in Germany, they say it is impossible to find out what His Majesty really feels about the present policy of the British Government: but it was not difficult for me to find out last night as he asked me what I thought! I told him, and he said: 'Yes! Yes! disgraceful, disgraceful!'

> I did not tell him that the Emperor had said that England must give up the idea of the two-power standard in the World's Navies! But I did tell him that the Emperor had said the best thing would be for a treaty to be made between England and Germany, and that his one desire was for peace and prosperity. The king thought for some time and then answered with a laugh: 'Yes, and what would France and Russia say?'

> I could not help replying: 'France, I imagine, Sir, could only be delighted to be one in such a treaty and feel at rest, seeing if there was a war between Germany and England, it would be France who would be the greatest sufferer, as the war would take place on her fields and in her towns and nowhere else. Germany is not going to risk losing any ships by coming to invade the English coast; she will march to England via France, as that country is in treaty with England.'

> 'Well,' he said, 'we must keep the peace somehow.'[56]

If the King's almost fatalistic acceptance of the political status quo was depressing, there was another memory to be cherished, "an example of King Edward's warm nature, kindly heart, and simple homeliness." During his last afternoon at Eaton Hall, the King had on the spur of the moment offered his company to Daisy on a visit to her grandmother Lady Olivia FitzPatrick at nearby Brynedwyn. Daisy was worried how her grandmother would react to the unexpected visit, but

> The King was not to be put off. ... When we arrived I hurried ahead to prepare Granny a bit. She had just come in from a drive. Her bonnet was crooked, her lovely white hair all blown about and her nose red. The idea

---

55 DPH, pp. 197-98
56 DPH, p. 202.

of seeing the King did not at all amuse her. She asked why he had come as she had nothing particular to show him.

However, the King was delightful, though he started badly by sitting down uninvited in Granny's favourite chair. He made outrageous love to the old lady and in a few minutes they were both flirting desperately. Granny could never resist flirting and neither could the King.

Granny's father, when he was Lord-in-Waiting to Queen Victoria, was a particular favourite of Her Majesty and his daughters had naturally been a great deal at Court. Gossip had it that the Queen thought Granny unduly lively and attractive.'

The King said: 'Is it true that my Mother sent you away from Court for trying to flirt with my father?'

'I can't quite remember, Sir; most likely I wanted to flirt with your father; he was a very good-looking man – besides, all the Coburgs inherited a roving eye. How humiliating it would be for a man to think that no woman ever wanted to flirt with him.'

'I doubt, Lady Olivia, if that is a form of humiliation on which either you or I could pose as an authority!'

That was the King's last visit to Eaton, and I like to remember how he voluntarily gave up so much time to going to see an old woman and how successfully he made her feel that even if youth had fled her, her attraction and charm remained.[57]

Few days remained for the King; he became more and more unwell and morose, his mind filled with gloom about the future of his country. To Mrs. Keppel, his closest companion during these years, the King confided his thought of abdicating the throne, once even exclaiming "My son will reign, but my grandson never will!"

On May 4, 1910, the news of King Edward's death reached Fürstenstein.

The one terrible moment that came as great shock to me was when I was alone at Fürstenstein and Hans in Breslau. My maid came in with my breakfast and the news: 'They say the King of England is dead; the English huntsman has had a wire from his wife in Bremen.' I tried not to believe it and wired the Embassy in Berlin, and got the answer that it was true.

On May 12, from Castle Pless Daisy wrote to King George:

---

57 DPH, pp. 203-04.

Your Majesty!
In remembrance of old days on the Britannia, over fishing at Newlands, and all the many many kindnesses, and dear remembrances I have of His Majesty King Edward. I beg you Sire to forgive this letter and accept it from someone who writes, with a very miserable heart to ask this Our King George to accept her deepest sympathy in this sudden and terrible sorrow, that has fallen over England. Which is felt by the *whole* World – and realized by every man and woman.

Yet, at the same time, in loving respectful devotion to His late Majesty, and although somehow it is hard to write these words. I most sincerely wish our dear King's Son – and now our King, a prosperous, strong, and long reign, with God's help from above, and the love of His subjects always at his side. I sincerely hope Queen Alexandra is keeping as well as can be expected under these sad circumstances. Thank God Your Majesty and the darling Mother love each other so well.

God bless King George and England and I pray it now, each of these nights; but it all seems so impossible to believe.

Begging Your Majesty to accept my most true and sorrowful sympathy, I have the honour to be Your Majesty's most humble and obedient servant.

Daisy Pless.[58]

The same day, Daisy received a disconsolate letter from Queen Alexandra: "... my life is finished, there is nothing left for me in the future."
For months, Daisy grieved about the death of her fatherly friend. To the Portuguese ambassador in London, Marquess de Soveral, she wrote:

The shock I may say has passed, but the feeling of a sudden dark cloud and great change will remain for very long, I am sure; in fact the whole face of England seems changed.[59]

Reading the papers filled Daisy with a sense of doom. Others who had been close to the late King struggled with similar emotions. Lord Fisher wrote that "I think we will find the landmarks of life greatly changed. ... I am still dazed by the suddenness of it all."[60]

58 Courtesy Archives Windsor Castle.
59 DPP, p. 242.
60 See Sir Frederick Ponsonby, op. cit., p. 273.

On a more personal note, Ponsonby said: "With King Edward's passing we lost a lovable, wayward human monarch. He was one who came to decisions by instinct and not by logic, rarely made a mistake in his judgment of men."[61] All of France was in deep mourning; President Poincaré's eulogy commemorated the King as a rare human being who "knew better than anyone else in England or abroad, the character of individuals, the mind of rulers, the feelings of the governed. He knew the strong and the weak points, the ostensible and the real character of every man and of everything."[62]

In Germany, the reaction to the passing of the British monarch was rather different. Although the Emperor cancelled his plans to receive President Roosevelt, ordered the English ensign to be flown at half-mast from all German warships, and decreed a period of twelve weeks of Court mourning, the German press did not stop decrying the King's role. "He was the great opponent who inflicted upon us immeasurable injury. ... We stand at his bier as that of a mighty and victorious antagonist," wrote the *Rheinisch-Westfälische Zeitung*, while the conservative Berlin *Reichsbote* did not fail to point out that King Edward "had the fortunate advantage that, in the political context, ... there was really no antagonist of equal – let alone superior – talent to take the arena against him." Probably expressing the feelings of most Germans, the *Leipziger Neueste Nachrichten* reminded its readers in grandiose words that "King Edward wove with masterly skill the Nessus robe that was to destroy the German Hercules!"

Years would pass before a German author would acknowledge the human qualities of King Edward VII:

> King Edward VII. began his reign with a larger number of personal friends than any monarch who had ever sat on the British throne. His love of people and his enjoyment of society had taught him wisdom. ... There was little he did not know concerning the frailties of human behaviour. He was aware of the perpetual clash of vanity, jealousy and ambition with the nobler qualities of human nature. When he became King of England he was equipped with the rarest of qualities a sovereign possesses: a deep understanding of his fellow beings.[63]

* * * * * *

---

61 Ibid., p. 272.

62 Virginia Cowles, *Edward VII and His Circle* (London, 1956), p. 363.

63 Emil Ludwig; in Virginia Cowles, op. cit., page 363

The Cornwallis-West Family

1. Colonel Cornwallis-West,
   Daisy's father

2. Mrs. Cornwallis-West,
   Daisy's mother

3. Daisy and her sister Shelagh
   (Constance)

4. Daisy's brother George

The Cornwallis-West Family

5.   Castle Ruthin in Wales (1980s)

6. Newlands Manor in Hampshire (1980s)

The Cornwallis-West Family

7. Daisy in Highland costume

8. Daisy on her 17th birthday

9. Daisy on her wedding day

10. Constance, Duchess of Westminster, Daisy's sister Shelagh

11. Hans Heinrich XI, Count of Hochberg and Duke of Pless, Daisy's father-in-law

12. Hans Heinrich XV, Count of Hochberg and Third Prince of Pless, Daisy's husband

13. Daisy and her husband on their honeymoon

14. Daisy wearing the legendary Pless pearls

Fürstenstein

15. The castle before 1905

16. The castle after 1925

Fürstenstein

17. Guests at Castle Fürstenstein attending the Imperial Maneuvers of 1905

18. Wilhelm II, German Emperor

19. Edward VII, King of England

Fürstenstein

20. Queen Marie of Romania

21. "Daisy Crowned"
by Boleslaw Szankowski

22. Jennie Churchill, first wife of
Daisy's brother George

23. Winston Churchill

Fürstenstein

24. Daisy's retreat *Ma Fantaisie* near Castle Fürstenstein

25. Daisy with her sons Hansel and Lexel

26. The three sons Hansel, Lexel, and Bolko

Fürstenstein

27. Booklet about the social welfare institutions for the miners of the Prince of Pless in Waldenburg, printed for the World's Fair at St. Louis in 1904

28. Casino 2 (one of the clubs for the Pless miners in Waldenburg)

30. Department store for the Pless miners

Fürstenstein

31. Silesian lacemakers

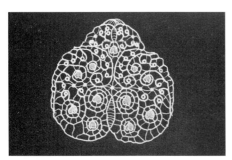
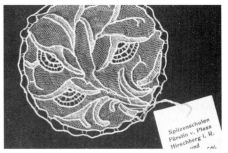

32. Silesian lace, certified as product of the *Lace Schools of the Princess of Pless*

33/34. Store of the *Lace Schools of the Princess of Pless* in Hirschberg, Silesia

World War I

35. Castle Pless, seat of the Imperial Great Headquarters 1914-17

36. Emperor Wilhelm II, Hindenburg, and Ludendorff at Castle Pless

37. Hans Heinrich XV accompanying Emperor Wilhelm II to church in Pless

World War I

38. Hans Heinrich XV in gala uniform

39. Daisy in Red Cross uniform

40. Daisy as volunteer at Tempelhof
Hospital in Berlin (August 1914)

41. Daisy with Professor von Küster,
serving on German hospital train
(St. Avold, France, 1915)

DD 13
DD 13

Bureau Seiner k. u. k. Hoheit des durchlauchtigsten Herrn G. d. K.
Erzherzog Franz Salvator, Protektor-Stellvertreter
österreichischen Gesellschaft vom Roten Kreuze und des Vereines vom Roten Kreuze der Länder
der heiligen ungarischen Krone.
Wien, I., Reitschulgasse 2 (Hofstallburg).

Nr. 31.390   DD 13

Ehrenzeichen.

Ich beehre mich mitzuteilen, daß Seine k. u. k. Hoheit der durchlauchtigste
Herr Erzherzog Franz Salvator, Protektor-Stellvertreter der österreichischen
Gesellschaft vom Roten Kreuze und des Vereines vom Roten Kreuze der Länder
der heiligen ungarischen Krone, Euer   Durchlaucht   im Namen

Seiner k. u. k. Apostolischen Majestät

das

Ehrenzeichen II. Klasse vom Roten Kreuze
mit der Kriegsdekoration

huldvollst taxfrei zu verleihen geruhten.

Wien, am   18.Oktober   191 8.

Der Vorstand:

An
Ihre Durchlaucht

die hochgeborene Frau Maria Therese Fürstin von PLESS,

freiw. Krankenpflegerin im ResSpital
"BRCKO"

in

BELGRAD.

42. Certificate accompanying Medal 2nd Class of the Red Cross with War
Decoration, bestowed by Archduke Franz Salvator on behalf of the
Emperor of Austria and King of Hungary on October 18, 1918, when
Daisy was serving at the Austrian Army Hospital in Brcko, Serbia.

43. The Hotel *Schlesischer Hof* in Bad Salzbrunn, converted to a convalescent hospital for wounded soldiers

44. Daisy among "my underofficers" in the gardens of the *Schlesischer Hof* in Bad Salzbrunn

45. Daisy after her divorce (1923)

46. Footmen at Castle Fürstenstein (January 25, 1925)

47. Hans Heinrich XV, Count of Hochberg and Third Prince of Pless

48. Hans Heinrich XVII, Count of Hochberg and Fourth Prince of Pless (Hansel)

49. Alexander, Count of Hochberg and Fifth Prince of Pless (Lexel)

50. Bolko, Count of Hochberg

Daisy's Residences after her Divorce

51. La Napoule, France
Villa *Les Marguerites*

52. Munich
Ismaningerstrasse 95

53. Castle Fürstenstein
Gatehouse with Daisy's apartment
in the wing to the right

54. Waldenburg — Villa Pohl in the
park of Castle Waldenburg, where
Daisy died on June 29, 1943

8 | *Into The Gathering Storm*

1909 had been *"a horrid year" for Daisy. 1910 did not start much different. A severe winter where starving birds fell out of the trees and froze to death was followed by an unusually early spring. But in May, Daisy watched a harsh frost kill all the blossoms on the terraces under her windows.*

* * *

Again, she was alone in Fürstenstein; only the five-year-old Lexel kept her company. Hans had taken Hansel along to Pless. When Secretary Freytag reported that "on His Highness's birthday it snowed all day," Daisy exclaimed in bitter sarcasm "thank Goodness I was not there!"[1] Hans would not have shared her sorrow anyway and Hansel was too little to understand. Nor would Hans accept her depressed mood about her pregnancy, which she had neither wanted nor expected. Reflecting on her own approaching birthday, Daisy wrote: "The years fly. ... I feel so old. ... There are so few years left before us. ..."[2]

In her loneliness and deeply depressed mood, Daisy called her sister-in-law Lulu Solms-Baruth to Fürstenstein. Since Vater's death, Lulu had become "a kind staunch friend. ... I used to go to her with all my difficulties and she never failed me. With a good brain and a strong character, she is my ideal of a real *Christian gentlewoman*."[3] However, not even Lulu could help Daisy who "suffered from a deep sense of forebod-

---

1   BLU, p. 258.
2   BLU, p. 259
3   DPH, p. 101.

ing which I could not throw off." After her return to Klitschdorf, Lulu sent Daisy a thoughtful, frank letter. On the last pages of her letter, Lulu talked about Daisy's failing marriage.

> I'll tell you first of all, my dear, a truth which is this: That men are childish, silly things, that think themselves cleverer than women, and are, and stay childish with their 'bigger brains' and all their superiority. And then they are so vain. ... I think we are apt to forget so often that they are big babies, and as we can't slap them as we would little babies, we have to get around them by flattering them and admiring them.

> I think this whole building in Fürstenstein also, is only a vanity of Hans. But I think one thing, dear, if you wanted to stay home Hans would let you, and I think he would by and by feel himself, that he too wants rest and quiet. ... Why are you continually moving? I really believe, it has a good influence on everybody, husband included, to know there is a *Mittelpunkt* [4] where they can come and rest and get advice and be petted.

> You say you have dark days before you. I don't think it is true what you say about Hans, he was *very much* in love with you when you married, and he used to tell us your many graces and accomplishments. And when we came to England and saw you, we naturally all went down before you.

> I believe every one of us has his pack to carry and I suppose it is all right. ... Naturally I would have arranged my life a little differently, had I had the arranging of it. When I think and remember *what* I thought life would give me when I was young! This is God's goodness, so it is with life, I can't ask anything more for myself, but God in His bounty still to use me to shelter those to come.

> YOURS, LOUISE.[5]

Even the sensitive Lulu had underestimated the depth of Daisy's depression, her fear of the unwanted pregnancy, and her sense of hopelessness when she talked of her marriage. As much as Daisy appreciated Lulu's comfort and advice, her inner restlessness and need to forget drove her to England again, into a whirl of social diversions. "Thank God, I feel well" she wrote between her accounts of the Ascot Races, visits with Queen Alexandra, Grand-Duke Michael in Kenwood, and outings from Eaton Hall with King Alfons and Queen Elena of Spain. There were only a few days of rest at Newlands where on Daisy's birthday, Shelagh gave birth not to the hoped for heir, but "only to a girl."

4　Centre, or focus.

5　DPH, pp. 216-17.

Shelagh's first child, a boy and heir of the Duke of Westminster had died at the age of three. Daisy's mother wrote from Newlands about the little baby "Shelagh has seen it only once in the dark and Bend Or[6] not at all. ... God help them both!"[7]

On September 11, Patsy accompanied Daisy to Berlin where a suburban villa had been prepared for Daisy's confinement. The passage across the North Sea was cold and stormy. "Little Patsy is with me, and Thank God the baby has not arrived yet – *unberufen*, but I had a horrid night. ... I am really frightened this time. ..."[8] From the day of their arrival in Berlin, everything seemed to go wrong. The highly recommended obstetrician Daisy had engaged had not returned from a conference in St. Petersburg. In his absence, the birth of her third son, Bolko,[9] on September 23, 1910 became a most painful ordeal for Daisy. The physician handled her

> like a piece of suffering flesh. ... Little Patsy [Daisy's mother] was marvellous and gave me drops of chloroform, but the whole thing was awful ... and no help or care or thought shown. ... Hans was not here. ... The little baby I love of course ... and I cuddle him.[10]

Disappointed in her hope for the little baby girl she had wanted, Daisy sadly held the weak, sickly looking creature in her arms. The little baby was not beautiful and, as yet, Daisy did not know of the heart condition he had been born with. Perhaps her sombre mood anticipated the short, tragic life Bolko was facing.

Hans came with Hansel and Lexel to stay in Berlin for a whole week – Daisy could hardly believe it. Lexel insisted on looking into every corner and cupboard of the building for the stork that had delivered his baby brother, because the Polish nursery maid had told him so. Bolko's godfather Crown Prince Wilhelm visited several times, and

> The Emperor came ... and stayed for one and a half hours. ... He brought me a bunch of dark red roses which he told me were his favourite flowers and said I looked like a coloured supplement in an English Christmas journal![11]

---

6 Shelagh's husband , the second Duke of Westminster. Bend Or or Bendor was his nickname.

7 BLU, p. 251

8 BLU, p. 266.

9 His legal names were Conrad Friedrich.

10 BLU, p. 267.

11 BLU, p. 269.

While the Emperor's visit momentarily cheered her up, Daisy felt very unwell and frightened, suffering from a persistent cough and severe pain in her legs. Not only did the clinic staff fail to take Daisy's complaints seriously, the treatment prescribed by the physician, as was realized too late, was wrong. How dangerous her condition actually was would later be explained in a letter by Daisy's chosen specialist obstetrician who had not been present at Bolko's birth.

Found in the archives of Castle Pless, this letter dated August 28, 1915 was to finally clarify the hitherto unsolved question of the physician's honorarium. Interestingly, the physician stated in his letter that as late as August 12, 1910, Daisy had advised him of her decision

> to remain in Fürstenstein. I therefore felt free to accept an invitation to an international congress in Petersburg which I could not cancel after the Princess changed her mind and travelled to Gross-Lichterfelde.[12] ... Three weeks after delivery, very late on a Sunday evening I was urgently called to see the Princess in Gross-Lichterfelde; I found her *up and around* but gravely ill. The wrongly diagnosed and untreated *bronchial catarrh* turned out to be embolisms in the lung.

> The illness ... was a consequence of already present varicose veins which, combined with deficient circulatory functioning promoted the formation of blood clots. The danger to the patient increased because of spending too much time in the damp environment of the clinic garden and frequent leg massages considered helpful for what were diagnosed as rheumatic pains, just about the worst and most dangerous treatment that could have been prescribed. ...

> Immediate measures introduced by myself during the night and the following day prevented the occurrences of further life-threatening embolisms. ... I also, during the night, after I found the Princess dangerously ill and suffering from embolisms in her lungs, explained to Count von Voss the extremely dangerous condition of the Princess and urged him to advise the Prince by telegraph of the critical condition of his wife.[13]

Six weeks after Bolko's birth, Daisy called a physician from London to her bedside. His diagnosis stressed the presence of a severe infection. Offended, the Berlin specialist referred to new complications, "since the thrombosis had now affected the other leg and the pelvic veins" and terminated his services. Everyone was angry at Daisy; nobody understood

---

12 A suburb of Berlin, the location of the clinic, where Daisy gave birth to her third son, Bolko.

13 Courtesy National Archives of Poland, Pszczyna (Pless) Branch.

why, in her worrisome condition, she did not know what to do anymore beyond calling for help from home. In August 1915, the original specialist was still waiting for his honorarium, and Daisy still waited for her full recovery. At this time a specialist from Breslau established "chronic, progressive circulatory disturbances."[14]

After six weeks in the Gross-Lichterfelde clinic, Daisy returned to Fürstenstein with a prolonged case of postpartum depression, aggravated by constant severe leg pains and difficulties in walking.

> Oh, how tired I am of it all. ... Sometimes I can't think anymore. ... Will I be ever really well again? ... Will people still care for me after illness has robbed me of my beauty! ... Perhaps all that is left is to try and grow old and live for one's duty![15]

* * *

In June 1911, a happy and obviously recovered Daisy wrote

> I had a very happy spring in England. ... I have to play hostess for Wolff-Metternich on Sunday. ... There are twenty-four German and Austrian royalties alone. ... Everyone is *so* nice and pleased to see me well again.[16]

Daisy had finally overcome her prolonged state of depression and self-absorption. She had enough strength now to return not only to social affairs but to political issues as well. At the Cowes Regatta, she spoke with King George, because "I was terribly distressed by the political situation and the disquietening look of European affairs."[17] Afterwards, using her proven recipe of confronting the Emperor with reality while flattering him at the same time, while holding the banner of peace and holding out the rewards he would reap if only he would accept her ideas of securing peace, Daisy wrote to Emperor Wilhelm from Bagnolles in Normandy, where she took another cure for her legs, while Hans did his cure in Marienbad.

> SIRE, YOUR MAJESTY, -
> The present moment in England is one of suspense and anxiety, also in France from where I write. The First Person in England[18] told me at Cowes

---

14   Ibid.
15   BLU, p. 269.
16   DPH, p. 222.
17   DPP, p. 258.
18   King George V.

(not privately, so I do not consider it wrong to repeat it to Your Majesty), that in May last, your promised word to him was that if further difficulties arose in Morocco a European conference would be summoned. He said to me: 'Is this calling a European conference, to send a war-ship suddenly to Agadir?' I said: 'Yes, it was absolutely right; it was a movement to bring things to a head and to force a Conference so that other Powers should not go to sleep and wake up some day to find Morocco a French Colony, while England looked on. ...'

Sire, even a woman may think and feel things sometimes, and I *cannot* see war coming; I *will not* believe it. ... If now (it is not too late) Your Majesty's Government calls this Conference all Europe will raise one voice in praise of Your Majesty, and will say, it is the Emperor who has kept the peace. ... It is the German Emperor who leads the world. ...

Sire, war would bring disaster to all countries for years, and at a moment when German commerce is on the verge of completely triumphing – as indeed she is doing in all things.

And if war is made and lost by her, it will be her Emperor who will be blamed by all the German middle classes, talkers, merchants, tradespeople and socialists; but if peace is maintained by a European Conference, the Emperor will be acknowledged the greatest man in Europe. ...

God bless you, Sire, always
Daisy of Pless.[19]

What Daisy referred to was the influence of his advisors, which the Emperor had fallen victim to again. She had heard in both Berlin and London that it had been the staff of the Foreign Service that had persuaded the Emperor to send the gun boat *Panther* to Agadir, which then provoked the second Morocco Crisis.

This crisis only served to accentuate the issues causing severe strain between England and Germany. The presence of a German warship, even a small gun boat, seemed an outright provocation of those English elements who continually voiced their fears about the increasing German naval strength. To Daisy, these fears were very real as factors contributing to the danger of war. Confronted with the increasingly anti-German mood in certain English circles, Daisy did not believe that the Emperor was always aware of the effects of recurrent provocative pronouncements made by him and some members of the German diplomatic and military establishment.

---

19   DPP, pp. 259-60.

Daisy did not restrain her emotions or anxiety in identifying such dangers in her next letter to the Emperor. After a passionate debate during the Emperor's visit in Pless, she took care to write her confrontative message with "sincerity, salt it with truth and sweeten it with a little necessary flattery":

The English will be the last to declare war and to this I can swear. ... Do you think I say things openly to you again and again to flatter you, Sire? Do you think I want anything – or hope to gain anything? My ambition would be to live in a little cottage by the sea with my children and flowers, and never go to any Court or enter Society again. Only I would be very very sorry never to see Your Majesty again. Do you think it was happiness for me that time at Pless – to have Your Majesty say things that you did not mean, but I was and am honoured to have Your Majesty's confidence, which I keep to myself. Was it happiness to me for someone also to come suddenly and sit next to me and say: 'Yes, there must be war, I am afraid.' And the band was playing and I had to laugh while I thought of the possibility of women made widows – children made fatherless. Was it for this God gave power to men? No: a thousand times, no. Sire, you know this and feel it too, for you are good.

The whole tone of the English Press has changed during the last month, as the cuttings I send will show. ... And I hope the gentlemen round Your Majesty have also perceived the change! ... How well I know what all the people I speak with in Germany think ...and to you they dare not tell the truth; to Your Majesty they prefer to say 'Yes' or even nothing, rather than argue the point! ... If only you would wait to increase your Navy Bill. ... Why increase it just this year? The very last thing on earth England wishes is to make war! ...

What do all those Gentleman whom Your Majesty brought to Pless know of the feeling in England, and do any of them really know Your Majesty? I scarcely think one of them does, for it is the people around you, Sire, who want to keep the power in their own hands and their agreed device is: 'Don't tell the Emperor.' Look at your own brother how he behaved five or six years ago, look how Bülow behaved. ... Germans are sometimes narrow-minded and suspicious. ...

Don't criticize and wonder and be influenced by people who say: 'Daisy is always in England.' I know Your Majesty thinks women are meant only for *Kinder, Kirche, Küche*,[20] but women have done good in the world. I am not ambitious for myself, but I want to see right always prevail: where right is there is peace. There is no hatred for Germany in England, I repeat ... I

---

20   A popular saying of that time: "Women are there for children, church, and kitchen."

should be the first to know. There is a great respect and admiration and *uneasiness at Germany's challenge to England!*

England is ready to stop building [warships] but must go on doing so as long as Germany does, and she has the money! Eighty millions is there to spend, so Winston Churchill told me, if this should prove necessary. England quite understands that Germany wishes to build, but only hopes that some day a sort of balance of building will be settled upon. ... And Your Majesty will lead the way, and it will not be by agony of death, or making the young corn-fields red with blood, and the world dark in misery and tears, but by doing good, and bringing strength and wisdom and religion to nations. ... Oh, Sire, *think* – and believe me. ...

I have marked the most important things in the newspaper cuttings. Please ... read them ... forgive me, Sire, for having sent them. (Herr von Jänisch will just miss them out, I am sure, the passages I have marked; he has little courage.)

Sire, Your Majesty promised the Empress Frederick to be my friend – please do not repeat what I write But oh! it would be good sometimes if only I dared tell Your Majesty the whole truth and all I hear, even in Germany.[21]

Amongst the profuse correspondence reported in Daisy's published diaries, this is perhaps the most remarkable letter from the pre-war years. Not only its length, but also its frankness is indeed astounding. With great courage, Daisy chose to ignore what she knew would aggravate the Emperor and provoke immediate outbursts that were never forgotten by those who were the victims of the Emperor's wrath and his unforgiving memory.

Daisy was well aware of the Emperor's opinion about women who dared express opinions on subjects such as politics. She was also aware that he treated her differently from practically all other women, because, she believed, she met him without fear and did not hold back the truth from him. Thus, she felt free to expose his weaknesses and state what she thought of his advisers who were, after all, hand-picked by the Emperor himself!

Granted, Daisy did mix "a little necessary flattery," but far too little, one would say, to balance the total sincerity and the bitter "dose of salt" with which the letter was written! It is known that the Emperor often sought Daisy's opinion, if not always advice, which she would give frankly and with respect. Her letter following the debate in Pless perhaps more than any other response took on the character of a message from one

21 DPH, pp. 32-34.

person feeling equal to the other. No matter how often Daisy begged "Your Majesty" to listen and to forgive, her true message did not spare the Emperor's feeling; there was no flattery but a challenge to the Emperor to show courage.

The Emperor's reaction is unknown, as none of his letters to Daisy have survived. If he was angry after reading this letter, he must have forgiven Daisy quickly, as the relationship between the two remained unchanged. No doubt, Daisy's conviction that the Emperor never wanted war positively influenced the relationship. Bülow was also convinced that the Emperor "did not desire war; indeed, he was dismayed when he realized that war was inevitable. ..."[22] Another "highly placed person" assured the British diplomat Lord d'Abernon that "I can give you my oath that the Kaiser never wanted war, I cannot speak for those who surrounded him."[23]

Those "who surrounded the Emperor,"were becoming more and more powerful. In May 1912, Count Wolff-Metternich became one of their victims. Long considered too much of an Anglophile by many in the German Foreign Service and distrusted because of his opposition to the German naval built-up, Wolff-Metternich was removed from the German embassy in London. This was termed a tragedy by one of his successors, Prince Lichnowsky:

> Metternich was an opponent of the fleet, of Anglo-German rivalry which would lead to war; he urged conciliation and giving in to England's desire for 'balance;' although he was notoriously unsociable, he was considered by the English as trustworthy and a great gentleman. ... The appointment of Baron Marschall von Bieberstein was but one of the many mistakes that characterized our foreign policy.[24]

Daisy broke into tears when she found the news of Metternich's dismissal in the papers. They were also tears of frustration; she knew Baron Marschall von Bieberstein personally, and his appointment horrified her. Not only did he lack in political acumen and diplomatic tact; for Daisy, he was the personification of German Anglophobia. Besides, she knew that with Bieberstein's arrival in London, she would become *persona non grata* at the German Embassy, which under Metternich's reign had been her social and political domain. Fate, however, interceded

---

22   d'Abernon, Lord Edgar, *An Ambassador of Peace – Lord d'Abernon's Diary* (London, 1929), vol. III, p. 261.

23   Ibid., vol. I, p. 152.

24   Ibid., vol. I., p. 174.

in an unexpected way. Baron Marschall von Bieberstein died shortly after assuming his post in London.

Even before Metternich's departure from London, Daisy had already looked for a different ally with more prominence in Berlin, who could give credible legitimation to her political pursuits, and on whose initiative she could depend. During one of the receptions at the German Embassy, Baron Ferdinand von Stumm, a member of the Foreign Service, had been introduced to her. Daisy was impressed with his unprejudiced attitude towards England and decided to invite him to Pless. Stumm arrived within days of the visit of the Emperor with whom Daisy had again debated "in full openness and frankness." The outcome of Stumm's visit fulfilled Daisy's hope for a kindred soul, for a true partnership:

> Berlin, Hohenzollernstrase 8, December 27, 1911
>
> Dearest Princess:
> I was so glad you invited me to Pless the other day and I hope you succeed in convincing your English friends. ... The most unfortunate situation that has arisen is due in greater part to mistrust, without any foundation. ... If you go to England you can be of very much use in always insisting on this point. ...
>
> As we agreed the other night, something positive should be done to bring about a change and the best way would be to come to some understanding of a political nature. It does not matter much on which question this could be the case. And I think it would be better, at the present juncture, not to mention any particular point. ... But I think, no harm can be done if you tell people that you know positively that we should be only too pleased to come to an understanding on some colonial or other question where we could meet the wishes of England and at the same time ourselves get something, in order to be able to convince those that are always pretending England grudges us everything, that they are wrong. Once such an agreement was concluded, matters would improve very quickly. ... Something ought to be done to disperse the clouds that are hanging over us.
>
> Hoping to see you and hear from you on your return from England, I ask you to believe me, dear Princess, Yours very sincerely,
> STUMM.[25]

On her way to yet another visit to England in February 1912, Daisy crossed paths with another ambassador of goodwill who was on his way

---

25 DPH, p. 226.

to Germany. Prime Minister Asquith was sending Lord Haldane to Berlin on a *mission of peace,* a controversial action loudly denounced by the Conservatives. But from Rome, Stumm dispatched a letter which truly delighted Daisy. Finally, someone of political prominence took her political efforts seriously:

ROME, VIA SARDEGNA 44, April 5, 1912.

DEAR PRINCESS,
I was so busy when in Berlin, that I found it impossible to ... answer your kind letter ... from Egypt. ... While the feelings are too deeply rooted in both countries ... Lord Haldane's mission ... has gone very far to remove distrust that existed on both sides. ...

I have heard of the work you did in London, and a very meritorious one it was. The Emperor received your cuttings and how much he valued them, you may infer from the fact that he sent them on to the Foreign Office. There they also passed into my hands, with your remarks on the margin. I may go to London in June, when I also hope to achieve some good. ...

If you pass through Berlin, do let me know. Otherwise, I shall be delighted to spend a day or two at Fürstenstein. ... Believe me, dear Princess, Very sincerely yours,
STUMM.[26]

Feeling quite ill, Daisy had to spend most of her weeks in London in a resthome. At her bedside, she had received a number of diplomats and other politically influential personalities before sending her report to the Emperor. Her observations and suggestions must have been of sufficient substance for Stumm to promise future collaboration. Whether her efforts as *ambassador of good will* had helped to bring about Lord Haldane's visit in Berlin, Daisy did not claim, "but the fact remains that the mouse has helped the lion!"[27]

One can say that at a time when unfortunate pronouncements made almost daily on both sides disturbed any small improvement in the political climate, Daisy's constant efforts, spurred on by Stumm's appreciation and encouragement to "explain the two countries to each other," must have paid some dividends; they were also important because of the prevailing ignorance among politicians and their reluctance to listen and examine their personal attitudes. Hans appeared bewildered when he wrote from London "here at the Foreign Office, they seem to believe

---

26   DPH, pp. 235-36.
27   DPH, p. 243.

that Germany wants war." Daisy reminded Hans of the Emperor's recent statement to the press that "I cannot and will not allow John Bull to dictate to me the speed of my ship-building." Insult was added to injury by the widely publicized conversation the Emperor had with a visitor from the United States, a Mr. Robinson, to whom the Emperor expressed his view that

> England is completely played out, the upper classes of society utterly demoralized ... corruption and incapacity are rampant in the army and navy ... and industry and economic life of the British Empire is in a state of stagnation. The world will see the decay and ruin of the British worldwide Empire proceed at an alarming speed.[28]

Daisy had been quite convinced for some time that the Emperor still wanted to approach the British. In Pless in November 1911, Daisy received the Emperor's loud complaint that there never had been a reply to his invitation to Sir Edward Grey to meet him in Germany. This was the kind of meeting Daisy had been trying to arrange for a long time. Now, she was confronted with the Emperor's hurt vanity and his outburst of hostility towards the British foreign secretary, whom Daisy considered a reasonable and objective man when it came to his attitudes towards Germany.

Immediately, Daisy wrote to Sir Edward Grey begging him to accept the Emperor's invitation "to talk from man to man." She felt that such a meeting could be arranged in one of her houses rather than the Imperial residence, where privacy was difficult to ensure.

Writing "on my knees in my sickbed," Daisy composed an eight page letter to Sir Edward Grey impressing on him to understand the deeply hurt feelings of the Emperor and believe his words that "I should enjoy nothing more. I had several conversations with Sir Edward Grey in London, and asked him to come and see me in Germany, the 25th of August or October, and I sent him the invitation by post, and am still waiting for an answer."[29] Offering her assistance to bring such a meeting about, Daisy gave Sir Edward Grey her assurance on January 23, 1912, that

> For over a year, I have encouraged the Emperor to meet with you and talk from man to man, not under the eyes of his courtiers but at a more private place such as my house or Kronberg. ...

---

28 See Count Robert Zedlitz-Trützschler, op. cit., p. 263.

29 DPP, p. 269.

I can only think, and this is private between ourselves, that he may really have intended the invitation to go – but that someone in his entourage, and some people dread him messing in politics, stopped the invitation ever reaching you. ... These sorts of things really upset him – as his one idea although none of you believe it, is to be cared for and appreciated by England – for a big man – he is strangely conceited and easily hurt. ... Keep all this private. ... I believe it is with you now to do a great deal to ensure peace and indeed, it is worth it, and if you feel so inclined to write me about this invitation episode, please do so, I have naturally not told a soul but I should like the Emperor to know.[30]

Daisy's letter caused an intensive search in the archives of the Foreign Office resulting in an entry dated 28 January 1912 that "Sir E. Grey never received a letter from the German Emperor inviting him to Germany," attached to a copy of a letter from Sir Edward Grey to

Her Serene Highness Princess Pless.
January 28, 1912.

Dear Princess Pless,
I was away from home for a few days or I would have replied to your letter before this.

I have certainly never received any letter of any kind from the German Emperor; if I had received one I should not have been so discourteous as to leave it unanswered. I might not in my present position have been able to do at the time what he desired, but whether that were so or not I should not have been open to any reproach of rudeness.

Yours sincerely,
E. Grey.[31]

* * *

This intercession between the Emperor and Sir Edward Grey marked the beginning of Daisy's most active period in international politics, which ended abruptly on August 3, 1914 with the outbreak of World War I. The thirty months between January 1912 and August 1914 were filled with numerous carefully chosen meetings as well as chance encounters with crowned heads, statesmen, diplomats, and generals. Using her intimate knowledge of both nations and her well-established position in both England and Germany, Daisy naturally devoted her efforts primarily to the relationship between the two countries. In this regard, she once

---

30   Courtesy Public Records Office, London.
31   Courtesy Public Record Office, London.

more approached the Earl of Rosebery, with whom she had had political discussions some years ago.

Since the days of the Chatsworth parties, Daisy believed Rosebery to be in favour of a sympathetic understanding with Germany; the years of his prominence in foreign affairs and his brief prime ministership had definitely been a period of harmonious relations with Germany. Daisy's high opinion of Rosebery was well-founded. As Winston Churchill astutely observed, it was Rosebery's good fortune that he "flourished in an age of great men and small events," but for Winston, Rosebery also remained "a master in the field of foreign affairs. He felt in ... his fingertips the vast forces of the Great War slowly ... assembling."[32]

It was Rosebery's political acumen and foresight that spurned Daisy to renewed efforts

> to bring Rosebery out of his political retirement, because his detachment from the more trivial side of party politics, his independence, great wealth and intellect, gave him a unique position in European affairs, and that, in a great crisis, he would be listened to as no other statesman would.[33]

Refering to this critical period in European history, Daisy urged Rosebery

> to give a series of public addresses designed to make it plain to Europe that the Franco-British Entente was in no sense a challenge to Germany, and that the sole aim of Britain's diplomacy was to stabilize the peace of the world.[34]

Perhaps Rosebery, as Winston Churchill suspected, did not consider the Entente[35] an instrument of peace; perhaps he was, as the Princess Radziwill said with great perception, "a politician more by chance than by real ambition."[36] With great tact, but with deep pessimism as well, Rosebery declined Daisy's urgent appeal to return to the arena of European politics.

ROSEBERY, GOREBRIDGE, MIDLOTH., *January* 25, 1912.

DEAR PRINCESS OF PLESS,
I am very grateful to you for your kind note. I am indeed uneasy as to our position, for we seem to be bound on the Continent by some invisible and

---

32 Winston Churchill, *Great Contemporaries* (London, 1937), p. 26.

33 DPH, pp. 265-66.

34 DPH, p. 266.

35 The Anglo-French Agreement of 1903.

36 See Princess Catherine Radziwill, op. cit., p. 24.

formidable bonds. But as this is the settled policy apparently by both parties it is not easy, perhaps not possible, to put things right. Anyhow, I cannot. I have tried it and found it a task both thankless and fruitless. And now I am, I hope and believe, definitely outside the political arena. Moreover, were it otherwise, I do not know enough. It is perhaps my ignorance that alarms me. ... But when I do come to London for good I shall be quite at your disposal. Believe me, Yours sincerely,
RY.[37]

As many other political personalities in British public life, Rosebery treated Daisy with great respect and gave her a remarkable measure of trust, greatly appreciated by Daisy who was well aware how unusual it was to be treated like that as a woman. Thus, it was hardly surprising that in certain circles the political engagement of the Princess of Pless which more and more seemed to border on active political involvement, met with increasing criticism. Leading the group of critics was Sir Ernest Cassel, who never missed an opportunity to vent his anger at the Princess of Pless. One of the late King Edward's closest friends, Sir Ernest, still retained his influence after the King's death. Because of his German descent, he was generally seen as favourably disposed towards Germany; a fateful misconception in Daisy's opinion, despite his close association with German bankers and industrialists. She saw in Sir Ernest the implacable foe of Germany.

Often enough, Daisy was witness to Sir Ernest's hostile comments about Germany. She regularly reported his comments to the Emperor and to Baron von Stumm at the Foreign Office. Sensing that the Emperor still considered Sir Ernest as his friend, Daisy resorted to a different ploy recommending that "Cassel be given a little plaster." Perhaps Daisy sometimes overestimated her influence, but shortly after her intercession, the Emperor decorated Sir Ernest Cassel with the *Order of the Red Eagle*. Yet, a few weeks later, Daisy was again confronted by the hostile Sir Ernest at a dinner given in her honour by Lady Minnie Paget to which

> Admiral Prince Louis of Battenberg, two generals, newspaper representatives, diplomats and so on were invited; ... they as usual turned to me. ... and asked when will Germany make war? I laughingly said: 'Ask Sir Ernest, he has just been to Berlin with the Emperor.' To my rage he said to them all: 'Well, I feel certain there will be war in April.'[38]

"I could have thrown a knife at him," reported Daisy to the Em-

---

37 DPH, pp. 232-32.
38 DPH, p. 238.

peror, as she urged him not to trust Sir Ernest. The Emperor replied "that he didn't, but was most surprised just the same."[39]

In late February, from her sickbed in a private resthome, Daisy directed another warning about Sir Ernest Cassel to Berlin, this time via Dr. Solf, the German Colonial Secretary who had just arrived in London for a "private visit." Stumm had asked Daisy "to get Solf in touch with the right people." Solf must have been bewildered by her letter and its almost conspiratory tone; he had never met the Princess of Pless before!

Private – absolutely for you alone
240 St James' Court, Buckingham Gate, S.W.

Dear Dr. Solf,
The papers say you have come here for no diplomatic purposes, but they naturally will not believe this. I telephoned last night to Herr von Kühlmann ... and I have just now received a telegram from Baron Stumm in Berlin. You will be surprised at my request which is if *you* will come and see me tomorrow *any time* you like before 4.45. *No one will know*, unless you would like to and if I dared ask you to meet Sir Edgar Speyer – he is a privy councillor and has the City at his fingers ends – he is also half German and pro-German, & is a friend, & does good, and knows very many people. Why I ask you to come and see me, is because being English I know *everything* here & have a very clear judgment, & in Germany where I have been married so long I am *proud* to say they give me their confidence which I keep. ... The Emperor was at Pless in Nov., but I have *not repeated* what he said there! Would you meet Sir Edgar Speyer & which day & which time would Sunday suit. I beg you to forgive this letter in pencil too, as I am doing a rest cure, in bed. My telephone number is 2360 Victoria. You can *believe me* that I hear far more than any ambassadors or gentlemen from the Embassy – & I know the *feeling* in England. I should be proud to meet you.
Daisy of Pless.[40]

Dr. Solf did not readily accept Daisy's invitation. The triple-underlined caption, the breathless urgency of Daisy's message written in one stream of words, and its secretive tone no doubt presented a near enigma to Solf. He did advise he could see Daisy on the following day, likely after having checked with Dr. Kühlmann at the Embassy and with Stumm in Berlin. Unfortunately, Daisy was on one of her rare outings when Dr. Solf called on her the next morning. Finding Dr. Solf's note of regret and also announcing his close departure, Daisy immediately sent another urgent note by messenger, again undated as was her first letter:

---

39 DPH, p. 238.
40 Courtesy Bundesarchiv Koblenz.

Private

St. James' Court, Buckingham Gate, S.W.

Dear Dr. Solf,
Will you come between 2 & 3 or *any time* after 4, you like to name.
I am very sorry not to see you to-day as we could have discussed your seeing
Sir Edgar Speyer – he would have been honoured to meet you – and as Sir
Ernest Cassel has *absolutely* turned *against* Germany -; Sir Edgar Speyer
might be very useful, as he at any rate in politics seems as far as I know very
sound – & being half-German is naturally Pro-German. I am sorry you are
leaving so soon. There are so many people who would have been glad to
meet you; & they would have believed your being here 'en visite' As England
is *very ready* to *listen*. I wonder if you will meet Winston Churchill I could
have so easily arranged that.

Yours sincerely, Daisy of Pless
Or if you like to come tonight early after dinner.[41]

No doubt, Dr. Solf would have handled any discussions with the
Princess of Pless very discreetly. Both were perhaps not so far apart in
their assessment of the situation and especially of the Emperor. In a
private letter to a friend, Solf had expressed his concerns quite openly:
"We are only too conscious of having to put up with many idiosyncrasies
of His Majesty from which we would gladly see our ruler free." It is also
unlikely that the name Sir Edgar Speyer meant much to Dr. Solf, but
Daisy's idea of cultivating Sir Edgar Speyer[42] as a contact and alternative
to Sir Ernest Cassel was certainly sound.

* * *

---

41   Courtesy Bundesarchiv Koblenz.

42   The son of a German-born banker in New York, Sir Edgar was the head of the London
     branch of the Speyer bank. Popular in society and well regarded at court, he was also
     highly respected for his philanthropic efforts and his decisive role in the expansion of
     the London underground trains and the consolidation of the entire London transport
     system, which earned him special recognition. Sir Edgar was also a well-known patron
     of the arts and a close friend of the German composer Richard Strauss who had
     dedicated his controversial opera *Salome* to "My Friend Edgar Speyer." It was during the
     opera's premiere at the opera house in Dresden on December 9, 1905 that Sir Edgar
     had been introduced to Daisy. Although she did not immediately share his enthusiasm
     "I did not like the theme or the music ... I think one must hear the music several times
     before understanding it," Daisy liked Sir Edgar and was alerted by his concerned
     comments about the Anglo-German relationships. Sir Edgar never denied his pro-Ger-
     man sympathies, which were to cause him great difficulties after the outbreak of the war.
     His enforced resignation from all public offices in 1916 brought about his return to the
     United States, a bitter, disappointed man.

During the Imperial visit to Breslau in September 1912, the Emperor decorated Daisy with the Order of the Red Eagle (First Class). What did Sir Ernest Cassel think about that? Hans was full of a pride, he had not felt for a long time. The following week, he had another occasion to be proud of his wife, when the Emperor came to Fürstenstein with the Crown Prince of Greece. As the castle was still under major reconstruction, the guests were accommodated in the fabulous new Grand Hotel in nearby Bad Salzbrunn. Hans was beaming when he reported to Daisy how

> everyone was speechless in awe of the hotel and its extremely tasteful and elegant furnishings; of course, I made certain that everyone realized that it was you who was responsible for it. [43] The Emperor exclaimed in admiration that he has never seen a hotel like this in his entire life![44]

While the Emperor did not spare with praise of Daisy's many talents, his visit in Fürstenstein was overshadowed by sharp verbal encounters between him and Daisy. This continued after the Emperor moved on to Pless. When Daisy again endeavoured to explain England to the Emperor, the Emperor lost his temper completely, and in front of the guests shouted "what the English want is a good thrashing, and they will get it if they don't take care!" Few people, certainly not a woman, would have dared to counter the Emperor's extreme anger as Daisy did when she coolly replied "Your Majesty ought to stop and think; we are not living in the fifteenth century!"[45] It was remarkable how unaffected their relationship with each other remained despite such repeated political debates. Daisy, however, did not dare to tell the Emperor at this time that she was planning to have Lord Winterton meet him at Newlands. After the Emperor's departure, Daisy bitterly confided to her diary:

> If Germany deliberately annoys England and tries for sheer devilry and conceited rivalry, to increase the taxation of both countries rather than tend the poor and use the money for the good of the poor, simply for the sake of the Emperor being able to launch more Dreadnoughts during his reign, then I shall close my door to him, and his policy. No one can conceive what

---

43 Ironically, there is a sad footnote to history: Some of the furniture Daisy had chosen for the hotel's main dining salon could be found in post-war Fürstenstein (since 1945 Zamek Książ) in one of the salons. Most of the castle's contents and treasures had already been sold by Daisy's husband before World War II; the rest fell victim to plundering at the end of the war. (The furniture from the Salzbrunn hotel has since been replaced.)

44 DPH, p. 244.

45 DPH, p. 229.

I went through during the Emperor's last visit to Pless; the band playing, and women in diamonds ... and there was talk about war. ...[46]

More and more in Germany, Daisy sensed a mixture of fatalistic acceptance of the inevitability of war and an obsession with the pursuit of power and glory at the same time. At court, no one seemed prepared to speak his mind openly in the presence of the Emperor. In Pless, his ministers pleaded with Daisy "to try and keep him quiet; he is mad about the navy, and can think and talk of nothing else."[47] Instead, Daisy confronted him with more than her usual frankness:

> Whom can Your Majesty trust? No one! You nominate your own ministers, and if they do not agree with you or refuse to act more or less on what you expressly desire, they can only resign; Your Majesty disgusts them. And the gentlemen you shoot with, they will only agree with every word you say, for fear you will not visit them again.[48]

Among these gentlemen, of course, Daisy counted her husband, the master of Pless and frequent host to the Emperor. Hans was known to never disagree with the Emperor; he was also disinterested in politics. On both counts, Daisy was his opposite:

> I was not the Emperor's servant and he could not therefore lose prestige in his own eyes by listening to me or following my advice; I was English; I was frank, outspoken and quite fearless and independent; last of all, I was a woman and when the Emperor really admired or cared for a woman he was far more influenced than he would ever have cared to admit.[49]

Daisy's personal life and her more and more fervent political engagement became a reflection of the accelerating events which gripped Europe during the last two years of peace. In 1912, Daisy had spoken with Lord Haldane again after his mission to Berlin, "bringing to his notice some points concerning Anglo-German relations which I thought might have escaped him..."[50] From Haldane, Daisy had turned to Lord Winterton; she received a very frank reply:

---

46 DPH, p. 246.

47 DPH, p. 228.

48 DPH, p. 229.

49 DPH, p. 225.

50 DPH, p. 242.

GRAVENHURST, BOLNEY, SUSSEX, 17.11.12.

DEAR PRINCESS,
I hasten to write and thank you for a most interesting letter. ...

Certainly, your theories are largely borne out by events. I myself am much less Germanophile since the Balkan war. I always hated the idea of a war with Germany. ... Now, I am much less certain of Germany's warlike intentions ... the next few years will be the really critical time...

I do not know what the course of business will be in the House of Commons, but I could run down for the day [to Newlands]. ... If you are in Germany in January or February, I wonder if I might come over for two or three days. ... perhaps I might come on short notice, since I gather you will be in Berlin, and I wouldn't bother you to put me up, but I could stay at the Adlon Hotel or somewhere.

There is one more thing I want to say. There will be distrust of Germany here so long as (apart altogether from armaments) German diplomacy seems to be always working underground. There is still a great dread here of Bismarck's methods, and the feeling is that Prussian diplomacy has retained its subterranean characteristics while losing its genius and objective. Deceitful for the sake of being deceitful. You must admit that this is deplorably evident in the Kaiser's Near Eastern policy of some years back and in Morocco.

Yours sincerely
WINTERTON.[51]

Daisy had considered Winterton's attitudes crucial; if she could modify them, he might influence his colleagues in the House of Commons; their attitudes towards Germany might become more benign thanks to the influence Winterton had among the members of both houses. Often tired of "constantly running against walls," frank reactions such as Winterton's spurned Daisy to renewed efforts. She must have a role to play, if the busy Winterton was willing to come to Berlin to meet her. She decided to ask Baron von Stumm to join her. Her continuing work with him would provide a favourable base for such a meeting. Stumm approved of her *political philosphy* and her plans. Daisy had reiterated them in a letter of many pages [about half quoted here] just six months earlier:

---

51 DPH, pp. 245-46.

Fürstenstein, Bez. Breslau, May 30, 1912.

DEAR BARON STUMM,

I hope you are not ... beginning to lose your patience and say: 'Well, if there has to be war, let there be war ... ' as neither side seems to wish to help the other towards a reasonable and possible understanding. I think Dr. Delbrück's[52] article in the *NORD UND SÜD*[53] the most dignified, clearly worded, patient, and reasonable. ...

Mr. Balfour's article is not worth discussing seriously. ... One must see that things are in a very grave and sad state ... if war was declared, I do not see what the victor could gain to any great extent that might make the horrible result of war worth the blood and money it would cost.

The time for diplomacy has passed. I enclose this article (written as a letter)... I ask you if some big man[54] in Germany could not publish it under his own name in the *NORD UND SÜD*, or any other paper or magazine to be translated into the English Press.

One of the important persons ... to influence is Winston Churchill. ... He absolutely believes that Germany is intentionally a danger to England on the sea and wants to fight ... [he] said to me, Germany, to protect her commerce, need only to build cruisers, not Dreadnoughts. What I answered you can guess; it would be too long to write ... but even an English Admiral agreed with me. ...

This is an idea I have – women as a rule go too fast, I suppose I do – but ... the smile and bow of the Ambassador will accomplish nothing! It is time an individual came forward and spoke like a man. Would it not be possible ... to assemble a private meeting, and have a 'sitting' as they do in every Parliament, and deal with the whole English and German question, as a *European* problem? Let the different ambassadors attend ... of Austria, France, Russia, America ... Italy and Spain; then the heads of the Cabinet in England and five influential men of the future government ... and eight or ten of Germany's most prominent men. The German Ambassador, of course, and Sir Edward Grey, would be the two who would speak and deal with outstanding questions; each Ambassador would speak afterwards. ... My dear Baron Stumm, this proposal may sound to you womanish and theatrical, but I ask you to think that if a political matter of the interior policy of a country is worth all the meetings and sittings ... is not a great and grave and solemn question like German and English Foreign Policy

---

52 German Minister of the Interior.

53 A cultural and political monthly published in Berlin and Breslau by the Silesian publisher Salo Schottländer.

54 i.e., an influential person, but not a woman.

worth the thought of all the most influential men, and should it not be discussed together in private behind locked doors? There are so many questions. ...

It is no use dawdling on, one man speaking after another – his remarks travestied by the free Press of each country. The old ways and paths have been trod long enough; let a new idea be tried and let someone act. ...

DAISY PLESS.[55]

Written in fear of an impending catastrophe, Daisy's letter expressed her sense of urgency. Beyond a diffusion of the present European crisis, Daisy also searched for ways which would lead to an enduring peace, to a world without war.

* * *

While her immediate concern was a solution of the Anglo-German crisis that would ban the feared outbreak of war, Daisy saw the need for a social, moral, and economic re-organization of Europe that alone could assure the true peace she was striving for. Across the Channel. she found a kindred spirit and ally, Sir Arthur Crosfield.

A member of a well-to-do, respected family, Sir Arthur was known for his interests in sports and particularly his campaign for the preservation of the dwindling forests on the British Isles, especially the unique New Forest near Newlands. Since 1906 he had represented his district as a Liberal member, but retired from the House of Commons in 1910, to spend most of his time in Southern France.

When he was introduced to Daisy at a dinner in Grand Duke Michael's villa, the two not only realized that they were neighbours, they also discovered the extent of their common interest in fostering a new political and social order in Europe, which both pursued with an almost missionary fervour. It was obvious that Sir Arthur's political and economic proposals and Daisy's social and humanitarian ideas for a better world complemented each other extremely well.

Daisy admired in Sir Arthur "a man of great foresight and statesmanship ... but like myself a private person." He, in turn, recognized in Daisy the strong-willed, committed, fearless person who, even though a woman, would be the ideal ally for publicly advancing their ideas. The ensuing productive collaboration resulted in a proposal about which Daisy reported in her diaries. Sir Arthur's political and economic analysis

---

55 DPH, pp. 236-39.

of Europe and Daisy's grasp of the moral and social issues of her time were integrated into a grand "Design for a New Order of Europe."

Clearly defined interests common to all nations were translated into a series of integrated political, economic, and social measures throughout Europe. Their purpose was to divert the energies of the nations, from armaments and preparation for war, towards peaceful goals; eventually a community of nations would evolve secure in its autonomy, but bound together by common interests, goals of prosperity, and the maintenance of peace.[56]

Recognizing the interdependence of political, economic, and social forces, Sir Arthur's and Daisy's design started from the premise that disarmament negotiations would lead to nothing, as proven by the existing political power structure that had remained hopelessly deadlocked for years. Instead, the first step towards a new order would concentrate on simultaneous economic and social reforms in Great Britain and Germany, the two greatest competitors in the economy of Europe and the entire world. Such co-operation between the two most advanced nations in Europe would promote economic integration and therefore reduction of wasteful competition; it would become the model for other European nations to follow in their own interest. At the same time, the eight-hour day would be introduced in all countries in order to diminish the enormous differences in economic strength between the various countries and to promote the equalization of economic and social conditions throughout the Continent.

Agreed-upon economic and social reforms would foster a more harmonious climate and more trusting attitudes throughout Europe, a pre-requisite to the next step: universal disarmament.

The disarmament envisioned would in reality be the re-organization of industries – the crucial factor for progress and prosperity – from having industries focused on preparation for war to industries promoting better standards of living for all people in Europe. Crucial for a successful transition was a carefully planned and followed sequence of economic and social measures as part of disarmament; this was vital in

---

56 Almost utopian for its time, Crosfield's and Daisy's proposal certainly strikes a chord in our present time, not only because of its ideals, but their practical applications through skillful blending of economic, moral, and social goals and through practical solutions to long-standing political and social issues which threatened the peace of Europe and the stability of individual nations. A fascinating observation cannot be ignored! With all the optimism inherent in the proposal, it is clearly designed for the western half of the Continent, expressing no trust or faith in the capacity of Russia to ever join the grand scheme of re-organizing Europe. Rather, one of its major benefits is the creation of a strong "bulwark" against the Czarist Empire!

order to avoid large-scale economic dislocation, unemployment, and human suffering. Only with such measures would all working people experience an immediate reduction in their tax load. The enormous capacity of the armament industry of the large nations would now be available for the benefit of the more disadvantaged, economically backward nations of Southern Europe and their chronically impoverished populations.

While an agreement to subscribe to the principle of the plan and its realization could relatively easily be reached between England and Germany, the relationship between Germany and France, burdened by a history of wars, would require complex measures. The stumbling stone was Alsace-Lorraine, the source of animosity since its annexation by Germany at the end of the Franco-Prussian War of 1870-71. For a successful European re-organization and integration, its return to France was an absolute pre-requisite; and France would have to compensate Germany for the loss of prestige and economic power. This could be accomplished by ceding parts of the vast French colonial territories in Africa and would have the added benefit of deflecting Germany's Imperialistic objectives from Europe to Africa. In addition, France would pay Germany a considerable sum of monies that could only be spent on social reforms.

Following removal of all issues impeding peace and co-operation between England, France, and Germany, the three countries would constitute a community of peace and prosperity while at the same time functioning as an insurmountable bulwark against Russia, which Daisy characterized as "the most reactionary and unstable country, a constant danger to the peace of Europe and the entire world."[57]

In early summer 1914, Sir Arthur's and Daisy's proposal for a new Europe was completed. On June 10, Sir Arthur sent a copy to Daisy, accompanied by a letter that enthusiastically predicted a time of peace for Europe:

> Then would follow, as surely as day follows night, that alliance between France, Germany and England, with which in turn other countries would be associated, which would be a permanent guarantee of peace among the great powers of the world. Such an alliance would make it rapidly and increasingly difficult for any of the smaller powers to kick over the traces.[58]

Daisy's immediate response to the letter was a plan to invite the Emperor to Fürstenstein or Pless to present the proposal to him, but she knew that the purpose of her invitation probably could not be kept

---

57 DPH, p. 116.

58 DPH, pp. 270-71.

secret. Many of the Emperor's advisers would be hostile to the proposal. The press would be told somehow and would spread the news to the general public prematurely, which both Daisy and Sir Arthur were determined to avoid. It proved difficult, however, to bring the proposal to the attention of a person who would have a benevolent attitude towards England and who could be trusted. Daisy could only think of Baron von Stumm. He might even find a way to lance its publication in *NORD AND SÜD*. Sir Arthur became impatient and urged Daisy to approach the Emperor as quickly as possible; he would just be the man to be fascinated by such a grand vision.

But the Emperor was on his *Northland Cruise* along the coast of Norway and had not indicated a visit to Fürstenstein or Pless in the near future, and Daisy hesitated to submit the proposal to the Emperor anywhere except on her "own territory." Sir Arthur then urged Daisy

> to lead a public crusade in favour of the reduction of Armaments and international amity and co-operation – in fact become a modern Joan of Arc – but unfurling the oriflamme of peace and not of war.[59]

But before Daisy could decide whether to become a crusader for peace and social justice, the fateful shots fell in Sarajevo on June 28, 1914.

On the day of the assassination of Archduke Ferdinand and his wife, Daisy was already in England. For years she would agonize over whether she had made the right decision. After the end of the war, when poor health and social isolation made her no longer feel the strong woman of powerful political and social convictions, she wrote:

> Armed with these arguments and this document should I have gone at once direct to the Emperor? Had I done so, would it have been of any use? History has made use at times of queer and feeble instruments. Could a frail Englishwoman, perhaps ignorant and ill-informed, certainly since years foreseeing war with her heart and feelings rather than with her mind, and moved by intuition rather than reasoned knowledge, have done anything effective to stem the tide of great and disastrous events? I often wonder and, even now, I do not know. Does the very presence of opportunity ordain that one should embrace it? Perhaps I ought, at any rate, to have made an attempt to see the Emperor. When one looks back, a most extraordinary thing about the years immediately preceding the Great War is that, although many highly-placed European personages were alive to the danger, no one did anything very definite to avert it.[60]

---

59   DPH, p. 270.
60   DPH, p. 271.

Did Daisy feel that there was no more hope to save the peace? Did she despair that at that late an hour she would not find anybody willing and capable to listen to such revolutionary ideas for a better, more peaceful Europe? Daisy gave the answer herself.

> I had a great belief in and respect for him [the Emperor] as a man; I had little of either for him as a Sovereign, He was surrounded by incompetent people and for this he must before the Bar of History bear the blame. ... He should have been strong enough to surround himself with capable advisers. ... The Emperor was never big enough to face the truth, or to find and keep near him those who looked upon indiscriminate flattery as unworthy.[61]

* * *

Tragically, Sir Arthur's and Daisy's thinking was far too advanced for its time. Sir Arthur's and Daisy's proposals remained in oblivion. For a brief time in the 1920s, Chancellor Gustav Stresemann of Germany, who shared the Nobel Peace Prize in 1929 with Prime Minister Aristide Briand of France, struggled in futility to create a secure Europe. Only after another war, far more destructive than World War I, would Europe enter the path of reconciliation and co-operation, that began in the 1950s. Thus, in an anonymous way, Sir Arthur Crosfield's and Daisy of Pless's vision came alive, the nations of Western Europe, primarily France and Germany took precisely some of those steps that Sir Arthur Crosfield and Daisy of Pless had proposed forty years too soon, before the need for survival, protection, and economic recovery finally began to unite the nations of Western Europe. The vast economic and social differences between the larger nations in the north and the smaller ones in the south gradually disappeared; borders between the countries opened and the arms race between the Western European nations became history. What Sir Arthur and Daisy had so clearly foreseen, however, remained a fact of life for decades, namely the seemingly permanent, tragic dichotomy between East and West, which excluded the Empire in the East from being a partner in this grand constellation; the Soviet Union and its satellites were being kept in check by the alliance of the Western nations as their enemy. Still, the fall of the Soviet Empire, while opening the door to a better life and bringing freedom to many of its people, has not extinguished the concern about an uncertain future in Eastern Europe and its effect on the western half of the continent, as Daisy had so clearly foreseen.

---

61 DPH, pp. 271-72.

In September 1938, Sir Arthur Crosfield died in Southern France under somewhat mysterious circumstances. The obituary in *The Times* took note of his humanitarian work for the League of Nations, but it did not allude to his political ideas and aims before 1914. In the same issue, a statement by the government of Greece eulogized Sir Arthur Crosfield as

> an indefatigable champion of the Greek cause ... and a vital link between Great Britain and Greece. ... Sir Arthur thought with his heart and, with characteristic, unobtrusive modesty, was a most helpful host. His memory will remain with us as that of a great and unselfish friend and a man of unflagging kindness and helpful sympathy in every aspect of Greek national life.[62]

* * *

One should not fault Daisy for refusing Sir Arthur's request to publicly crusade for peace and disarmament. More than any other woman of her class she had already transgressed the boundaries set by etiquette and convention, and by male prejudice against women who concerned themselves with social justice, politics, and peace. Furthermore, Daisy believed that public opinion in Germany was still far from accepting even some of the basic ideas underlying Sir Arthur's and her vision of the new Europe. This inimical political climate she was conscious of was explained by the German historian Delbrueck in his comments on the German government's refusal to support the aims of the Hague Peace Conference:

> They omitted to do this on purpose because Germany was still a young nation with a great future, and it did not think that such institutions should be allowed to destroy its future opportunities.

To the very last moment of peace, Daisy fought for the proposal she and Sir Arthur Crosfield had created with so much enthusiasm and idealism. Soon after her arrival in London in June 1914, Daisy turned to Lord Roberts, while still "considering Sir Arthur's sensible suggestions and hesitating how best to act." Lord Roberts figured prominently in the current debate on National Service and "naturally he had many hard things to say against Germany," but Daisy considered Lord Roberts an important link in "pursuing my policy of always trying to bring together leading men in every country." In her reply to his letter, Daisy invited Lord Roberts to Fürstenstein

---

62 *The Times*, September 23, 1938.

to come to us to a short visit in autumn. ... It will only be a small shooting party in November. Besides, the Emperor would like to sit with you in a small corner and talk. Indeed, the more one knows him, the more one realizes how he likes peace, not only in a room to make conversation, but amongst the nations of the world. He will be interested about current affairs in England ... and, at the present moment, must be very sarcastic at the terrible state of things. ...[63]

One person in whose influence Daisy placed her highest hopes during these last weeks of peace was her friend Prince Karl Max von Lichnowsky, who had succeeded Baron Marschall von Bieberstein as German Ambassador in London in 1912. Lichnowsky had previously served in the German diplomatic service, but in 1904 he had decided to leave the Foreign Office in order to administer his vast estates he had inherited from his father that were located in Bohemia, just across the border from Pless. Thus, Lichnowsky had become a close neighbour and friend of Hans and Daisy; his castle at Kuchelna was only a short hour's drive from their home.

Over the years, Daisy and Lichnowsky had exchanged many political and social views. They were both concerned about the desperate situation of the rural proletariat in this remote corner of Prussian Upper Silesia and Austrian Silesia. Daisy respected Lichnowsky highly not only as a personal friend, but also as the first landowner in the Habsburg monarchy to introduce a land reform on his estate.

Lichnowsky's sudden return to public service had raised a good deal of speculation in diplomatic circles. It was generally assumed that his recall to the Foreign Office was to please the Polish nobility in the Province of Posen, which Daisy thought ridiculous since "although of Polish extraction, Lichnowsky hates the Poles and works with the government against them." For Daisy, who had long appreciated his European perspective, Lichnowsky's appointment as ambassador in London was nothing but a good omen. Soon after his arrival in London, Daisy wrote to Hans about how highly the King spoke of Lichnowsky and how well the new ambassador was received by the diplomatic community. She was a little concerned though, about the ambassador's wife, an artistic, slightly eccentric personality:

> Princess Lichnowsky ... is handsome, I think, and I like her; but I know all the Court people won't. They will think her rude because she is almost too natural and she doesn't care a hang for anyone or anything.[64]

---

63 DPH, p. 274.
64 BLU, p. 240.

Lichnowsky was "absolutely un-Prussian," of a harmonious nature, and always tactful and diplomatic; in other words, the ideal ambassador for whom Daisy had always wished. A very positive relationship, based on mutual respect, had also developed between Prince Lichnowsky and Sir Edward Grey which, however, remained on a personal level and was, unfortunately, much overrated in its political implications by Lichnowsky himself; something he realized too late. Long before, the always observant Daisy had already realized that Lichnowsky had the dangerous tendency to interpret Grey's personal friendship with him as an indicator of his feelings towards Germany. She tried her best, especially after her return to London in June 1914, to convince Lichnowsky to see things her way, but he remained unconvinced, even though he usually held Daisy's opinion in high regard.[65]

Daisy also had the strong impression that Lichnowsky was on purpose ignored by his German superiors. She strongly suggested that he approach the Emperor directly and seek his help for the best of Germany and of peace. However, the Emperor was not in Germany. Although so deeply convinced of England's sinister design against him, he absented himself from Berlin during these last weeks of peace. Far removed from the centres of decision-making, the Emperor sailed along the Norwegian coast, all the time adhering to his traditional routine of a carefree life and entertainment on board the Imperial yacht. For his absence from Germany at this crucial time, the Emperor has been widely criticized. Later, the Emperor placed considerable blame on the Foreign Office and on his chancellor who had encouraged him to embark on his annual cruise while peace was clearly at peril. It also remains an enigma why he was not routinely supplied by the Foreign Office with all the confidential reports on the changing situation, or why he did not insist on receiving such information. The Emperor himself reported in his memoirs that

---

65 Much later, on January 30, 1916, Daisy reported about Lichnowsky's upsetting visit at her house in Munich: "To talk to poor Prince Lichnowsky last night was really sad; and to see him again as I did at tea to-day. He is frightfully depressed, feeling that the Emperor and others blame him for the war between England and Germany. He seems to think still that because they were so nice to him and his wife Mechthilde in London that it meant that the political feeling against Germany had absolutely died. I cannot quite think this is so. ..." The Emperor could never forgive Lichnowsky for what he saw as faulty judgment and blind faith in his English friends. But Sir Edward Grey wrote that "had Lichnowsky continued to be the trusted representative of his government, had they dealt frankly with him, and through him, with us, after the murder of the Archduke, war might have been avoided."

I received only meager news from the Foreign Office and was obliged to rely principally on Norwegian newspapers, from which I got the impression that the situation was growing worse. I telegraphed repeatedly to the Chancellor and the Foreign Office ... but was asked each time not to interrupt my journey. ... But when I learned from the Norwegian newspapers – not from Berlin about the Austrian ultimatum to Serbia, and immediately thereafter, about the Serbian note to Austria, I started without further ado my return journey.[66]

Whether the Emperor maintained close communication with Berlin or not, his pursuit of pleasure, sailing in the North Sea, remains somehow congruent not only with his personality, but also with the strange, ambiguous mood of these days. On the one hand, daily life seemed determined by an almost compulsive denial of any risk of war while, on the other hand, events, reactions, and political decisions seemed to herald the outbreak of hostilities almost any day. Survivors remember the exceptionally beautiful, serene summer of 1914, when Germany seemed at the height of her prosperity, and people were almost frantically enjoying life hour-by-hour in the face of impending disaster.

Daisy enunciated the reality and ambiguity of this last brief period of peace in the old, never-to-return Europe as

the most brilliant and prosperous of modern times, and yet anyone in the least behind the scenes was uneasy. ... As Algernon Blackwood has somewhere said: 'Everywhere behind the fun lay the fear.' ...This feeling of apprehension grew. ... In spite – perhaps because of – this haunting foreboding, people, driven by some fiendish, overmastering fate, went on with their business, making money and amusing themselves; it was almost as if they dared not to stop to look or listen.[67]

On June 28, 1914, the world received the news of the assassination of the Archduke Franz Ferdinand and his wife in Sarajevo. For Daisy, this was

the moment I had so long dreaded, the fatal moment when diplomacy, reason and common sense abdicated their natural functions had arrived. The time for words had passed, and the earthquake action of war was at hand. ... And being an Englishwoman married to a German in a foreign country![68]

---

66 *The Kaiser's Memoirs – Wilhelm II, Emperor of Germany*, translated by Thomas R. Ybarra (New York and London, 1922), p. 246.

67 DPH, p. 266.

68 DPP, p. 301.

There was no point writing to Hans, Daisy concluded. For years, he had casually accepted the inevitability of war between Germany and England. Only recently, he had shocked her brother George with his matter of fact statement that "you cannot have two top dogs in one kennel."[69]

* * *

Bad news followed each other; Daisy and Lichnowsky still hoped that at least between England and Germany, war could be prevented, even though on the Balkan, events seemed irreversibly out of control. The Austrian ultimatum transmitted to Belgrade on July 23, requested that Serbia cease all propaganda and action against Austria-Hungary's territory and immediately proceed with legal action against the assassins of Sarajevo. On July 25, Russia declared her support of Serbia in the event of an Austrian invasion and simultaneously announced the partial mobilization of her forces. Russia's sympathetic attitude provided sufficient encouragement for Serbia to respond to the Austrian ultimatum in a vague fashion; and in the evening of the same day, Austria and Serbia broke off diplomatic relations and proclaimed full mobilization. Last minute attempts at conciliation by Berlin and London failed and, on July 28, Austria declared war on Serbia.

What happened within the next forty-eight hours illustrates the dramatic disintegration of mutual loyalty thought to rest firmly in the hands of the three Emperors. On July 29, the total mobilization of Russian armies to which Czar Nicholas II had reluctantly agreed, was reduced by the Czar to a state of partial mobilization in response to an urgent telegram from the German Emperor, who hoped that German conciliation might avert a European war. One day later, the Russian foreign minister Sazonow persuaded the Czar to re-authorize full-scale mobilization – it had never been stopped by the general staff anyway – which resulted in a telegram sent by the German Chief of Staff Generalfeldmarschall von Moltke to his Austrian counterpart Conrad von Hötzendorf requesting that Austria fully mobilize against Russia. Moltke gave his assurance that Germany's full mobilization was also imminent. Dispatched without the knowledge of either the Emperor or the German Chancellor, this fateful telegram had far reaching consequences, because Moltke's action contributed significantly to Austria's decision to proceed with military action against Serbia. Within twelve hours, on July 31, "der Zustand drohender Kriegsgefahr"[70] was proclaimed by Germany; two

---

69 See George Cornwallis-West, op. cit., p. 237.

70 "the state of threatening danger of war."

ultimatums were dispatched, one to Russia threatening German mobilization, and the other to France requesting assurance that France would remain neutral in the event of German-Russian hostilities. Russia was given twelve hours to respond to the German ultimatum, while France's response was expected within eighteen hours.

On August 1, Germany declared war against Russia; on the following day, German troops occupied Luxemburg; on August 3, Germany declared war against France. Since Germany's strategy against France, based on the plan of General Schlieffen, involved the invasion of France via Belgian territory, urgent negotiations were held with Belgium requesting the country's benevolent neutrality during the crossing of the German armies. When Belgium refused, German troops entered the country as hostile forces on the first day of Germany's war with France. It was a question of time, how long England would stand aside, after Germany's violation of Belgium's neutrality had become a fait accompli.

Daisy saw the swiftness of events overpowering any hope of retaining peace even if only in some parts of Europe. Only one day before Germany's declaration of war against Russia, and only three days before her troops crossed the Belgian frontier on their march into France, Daisy had lunched with the French Ambassador Paul Cambon, who "thought that Austria and Serbia would fight it out alone and no general European crisis would arise."[71] From the first day of August, however, Daisy could only put her hopes into England and Lichnowsky, who with his daily visits to Sir Edward Grey and the increasing number of telegrams fired off to Berlin, desperately tried to defuse the reasons that could force England into war against Germany.

Daisy visited the German Embassy at least once every day and listened to Lichnowsky's hope after he had sent a positive message to Berlin, and his despair when as an answer only a vague reply arrived from Germany. What Daisy witnessed with a sense of foreboding is reflected in the numerous telegrams forwarded by Lichnowsky to the German Foreign Office every day, from July 24 on, which, in the end were dispatched almost every other hour.[72]

TO THE FOREIGN OFFICE,
LONDON, 24th July, 1914
Sir Edward Grey has just sent for me. The Minister was obviously deeply

---

71 DPH, p. 275.

72 Lichnowsky's telegrams quoted on the following pages are excerpted, rather than given in their original length.

affected by the Austrian Note,[73] which in his opinion went beyond anything of the kind he had ever seen. ... The danger of a European war would become imminent should Austria *invade Serbian territory*. The results of such a war between *four* nations ... were absolutely incalculable. However the affair might end ... Revolutionary movements such as those of the year 1848 would follow as a consequence. ... He told me he would be prepared to join with us as *a way out might then perhaps be found*. ... England, Germany, France and Italy, should ... mediate between Russia and Austria. This proposal, too, he requested me to submit to Your Excellency. The Minister is obviously trying to do everything to avoid European complications.
LICHNOWSKY.[74]

TO THE FOREIGN OFFICE.
LONDON, 25th July, 1914
Here, too, the view is general that ... we share Austria's moral responsibility. ... Unless we participate in the mediatory action, all confidence in us and in our peaceful intentions will be shattered here for good and all.
LICHNOWSKY[75]

TO THE FOREIGN OFFICE
LONDON, 25th July, 1914
Would urgently advise not to refuse Sir Edward Grey's proposal with regard to extension of time limit, as otherwise we will be reproached here with having left nothing untried for the maintenance of peace. An attitude of refusal might greatly influence England's future conduct.
LICHNOWSKY.[76]

TO THE FOREIGN OFFICE LONDON, 25th July 1914
PRIVATE FOR THE SECRETARY OF STATE VON JAGOW
I should like to call your attention once more to the importance of Grey's proposal of a mediation by the Four Powers between Austria and Russia. I see in this proposal the only possibility of avoiding a World War. ... If we decline, Grey, too, will make no further move. ... I do not think that England could possibly remain disinterested should France be drawn in. Once more urgently advise the acceptance of the English proposal and that this be announced in Vienna and St. Petersburg.
LICHNOWSKY.[77]

---

73   Austria's ultimatum of July 23 to Serbia requesting a reply within 48 hours.
74   Karl Max Fürst von Lichnowsky, *Into the Abyss – Reminiscences by Prince Lichnowsky*, (New York,1928), p. 391.
75   Ibid., pp.391.
76   Ibid., p. 392.
77   Ibid., p. 393.

TO THE FOREIGN OFFICE
LONDON, 25th July, 1914
Have just seen Sir Edward Grey and have spoken as suggested in Telegram
169. ...Without our co-operation, he said, all attempts at mediation would
be hopeless, and he could not approach Russia and Austria alone. ... He
wanted therefore to go hand in hand with us ... he hoped that by our joint
mediation ... an Austro-Russian war might be averted

I regard it as my duty to point out to Your Excellency that the British
Government will ... strive to maintain as friendly and impartial an attitude
as possible towards us, so long as it believes in our sincere desire for peace
and in our endeavour to go hand in hand with England in trying to ward
off the threatening European storm. The rejection of this proposal ... or a
brusque attitude would probably have the result of driving England unconditionally to side with France and Russia.
LICHNOWSKY.[78]

TO THE FOREIGN OFFICE
LONDON, 25th July 1914
Have just received the following letter from Sir Edward Grey in his own
handwriting: 'I enclose a forecast that I have received of the Serbian reply.
It seems to be that it ought to produce a favourable impression in Vienna
... if the Serbian reply ... corresponds to this forecast, the German Government may feel able to influence the Austrian Government to take a
favourable view of it.'
LICHNOWSKY.[79]

TO THE FOREIGN OFFICE
LONDON, 25th July, 1914
Supplement to Telegram No. 16. – Telegram from Mr. Crackanthorpe,
Belgrade, 25th July, 1914. 'Council of Ministers ... reply to Austrian Note
... will be drawn up in most conciliatory terms and will, in as large a measure
as possible, meet Austrian demands.'
LICHNOWSKY.[80]

TO THE FOREIGN OFFICE
LONDON, 25th July, 1914
Prince Henry requests me to report to Your Excellency that His Majesty the
King has expressed to him his keen desire that Britain and Germany acting
together, with the assistance of France and Italy, may in the interest of peace
succeed in keeping the exceedingly grave situation in hand.
LICHNOWSKY.[81]

---

78 Ibid., pp. 393-94.
79 Ibid., pp. 395.
80 Ibid., p. 396.

TO THE FOREIGN OFFICE
LONDON, 26th July, 1914
Since publication Austrian demands here, no one any longer believes in possibility of localizing conflict ... from this sort of procedure on part of Austria world war must result. Consider moment come to inaugurate mediation along lines suggested by Sir Edward Grey.
LICHNOWSKY.[82]

TO THE FOREIGN OFFICE
LONDON, 26th July, 1914
Have just had a conversation with Sir A. Nicholson and Sir W. Tyrrell. ... Both gentlemen see in ... conference *à quatre* here the only possibility of avoiding a general war. ...

I should like to utter an urgent warning against continuing to believe in the possibility of localizing the conflict. ... the German people has nothing to gain and everything to lose.
LICHNOWSKY.[83]

TO THE FOREIGN OFFICE
LONDON, 27th July 1914
Sir Edward Grey... was now turning to us ... with the request that we should use our influence in Vienna.

I found the Minister in a depressed mood for the first time. ... people here see in Austria's procedure every sign of evil intent. Everybody here is convinced ... that the key to the situation is to be found in Berlin ... to restrain Austria from, as Sir Edward Grey puts it, pursuing a foolhardy policy.
LICHNOWSKY.[84]

TO THE FOREIGN OFFICE
LONDON, 27th July, 1914
Should therefore Austria's intention to make use of the present opportunity 'to crush Serbia,' as Sir Edward Grey puts it, become more and more apparent, England will of this I am convinced place herself unconditionally at the side of France and Russia. ... If under these circumstances it should come to war, we shall England have against us.
LICHNOWSKY [85]

---

81 Ibid., p. 397.
82 Ibid., pp. 397-98.
83 Ibid., p. 398.
84 Ibid., p. 400.
85 Ibid., pp. 400-401.

TO THE FOREIGN OFFICE
LONDON, 28th July, 1914
Count Mensdorff[86] ... never made the slightest attempt to conceal the fact
that Austria's sole concern was to overthrow Serbia and that the Note was
intentionally so drafted that it would have to be rejected.
LICHNOWSKY.[87]

TO THE FOREIGN OFFICE
LONDON, 29th July 1914
Sir Edward Grey ... communicated to me a telegram from Sir George
Buchanan according to which ... Russia found herself obliged to regard the
violation of Serbia's territory by Austrian troops as a *casus belli.*
LICHNOWSKY.[88]

TO THE FOREIGN OFFICE
LONDON, 29th July, 1914
Sir Edward Grey ... received me with the words that the situation was
growing more and more acute, Sazonov ... now that war had been declared
... had requested them here again to *take up mediatory efforts.* ... Sir Edward
Grey repeated that we should take part in a mediation *à quatre.* ...

Sir Edward Grey then told me ... that as long as the conflict was confined
to Austria and Russia, it[England] could stand aside, but if we and France
were drawn in ... the British Government would then be forced to make up
its mind very quickly.
LICHNOWSKY.[89]

On July 30, Lichnowsky sent seven telegrams to Berlin, three cables
on the 31and eight on August 1. On the following day, the fourth of ten
telegrams dispatched this day, reads as follows:

TO THE FOREIGN OFFICE
LONDON, 2nd August 1914
The question whether or not we violate Belgian territory in the war with
France will probably decide whether England is to remain neutral or not.
My impression on this point is strengthened not only by Sir Edward Grey's
remarks ... also by ... the British Press. Should we violate Belgian neutrality
and should a war against Belgium ensue, I believe the government will no
longer be able to remain neutral in the face of the storm. ... Public opinion

---

86   The Russian Ambassador.
87   Ibid., p. 402.
88   Ibid., p. 404.
89   Ibid., pp. 404-05.

here has been aroused. Should we on the other hand respect Belgian neutrality, there is still a possibility of England's remaining neutral. LICHNOWSKY.[90]

TO THE FOREIGN OFFICE
LONDON, 3rd August 1914
The Minister [Sir Edward Grey] appeared to be very much put out and indicated that England would not be able to take so calmly the violation of Belgian neutrality, which she had expressly guaranteed. ... I repeat that they would like to remain neutral and are counting on our support in order to be able to do so.
LICHNOWSKY.[91]

TO THE FOREIGN OFFICE
LONDON, 4th August, 1914
Sir E. Grey's speech ... I am compelled to modify my view I took yesterday. ... I do not now believe that we can reckon much longer with the neutrality of Great Britain.

I do not see ... how the British Government could draw back unless we ... evacuate Belgian territory in the very shortest period. We have accordingly to reckon with the hostility of England ...

The news ... of the invasion of Belgium by German troops provoked a complete reversal of public opinion to our disadvantage.
LICHNOWSKY.[92]

TO THE FOREIGN OFFICE
LONDON, 4th August, 1914
Conversation with Sir W. Tyrrell confirms my impression that after receiving the news of serious German-Belgian collisions, continuation of English neutrality can no longer be counted on and that a rupture of relations is imminent.
LICHNOWSKY.[93]

These telegrams were only part of the forty-one dispatches forwarded by Lichnowsky to the Foreign Office in Berlin within the short span of twelve days, between July 24 and August 4, 1914. Several cables indicate that they had not received a reply. This meant that too often, the embarassed Lichnowsky had to come with empty hands to see Sir

---

90   Ibid., pp. 419-20.
91   Ibid., p. 423.
92   Ibid., p. 425.
93   Ibid., p. 426.

Edward Grey during his daily meetings. After he finally had given up all hope, Lichnowsky received a cable from Berlin instructing him to advise Sir Edward Grey that "Germany's disregard of Belgian neutrality was a question of life and death." At this late hour, Lichnowsky could not but feel that events had passed the point of return. When learning of Germany's invasion of Belgium, Prime Minister Asquith exclaimed "this simplifies matters." Two days earlier, Sir Edward Grey had explained England's dilemma to Lichnowsky:

> If, in a crisis like this, we run away from those obligations of honour and interest as regards the Belgian Treaty, I doubt whatever material forces we might have at the end would be of very much value in the face of the respect that we should have lost.[94]

On the evening of August 4, the day of England's entry into the war, Sir Edward Grey watched from his window the lights being lit along The Mall. To his visitor Mr. Spender, the editor of the *Westminster Gazette*, he remarked "the lamps are going out all over Europe; we shall not see them lit again in our lifetime. ..."[95]

England's entry into the war was followed by declarations of war on Russia by Austria, on Germany by Serbia, and on Austria by France and England. Over the course of two weeks, Lichnowsky's prophecy began rapidly to fulfill itself: the initial conflict between Serbia and Austria widened into a European war involving all major powers, to be followed by the smaller powers, as the war proceeded towards becoming a world-wide conflict from which few countries, victorious or vanquished, would emerge unchanged.

Lloyd George wrote a few years later:

> Nobody wanted war, "but ... there was no arresting voice anywhere to call a halt; no dominating personality to enforce attention or offer acceptable guidance amidst the chaos. The world was exceptionally unfortunate in the quality of its counsellours in this terrible emergency. Had there been a Bismarck in Germany or a Palmerston or Disraeli in Britain, a Roosevelt in America, or a Clémenceau in authority in Paris, the catastrophe might, and I believe would, have been averted." The men in power "were all able, experienced and conscientious and respectable mariners, but distinctly lacking in force, vision, imagination and resource which alone could have

---

94   Ibid., p. 427.

95   Edward F. Willis, *Prince Lichnowsky, Ambassador of Peace – A study in Prewar Diplomacy 1912-1914* (Berkeley, 1942), p. 284.

saved the situation. They were all handy men in a well-behaved sea, but helpless in a typhoon."[96]

* * *

On August 4, 1914, a long chapter in the history of German-English friendship came to an end; for some it seemed if not forever, at least for a long time. How conscious people were of this event, how much regret there was, manifested itself in the extraordinary preparations of the British government for the departure of the German Ambassador. For-ever memorable were those last hours with the special farewell extended to Prince Lichnowsky, which signified the remembrance of happier years of friendship and respect between the two countries. Deeply moved, Prince Lichnowsky wrote how

> after the declaration of war, and before my departure, I went to see Sir Edward Grey at his special wish, to say Good-bye. On this occasion the Minister gave me to understand that England had hoped that the war might be over as quickly as possible, and said that he would always be ready to mediate in the event of our not achieving the successes we hoped for. 'We don't want to crush Germany,' were his words.[97]

When he returned to the embassy, Lichnowsky found Sir Frederick Ponsonby waiting "who came to express His Majesty's regrets that he could not receive the Ambassador to say Good-bye."[98]

Among those hurrying to the German Embassy was Daisy, who had run into Mechthilde Lichnowsky "walking around St. James Park with tears streaming down her face."[99] Like a symbol for the rapid political developments, Daisy observed the workmen busy with removing the German insignia and the German Imperial Eagle above the door of the embassy. And in the hall, "poor Prince Lichnowsky, terribly distressed and pale ... said to me with his two hands stretched out: 'Just look how things are after all I have done!"[100]

Within days, the German diplomatic corps left London, and the large embassy building stood empty. The British Government was ex-tremely solicitous

---

96 Ibid., p. 285.

97 See Karl Max Prince Lichnowsky, op. cit., pp. 15-16.

98 See Edward F. Willis, op. cit., p. 288.

99 DPH, p. 278.

100 DPH, p. 276.

of the welfare of the German Ambassador and his staff. The First Lord of the Admiralty, Winston Churchill, was entrusted with the duty of making all arrangements for their departure. He sent his Naval Secretary, Rear Admiral Hood, to enquire the Ambassador's wishes. ... A special train would convey them to Harwich where they would embark on the steamship *St. Petersburg*, placed at the Ambassador's disposal by the Admiralty. ... At Harwich a special guard of honour stood drawn up for Prince Lichnowsky. Besides Rear Admiral Hood, Sir Edward Grey had sent his Assistant Private Secretary. ... They formed an escort for the Prince and Princess Lichnowsky, Dr. and Mrs. Kühlmann, the Embassy Staff, and about two-hundred-and-fifty Germans accompanying them. ... Soldiers and sailors presented arms, and lined the streets, and in the Ambassador's words, 'he was treated like a departing sovereign.'[101]

This moving farewell was like a requiem to the dying chivalry and decency of Europe, never to be repeated on like occasions.

Deeply touched by these last great gestures, Lichnowsky dispatched a telegram to Sir Edward Grey upon the German party's arrival at Hoek van Holland. "Please express to His Majesty and His Government our sincere thanks for the great courtesy shown to us during our journey."[102] No such courtesy awaited the German Ambassador in Berlin. Angrily, Lichnowsky wrote that

as soon as I arrived in Berlin, I saw that I was to be made the scapegoat for the catastrophe for which, despite my advice and warnings, our Government had made itself responsible.[103]

Worse disappointment had been waiting for Daisy in Germany on July 31. She had, with true regret, declined Lichnowsky's offer to wait for a few more days and join the party of German diplomats leaving for Germany on August 4. Daisy was anxious to be reunited with Hans and her three boys as quickly as possible. The "charming little house in Savile Row" which she had occupied since June, felt like a trap. Only a telegram from Hans to advise of the travel arrangements he had made would free her. However, there was no sign from Hans as yet. Daisy decided to make her own arrangements, joining the crowds of German citizens that beleaguered the offices of the German steamship companies. She was fortunate to get a passage to Bremerhaven, but when she sent Schulz, her German chauffeur, to pick up the travel papers on July 27, he was

---

101 See Edward F. Willis, op. cit., pp. 288-89.

102 *The Times*, August 7, 1914.

103 See Karl Max Prince Lichnowsky, op. cit., p. 78.

advised that the earlier boat that Daisy had hoped to take for Germany had never left Bremerhaven. The excited clerk also confided to Schulz that even the luxury liner *Imperator* had, by orders from Berlin, already returned from Southampton to Bremerhaven, instead of continuing her regular route to New York! There would be no earlier passage available to Germany than the boat she had booked for July 31.

Unexpectedly, there was time for one last visit to Newlands. The terraces and their flowerbeds were in full bloom; the lake looked golden in the late afternoon sun. Daisy did her best to act cheerfully in the presence of her elderly parents. The train bringing her back to London was almost empty; she was the lone passenger in her compartment. Tearfully, she realized that she might never see her 82- year-old, already so frail *Poppets* again. Holding the diary on her knees in the rocking train, Daisy wrote

> It is really strange and sad to think that everything I prophesied has come true; I told Hans six years ago not to build at Fürstenstein, as there would be war.[104]

On July 30, Daisy obtained a laissez-passer at the German Embassy and said good-bye to Prince Lichnowsky and his wife. They all had tears in their eyes. The rest of the somber day was spent with George and Shelagh. There was still no telegram from Hans; no reply to her cable announcing her arrival in Berlin on August 1. In the evening before her departure, Daisy experienced a brief moment of exhilaration that turned into a shattering realization.

> The night before I left (Friday), a telegram came at eight-thirty to say the motor car with Schulz the chauffeur was to return to Germany at once. I was very surprised that no message came for me. It was one of those surprises one remembers all one's life.[105]

Hoping against hope that a separate personal message from Hans for her might have been lost, Daisy embarked on her return journey to Germany, sharing the overcrowded ferry and the train to Berlin with anxious, downcast Germans and Austrians. But there was no one waiting for her at the train station in Berlin, and "there was still no message for me at the station, and I had no idea where Hans was."[106]

---

104 DPP, p. 303.

105 DPP, p. 304.

106 DPP, p. 304.

The German capital seemed in chaos; streets and railway stations were overflowing with thousands of foreigners trying to leave Germany at the last minute. Leaving her entourage and her luggage behind, Daisy managed to commandeer a cab by pushing herself next to the driver and "putting two marks in his hand." But at the *Hotel Bristol,* no one seemed to know where Hans might be. Only next morning did Daisy find out that Hans and Hansel were now staying at the regimental headquarters in Potsdam. Daisy suffered through the hour-long ride to Potsdam, agonizing over all the possibilities that might have prevented Hans from meeting her at the train.

Another brief, unemotional entry in Daisy's diary signalled the beginning of a new, different stage in her marriage:

> I ... went ... to Hans's Regimental Barracks and saw our motor car waiting at the gates. I found them both at lunch, very surprised and not pleased to see me. ... *I shall never know all my life if Hans really wanted me to remain in England or to come back to Germany!*[107]

Much to the anger of Hans, who wanted her to return to Fürstenstein immediately, Daisy decided that "for the next few days I shall move nowhere!" And one more time, Daisy tried to influence the course of events. In the morning of August 3, she dispatched a telegram to King George. England had not yet declared war on Germany and, in typical telegraph style, slightly mutilated in transmission, Daisy implored the King in urgent words to take action before it was too late:

AUGUST 3rd, 1914, GIVEN AT BERLIN AT 9:48 AM – RECEIVED AT PALACE AT 9:53 AM – SENT OUT FOR DELIVERY AT 9:54
Private to His Majesty the King – Buckingham Palace England

Have arrived here – Germany asks what England will do as in England all wondered if Germany could produce peace in Europe – Sire Your Majesty drop parliament's advice or the fullfillment of promises made – hold England yourself as King of a great Empire – join now with Germany – drop a friendship that brings disaster to all Europe – let all the world look up to you now as peacemaker and benefactor to cease a war & bring magnificent power & grand peace to great nations for future power and protection against all evil and grave danger – Italy has retracted – Europe is past the time to accept politeness & expect fullfilled promises – England wants her King to stand out firmly on all points – do it Sire – I beg you to forget the word constitutional monarch – speak for yourself – England and all Europe

---

107 DPP, p. 305. Original partly in italics.

will listen and thank God – may he bless you.
Obediently Daisy Pless.[108]

In the early afternoon of the same day, Daisy sent a second cable to the King. The deteriorating situation is reflected in the extra time required for its transmission, compared to the morning when Daisy had dispatched her first cable to the King. In the meantime, orders had been received that all telegrams to foreign countries must now be dispatched in German only. Censorship had also begun its reign!

GIVEN AT BERLIN AT 2:18 PM – RECEIVED AT PALACE 3:57 PM – SENT OUT FOR DELIVERY 3:58.
Private – His Majesty the King – England Buckingham Palace.

Majesty – all telegrams must now be sent to England in German. England cannot imagine what war means – I do not have servants or horses anymore – For the love of God & everything that is good I ask Your Majesty to abandon a treaty which cannot bring anything good – only blood and devastation of all nations – I ask you to move away from Russia – Italy is remaining quiet – Your Majesty please remain now and forever at Germany's side so that all Europe may be protected – England & Germany would find ways to co-operate – What do ministers in office know about these big questions – Europe would forever be grateful to you – Constantinopel & the Dardanelles would fall to England – India would be under strong protection – A German word is always true – I do not speak in ignorance – will soon serve with the Red Cross – I am asking Your Majesty to believe me – I personally know more than the present Ambassador – If between the two countries there is something to forgive one must not remember such matters in such grave times – I am writing not in ignorance – England and Germany should determine the fate of all Europe – May God protect Your Majesty - Daisy Pless.[109]

Aside from the urgent appeal to the monarch to save the peace, this passionate message, overflowing with emotions, also contained some remarkable challenges. Aside from her fear about her personal future, Daisy's horror of war drove her to extremes of warnings and suggestions. Only liberation from the chains of present treaties would open the path for England to save the peace in Europe in concert with Germany; and only success in maintaining peace would secure the British Empire and satisfy Germany in its aspirations in Europe, securely under control through its friendship with England. No one except His Majesty would

---

108 Courtesy, Royal Archives, Windsor Castle.
109 translated by the author. Courtesy, Royal Archives, Windsor Castle.

be able to accomplish this, and only by courageously transgressing the constitutional limitations placed on the monarchy. What Daisy challenged the King to do was nothing less than to commit a coup d'état!

One might want to take Daisy's appeal to the King seriously – her mistrust and lack of belief in the competence of politicians was certainly born out by later events. One might look at Daisy's missive to the King as the emotional outburst of a woman despairing at her personal fate during the coming times of war. But it might not be fair to Daisy to ridicule her lonely appeal to the King. After all, as Lloyd George later deplored, during these days, no one in Europe seemed to have possessed the will-power and determination to attempt to save Europe from this catastrophe.

Daisy's oldest son Hansel remembered his mother's prophetic words on August 4, 1914 when the fourteen-year-old impatiently waited for the day to enter the German army as a volunteer: "The end of this terrible war will find most of Europe's rulers swept from their thrones!"[110]

* * * * * *

---

110 In conversation with the author.

9 | *Sister Daisy of the Red Cross*

I *nspite of my varied interests and occupations, I sometimes feel terribly lonely. Not the loneliness of being alone, but the loneliness of being one in a crowd in a country where everyone's sympathies and opinions are so terribly in opposition to my own. I sometimes feel fairly rent in two, between love of my family and native land, and love and loyalty to my husband and his country for his sake.*[1]

Princess Evelyn Blücher, August 1914.

* * *

With these words, the Princess Blücher described her emotions to her friend Daisy of Pless on August 10, 1914. The two women were on their way to attend a lecture at the Army Reserve Hospital II in Berlin-Tempelhof. Like Daisy, the Princess Blücher was an Englishwoman married to a Prussian nobleman. The Blücher estate at Krieblowitz[2] was only an hour's drive from Fürstenstein. Now, during the second week of the war, she felt she "must take up some work, for this passive waiting is too much for my nerves. So I have been to see Princess Pless about Red Cross work."[3] Thanks to the "good offices" of the Emperor's brother Prince August Wilhelm, Daisy had already been working for several days as an auxiliary nurse at the Tempelhof hospital. She thought it best to enroll her friend, the Princess Blücher, in a First Aid course.

---

1   Evelyn Princess Blücher, *An English Wife in Berlin (London, 1920), p. 195.*

2   Since 1945 Krobielowice.

3   See Evelyn Princess Blücher, op. cit., p. 196.

As with many ladies of the Prussian nobility, Daisy had spontaneously offered her services as a volunteer. Hans, who had already been transferred from Potsdam to the Imperial Headquarters as aide-de-camp to the Emperor, had been most insistent that Daisy return to Fürstenstein immediately despite the news from Fürstenstein and everywhere in Silesia that there was rising anti-English sentiment among the population.

Hans had decided, without consulting Daisy, that his oldest son would complete his education in Berlin. School was the last thing on Hansel's mind during these early days of the war. In the absence of his parents, Hansel had gone to Waldenburg on his own in order to enroll as a volunteer in the army. As Daisy wrote in her diary on August 6, 1914:

> As soon as Hans left Fürstenstein to come here to Berlin, the boy at once ran off. ... He wanted to join a Regiment and be a soldier. As he is only fourteen and a half of course they would not accept him; but I love the spirit of him, as it is just what I would have done if I had been a boy. In a way it is rather like what I have done now when they said I could not leave England, and I did. They also thought here of sending me back to Fürstenstein at once to do my jobs and play in the garden, instead of which I shall go off to the front as soon as possible as I can with the Red Cross![4]

The decision about where to give Hansel his education had been another source of friction. To her old friend, the former Ambassador Count Paul Wolff-Metternich, Daisy complained as a mother whose responsibility for her child has been removed from her:

> I am sorry to say poor Hansel instead of having been ALLOWED TO STAY in Silesia and study in Waldenburg at the Gymnasium ... he was ordered to stay in Berlin at the HOTEL BRISTOL with my mother-in-law; ... at least I *thought* I had a right to change it ... instead of that which would have been awful for a boy of that age next door to the vulgar streets, to at least stay in Potsdam with my sister-in-law and study there privately, as he is not allowed to go to the gymnasium here ... my husband thinks the son of a 'Fürst'[5] cannot do this!!!

> My mother-in-law never reads the papers or sees anybody. ... He never will know there is a war. In Silesia Hansel would have seen the men in the country to which his *name* belongs, going out to the front. ... *He is very intelligent and I am extremely sorry for him, but somehow this mark in his life is missed forever.* ... [6]

---

4   DPH, p. 277.

5   The son of a prince.

6   DPH, p. 276.

The war drastically changed the nature of Daisy's marriage. As with countless other men, Hans would see his wife only on rare days of leave. Interestingly, the enforced separation had a noticeably positive effect, especially on Hans, who all of a sudden seemed to care a lot about the welfare of his wife. For the next four years, Hans did his best to maintain as close a contact with Daisy as circumstances allowed; by letter, by cable, or by telephone. By their frequency, their intervals, and their content, Hans's letters took on a new character. There was genuine concern for how Daisy would manage to survive in a hostile environment, and much more frequent expression of feelings approaching love and admiration for Daisy. But Hans remained Hans in other ways: he composed long reports from bloody battles, which must have made Daisy's heart shiver; he was jubilant about the triumphs of the German armies; he did not appear to think much about how Daisy felt about her separation from her parents.

The mood in the country, though, forced Hans to be conscious of the sensitive, vulnerable position Daisy occupied. Partially to protect his wife from harm, partially to keep the name of his family out of the papers, he exhorted Daisy in each of his letters to exercise utmost discretion and caution, as the hatred against England rose to a fever pitch. All foreigners were suspected of acting as spies for their homeland, Hans wrote; and in Breslau, a number of foreigners had already been imprisoned. Daisy's impulsive nature made Hans especially anxious. He even thought her work at the Tempelhof hospital exposed her too much to the public eye. He again urged Daisy to leave Berlin. Daisy already felt persecuted by the public, and did not react kindly to Hans's sincere concern for her. "I have come to the conclusion that whenever I want to do anything I must just do it myself and ask no questions,"[7] she wrote in her diary.

Daisy had indeed never been so dependent on her own counsel before in her life. More than before, she seemed to stand in the limelight of the press. There was little to report about the glamour of life at court where the Princess of Pless was often the centre of attention. Instead, the papers turned their attention on the Princess of Pless as a spy in the service of her homeland and accused her of disloyalty towards her husband's country.

Nothing was further from the truth, but no matter how Daisy conducted herself, the Princess of Pless remained the subject of interest. What the public did not know was that Daisy felt less and less well. She was constantly worried about little Bolko's delicate health, and her

7   DPP, p. 306.

circulatory disturbances made walking more and more painful, a fact she hid successfully during her work as an auxiliary nurse. Emotionally, she was trying to solve her conflict of loyalty towards England and Germany.. The mistrust and suspicion she encountered, and the obsession with her English birth and her well-known close relationships with many members of the royal family did not fail to provoke strong, sometimes rebellious reactions in Daisy that she expressed in impulsive, defiant actions.

* * *

The burden of the war and its consequences for Daisy are evident in diaries she penned during those years. Daisy devoted half of her published diaries that she maintained between 1894 and 1918, to the four years of World War I. Her reminiscences and commentaries from the war years are remarkably rich – but also remarkably free of gossip and *klatsch*. Instead, they are composed of personal experiences, constant observations, commentaries, and fascinating correspondence, sufficient to fill the pages of an entire book.

So much happened in Daisy's life during these fateful years, that this chapter about *Sister Daisy of the Red Cross* has almost become a series of vignettes. Out of necessity to limit the length of this chapter, many significant events which critically touched upon Daisy's life had to be disregarded. Daisy wrote later,

> In August 1914, it was very hard to know what to do for the best. The natural thing to do would have been to go to Fürstenstein, turn it and the Hotel at Salzbrunn into Hospitals and, when I had got them going, to make my headquarters among our own people at Pless, do what I could for the wounded from the Russian front, and, generally, visit, encourage and give practical help to Hospitals and similar institutions in my own part of Silesia.
>
> I had no husband or near relative to advise me; moreover, Hans ... was averse to any large expenditure. ... Moreover, I soon learned that I was not wanted in Silesia, as it was too near the Eastern Front and already there were violent anti-English demonstrations in Breslau and elsewhere.[8]

Daisy knew what needed doing and what she could contribute, but without the support of Hans, who was stationed far away at the Imperial Headquarters, she felt incapable of facing the hostility she would encounter in Silesia from the provincial administration, from the military, and even from the Silesian noblewomen also engaged in the war effort, but in a different capacity from what she envisioned for herself. It seemed

---

8   DPP., p. 306.

best for her to remain at the Tempelhof hospital until her superior Professor Baron von Kuester had obtained permission for Daisy to work as an auxiliary nurse at the front.

In the meantime, the first letters from across the Channel arrived with the help of another Daisy, the Crown Princess of Sweden.[9] The first letter Daisy opened came from Ruthin:

THE CLOISTERS, RUTHIN, NORTH WALES,
August 24, 1914.

DEAR PRINCESS OF PLESS,

Mrs. West has just told me that it is now possible for letters to get through to you. I should like you to know that we are thinking of you here in Ruthin. We have special prayers in St. Peter's which include all those tending the sick and wounded either our own or others — as you are doing. ... It is difficult for us to realize it all here in peaceful little Ruthin but our sympathy with you in this hour of trial is very sincere. It seems only a few Sundays back since you were singing in dear old St. Peter's.
May God bless and keep you and yours,
Yours very sincerely,

LEWIN PRYCE, Warden of Ruthin.[10]

And Daisy's mother Patsy wrote:

My early morning letters just come in and one from you, my precious darling. It is censored. ... We are all well here ... Biddy[11] is wonderfully well; she comes to Newlands on the 24th and I go back with her to the hospital in La Touquet. ... George is so different and loves soldiering again. ... George's wife Stella made five hundred pounds for Biddy and her hospital by one matinee out in America. Daisy, do you know I like that woman; she is nice to me, which the other[12] never was. ...[13]

More letters came, many of them inquiries about the fate of the first British prisoners of war transported from the Western Front to Germany. Daisy also worried about George. An inquiry to the Imperial Headquarters produced no result; Hans could offer little hope:

---

9   There was no mail service between hostile nations, but letters still reached their destination via friends living in neutral countries.
10   Courtesy Mr. McGowan.
11   Daisy's sister Shelagh.
12   George's first wife Jennie (Churchill).
13   DPH, p. 314.

> The English force has been beaten three times. ... Lots of prisoners have already been made, but as they are sent at once to Germany and no names are taken ... it will be quite impossible to find out who is killed, wounded or made prisoner. ... I would advise you to write ... to some neutral Embassy and find out if George has gone to the front or not.[14]

In the middle of September 1914, Daisy committed a mistake the consequences of which would pursue her for the rest of the war.

Devoted to Daisy and an Anglophile himself, Fritz Hochberg[15] suggested that the two drive to the prisoner of war camp in Döberitz near Potsdam. Döberitz was the major army base near Berlin; it would have been unwise to go there at the best of times. However, with Daisy in her nurses' uniform riding in a car with the Hochberg coat-of-arms, passing the camp gates presented no difficulties.

> We passed a sentry at a gate and went into a big field where I saw a lot of men. I was in my Red Cross uniform, spoke to no one, did not even smile, and ... was hardly in the place ten minutes. ...Two days later my mother-in-law said: 'I hear you have been to see the English prisoners. ... Mitzie Ratibor[16] is furious and says she will take the Red Cross from you for having done such a thing.' I paid no attention ... there was much gossip ... amongst my friends and this I ignored until I heard the story had been carried to the Emperor. Then I wrote to Hans and told him everything.[17]

Within days, an outraged press published sensational reports: Wearing the uniform of a high-ranking Red Cross member, the Princess of Pless had entered the camp under false pretenses and was followed by a large lorry filled with hundreds of roast chickens, hundreds of pounds of chocolate, and packages of cigarettes. Without any guards nearby, the Princess was able to exchange vitally important information to be transmitted by her to England. There was no question, the Princess of Pless was actively spying for England.

On October 7, Hans informed Daisy about the storm the Döberitz affair had created at the Imperial Headquarters. He would advise the Emperor of what actually had happened. During the next few weeks, Hans, the Emperor, General von Plessen, General von Boehm, and General von Löbell were all occupied with the clarification of Daisy's conduct at Döberitz. General von Löbell had forwarded the report of his

---

14 DPH, p. 304.

15 Daisy's brother-in-law.

16 The Duchess of Ratibor.

17 DPH, pp. 293-94.

official inquiry to the Imperial Headquarters, which more or less stated what had been said in the press, but did not include a statement by the Princess of Pless. Hans was incensed and requested by urgent telegram an immediate declaration drawn up by an attorney and signed by Daisy stating

> 1. if you went to the camp with or without permission and, if with one, who gave it to you;
> 2. if you spoke to the prisoners and what;
> 3. if you gave them anything.[18]

An angry Daisy immediately dispatched a letter to General von Plessen:

> This Report is false from the beginning to the end. As what I have already repeatedly written is not believed I beg to request an Official Inquiry, in order that I may make a statement on oath, and be able to summon witnesses. I hope that a woman will not be refused what a man would be granted.[19]

The times, or at least General von Plessen, were not ready to grant to a woman what Daisy asked for. In a "suave" letter, General von Plessen advised Daisy that

> I most respectfully submit that you should leave to His Highness the Prince, your noble husband, the rectification of this affair ... and that you will allow him to undertake the representation and the defence of his noble wife.[20]

Daisy received Plessen's letter "as a slap in the face of a modern woman." Determined not to be "browbeaten," she asked her friend Prince Eitel Friedrich, the Emperor's brother, for his intercession.

The Prince assured her of his assistance, but begged Daisy to exercise the utmost discretion in all situations in her current life. It was no consolation that she received the same kind of message regarding her position in her homeland. From New York, Daisy's American friend Mrs. Davis, who had just returned from London, wrote about the storm of indignation Daisy's open letter to General Sir John Cowans had raised in the English press and even in some of the New York papers. As in the past years of imperiled peace, Daisy had decided once more to explain the two nations to one another hoping to smooth the waves of hatred

---

18 DPH, p. 297.
19 DPH, p. 298.
20 DPH, p. 299.

between England and Germany. Mrs. Davis urged Daisy to exercise extreme caution:

> A voice in London telling of German success and denying German atrocities was indeed a voice in the wilderness!

> No one wished to hear good of Germany, and every one urged me to tell you how impossible it would be even for you to think of returning to England. You and I who have known the calm, British nation could not believe it possible to arouse this bitter racial feeling against everything and every one German. It is bitter – bitter – venomous.[21]

George Cornwallis-West's biographer Eileen Quelch described the near-manic spy hysteria that gripped all of England. She described how Mrs. Cornwallis-West found herself among the victims of a hostile press, which claimed that she visited camps housing German prisoners of war every day, and that among friends and in public, she even boasted of having a German grandson, the child of an English mother, who in spite of his tender age of fourteen, already fought in the ranks of the German army.

And Hans wrote from the Imperial Headquarters:

> Of course your position is difficult, I mean, you must have feelings for both countries. ... I knew too, and have told you often (I remember that it always made you angry), that the war between Germany and England was sure to come sooner or later. ... And this war is not like a football match or a game of Bridge, when one shakes hands again after it is over. The hatred between the two countries will be immense, and last much longer than we will live. ... I don't tell you all that, darling, to make you sad, but to prepare you for the state of things, as they will be when the war is over.[22]

These were two letters, both extending sympathy to Daisy, but also confronting her with being a foreigner in a country at war with her homeland and, vice versa, of being away from her homeland during times of war and married to a citizen of a hostile country. Daisy felt misunderstood and attacked from all sides. In her dejection, she decided to return to what had helped her in past times of severe distress. She would try to help people in far deeper distress and danger than she was herself. While the Döberitz affair was still under investigation, Daisy travelled more or less clandestinely to a prisoner of war camp at Eisenach in Thuringia to bring English officers and soldiers news from their

---

21 DPH, pp. 301-33.
22 DPH, p. 304.

families. Fortunately, no one in Berlin found out, as the camp commander, First Lieutenant Brandis, the son of an Irish mother, was friendly and helpful and never reported Daisy's visit to his superiors.

When King Alfonso XIII of Spain enlisted Daisy's help, her network of friends and acquaintances all over Europe was most useful.Using the Spanish Embassy and other representatives of neutral countries in the German capital, Daisy worked with the Spanish King in the exchange of information and news between soldiers and civilians in countries belonging either to the Central Powers or the Allied side. Before Christmas 1914, Daisy had successfully assisted in the exchange of wounded or ill prisoners of war.

In November, Daisy finally received the anxiously awaited news from an obviously much relieved Hans, who for the first time in years wrote to his wife in a genuinely affectionate manner:

GROSSES HAUPTQUARTIER, November 11, 1914.
MY DARLING LITTLE DANY[23] WIFE,

At last I had a chance of talking the Döberitz affair over with the Emperor. He understood everything and told me to tell you so. There was never a question of my not believing what you or your friends wrote about it, but, as a report from Berlin was asked for, one had naturally to wait for it. Your declaration proves now that the official report is full of lies.[24]

Daisy's exoneration and intended rehabilitation, however, turned out to be a short-lived victory. Only two days after Hans's letter brought some relief, General von Boehm announced his visit at the Hotel Bristol. Forever cautious and convinced that her movements were observed and her letters censored, Daisy arranged for her friend Count Clement von Schönborn-Wiesentheid, the President of the Bavarian Red Cross to be present during the general's visit to her suite. General von Boehm advised that by "higher order ... the Princess of Pless must leave Berlin at once." The old general declined to give any reasons other than that the order was a consequence of Daisy's Döberitz affair and her voluminous correspondence with persons residing in hostile and neutral countries. General von Boehm presented Daisy with a written order which Daisy obeyed immediately, but only in her fashion.

---

23 Daisy's nickname as a child.
24 DPH, p. 303.

Nothing would induce me to leave Berlin. To show this I left the Hotel and moved into a furnished flat. ... I never showed fear, even if I felt it! What I did do was to sit down immediately and write to the Emperor.

YOUR MAJESTY, SIRE,
I thank Your Majesty for the wire received yesterday. I hold it in my hand now as comfort, but not to show it – as General von Boehm came to see me and calmly said there was an order that I had to leave Berlin at once and remain in Fürstenstein till the end of the war. ... I shall remain in Berlin until I receive an order from Your Majesty or the Empress. I have been all these years Your Majesty's true subject not only by marriage but in heart and in every word I have ever said or written before and since this war, and you know this, Sire. I care for nothing at this time; you can do with me what you wish, but nothing will induce me to leave Berlin where my children are, until these orders are confirmed.
I cannot be treated like a spy being oh! so truly honest, without an examination and reason given.

I await the orders of Your Majesty.

DAISY PLESS[25]

In Tempelhof, Professor Kuester had also received orders for the immediate dismissal of the Princess of Pless. While he had to obey this order, the sympathetic Professor Kuester at least permitted Daisy to enter his hospital as a private visitor and bring small gifts to his soldier patients. At her farewell tea, he presented her with a testimonial that Daisy afterwards carried with her personal papers like a treasure until the end of the war:

> Her Serene Highness the Princess Marie Therese of Pless, called *Sister Daisy*, has, during the months of September and October and part of November, been working in the outer department of the Reserve Lazarett, which is under my direction. With great sacrifice and love she has taken care of the wounded, and comforted and gladdened them by her cordial manner. Untiringly she endeavoured to cheer them up and to refresh them and to ease their sufferings. *Sister Daisy* may be called a benefactress in the truest meaning of the word. Professor Freiherr von Kuester.
> Berlin-Tempelhof. 15. 11. 1914.[26]

* * *

---

25   DPH, pp. 210-11.
26   DPH, p. 316.

Winter had arrived and the war showed no signs of coming to an end. The enthusiasm, which had accompanied the soldiers on their way to the front during the beautiful days of last August, when everyone seemed so sure that "by next Christmas we will all be united at home again," had begun to yield to a much more somber mood. The rapid advance of the German troops through Belgium into France, the constant announcements of one glorious victory after another, had given the people the hope that at least in France, the war would soon be over. But after the Battle of the Marne, which saved Paris from German siege or occupation, the stabilization of the Western Front signalled the beginning of bloody trench warfare.

The situation at the Eastern Front had been much more worrisome. While the population of Silesia was spared an invasion by Russian armies, vast areas of East Prussia had to be abandoned to the enemy soon after the start of hostilities. On August 22 1914, General Colonel von Beneckendorff und von Hindenburg had been called to the Eastern Front. After being victorious during the battles of Tannenberg and the Masurian Lakes, Hindenburg liberated East Prussia by the end of September.

In the southern section of the Eastern Front, the armies of Austria-Hungary were less successful. Lemberg[27], the capital of Austrian Galicia, was quickly occupied by the Russian armies that also laid siege to the strong fortress of Przemysl to the west of Lemberg. It required the support of the German Ninth Army to force a retreat of the Russian armies. At the same time, *the Russian steamroller* endangered the German provinces of Posen and Silesia. By Christmas 1914, the Eastern Front seemed frozen in trench war as well. All hope for a short, victorious war seemed crushed.

Adding to the disillusionment of the population was the unexpected neutrality maintained by the allied countries of Italy and Romania, which provoked the sarcastic comment of the Emperor in one of his notorious marginal notes that "hardly that the war has started, our allies are falling away from us like spoiled apples from a tree!"[28]

Daisy could not escape the somber, pessimistic mood of these days. After her forced dismissal from the Tempelhof hospital, she wrote

> My greatest grief was that I could no longer work at the Tempelhof Lazarett. ... The military party, which eventually ruined Germany, was doing its best to ruin little me. ... For the moment, the Emperor was still a power in the

27   After 1919 Lwów in Poland; after 1990 Lviv in Ukraine.
28   Karl Georg von Treutler, *Die graue Eminenz*, (Frankfurt, 1971), p. 131.

land. ... But the military had already determined to dominate everybody and everything. ...

At the beginning of the war, I started out with a threefold determination: Loyally to do my utmost for the country of my husband and my children by continuing my lifelong, sincere, efforts to do everything that might make for peace between England and Germany; and to nurse Germany's sick and wounded; and to do everything in my power for British and Allied prisoners.

Not until the beginning of 1915 did I begin clearly to realize the hatred, suspicion and jealousy which were directed towards me personally from all sides. ... It did not occur to me that people might hate me or doubt my loyalty. I closed my mind to the rights and wrongs of the nations and only saw the terrible suffering.

Perhaps ... I ought to have buried myself in obscurity. ... But that is not the way Englishwomen are made. It certainly was not the way Daisy Cornwallis-West was made, and long years of trying to be Daisy of Pless had not, I am afraid, modified her to any great extent.[29]

Too tired from the constant suspicion and the hostile attitude of the public towards her in Berlin, Daisy resolved "to escape it all." After a last tearful visit to the Tempelhof hospital, Daisy left Berlin with Lexel and Bolko for a peaceful Christmas 1914 in the quiet environment of Meran in the South Tyrol. In January 1915 she rented the little Villa Gibson in Partenkirchen in the Bavarian Alps, that "seemed an island of peace." But the newspapers sent from Berlin proved that the persecution by the press had not ended. An incredulous Daisy read the story that after the death of Mr. Todd, the Scottish head-gardener in Fürstenstein, she had ordered his remains to be transferred to England, but not before personally filling his coffin with highly confidential information about the movements planned for the German armies at the Western Front. A few days later, it was reported that the Princess of Pless had finally been imprisoned and, a few days later again, that because of her espionage activities, her husband had killed the Princess of Pless and committed suicide afterwards.

What could have been a ray of sunshine during these gloomy winter months caused new bitterness. For the first time since the beginning of the war, Daisy had received a letter calling her back to Silesia to sing at a charity concert in Waldenburg, but the letter arrived too late. Daisy was convinced, that the censor had held back the letter on purpose. It was too late to respond to the invitation. By the end of March, Hans had obtained permission for Daisy to come to Potsdam to attend Hansel's

---

29 DPH, pp. 319-22 passim.

confirmation. Afterwards, Hans, who planned to spend two days in Fürstenstein with Hansel, took Daisy back to Silesia. It was a glorious day of spring; it reminded Daisy of the days when she felt she could love Fürstenstein and its beautiful nature after all. Unfortunately, Daisy could not restrain herself from showing Hans a copy of a letter she had sent to the Emperor that ended with the following postscript:

> God take care of Your Majesty and all that are yours; and do this for me. Your obedient subject and – – – ![30]
>
> DAISY OF PLESS
>
> P.S. I have been dismissed without trial or judge to defend myself – so I am a servant no longer![31]

Hans coolly explained to Daisy that the defiant gesture in her postscript "was quite useless, that everything now went by rule in Germany, and not even the Emperor himself could personally do anything."[32] On the train to Partenkirchen, Daisy wrote in her diary

> The Court can give me no orders now; I remain a German subject ... but I am no longer an 'obedient servant' which is the way one signs oneself, and which I signed so often to the Emperor. No – I am no longer that, I am nobody's servant; neither shall I play the role of the dressed-up house-keeper![33]

The brief stay in Fürstenstein had not brought Daisy closer to her husband and his attitudes.

Hoping to end her enforced isolation in Partenkirchen Daisy wrote to Prince Ludwig Ferdinand of Bavaria offering her services to the Red Cross, but his reply stated that too many ladies wanting to serve had already been placed on a waiting list. The Prussian Crown Princess Cäcilie also refused Daisy's offer because work in a hospital at the front would be far too hard for her. Not until June 21, 1915 would Daisy's wish be fulfilled; Professor Dr. Kuester wrote that he would soon have a position for Daisy on his hospital train.

Daisy immediately returned with Lexel and Bolko to Fürstenstein, where the children would be staying from now on. The atmosphere in

---

30 Daisy usually signed her letters to the Emperor as "Your obedient subject and devoted servant."

31 DPH, pp. 338-39.

32 DPH, p. 339.

33 DPH, p. 340.

Fürstenstein was noticeably tense. Louis Hardouin, the French chef of the castle's kitchen, had already been imprisoned in Breslau.[34] The rest of the English staff and their families expected to be interned any day.

As a French citizen, Louis Hardouin had become one of the first victims of spy hysteria. He had been apprehended during the early days of the war; his frightened wife discovered an editorial in the *Freiburger Bote* suggesting that her husband should immediately be shot without trial. His son related to the author how Princess Daisy and his mother had visited his father in his prison cell in Breslau. They had found him, an always optimistic, active and healthy man, physically and mentally in deplorable shape. Louis junior was convinced that only the determined intercession of the Princess had effected the transfer of his father out of this punitive prison to the internment camp in Holzminden an der Weser, not far from Hannover, but very far from Fürstenstein.

The Holzminden camp accommodated thousands of civilians, men, women, children, and old people from all parts of Europe occupied by the German armies. It was perhaps the last camp in European history where a humane administration permitted the inmates to retain their dignity. Thus, it was possible for Louis Hardouin to send for his photographic equipment. Over a period of two years, he created a unique pictorial documentation of life in an internment camp, where the indomitable human spirit survived the loss of freedom. But while Louis Hardouin was interned 400 miles from Fürstenstein, his sons Louis and Maurice were forced to assume German first names in order to continue attending the high school in Freiburg. Their father returned to Fürstenstein in November 1916. His son Louis assumed, this was once again a result of Princess Daisy's intervention, although he had no proof for his firm belief.[35]

* * *

---

34 Louis Hardouin senior, who had been chef in Fürstenstrein since 1905, was born in the little village of St. Bénoit near Le Mans in France and had been "discovered" by Daisy's husband in London. His son Louis Hardouin junior shared with the author that his father's photographic talent and oeuvre had fascinated Hans as much as Hardouin's culinary art. Over a period of two decades, Louis Hardouin, the photographer, captured on glass plates Castle Fürstenstein and its environs, the Prince of Pless, his family, the Hochberg relatives, the illustrious guests flocking to Fürstenstein, and the people working in and around the castle during their daily life, on holidays, and on feast days. Louis Hardouin's legacy of over 3,000 artistically and technically superb photographs assisted the author in the completion of his book about Castle Fürstenstein in 1989.

35 Conversation London, summer 1982.

On July 26, 1915, Daisy was called on short notice to Castle Pless, the seat of the Imperial General Headquarters. Hans advised her by telegram that the Emperor had requested Daisy's presence for a period of two days. As there was no room in Castle Pless, she would have to stay overnight with the Larisches at nearby Solza. On the morning of July 28, the Emperor wished to congratulate her on her birthday. Having been barred from her second home, Daisy was in no mood to follow the Emperor's orders, as she replied to Hans. But

> a very nice letter from Hans came with the motor-car sent by the Emperor and ... on thinking quietly and carefully ... I decided it would be best to go to Pless – but on conditions which in my own mind I had clearly fixed. There was much to be gained from a visit to the sacred Great Headquarters![36]

In the end, Daisy also slept in her own bed in Castle Pless. But she hardly recognized the little town. Pless was overflowing with military; there was a steady coming and going of courier automobiles; like a spider web, hundreds of telephone cables connecting the Imperial Headquarters with the front in the East, West and South, radiated from the castle above the houses of the town in all directions. The Emperor, accompanied by a distressed and preoccupied Hans came to see Daisy in the afternoon. Daisy wished she could have spoken to the Emperor alone, but then, in the evening just before dinner, Daisy was called to the Emperor's apartment where

> He took out a little brooch out of his pocket and gave it to me. ... Had I had more time with him alone ... I could have made him happier, as he is a very sad man, feeling terribly hurt by the one country he loved – England. He never forgets it; he tried all these years to keep peace, and although I am English and they might hate me at home for saying this, I shall always proclaim it to every man and woman I know![37]

The next morning, on Daisy's birthday, the Emperor was in the best of moods and congratulated Daisy with the words, "I suppose you are twenty-nine today; at least you look it!"[38]

Accompanied by Hans on her return trip to Fürstenstein, Daisy followed her own thoughts. She was worried about the Emperor. It seemed easy to get him excited and upset. For the first time, she had been careful not to hurt his feelings. They had hardly left Pless when

---

36 DPH, pp. 348-49.

37 DPH, p. 351.

38 DPH, p. 353.

Hans said that her presence had not been welcomed by the generals. Daisy assured Hans she had no desire to return to Pless until the war was over.

But on August 13 in Berlin, Daisy was to her great surprise again called to Pless. Again, she refused, but Baron von Stumm appeared with an urgent message from the Emperor, who asked for Daisy's presence as hostess to the Empress, who was already on her way to Pless. Upon her arrival in Pless, Daisy was received with unexpected honours. At the railway station, the *Fürstenzimmer*[39] had been opened for her; from there, General von Plessen took her past an honour guard of soldiers to her carriage. During the next few days, the Emperor and the Empress were "most cordial;" there was also enough time to give Hans some comfort; he was recuperating from an unexpected appendectomy. Daisy was introduced to General Ludendorff and had to field too many painful questions from the other generals and politicians. "But as always, I played the role expected from me and let no one know how my heart hurt. ..."[40]

In July 1915, Daisy had followed the invitation of the Grand Duchess[41] to visit Neustrelitz and spend time with her in Bansin at the Baltic Coast. The Grand Duchess's grandson Adolph Friedrich[42] happened to be on leave from the Western Front. Daisy had always been quite fond of the young Grand Duke. Perhaps out of her own unhappiness and loneliness, she failed to exercise some caution, doing little to discourage the Grand Duke's obvious infatuation with her. Young and inexperienced, and in love, he did not appreciate the likely political consequences of this basically harmless relationship. He openly adored Daisy in his letters, which were all censored, but Daisy, as in her relationship with Maxl before, remained within the conventions dictated by her position as a married woman:

> I had felt strongly for some time that the Grand Duke of Mecklenburg-Strelitz would be happier if he were married. ... He was terribly alone, and had no one to confide in. It was in these circumstances that he and I became real friends. We often discussed marriage. ... I had some time before thought of a young and charming Princess, a relative of our own. The suggestion was acceptable to both sides. I was pleased about it all and so was Hans, who knew everything, and fully approved.[43]

---

39   A special salon at the railroad depot reserved for royalty and high nobility.

40   DPH, 412.

41   Augusta Caroline, Grand Duchess of Mecklenburg-Strelitz.

42   Adolphus Friedrich VI, Grand Duke of Mecklenburg-Strelitz.

43   DPH, p. 437.

For Daisy, the weeks in early fall were occupied with looking after the military hospitals around Fürstenstein, in Bad Salzbrunn, Waldenburg, and Kunzendorf. Everything went well except at the Grand Hotel in Salzbrunn, once built to accommodate the Emperor, but now transformed into a convalescent home for officers. Being the wife of the owner, Daisy insisted that part of the Grand Hotel ought to be made available for ordinary soldiers as well. Daisy did not get her way until she threatened the officer in charge with turning to the Emperor. In a letter, she reminded the Emperor how impressed he had been with the hotel only a few years ago. Now, "62 ordinary soldiers could spend their reconvalescence in these beautiful surroundings."[44] In a Christmas letter sent to her friend Count Wolff-Metternich in Constantinople, Daisy enclosed a photograph with the explanation: "Here I am with my soldiers and under-officers."[45]

When she turned her attention to the Kunzendorf Hospital[46], Daisy discovered an entire unused floor and immediately decided to establish a rest home "for poor soldiers' wives who cannot afford a holiday, where every woman can bring along one of her children so that she may not feel too lonely."[47]

By October 1915, Daisy was still awaiting a call from Professor von Kuester to join his hospital train. She knew he had experienced difficulties and was still waiting for permission to recall her. Daisy decided to write to the Emperor, who again did not fail to help her. Soon, Daisy entered the good news in her diary. She had not sounded so happy in many months:

November 3, 1915. Military Lazarett Train Y.
What an address, thank God I *can* give it. I left Berlin in a fearful hurry – lots of wires and so on; one saying that His Majesty wished that the Princess of Pless should go to the Serbian frontier; so here I am ... the *greatest* luck that somehow has come at last. ... To be on this very train which is under Professor von Kuester. ... This Train is like a street, it is at least six hundred yards long, and will hold at a time two hundred and sixty wounded, who, we go now to fetch. ...

---

44 Letter to the Emperor, July 5, 1916. Courtesy Bundesarchiv Koblenz.

45 Letter to Count Wolff-Metternich. Courtesy Paul Joseph Graf Wolff-Metternich.

46 Formerly a seniors' home built by the Prince of Pless in Kunzendorf; since 1945 Mokrzeszów.

47 Daisy to the Emperor, July 5, 1916.

> I have always said, give me people who are not in Society. It is in this class
> of men and women one finds a true feeling which is just happy doing good
> to others. ...

> How old General von Perthes in Berlin must be grinding his teeth! When
> I got on the telephone to him to ask for a Pass he said it was out of the
> question. ... So I telephoned at once to Pless for a Pass – and here I sit a
> conqueror – with a smile and very dirty hands![48]

However, as so often in the past, Daisy's triumph turned out to be
short-lived. When the hospital train stopped at Magdeburg on its return
from Serbia, Professor von Kuester received orders from Berlin to
immediately remove the Princess of Pless from his train, as she had
received permission for a single journey only. An insulted Professor von
Kuester threatened to resign, while Daisy telephoned Hans in Pless to
tell the Emperor that if she would have to leave Professor von Kuester's
hospital train, she would never set foot in the Imperial Court in Berlin
again for the rest of her life. Only after the military administration in
Magdeburg was advised by the Imperial Headquarters in Pless that the
Princess of Pless was to remain with Professor von Kuester, did the train
proceed.

Daisy travelled with this hospital train from Berlin to Serbia and
back one more time. Returning on her third trip, she left the train in
Budapest to meet Hans in Vienna in order for the entire family to spend
Christmas together in Partenkirchen. Hans did not reach Vienna in
time, but after a journey of sixteen hours, Daisy and her maid Henrietta
arrived in Partenkirchen, happy to find Hans and the boys waiting for
her. How tenuous the family relationships had become is indicated in
Daisy's diaries:

> Nothing but rain, Hans got bored, so he went to Fürstenstein to see his
> blessed building operations, and Hansel went to Munich to the Schön-
> borns[49] for Christmas. Except for Lexel and Bolko my Christmas was
> therefore a lonely one, but I made the best of things. My greatest source of
> happiness was the knowledge that in the Lazarett Train I had been of some
> use and that the Staff and the poor wounded loved me.[50]

* * *

---

48 DPH, pp. 382-84 passim.
49 The future in-laws of Hansel.
50 DPH, 386.

Work on the hospital trains had restored much of Daisy's self-respect; it had also given her some inner peace. Early in October when she had still desperately waited for a call from Professor von Kuester, and when she had been deeply depressed and dejected, she had made her will. Eight weeks later, she added an appendix. As with many other things in Daisy's life, this was a rather unusual request, but it did say much about her improved mood.

SCHLESISCHER HOF Dec. 1st, 1915
My Testament is in Pless with the Administration and with Mr. Pünder in Berlin. I beg – and request that what is said in it, will be executed. The costs will be minimal – *there will be no funeral.*

My friends shall all come – with understanding and in happy mood – it will be my birthday[51] - and no one shall dress in mourning.

No etiquette and formalities – there shall be a party for the children, and they shall be allowed to pick flowers in the park.

Princess of Pless.

This Testament has been written a month or more after the first testament. Everything shall remain the same.[52]

This is a touching document written by Daisy without the assistance of her secretary or her maid. While composed in clumsy German, it nevertheless conveyed Daisy's wishes quite clearly as much as her resolve to leave this world without the pomp and circumstance she had endured so often against her will. That she did not wish to be buried in the gloomy depths of the family's mausoleum in the park of Fürstenstein, but outside its sunny southern wall, had already been stated in the original testament. She would leave this world with an easy heart; nobody should mourn, everybody should feel as cheerful as always in her presence in the past. Once more, Daisy seemed far ahead of her times!

At the end of 1915, Daisy found some consolation that at least partly, her name and reputation seemed rehabilitated. Her enemies, however, never really ceased trying to harm her through spreading lies and rumours, hoping that their efforts would finally achieve their aim of forcing the Princess of Pless to step out of public life completely. Early in 1916, they appeared to have succeeded. Daisy found herself without

---

51 this was obviously meant figuratively; but, strangely, Daisy died one day after her birthday; she was laid to rest four days after her 70th birthday.

52 National Archives of Poland, Pszczyna branch.

work on a hospital train. Under continued attack, Professor von Kuester had been forced to terminate his service on the Lazarett Train Y, and the press had found another victim, reporting that Professor von Kuester had always attached an elegant *Salonwagen*, to his hospital train, which was for the exclusive use of the Princess of Pless and her huge entourage. In reality, Daisy, her maid, and the other personnel of the hospital train had shared an ancient fourth class coach provided only with some wooden benches alongside its walls.

In these trying days, it was great comfort for Daisy to know that Hans would stand by her, as the Emperor always did. Of all her friends, the Emperor had been the most faithful, although Daisy had gradually become aware of his diminishing authority at the Great Headquarters. Daisy also developed a new respect for her husband, whose dual role of aide-de-camp to the Emperor and host at Castle Pless was rather complex, a task Hans nevertheless mastered admirably.

Among those at the Pless Great Headquarters who admired Hans was Baron von Treutler whose Silesian estate in Alt-Lässig was only a stone's throw from Fürstenstein. In his memoirs *The Emperor's Advisors*, Baron von Treutler remembers with sympathy and respect the difficult tasks mastered by Hans and Daisy:

> Among the other members of the Great Headquarters one must especially mention the Prince of Pless. ... He was at the height of his life's career when the Great Headquarters were transferred to Pless, where he functioned simultaneously as aide-de-camp and as host. With sensitivity and tact, he mastered his dual role so admirably that the King of Bavaria observed: 'If one wants to see how the solutions to delicate situations can be accomplished supremely, one must come to Pless.'

> One must even give higher credit to the Princess of Pless, if one considers the incredible situation created by the tactless, crude generals. ... [She] had already tried her utmost in peacetimes to improve the relationships between our and her country; that was resented in England as much as in Germany. She ended up sitting between two chairs, just as the Empress Friedrich whose life was made so miserable by so many people in London and in Berlin. It was therefore no wonder that with the outbreak of war, the Princess Pless, at least for a certain influential highly-placed clique, became persona-non-grata. ... During the war, the Princess needed and deserved support. Together with Reischach,[53] I asked the Emperor to call General Kessel and General Löwenfeldt to Pless and have them account for their attitudes and actions against the Princess of Pless; both generals had behaved in a particularly rude manner towards the Princess. We also begged

---

53   The Emperor's Court Marshal.

His Majesty to rehabilitate the much maligned Princess by personally inviting her to Pless. This was done promptly, although for the gracious lady, such an invitation was perhaps more a sacrifice than a pleasure.[54]

Far away from the troubles and unpleasantries of Pless, Daisy spent New Year 1916 with Duke Leopold and other members of the Royal Bavarian family in Berchtesgaden. The difference between Prussia and Berchtesgaden could not better be characterized than by Daisy herself:

> I wish I could describe the natural homeliness of Bavaria, and the naked-kneed but charming Bavarian Royal Dukes who used to constantly come and see me in Partenkirchen. ... Herr Martner had given me a Tyrolean dress, a red silk bodice with a dark-flowered silk skirt ... and Duke Luitpold said I looked like a Rubens picture. Afterwards all the servants came in and danced, and my chauffeur sat and smoked as an equal with the Royalties and others. In Silesia, as I know it, this would be unimaginable. ... But Bavarians are extraordinary people. The next day the staff were all perfect servants again as if the music and dancing of the night before had been a dream. I loved it. ... I was so tired of what is called Society.[55]

Daisy did not look forward to her return to Fürstenstein. She thought it best to leave Lexel and Bolko in Partenkirchen for the remainder of the war; especially little Bolko in his delicate health, who should do better in the climate of the Bavarian Alps. Daisy knew she could not stay in Bavaria for too long, and desperately looked for a way to escape the depressing atmosphere in Germany, if only for a few weeks. Daisy's brother-in-law Conrad von Hochberg, who had consciously chosen England as his home for the rest of his life, had been forced to return to Germany after the outbreak of war. Now that he was staying in Switzerland, he suggested to Daisy that a prolonged stay in Switzerland would do wonders for her health and her mood. However, a worried Hans wrote Daisy,

> People in Silesia are talking a lot about Conny being in Switzerland and meeting so many Englishmen. If you went too, it would be madness. The war is nearing its very end now so you can wait for a few months longer before you see Shelagh.[56]

The only other chance for a change from daily life in Germany would be a visit to Count Wolff-Metternich in Constantinople – Turkey

---

54 Karl Georg von Treutler, Ibid., p. 158-59.

55 DPH, pp. 390-91.

56 DPH, p. 397.

was still an ally of Germany. Daisy's brother-in-law Fritz Hochberg, who had just returned from an assignment in the Turkish capital encouraged Daisy to write to Metternich which she did on the day of her return to Fürstenstein:

FÜRSTENSTEIN, February 3rd, 1916

DEAREST COUNT METTERNICH,
and dear *Friend* of so many years. How sad you could not come to Partenkirchen. We would have had such *wonderful* days together, with conversation and walks, although I *cannot walk very far at all any more*. ... I have just come back from Salzbrunn (at the Hotel) where I have a Lazarett for convalescents. I gave them an evening which I do very often and they all sang ... and were happy. One of the doctors ... sang a song ... *it was all against England*. ... Oh!, my dear I have *acted* and *smiled* all my life, *as you must know*. ...

I am so tired and weary, and someone whose name I bear did *nothing* to help me; only by doing *nothing* he made things look worse.[57] I want a change before I start working again either in a Lazarett Train or in Breslau.

I have been through hell, Ct. Metternich dear ... but my ambition for this country has been bigger than that of *many Germans*! ... What I write you for is to ask you honestly IF I came to Constantinople would you be nice to me and have you time to spare to even little cozy talks together like we used to have in *the happy old days in London*? Do you remember when I left my slippers under your breakfast table?!! ... Coming to Turkey is to see you and have a little peace. I have the permit of course, and a letter from the Ambassador etc. in Berlin for my servant and maid and myself. Write me Express Insured. ... I would come anytime as I start work again soon. ...

All the *nicest* thoughts – yours always the same friend,
PRINCESS DAISY.[58]

The rest, change, and comfort of a few weeks in Constantinople, the warm and uncomplicated companionship Daisy had asked her old friend Metternich for, did not come true. Just days before her departure for Turkey, Daisy was called to serve on a new Lazarett Train sponsored by Mr. Friedländer-Fuld, a Berlin industrialist. On April 29, 1916, Daisy wrote in her diary:

---

57 Daisy is referring to her husband.

58 Courtesy Paul Joseph Graf Wolff-Metternich.

April 29, 1916. Lazarettzug D.3.

As I write this a train passes loaded with *coal*; and I suddenly realize I am the wife of a German coal-owner. ... And I should be treated here as a *rebel*, and not allowed to see my boys again. I have been through so much that somehow my courage seems to have left me; such an attempt would require bodily courage as well as careful thinking. I had better wait.[59]

And later, after visiting a hospital for English prisoners of war:

CAUDRY, LAZARETT TRAIN D-3. June 9, 1916.

Just back... A charming old Oberleutnant ... let me speak to the Englishmen. ... I had just time to slip into the hand of an officer called Major Craig a piece of paper ... on which I had written ... that I was the sister of the Duchess of Westminster, and that my heart was with them all. ... I only pray to God he will keep it a secret ... otherwise they will say the most devilish things against me here. ... I should be shut up in Germany.

The guns are booming. ... God help me! A miserable Lazarett Train stopped close to ours; we found ... it was full of wounded English. I spoke to two of them. ... One was a Major Brown, he gave me his address asking me to write to his mother, close to Winchester. I spoke to another, but did not dare go in for fear some one might see me; it smelt dreadfully and the soldiers told me it was full of lice! One soldier on board was dead and I longed to find his body and put a little flower on it! Now more English are coming; but I shall stay in my cabin, I cannot bear it; as I may do nothing for them, nor talk with them, except on the sly. I am a German nurse in German uniform. ... God help me soon, but only death can set me free![60]

Daisy was not only faltering under the stress of her work and of seeing thousands of wounded and dead every day; she was also increasingly gripped by a sense of alienation. Her heart went out to the wounded from her own country, but she could do nothing to help them, even run the risk to talk to them. A short leave to see her children came as true relief, but being back in Germany also meant new problems! On another hospital train, she wrote to the Emperor asking again for his help:

Verpflegungsstelle für Lazarett Zug D.3 Aachen, Burtscheiderstrasse 8

July 5th, 1915[sic][61]

Sire Your Majesty.

I have been at work now ... on a Lazarettzug ... the horrors one sees and

---

59 DPH, pp. 399-402 passim.

60 DPH, pp. 407-08.

61 Date incorrect; should be 1916 rather than 1915.

does. But I work proudly. ... I have the operation room and eight carriages; I beg that Hans would show Your Majesty what the chef artz[sic][62] here, a great rough man with a big heart wrote about me. ... I write to ask Your Majesty to insist on my right which I deserve and because of all the examinations I have passed to receive the Hilfs-Schwestern Brosche[63] – which is really absurd for me to beg for as the three girls I have in Salzbrunn for Convalescents *have* it ... that when I go to Wohltätigkeit[64] in Silesia I shall not be ashamed. ... But they have refused from Breslau to give it to me; Hans wrote to Princess Charlotte of Saxon-Meiningen,[65] but the brooch was refused me. ... How *dare* they after all I have done in that Province – my clothes from there and not from Paris or Vienna – my cripple school in Waldenburg; 14 lace schools in Hirschberg & all kept going; they blame *me* for the many horses from England and France!! the new building at Fürstenstein! I have stood more than most women *could have stood*; and yet my heart is still true; truth can never change. ...

The chef artz here says (& without me even speaking with him, he *knows* from Berlin) – if *only a single line* came in the papers that the Princess of Pless has received the Red Cross and that His Majesty wishes to receive me to hear all about Salzbrunn, or Kunzendorf. ...

About my work Hans knows it all, if he will try & remember. I wrote it to him:

1914 – on Thursday 8th August for three weeks with Professor Grauert, Professor Beer; till September I was at Tempelhof in operations room – and bandaging room under Professor von Kuester.

May 15 in Salzbrunn Lazarett.

Sep. till Dec. in Lazarettzug with Prof. von Kuester.

Apr 16 here in this train three months – in between I was at Partenkirchen with Baby and in Silesia three times between looking after everything and one man said in Salzbrunn he could stand the 30 years war there.

Others have a Red Cross ribbon & I have *nothing*! They must wonder; & still as usual my life goes on & I have to smile; & *I do it*; but there is *cruelty* around me; and no one *outside* knows or *could guess* all I do & see now; I want *my sword in my hand* which is just a little *right* I ask for; surely Hans must understand. I *implore* Your Majesty to help me; that little brooch is a

---

62 physician, "Arzt" in German.

63 the auxiliary nurse's pin.

64 charity functions.

65 Protector of the German Red Cross.

safty[sic][66] . ... I have to travel in a Schwestern dress [67] when I leave this train or join it; and without it (so Countess Brockdorff wrote me) I have not even the right to go to church on Good Friday – *who was there*; how did they *know!!!* Berlin still wishes to harm me; it is cruelty against a *woman* who has never hurt any one. With all thoughts to Your Majesty & prayers to God in *true* & deep devotion

DAISY PLESS

If Your Majesty did not trust me; I would never return to this country – I have had too much to bear, in many ways. – Our Train with the wounded *comes* P.[68]

In her excitement, Daisy had mixed up the years while dating this letter which, as its contents prove, was written on July 5, 1916 rather than 1915. Daisy really did not ask for very much except for some recognition and protection at a time when again she felt entirely alone. The Emperor must have received the letter in good grace with much understanding of Daisy's plight, as a long letter from Hans received shortly after, indicates:

GROSSES HAUPTQUARTIER, July 21, 1916.
Germany is, as you know, the country of regulations, therefore everything is überlegt[69] about several times, carefully looked after, and then it goes through the official channel, which takes a lot of time. If somebody dares to do it differently, he gets at once into hot water. That was also the reason for the report that you went to church in Berlin in nurse's dress. ... When I explained to the Emperor that you wore it because you had to catch the train directly after church, it was all right.

I am glad little Bolko is better. ...

The newspapers which announced that on your birthday the English flag was hoisted in Salzbrunn, had all to deny it. It was simply the West colours, red and blue, which some idiot mistook for the English colours[70]. ...

We are just in the midst of what I think is a decisive battle on the Somme. ... I am glad you saw Hansel. He must look very nice as Hussar. ... If you

---

66 Safety.

67 Nurse's uniform.

68 Letter to the Emperor courtesy Bundesarchiv Koblenz.

69 Endlessly deliberated.

70 The colours of the Wests were flown at Fürstenstein and Salzbrunn on June 28, Daisy's birthday, a long-standing tradition. On that day, Daisy was hundreds of miles away at the Western Front.

meet English wounded out where you are, be very careful with them, or there will be some new gossip.[71]

Even though Hans's worry about Daisy's tendency to get into trouble can be read between the lines, this letter and many others at that time were sincerely affectionate and demonstrated the concern and care Daisy so badly needed. If what seemed like an obsession "of having the Red Cross brooch" sounds slightly petty, Hans's explanation of how Germany was run, how everyone made sure to follow directives and not burn his fingers, said it all. Daisy's appearance at church in the nurse's uniform had been promptly reported to the Countess Brockdorff at the Court in Berlin. It speaks for the Emperor, who was after all the epitome of everything German, as Hans had characterized it, that he fully understood Daisy and promptly helped her. For a person as exposed to public scrutiny as Daisy, having the Red Cross nurse's brooch was protection in public; her nurse's uniform had become a protective shield in these years; a visible sign of legitimacy. It had become part of her identity; just as serving the sick and wounded had become the only raison d'être for Daisy to remain in Germany during the war and maintain a measure of self-respect. Not even during her days of leave and rest in Partenkirchen did Daisy put her uniform aside. As a number of photographs show, whether resting in the garden, going for short walks, or playing with Lexel and Bolko, Daisy was always seen in her beloved nurse's uniform.

* * *

The persecution of Daisy in the German press brought more distress.

One morning, the nurses on the Lazarett Train expressed their condolences. A confused Daisy learned that the papers had reported the death of her father. Having received word of the death of her beloved Granny Olivia only a few days before, Daisy longed to meet her mother in Switzerland more than ever. She had already begged Hans to find a way for her to go to Switzerland. He had tried his very best, but at the end of August, General Ludendorff, who had recently received extensive powers of control over the military as much as over the civilian affairs of the country, had ordered new restrictions which made travel to neutral countries practically impossible. On September 10, Hans was relieved to advise Daisy that her *Poppets* was quite well.

---

71 DPH, p. 410.

PLESS, September 10th, 1916.

MY DARLING DANY WIFE,
I cannot tell you how pleased I am that the news about Poppets is good. ...

Hermann[72] probably addressed himself through a neutral power to Beneck-endorff,[73] his brother-in-law, and got the answer at once. What a dreadful time you must have passed. ...[74]

December 8, the day of their silver wedding anniversary, found Hans in Pless and Daisy in France. "How can we be glad about anything?" Daisy asked her diary, "Private sorrows and public griefs jostling one another so quickly ... " But Hans had not forgotten the anniversary. On December 8, two letters arrived, one wrapped around a small package:

> I have bought a little brooch for you the other day in Berlin and told them to send it so that it arrives on the 8th in your hands. This is not a proper silver anniversary present, but only a little trifle to show you that I have not forgotten the day. The rest we can talk later.[75]

PLESS, December 6, 1916.

MY DARLING DANY WIFE,–
I hope this letter will just reach you on the morning of the 8th, as your letters don't seem to be any more delayed. Well, it is twenty-five years that we are married, and I can only say, that I feel very proud, that I had such a brilliant idea twenty-five years ago. You have decidedly succeeded in making me extremely happy during this long time, and I trust to God, you will find your happiness again too, when this beastly war is over and Hansel is safely at home. I am sure that in a year's time we will have peace and, surrounded by our three dear boys, we can have proper silver wedding festivities (which would also please the people) either here or in Fürstenstein, which will be ready by then, or in both places, one after the other.[76]

Hans also promised an official silver anniversary present of 200,000 Marks.

Except for a brief few days here and there, Hans had been separated from his wife since the first days of the war, but he seemed to feel closer to his wife than he had in years. No doubt, Hans could not help but

---

72 Prince Hatzfeldt.
73 The Russian Ambassador in London.
74 DPH, p. 412.
75 DPH, p. 424.
76 DPH, p. 425.

admire Daisy who, in spite of increasing health problems, continued to do her demanding work as an auxiliary nurse on hospital trains, even though her dedicated service to the sick and wounded earned her nothing but hostility among the German public and never- ending machinations by the military. Although Hans could not completely absolve his wife from any blame for the persecution she had to endure during the war, the Emperor's never-failing concern for Daisy filled him with pride.

One must not forget that as aide-de-camp to the Emperor and host at the Great Headquarters in Pless, Hans was responsible for complex tasks and duties and faced challenges that his rather cautious and phlegmatic nature had never before been confronted with. For years, Daisy had tried to "find something to do for Hans" and bring him out of his reserve and his shyness in public. Perhaps Daisy had never understood the reasons for her husband's frequent mood swings and his proverbial "bad temper" she so often complained about. Perhaps Hans was a person who needed to be challenged to feel fulfilled and rewarded, and who, without challenge, would easily retreat from others and fall into listlessness and depression. Chancellor Bülow had characterized Hans as "unimportant."[77] Seymour Leslie, Jennie Churchill's nephew, remembered Hans as "overly reserved, morose and looking depressed."[78] But Baron von Treutler and others remember an energetic, tactful, and diplomatically resourceful Prince of Pless in his role as host at the Great Headquarters. Hans must have done his job well and enjoyed it too!

His frequent letters to his wife between July 28 and December 2, 1916 indicate how Hans and Daisy's Castle Pless had become the political and military nerve centre of Imperial Germany and her allies.

> At nine p.m. the Emperor got here with all his people and Jagow ... at eleven Bethmann-Hollweg the Chancellor ... the next morning Hindenburg with Ludendorff. ... Yesterday the Crown Prince Boris of Bulgaria arrived with General Tchov ... one hour later Archduke Friedrich arrived from Teschen.[79] General Conrad von Hötzendorf[80] arrived for dinner. ... The absence of General von Falkenhayn[81] was much commented on; 'he had a bad tooth ache!'... Important decisions have been taken. ...

---

77 See Bernhard Fürst von Bülow, op. cit., vol 2, p. 421.

78 In conversation, October 1977.

79 The Headquarters of the Austrian Armies.

80 Commander-in-Chief of the Austro-Hungarian Armies.

81 Chief of Staff; relieved of his command and succeeded by Hindenburg on August 29, 1916.

We are so full up that all the younger gentlemen live in the train at the Station. ... The Empress is here, also King Ferdinand and the Crown Prince of Bulgaria ... to-night Enver Pascha (the Turkish Minister of War) arrives and Archduke Friedrich and all the Austrians came over from Teschen. I had to go to Mass with the Bulgarians at 8:30, at 10 to the Protestant church with our Sovereigns, then walk with the King in the Park, and then to lunch with lots of people to talk to. ... The work is terrific!

You have no idea how much there is to do around here. Politically this Polish question[82] gives one heaps to do ... to meet the new state of things. And what this will really be, God only knows. The Poles here are very quiet. ... Yesterday the Emperor Karl and the Archduke Friedrich came over (48 people). ... A big kiss for Bolko and a very big one for you![83]

If Hans felt fulfilled with his work, Daisy felt more excluded from his world and their home than ever. How much she could have helped, functioning as hostess of Castle Pless to the hundreds of guests! She made one attempt to be "admitted" to her own home; not to the big Castle, but to the hunting lodge a few miles away, but the answer from Hans was shattering:

You cannot come and live at Promnitz,[84] as the whole place is in a dreadful state. ... There is a list kept at the Secretary's Office of all the people that have been staying at the Castle since the War began, with dates and the names of the rooms. ...[85]

Daisy was confused. Did Hans not care for her enough to have the hunting lodge in Promnitz cleaned up for her? Was he too busy to have any time for her? Did he try to save her feelings? Or was it just an excuse to hide the fact that he did not get permission to have his wife come to Pless?

In retrospect, it appears a tragedy that Hans and Daisy had so few opportunities during these decisive years to be together for more than a few days at a time, and these few were too often in settings where there was no privacy. It was now too late for Hans to win back the love and affection of his wife. Too much had happened in their marriage and Daisy could not forget or forgive. Daisy's letter to Metternich, written only days after Hans's affectionate silver anniversary letter, betrays how little her attitude towards her husband had changed in spite of his

---

82 Germany and Austria were planning the creation of a Kingdom of Poland.

83 Letter by Hans dated July 30, 1916. DPH., p. 412.

84 The hunting lodge of the Prince of Pless in the forest near Pless.

85 DPH, p. 417.

obvious attempts to find a way back to a closer relationship. The inner turmoil that plagued Daisy, her pessimistic view of her marriage, her anger at the hostile attitudes and actions she had to endure in Germany, and the description of her physically and emotionally deteriorating health must have frightened Metternich.

BERCHTESGADEN, BAYERN
GMUNDSCHLOSS
Dec. 14, 1916.

MY DEAR COUNT PAUL,
I cannot tell you how I long to see you, how miserable I was ... not being well enough. ...

I stand absolutely alone. Friends – yes, but they are mostly in Austria for which one has to get now a special permit to go, or else they are in Berlin, a town I wish to turn my back upon. ... You know how I worked and how truthful I have been! The cruelty which a person like myself seems to have to suffer is to me a surprise ... the older I get the more I realize that I lived in my own artificial cloud not wishing to *know the truth*. ...

Hans was coming here for Xmas, but has now changed his mind. ... What Hans will do I generally do not know. To ask questions I have given up. He is now free till the 20th of this month, but he does not choose to come here, which is from Dresden a through journey with a sleeping car. ...

Hansel who is only 17 in February is already out there, for the sake of winning the Iron Cross which Hans wished him to do even earlier; but Thank God the Emperor did not allow this. ...

Hoping ever so much to see you any time you like. ...
Yours just the same!
PRINCESS DAISY[86]

Two days after dispatching her letter to Metternich, Daisy decided to go to Silesia on the spur of the moment. She stayed only long enough to complete the traditional distribution of Christmas presents in Fürstenstein and visit the hospitals. She returned to Partenkirchen in a state of exhaustion. On New Year's Day 1917, she fell ill with pneumonia, circulatory disturbances set in, and walking became almost impossible. The planned return to the hospital train was now out of the question, especially since her recovery was exceedingly slow. The island of peace in beloved Bavaria was turning into a prison. Like a momentary ray of

---

86 Courtesy Paul Joseph Graf Wolff-Metternich.

sunshine during these gloomy days, a telegram arrived from the Emperor. It had been dispatched prior to the transfer of the Great Headquarters from Pless to the Western Front.

> PLESS CASTLE, February 11, 1917.
> On my departure from Upper Silesia, I would like to tell you how well I have been looked after here and to let you know how thankful I was to feel how carefully everything had been thought out to make my careworn life as agreeable as possible. With best greetings,
> WILHELM I.R.[87]

When it came to Daisy, the Emperor always showed great sensitivity and care, contrary to his image of a boisterous, thoughtless man without tact. Even though Daisy had been unable to make his life more "agreeable" in Pless, the Emperor did not fail to give her his respect as the hostess of Castle Pless. His telegram reminded Daisy again that, except for two very brief occasions, she had been banished from her home in Pless. That the Emperor had not forgotten her true position, cheered Daisy only momentarily; after the first moments of delight about the Emperor's gesture, bitterness took over again.

* * * * * *

---

87 DPH, p. 430.

10 | *Whither Loyalty?*

We are in Ste. Avolde in Lorraine, waiting to go up somewhere and bring the wounded down. ... The whole of the field and all the "world" outside Metz seems a bare desert as the trees have been cut down for clearer sights, Schützengräben, hidden mines and so on.

And I have a longing like a thirst to speak with those I love. As I crossed into France yesterday, and as we shall go to Mars La Tour from Metz, I thought how easy it would be for me to cut my hair, dress up as a man, live hidden while I am searched for, and somehow get into the French lines and be sent to England.[1]

Daisy of Pless, April 29, 1916

* * *

Few experiences during the war had insulted Daisy as much as her exile from Pless. The Emperor's well-meant gratitude seemed only to ridicule her situation, since as the legitimate hostess of Castle Pless, she had not had a single opportunity to fulfill her role during the Emperor's prolonged stay at her home. Daisy felt excluded from a world which, after all, had been her own for her entire married life, even though Hans tried his best to give her a sense that she was still part of this world. It became impossible for Daisy to distinguish between the orders and controls Hans had to accept himself, and what in all sincerity he attempted to do for her under difficult circumstances.

In past times when she was still hoping for a meaningful relationship in her marriage, Daisy had been grateful for every little sign of trust and

---

1   DPH, pp. 399-402 passim.

concern from Hans. Now, Hans demonstrated so much more empathy for her feelings and her deplorable situation. He stood up for her and defended her more than ever before; he recognized her qualities and her efforts, and as a sign of trust, he often shared rather confidential news with her. This remarkable change in his attitudes, however, no longer affected Daisy's feelings for Hans to any degree.

Besides, it was now impossible to determine to what extent the *new rulers* at Pless governed the relationship between Hans and Daisy and even between the Emperor and Daisy. The absence of General von Falkenhayn, mentioned by Hans, was the first indication of the already secretly decided change in the structure of the Supreme Command. The historic decisions made at the Great Headquarters in Pless started with the transfer of almost unlimited autocratic power to the generals Hindenburg and Ludendorff on August 26, 1916. On November 5, 1916, also at Pless, followed the proclamation of the new Kingdom of Poland, which was the starting point for Ludendorff's design for an Eastern Europe under German domination. Ludendorff's plan found only some initial resistance among members of the German government.

These were decisions of militarily and politically enormous consequences; they immediately changed the power structure within Germany and restricted the already weakened authority of the Emperor; it was a fateful turn of events deplored by more than one influential person in Germany, and it was fateful for Daisy herself!

The Emperor reacted visibly to the changes of summer 1916 and his loss of power. Admiral von Müller reported that the Emperor was practically taking refuge at the Great Headquarters in Pless. The Emperor was loath to leave Pless even for a few days. While there, he occupied his time with shooting parties and all sorts of festivities; besides, the Empress came to Pless far too often and for far too lengthy visits. The mood at Pless was not very optimistic in these days, especially after Romania's entry into the war on the side of the Allies on August 26, 1916. There was also great worry about the continued strength and loyalty of the Austrian ally, especially after the death of the old Emperor Franz Joseph on November 21, 1916.

The Poland envisioned by Germany and Austria was never intended to be truly independent, but rather remain under the suzerainty of Germany. Her king was to be chosen from amongst Germany's nobility. This became a drawn-out process, as practically no one was ready to assume the difficult position of being a German occupying the throne in a country of Polish people, while at the same time being primarily loyal to the German Emperor.

The new Polish state never became a kingdom, which could have had a significant effect on Daisy's family. Those in charge were still "searching in the dark"[2] when the Kingdom of Poland had already been proclaimed. Eventually, the possibility of offering the Polish crown to the Prince of Pless was considered, as the Prince was seen as quite popular among the Polish population of at least Upper Silesia. Daisy mentioned that Hans had refused the offer of the Polish crown for various reasons, not the least of which was the near certainty that his large properties in Upper Silesia might become part of a new Polish kingdom. Daisy also insisted that the Polish crown had been offered to Hans for one of his two older sons, and that for that reason Lexel was to convert to the Catholic faith, a version which has never been confirmed or authenticated by members of the Hochberg family.[3]

The Kingdom of Poland was only part of a grand design that placed German princes on the thrones of countries to be created, including Courland and Livland,[4] Estonia and Lithuania, and possibly parts of Ukraine in the East; in the West, Belgium, French Lorraine, and possibly part of the French Coast were to be economically integrated into the German Empire. This design was fervently pursued by Ludendorff whose goals, however, went much further:

> I was determined to utilize the manpower reserves of the Eastern territories to the utmost, partly through setting up new regiments, partly through bringing workers to Germany and thus free fresh manpower for our armies at the front.

> I clearly moved beyond military necessity ... I wanted to strengthen the German element in the East and make it more powerful and influential. What occupied me day and night was my favourite plan of resettling in our new Eastern territories all the millions of Germans who had been living throughout the vast Russian Empire for many generations, next to millions of our soldiers discharged from our armies at the end of the current war. In this way, I clearly represented the causes and interests of the German race.[5]

---

2 Admiral Georg Alexander von Müller, *The Kaiser and His Court* (Göttingen, 1959), p. 342.

3 Interestingly enough, Lexel did convert to Roman Catholicism on October 17, 1920. After his death on February 22, 1984, Polish historians began to delve anew into the question of Lexel or another member of the House of Hochberg having been close to accepting the crown of a re-born Kingdom of Poland. Lexel had accepted Polish citizenship after 1922 and had served as a lieutenant in the Polish corps under the British Eigth Army in the Middle East and Italy during World War II. Lexel has therefore remained quite popular among the Poles of Upper Silesia to this day, which promotes the belief that he might have been a candidate for the Polish crown.

4 Out of Courland and Livland, Latvia was created in 1918-20..

5 General Ludendorff, *My War Memories 1914-1918* (London, 1929), pp. 5534-35.

In spring of 1918, the Polish question still awaited its solution.[6] In the meantime, the third of the far-reaching decisions had been made at Pless, which would determine the outcome of the war. On January 9, 1917, the introduction of unrestricted submarine warfare against the Allies was finally decided. On January 31, the German Ambassador in Washington received a message from Berlin that the unrestricted U-boat warfare would start at the beginning of February. Two days later, diplomatic relations between Germany and the United States were broken off, and on April 1, the United States declared their entry into the war against Germany. Although few wanted to believe it, the fate of Germany and her allies was now sealed.

Hans was shocked by the submarine warfare proclamation made at Pless on February 1, 1917. In deep dejection he wrote to Daisy that the entry of the United States into the war would destroy all hope for peace for at least another two years. Hans had come to that conclusion after a meeting with the American Ambassador James Gerard, who had come to the Great Headquarters, now at the Western Front, to warn the Emperor that unrestricted submarine warfare would mean the entry of the United States into the war on the side of the Allies. Mr. Gerard personally reiterated his warnings to Hans when "one day I had tea in the garden of the villa occupied by the Emperor, with the Prince of Pless (who is always with the Emperor and seems to be a prime favourite with him). ..."[7] And Hansel wrote his mother in an unusually pessimistic vein:

> FROM THE WEST, April 30, 1917.
> Germany, I think, will never be able to make anything out of Austria because they hate us and will not let us interfere in their business – which from their point of view I can very well understand. I don't think there will be peace either before two years, or a year and a half. I don't see any reason for the others to stop. I don't even quite believe that we can starve England by our Submarines. ...

I hope your legs are all right again! Perhaps you walk too much.[8]

This was not an item of news from or about Hansel that made Daisy happy, as the Emperor's brief but thoughtful message did – he must have sensed how much Daisy needed some sympathy and comfort:

---

6   The Polish question was never solved according to the plans of Germany and Austria for a Kingdom of Poland. Poland became a republic as a result of the Treaty of Versailles in 1919.

7   DPH, p. 439.

8   DPH., p. 439.

ON THE FIELD, March 28, 1917.
Yesterday when on an opportune visit to the First Garde Division I saw to my delight your little big boy. Heartiest greetings.
WILHELM.[9]

Between the discouraging letters from Hans and Hansel, Daisy received alarming news. On March 17, she learned of the stroke her beloved father had suffered at Newlands. In May, still not feeling well, Daisy decided to go to Fürstenstein despite Hans's urgent warnings that, if she insisted on going, she must not receive any visitors and would have to avoid all contact with the public. If Daisy thought that Hans was overreacting again, another letter proved even more perturbing. Kind, generous old Uncle Bolko, who lived only an hour's coach-drive from Fürstenstein, wrote in deep concern:

ROHNSTOCK, May 13, 1917.

DEAR DAISY,
That you will shortly come to Fürstenstein I have learnt elsewhere and we trust then also to be able to see you. Like Hans Heinrich, I would also like to ask you to be very careful and *not show yourself at other places*. As I have often told you there are the most adventuresome and silly rumors abroad about you, which have even led to enquiries being made of us, which we naturally have rejected as being silly and without taste. It is said that you are an English spy and as such, have been arrested or even already shot.

In any case among the people there exists a bitter feeling against you and you must not be surprised if you possibly get insulted. ...

YOUR FAITHFUL UNCLE BOLKO.[10]

Remembering how the people around Fürstenstein had never hesitated to demonstrate their love for *Our Daisy*, Daisy did not give full credence to the warnings from Hans and Uncle Bolko until she arrived at her home. Everything had been prepared for her stay, not in the castle, but at her cottage *Ma Fantaisie*; neither the public nor the personnel from the castle had access to the remote, isolated Schwarzengraben without special permission. Meals prepared by the faithful Louis Hardouin, who had returned from the internment camp at Holzminden a few months ago, were sent daily to the cottage. Louis Hardouin himself never dared going to see the beloved Princess for fear that even a single

---

9   DPH, p. 436.
10   DPH, pp. 437-38.

visit to the cottage in the Schwarzengraben would result in his renewed imprisonment and more spy stories about the Princess of Pless.

On June 3, a letter from Hansel arrived:

> Just a few lines to tell you that I got the E.K.I.[11]... Please don't believe everything people tell you — especially now in war-time, because ninety-nine per cent is bosh! ...[12]

Did Hansel appreciate the extent of the distorted news and lies in the press, of the hatred which followed Daisy everywhere in Germany? Except for some news advising Daisy of her success in the exchange of prisoners, letters and telegrams brought nothing but sad, depressing messages. Early in June, Patsy wrote that *Poppets* had been very ill, and after Daisy had fled the unbearable situation in Fürstenstein, a single-line telegram dispatched from Ruthin via Sweden reached Daisy on July 7 in Bad Nauheim:

> July 4, 1917 – A Great Heart is dead – Patsy -[13]

In grief, Daisy wrote:

> I had been uneasy for some time, but not anxious, as Patsy had said how well Poppets was again in the beginning of June. It was the greatest blow I experienced during the War. To be away from him when he needed me most. ...[14]

Daisy was still battling the bitter experience of her last visit to Fürstenstein. How could the population of the district and the people of Waldenburg she had always felt so close to, so turn against her after all the reverence and gratitude she had found there before this terrible war?

In August, a little pleasure came with the current issue of *Die Woche*, a German weekly read by the middle and upper classes. Prominently referring to the Princess of Pless, it included an illustrated report about her rest home for soldiers' wives in Kunzendorf. Shortly after the article appeared, Prince Hatzfeldt offered to arrange a position on a hospital train somewhere on the Balkans, or perhaps in a hospital in Serbia, definitely under the jurisdiction of the Austrian Army. In his mind, Prince Hatzfeldt had already decided that Daisy's return to the Western

---

11 Iron Cross First Class

12 DPH, pp. 440-41.

13 DPH, p. 443.

14 DPH, p. 443.

Front would be out of the question; the hate campaign against her continued unabated.

Daisy's later reminiscences of the painful waiting for the call to the Serbian front might seem to the reader as often one-sided and too black and white; even though influenced by her negative experiences of that time, they do contain a remarkable core of truth:

> At the behest of the extremists ... the Emperor sacrificed Bethmann.[15] From that moment his own doom was sealed, because, win or lose, he never again would be anything but a tool, a puppet in the hands of Hindenburg and Ludendorff, of the military and naval dictatorship. ... The military machine ... ruined the Emperor and the Dynasty and ... lost the War. I repeat, *the German Militarists lost the War.*

> That the Emperor was too weak to withstand them was his misfortune rather than his fault. ... All his life, and all through the War ... the Emperor desired Peace. To my mind, in modern times it is the people who make their Kings; not Kings who make their people. In 1917 the whole German people demanded *frightfulness.*

> Before the War the Emperor was loud, swaggering, aggressive, showy, because there is an element in the German character that is all these things, and admires them. He was narrow in his outlook, bigoted in his sympathies, intolerant in his attitude to foreign nations, because the Prussian spirit in Germany is all these things. The Prussian likes to ride rough-shod over others and thinks he has a right to do so.

> It suits them all now to blame the Emperor for these things and to call it Hohenzollernism. Hohenzollernism is only Prussianism in the open. They say its spirit has (with the Emperor) completely disappeared. It may be so, but I for one think that sudden national conversions are as rare and unsatisfactory as sudden individual conversions![16]

In October, Hansel's regiment was moved from the Galician front to France. Speaking Polish had stood him in good stead; now his excellent French would be useful. Daisy immediately rushed with Lexel and Bolko to Fürstenstein to meet Hansel, who had a few days of leave. Again, Daisy had to avoid the castle, but "in the Schwarzengraben, we all spent a happy time there in perfect weather."[17]

---

15 von Bethmann-Hollweg, German chancellor.

16 DPH, pp. 446-48 passim.

17 DPH, p. 451.

Before returning to Bavaria, Daisy had to make important decisions. All of a sudden, Daisy felt her true self again. Nobody interfered with her decision about how Lexel and Bolko would be looked after while she would serve on hospital duty in Belgrade beginning November 1, 1917. Although Lexel had already been registered at the high school in Görlitz, he would have to remain in Fürstenstein, as his tutor Herr von Selle was called up for military duty. *Baby Bolko* would return to Bavaria with his nanny Fräulein Staehle. Hansel would be with his regiment in France, Hans would remain at the Imperial Great Headquarters at the Western Front, and Daisy would commence her work as an auxiliary nurse on the Balkans in a few days. United with her children for four radiant autumn days, happy and unforgettable, but not free of a bit of melancholy, Daisy realized that the five members of the family would soon be swept in all directions like leaves in the fall wind.

On October 30, 1917, Daisy and her maid Elsa arrived in Belgrade. In an exuberant mood, she entered her first experiences in her diary:

> Belgrade of course was full of Austrian soldiers, and the hospital I was to serve in was an Austrian official one with the very grand name of Royal Hospital Brcko. I was met by a very nice fat Hungarian Professor who conducted me to a little three-roomed house formerly belonging to a Serbian officer and his family of seven! ...

> That night I slept very well ... for weeks I had suffered from insomnia and used to lie awake swallowing my thoughts. ... I was in a beautiful dreamless oblivion when suddenly ... up went my feet and down my head. The back of the bed had come off. ... I had been told to 'keep my feet up,' but this was carrying things too far. ...

> The food we get is awful. Anchovy paste smeared on war bread is considered a great delicacy. Onions and garlic are in constant use. I think one associates a smell with each city one knows. London (best smell of all), Paris, Madrid, Berlin, Vienna, Moscow, Calcutta, Dublin, Buenos Ayres, Oslo, Budapest, Breslau have all their own individual and peculiar odour, but I can never think of Belgrade except as a mixture of anchovies, garlic and drains![18]

Living conditions in Belgrade were primitive; the work at the hospital was hard; but there was an atmosphere of collegiality that Daisy cherished. Every day she realized anew how far away from Germany she was. Still, the war was going badly. Everybody was anxious and Daisy worried about her children and her mother. The daily work at the hospital helped a great deal; Daisy delved into her work.

---

18 DPH, pp. 452-54 passim.

The Brcko Hospital not only receives soldiers, but civilians, including women and children. Soon after my arrival I disgraced myself (in my own mind) very much ... I was on duty during an operation during which a man was having a piece of diseased bone cut away. I was holding open the incision ... as soon as the piece of bone was removed matter gushed up and all over me. I became faint but dared not let the wound close ... I was ... soused with cold water. I was both annoyed and angry and full of attrition. The operating Doctor said it did not matter, as something of the sort happened to every Doctor and nurse at least once in their lives. ...

I was feeling very depressed and wrote to Hansel saying I would soon be catching crayfish – an amusement we both loved and often shared at the Daisysee near Fürstenstein – but in heaven with Poppets.[19]

An amused Hansel replied:

FROM THE WEST, December 21, 1917.
... There will be no nonsense about your going on catching crawfish in Heaven. You will first catch a few thousands in the Schwarzengraben and Daisysee[20] with the family and then eat them, before you are allowed to sneak away and catch them all alone! I never knew you were so greedy! Haben Ihrer Durchlaucht verstanden? – Has Your Serene Highness understood?

I think now we will have Peace in a year. Russia is absolutely finished. ... When we get our troops from the East to the West ... England and France will have to give in before America can help them one little bit.

I thought you would not like Belgrade and all the garlic. ...[21]

Gratefully, but not without some sadness, Daisy realized how under the experience of war, Hansel was changing fast from the loving adolescent son to the man and protector of his mother. How much she longed to see him, before he had lost all the attributes of his young years! There was little chance, as Daisy had been signed up for hospital duty for the Christmas days. But unexpectedly, Hans had arranged a brief leave for her and Hansel at New Year's. Time was too short for the entire family to gather at Fürstenstein, but

---

19 DPH, p. 454.
20 A small lake with a teahouse near Fürstenstein, still carrying Daisy's name (Jeziorko Daisy).
21 DPH, p. 455.

I did manage to go to Berchtesgaden to Bolko where Hans, Hansel and Lexel joined us. We all had the feeling that somehow, in one way or another, 1918 was going to be a decisive year. ...[22]

* * *

From the very beginning, 1918 became a year of crucial personal decisions and tragic events for Daisy. In a way, Serbia offered Daisy a refuge from the desperate condition in Germany, the increasingly felt deprivations resulting from the prolonged war against the overwhelming forces of the Allies, and the horrible winter of hunger, the infamous *1917/18 Rübenwinter*,[23] about which Daisy's compatriot Princess Evelyn Blücher reported:

> We are all gaunt and bony now, and have dark shadows around our eyes, and our thoughts are chiefly taken up with wondering what our next meal will be. ... The hunger was bad enough, but the bitterly cold weather increased the misery. There was no coal to be had ... people are beginning to think that the torments of Dante's inferno are capped by the hardships of this deadly winter. ... As for the mood of the people, the heroic attitude has entirely disappeared. Now one sees faces like masks, blue with cold and drawn by hunger, with the harassed expression common to all those who are continually speculating about the possibility of another meal. ...[24]

Daisy was packing her bags to return to Belgrade when a telegram from her sister Shelagh arrived in Berchtesgaden that Patsy was seriously ill. Postponing her departure for Serbia, Daisy telegraphed to Hans for help, but Hans could only advise that

> under the current circumstances getting to England was absolutely out of the question. ... So I thought it much better to distract my mind by returning to Belgrade to nurse.[25]

Expecting the worst from day-to-day, two weeks later, with trembling hands, Daisy opened a letter from her sister-in-law Stella.[26] With great relief, she read that

---

22 DPH, p. 455.

23 During this hardest winter of the war, the population literally subsisted on a diet of beets, which provided the base for hot meals, for bread and other foodstuffs.

24 See Princess Evelyn Blücher, op. cit., pp. 181-82.

25 DPH, p. 457.

26 Mrs. Stella Patrick-Campbell, *My Life and some Letters* (Toronto, 1926), p. 283.

Your mother is much better and through the worst. I saw her again to-day and was deeply moved by her inner strength and her will to live. ... I am begging George to try and come to England to see his mother. ...[27]

George did receive a short leave to visit his ailing mother. When he was met at London's Victoria station by Jennie's sister Clare, he learned that his first wife Jennie had decided to marry again. George, whose marriage to Stella had lost all its romance was quite troubled by the news; he immediately wrote to Jennie confiding in her as in past times, and affectionately wishing her the best. Jennie replied with remarkable kindness and generosity of heart:

My dear George,
I heard all about you from Clare. ... I am glad you wrote ... and in your heart of hearts you must know that I never could have any but kindly feelings towards you. I never think of you but to remember all those happy days we spent together. ... I have forgotten everything else. I do wish you all the best. ... Peace is an essential to life and if you have that you are on a fair way to happiness. Life is frightfully hard. One's only chance is within oneself. ... Bless you ...
Always your best friend
JENNIE.[28]

At the end of February 1918, Daisy reached the most shattering news of all, of the never expected loss of a friend: The Grand Duke Adolphus Friedrich von Mecklenburg-Strelitz had drowned in a canal in the park of Castle Neustrelitz under as yet uncertain circumstances. Hoping against hope that this news, found in the daily paper, was simply another malicious rumour, Daisy refused to believe that her friend was dead.

I could not believe it. I had written to him at Christmas and received in reply a nice chatty letter from Strelitz where he was on leave. He ... spoke of the young Princess whom I hoped he would marry. ... It was a dear letter, quite hopeful and dated January 10. Yet in less than seven weeks he had gone ... voluntarily. One says that; but was it voluntarily? All one can know is ... a human soul must feel utterly defenceless and alone. Then the consuming grief and regret that one was not there at the time of greatest need to help, perhaps even to prevent![29]

---

27   Mrs. Stella Patrick-Campbell, ibid., p. 283.
28   See Eileen Quelch, op. cit., p. 148.
29   DPH, p. 458.

Immediately, the press grabbed the sad news of the terrible event, exploiting it to the sensational utmost. The Princess of Pless supposedly had involved the Grand Duke in a love relationship and other unsavory affairs from which he could no longer extricate himself except by taking his own life. There was no question, the Princess had also used the Grand Duke in her long suspected espionage activities for England. For weeks, headlines such as "The Secret of Mecklenburg-Strelitz" or "Why the Grand Duke of Mecklenburg-Strelitz had to Choose Death" dominated the papers in Germany and Austria:[30]

> By the end of January 1918, the Princess of Pless can no longer control her in Court circles well-known infatuation with the Grand Duke. ... With begging and flattery at Court and supported by her unsuspecting husband who is delegated to the Imperial Headquarters, she succeeds in travelling to the Western front close to the section where her friend the Grand Duke is stationed.

> In the meantime, the commander of this section has come to the conclusion that ... somehow, the enemy is receiving *intelligence* from a third party. ... It is therefore decided to plan a fictitious offensive of which except for the commander, only the Grand Duke is aware. The English grab the bait!

> *The Princess of Pless has been caught!* 'The faithful friend of the Emperor' simply turns out to be *a traitor to our country*!

> The innocent and youthfully carefree Grand Duke wakes up. Degraded and heaped with shame, he is sent to his castle Neustrelitz. This is where, filled with self-hate and disgust for the woman who had tried to destroy his relationship with another woman, an Austrian singer, the Grand Duke shoots himself. Within hours, the Princess of Pless arrives in Strelitz to remain at the side of the mother of the departed. ...[31]

Except for the Grand Duke's suicide, there was not a kernel of truth in this story. But even for Hans, it was impossible to ignore stories such as this particularly libelous one, which cast the worst suspicions on his wife. Daisy was grateful for being in Serbia and not having to face anybody in Germany at this time. From a letter of one of her closest

---

30 After the end of the war, the *Grünen Briefe für Politik und Wirtschaft* embellished the original story which had first been published in the *Gleiwitzer Voksstimme* in Upper Silesia. Even ten years later, the right-wing monthly *Die Wahrheit* dug up the story again on January 29th, 1929.

31 *Oberschlesische Volksstimme* (Gleiwitz, April 3, 1918); reprint in *Die Wahrheit* (January 26, 1929).

friends, she derived much consolation and, finally, certainty of what actually had happened:

> At the end of January we were for some days in Berlin together, where he [the late Grand Duke] was pleased and contented and so full of future plans. One cannot understand what made this horrible issue possible. So far as I can judge, his character was not at all disposed to melancholy. Lonely he certainly was, but I had not the impression that this troubled him. ...

> The facts which are known to me are as follows: He went out with his dog at four o'clock on the 23rd inst.[32] As he did not come back to dinner his people began to be disturbed. They made a search at once but found nothing. Military Police with dogs then searched further and at mid-day the next day the Bodyguard first found his dog sitting near his cap at the Canal. After dragging the Canal they found the body with a shot wound in the temple. So far the weapon has not been found. ...[33]

Even the serious German newspapers respected for their integrity discussed the Mecklenburg-Strelitz affair at great length, often without going to the trouble of discounting the rumours and falsifications that filled the pages of the yellow press. The English papers quickly discovered the affair and sensationalized "this scandal" to the utmost:

> Every one who is acquainted with Strelitz and its surrounding knows the real motive. ... The influence of the deceased (as a big Berlin newspaper had already mentioned) is the wife of a German Prince and magnate who is an Englishwoman by birth and – as many symptoms in her surroundings have indicated – has remained English in her thoughts and in her mind. (The lady in question can only be the Princess of Pless – the Editor of the Paper). This lady, a greatly celebrated beauty, had won a fatal influence over her Grand Ducal friend. The mutual relations finally ended in a public scandal. The consequence of it was that the Grand Duke ... as the head of his country, and as a soldier, was no longer acceptable to his subjects. Shortly before his death he is said to have received the visit of his sweetheart. It came to a tragic issue and those who have followed the course of the conflict were not surprised by its end.[34]

On May 29, Hans wrote from the Western Front:

---

32 DPH, pp. 459-60.

33 Identity of writer not revealed.

34 DPH, pp. 468-69.

About those insulting newspaper cuttings: the Emperor was not furious about you, but about the papers. It was I who showed him the cuttings, and he agreed with me that proceedings should be taken at once![35]

On June 1, Daisy received a long comforting letter from her friend Princess Margaret (Daisy), the Crown Princess of Sweden, which closed with the encouraging words "I hope you are getting the best out of the nursing you can, it may of course be a help in spite of the hard work"[36]

And on June 10, Princess Margaret of Hesse, who had fulfilled Daisy's request to transmit one of her letters to her brother, the Emperor "privately" wrote:

DEAR DAISY,
Just a line to say, that the Person I am very fond of, and to whom you wrote through me, let me know that he had received the letter, and would do what he could to help you, and put your mind at ease. ... You can be sure that you will never be forsaken by your friends so there is no reason to worry, nor to believe that they distrust you. Just do as they advise, and put up with all the complications and difficulties of these terrible times. I can assure you it is not easy for anyone, and all have their share of trouble. Hoping you are pretty well, and with much love, Yours affectionately,
MARGARET[37]

The Emperor took immediate steps to rehabilitate the name of the Princess of Pless, primarily through the Chief of his Personal Staff, Colonel General von Plessen. Daisy correctly assumed that he adopted this method in order to make his attitude in this matter widely known.

Daisy gratefully acknowledged that his public condemnation of the persecution of the Princess of Pless by the press carried the weight of an official action by the Emperor.

This was the last personal kindness the Emperor did for me. It was done at a time when his country, his throne and even his person were in grave danger. In such circumstances not many men or women would have stepped aside from stupendously important affairs to interfere on behalf of a perhaps silly woman who had been libelled by a scurrilous rag.[38]

What General von Plessen conveyed on behalf of the Emperor was clad in elaborate phrases:

---

35 DPH, p. 468.
36 DPH, 463-64.
37 DPH, p. 471.
38 DPH, p. 472.

GREAT HEADQUARTERS, 10.VI.18.

YOUR SERENE HIGHNESS, MOST GRACIOUS PRINCESS,
His Majesty sends you his best greetings and thanks for your letter of May 19th and directs me to reply as follows:

You may be sure that His Majesty did not believe one word of the gossip concerning the late Grand Duke of Mecklenburg-Strelitz. The newspaper article which treats this matter in such a brutal way had been forbidden by the Chief Censor. The author of the article nevertheless published it and – at the request of the Prince of Pless – will be prosecuted by the State Attorney. The investigation is still proceeding.

The authorities have been instructed not to in any way inconvenience Your Highness. However, in order to prevent any misconceptions, it would be well for Your Highness to avoid in public life everything that might appear in the least unusual.

His Majesty would be glad if Your Highness would lend your time and valuable strength more to the narrower home country in place of the unquiet activity in Hospital Trains and foreign Hospitals.

With the expression of my most complete esteem, I have the honour to be,
Your Highness's devoted servant,
VON PLESSEN, Aide-de-camp, General.[39]

The unequivocal declaration of the Emperor, which supported the lawsuit pursued by Hans in Upper Silesia, was most effective. Also, Hans had already started legal proceedings at the General State Attorney's office in Gleiwitz on May 3:

On April 3rd 1918, the *Oberschlesische Volksstimme*[40] published an article under the headline 'Why the Grand Duke of Mecklenburg-Strelitz Committed Suicide.'

Referring to my wife in specific terms, the article claims that she had been the lover of the late Grand Duke of Mecklenburg-Strelitz and, further, that it had been precisely this love-relationship which had driven the Grand Duke to commit suicide.

I beg to request the start of proceedings leading to the prosecution and punishment of the author and distributor of the said article causing the public slander of my wife the Princess of Pless.[41]

39 DPH, pp. 472-73.
40 A daily paper in Gleiwitz (since 1945 Gliwice), Upper Silesia.
41 Courtesy National Archives of Poland, Pszczyna Branch.

Hans had initiated a similar lawsuit in Berlin where the author of the original article operated a bureau through which he had effected the distribution of the slanderous article to hundreds of newspapers throughout Germany and Austria. On July 31, the author of the article approached Hans with a pathetic letter; its grovelling, tearful wording cannot be fully expressed in an English translation:

> I would beg the Prince of Pless to consider my proposal to prepare public declarations in a manner fully to the satisfaction of Your Highness. Readers of these declarations would realize without ambiguity that the newspaper had realized the falseness of this information on its own without having been encouraged or forced by a third party to publish an official denial.
>
> After stating the above, may I hope that I will be given an opportunity to satisfy Your Highness without enduring further legal action.
>
> Eagerly awaiting a gracious reply, I remain Your Highness's most devoted servant.[42]

The lawsuit was settled out of court, first in Gleiwitz and a week later in Berlin. Although this arrangement saved Hans and Daisy from prolonged court proceedings, which again would have been reported at great length in the press, the decision to settle the matter out of court was probably a mistake that would haunt Daisy for the rest of her life. Her reputation never appeared to have been fully restored. It was unfortunate that her name had not been publicly cleared in court.

In May, Daisy had received an offer of the directorship of a newly opened convalescent sanatorium for Austrian and Hungarian soldiers at the Black Sea resort of Constanza in Romania. Too exhausted emotionally after the death of her friend, the Grand Duke and the ongoing hate campaign in the press, Daisy felt unable to make a decision and asked for a brief leave from her hospital work instead. This gave Hans an opportunity for the belated celebration of the silver wedding anniversary in Munich. To his deep disappointment, Daisy seemed distant and removed on this special day; early the following morning, she left for Fürstenstein. Again hiding in the Schwarzengraben for a few days of peace and rest, Daisy was surprised by the unannounced arrival of Hans. If Hans had followed his wife to Fürstenstein to help her over her sad mood, his effort was without success. In a curiously removed, perhaps distrustful mood, Daisy wrote,

---

42 Ibid.

Hans dashed to *Fürstenstein* to see either me or the building operations – I was not in the least sure which. Anyhow men never grow up and must always have some ploy or another [43]

Daisy's relationship with Hans and even with Hansel was burdened with fresh tension arising out of the turn the war was taking. In July, the fifth German offensive of the summer along the Marne and in the Champagne had hopelessly stalled after some initial advances. The German initiative had provoked a strong counter-offensive by the French army, followed by the English offensive in the Battle of Amiens which Ludendorff characterized as "the black day of the German army." During the first week of September 1917, the German forces retreated to the *Siegfried Line.* [44]

At this stage, Daisy considered the war as definitely lost for Germany, and could not comprehend how not only Hans and Hansel but so many of her German friends deluded themselves with their hopes for soon-to-be won battles in the West followed by a victorious conclusion of the war before the end of the year. Hans remained the faithful letter writer describing over and over again in greatest detail countless battle scenes and enumerating the losses of the English and American forces, while never mentioning those of the German armies. He seemed totally oblivious to the effect his enthusiastic descriptions of the attacks of tanks and planes, the use of poison gas, and his jubilant announcement of the renewed shelling of Paris was bound to have on Daisy. Too many of her friends and even relatives were fighting on the other side in the battles Hans wrote about. Did Hans ever wonder what went on in Daisy's heart when it came to wishing which side should come out on top of this horrendous struggle?

Like bulletins from the front, Daisy received Hans's letters almost every other day. It was too painful to read them in all detail, Daisy realized that Hans, like others in Germany, was chasing a dream, while Daisy was convinced Germany had already lost the war.

June 4, 1918.
Here are two of the last photos of Hansel and me. On the one of them you can see his E.K.I. ... That we got in such a short time to the Marne, is beyond every expectation. Yesterday ... we went with the Emperor onto the top of a hill, from where we could see with the naked eye a great part of the fighting. Everything is going on so marvellously well, that it can only be now a question of a few weeks till, at least the French will give in. Our line is at

---

43 DPH, p. 475.
44 The new line of defense at the Western Front.

present seventy kilometres (forty-four English miles) from the centre of Paris! A few kilometres further, and we can place our *ordinary* big guns, of which we have scores. This means that in a few days Paris will be shelled so that not one stone will be left on the other, simply wiped off the face of the earth, like so many other French towns which I have seen. Would not the French prefer to make peace, to avoid this disaster? ...[45]

July 27, 1918.
On the 15th in the morning at 1 a.m. our Artillery fire began, and continued till five o'clock. ... [And four pages further into his letter] ... it would take too long to explain everything to you, but you can perhaps imagine what it all means.[46]

And in the next letter, between endless descriptions of bloody battle scenes, it finally occurred to Hans to remember Daisy's plight; she had been put under renewed pressure by members of the General Staff:

August 1, 1918.
I had breakfast with the Emperor alone. I had Count Freytag's letter ... and told the Emperor about you and read the letter to him. He was very angry about this behaviour towards you and told me to give the letter to Plessen and to tell him to write at once to the *Generalstab*. This was done, of course, the same day. The Emperor asked me why you wanted to stick to Belgrade, instead of nursing in Germany. This was just my chance and I said: In the beginning of the War, my wife tried to occupy herself with the Silesian Hospitals and Breslau, but they kicked her out. So she went to Berlin, where the same thing happened. Then she travelled in Hospital Trains ... then went to Belgrade. He said it was disgraceful the way you had been treated. I answered, especially after all she has done for Silesia and Germany ... and her lace schools, cripple-homes and hospitals. He is full of sympathy for you, and I am sure, he will always be a true friend to you, and you will see it after the War is over.

The Emperor asked why you did not occupy yourself in Germany. ... I think that the West front with the English wounded would not be advisable, as it would only be a cause of new gossip. ... I pray ... for Hansel. He has been in a hell of a fire on the south of the Marne.[47]

Did Daisy have a sense of satisfaction, perhaps even of triumph, now that Hans not only defended her, but explained her and her past humanitarian work in Silesia and in Germany to the Emperor; and did this – finally – with a sense of pride in his wife? Daisy did not mention her

---

45 DPH, pp. 470-71.
46 DPH, p. 474.
47 DPH, pp. 475-76.

feelings. There was too much that made maintaining a feeling of loyalty to Hans and his country, while her heart was beating for the country of her birth, impossible to achieve. Not only the losses on the German side, the losses on the Allied side were also extreme.

Hans announced in a matter-of-fact tone:

> August 10, 1918.
> The Americans published the names of sixty-four thousand officers and men killed, wounded, made prisoners and missing of their seven Divisions. ... This means ... practically the annihilation of these seven Divisions.[48]

And then, again with excitement and enthusiasm that Daisy considered almost insane:

> September 4, 1918.
> The situation is good. The continual attacks of the enemy are only the proofs that *they* must finish the War before the winter. ... But it is also possible that England at last comes back to her senses . ...[49]

> September 16, 1918.
> What do you say to Lansdowne's new party and his programme? I think it might lead to peace![50]

No matter how optimistic Hans sounded in his letters, Daisy knew that *the Great Retreat* had begun. Much more than his father, Hansel sensed the approaching breakdown, at the front as well as at home. On September 29, the day of Bulgaria's capitulation, he wrote to his mother:

> One hears from men who come back from leave that the frame of mind is not very good at home. The people have forgotten the war and only think of gaining money and feeding themselves. Even the educated classes hardly realize that their country is fighting for its existence. They cannot understand what this little word 'existence' means, because they have not seen how France is ruined, thousands of villages burnt and plundered, and how their women and children are killed by shells and bombs.[51]

A suddenly cautious Hans wrote on October 7, "We seem to really get nearer Peace, only God knows *what* sort of Peace it will be. ..."[52] And on October 8, the Emperor's sister, Daisy's friend Princess Margaret of

---

48 DPH, p. 476.
49 DPH, p. 477.
50 DPH, pp.478-79.
51 DPH, p. 480.
52 DPH, p. 480

Hesse lamented "Oh Daisy! What a mess the world is in and how dark everything seems! ... We must keep our courage. ..."[53]

On October 1, Daisy left Belgrade for Constanza accompanied by her secretary Helene Wagner, whose assistance would be needed for the management of the convalescent sanatorium. The Balkan front was already in a state of collapse. At Herkulesbad in southern Hungary, the train could not proceed any further, as the bridge across the Danube was destroyed. There was no hope to reach Constanza by different routes; lines of communications were fast breaking down everywhere. Daisy decided to return by steamer to Belgrade, collect her belongings and, with her maid Elsa and her valet Seidel, try and reach Budapest by any means whatsoever. After her arrival in Belgrade Daisy wrote in her diary:

> It seemed almost an absurdity to arrange one's personal life while Empires were breaking into pieces before one's very eyes. ... Our journey was heart-breaking, the boat was small, terribly overcrowded and filthy and took about sixteen hours to do the journey instead of ten. We travelled ... with refugees of all countries, so it seemed to me, one dirtier than the other, Helene got a louse on her coat.

> When we got to Belgrade at three in the morning only poor Dr. Bender was there, sent by General von Rhemen to meet me. Thank God for this, as we saw no one in civil clothes and could not find Seidel. Dr. Bender told me that Seidel and Elsa had gone. ... But the General would want to see me. He practically ordered us to proceed immediately to Germany, as Belgrade by this time was unsafe and in utter turmoil. ...

> In great hurry, General von Rhemen took us on board of the last steamer leaving for Budapest within ten minutes. There was no time to go to our house in Brcko. We needed more than two days to reach Budapest.[54]

Minutes before her precipitate departure from the Serbian capital, General von Rhemen presented Daisy with the *Medal Second Class of the Red Cross with War Decoration*, accompanied by a document addressed to

Her Serene Highness, the gracious Lady Maria Therese Princess of Pless, voluntary nurse in the Reserve Hospital Brcko in Belgrade.
I have the great honour to advise you that His Imperial and Royal Highness the Most Serene Archduke Franz Salvator, Protector of the Austrian Society of the Red Cross and of the Society of the Red Cross of the Lands of the Holy Hungarian Crown has, on behalf of His Imperial and Royal Apostolic

---

53 DPH, p. 484.
54 DPH, pp. 481-82.

Majesty, most graciously decorated Your Serene Highness with the Medal Second Class of the Red Cross with War Decoration[55], most benevolent and tax-free.

Vienna, October 18, 1918.
The President.[56]

Daisy left Belgrade with her medal, but not too much else. Her valet Seidel had already sent all her luggage to Üsküb and, together with Daisy's maid Elsa, had fled for Vienna.

Conditions in Belgrade had been chaotic, but Budapest did not seem to be much better. Daisy recognized the signs of the dissolution of the Habsburg monarchy everywhere, and she wondered what would Germany be like now. Her heart almost stopped when she read the headlines of the daily papers; the Allied Powers had advised that the abdication of the German Emperor would be the absolute pre-condition for an armistice. Before nightfall, Daisy returned to her hotel. The next day, she was forced to spend the entire day in her room as she had been warned that the streets were unsafe and overflowing with agitated masses. From her window, Daisy could hear shooting right in the centre of the city. Daisy spent hours over her diary:

> October 26, 1918. Budapest, Hotel Ritz.
> It is terrible that they now propose the German Emperor should give up his Crown for the sake of peace. ... The King-Emperor[57] had a big meeting to-day. Well, as Count Esterhazy said, there is little use in all these meetings as there is no Chancellor. ... All Austria is now in bits and every part wishes to become an independent state, the Croats, Bohemians, Hungarians, and the Poles.
>
> Yesterday, Count Schönborn-Buchheim came to see me. ... He promised to return to-day, but to my astonishment this morning I heard he had gone. ... This afternoon the Head Surgeon from the Brcko Hospital came to see me ... then Dr. Hüttl came. ... We worked so happily in Belgrade! ...
>
> During the night, there was a throwing of bombs and heavy shooting on the other side of the Danube. ... Many hotels are shut.
>
> I have been here for three days and have not moved. ... There is such an unrest. ... It is more ... safe to stay in. ...[58]

---

55 Ehrenzeichen II. Klasse vom Roten Kreuz mit der Kriegsdekoration.

56 Courtesy Bundesarchiv-Militärchiv Freiburg i. Breisgau.

57 Karl, Emperor of Austria and King of Hungary.

58 DPH, pp. 482-84 passim.

Little did Daisy know that in Germany, the disintegration of the country and its government had proceeded even further. As the Princess Blücher reported in her diary on October 24, 1918, less than three weeks before the revolution rolled across Germany:

> Last evening there was still another demonstration. ... The people are gradually awakening to a sense of their power, but ... there are still invisible hands ... ready to nip any pacific movement in the bud...

> Whilst depicting the last agony of the country at large, one is apt to forget the sufferings of the individual, but what the war is not destroying in human life, the terrible grippe epidemic is carrying off. One hears of whole families dying out. ...

> Everyone feels something momentous is going to take place. ... The whole public spirit is so depressed and the universal suffering so great that the people are threatening to take matters in their own hands. ... Wounded men refuse consent to operations ... on the ground that they might then be sent back to the front ... they have no intention of going there. Capitalists and large landowners ... talk in earnest about their land being confiscated and their property divided up in the Bolshevik manner.[59]

* * *

On November 3, 1918, the day the German Revolution was started in Kiel by soldiers of the Imperial Navy, Daisy left Budapest. During two days on the overcrowded train, neither the schedule nor the accommodation were what used to be standard for the Princess of Pless before the war. Several times, the train was stopped and searched for communists and spies. Daisy's health seemed surprisingly good, a result perhaps of the excitement of fending for herself, of being entirely on her own and travelling incognito, a lonely woman and her companion amongst hundreds of thousands of people streaming westwards through countries on the verge of disintegration.

> Budapest and Vienna were now very uncomfortable and quite dangerous. I rather liked the idea of being in the midst of turmoil and revolution as I am not in the least afraid of crowds and find danger of any kind exhilarating.[60]

Daisy arrived in Munich on November 5. Four days later, a tired man in torn clothes, the usually impeccable Seidel, and a dishevelled

---

59 See Evelyn Princess Blücher, op. cit., pp. 256-57.

60 DPH, pp. 484-85.

woman, the pretty Elsa, stood at the door of Daisy's apartment in the Romanstrasse in the Munich suburb of Nymphenburg.

In the Bavarian capital, revolution broke out on November 7. The King was forced to flee across the Austrian border to Salzburg, the monarchy was declared abolished and, on the following day, Bavaria was proclaimed a Free State. In Berlin on November 9, the Social Democratic Reichstag deputy Philipp Scheidemann proclaimed the German Republic from a window of the Berlin Castle. The Emperor declared his abdication; Prince Max von Baden, the last chancellor of the Empire, resigned and transferred the responsibility of governing the country to Friedrich Ebert, the chairman of Germany's Social Democratic Party. On November 10, the Emperor crossed the Dutch border into his exile.

On the day before, Prince Max von Baden had addressed the Emperor in a decisive conversation over the telephone, which was recorded by the Chancellor's aide von Prittwitz:

> Your abdication has become a matter of necessity, if civil war is to be averted. ... If that succeeds, Your Majesty's name will be revered in history. If it fails, the Reichstag's demand will be made. ... We can no longer rely on the troops. ... Abdication ... must be voluntary – so only will Your Majesty's name live in history![61]

Silesia was also seized by civil disturbances and revolt almost everywhere. Daisy's hope to return to Fürstenstein after the end of hostilities came to naught. Hans had returned to Fürstenstein immediately after Armistice was declared. While the castle district still seemed an island of peace, he was shocked by what he found in Waldenburg and the surrounding area. Almost in disbelief, but greatly alarmed, he informed Daisy that the streets of Waldenburg were overflowing with thousands of demonstrating workers. Those working in the Pless mines had continued to the Castle Waldenburg [the seat of the Pless administration] shouting "Hang Keindorff."[62] And much of the press still had nothing better to report than the high treason of the Princess of Pless. At this stage, Daisy's return to Fürstenstein or Pless would be absolutely impossible – it would literally mean risking her life. Even the Polish population in Pless seemed in a state of excitement and restlessness.

What was left for Daisy, but to return to her "private exile" in Partenkirchen! Things had changed there as well. Daisy would have

---

61 See Emil Ludwig, op. cit., p. 436.

62 "Hängt den Keindorff!" general director of the Pless properties in Lower Silesia.

never expected to find five members of the local Workers and Soldiers Council living in her villa.

> November 15, 1918. Partenkirchen.
> They are all very, very nice to me and I have given parties for them and their friends twice in my little house; and then in the village hall two big parties for two hundred men; this means simply providing cigarettes and beer, otherwise it is all done at the expense of the community. The little I do is simply done most truly from all my heart, as one must not forget these men have all been at the front since four years and in my eyes, as I see things clearly coming, they are our only defence against Bolshevism.
>
> They simply want, as far as I can learn by talking to them, a certain right to what God made the world for, and that is that the poor shall not hunger and want, and that fields and green grass shall be free for men and women to walk over. ... Since Vater died I have hated to see at Fürstenstein and Pless new roads built to hide every single soul that could pass near us, chains hung everywhere with the word upon them *Verbotener Weg*.[63] God's heavens are not *verboten* and there all, thank God, will some day be on the same level and only the soul and heart may speak. Work we shall have to do but it will be a work of kindness to all.[64]

Daisy waited for the magic word; that it was safe to return to Fürstenstein. She waited to see her children Hansel and Lexel, and she waited for news from Patsy – for weeks no mail had arrived from England. But at least, the war had come to an end. Despite all her worries and sorrows, Daisy now looked forward to a better future, but what did she know about the future that was waiting for her! Her hopes for England and Germany eventually became true, but only after another world war. Her hopes for her own future could not be more disappointed. On November 27, 1918, Daisy wrote:

> I see so distinctly a future when England and Germany will be (and have to be) friends – not alone, but with many others; that means without signed treaties, which are no use, but with just a good understanding, and what the Soldiers' Council call *Kameradschaft*.[65]

* * * * * *

---

63 Private Path – Access Forbidden

64 DPH. p. 486.

65 DPH, p. 488.

11 | *Forgotten by the World*

The princes went. Hohenzollern and Wittelsbachs, Wettiner and Guelphs and Zähringer, the dynasties which for a thousand years had shared or decided, as they did in 1848, the fate of Germany – within two days they all vanished. ... They were not hated ... and there was no reason to hate them. They were sent packing because there was a revolution. ... No hand was raised on their behalf. ... Something that died so easily could not have had any vitality. ... It is possible to think that it might have been better to keep them. While they could not achieve much nor prevent much, they were at least centres of tradition and style. Perhaps they would have later acted as a restraining element – with a king in Munich or Stuttgart it is difficult to imagine a victory for National Socialism.[1]

Golo Mann

* * *

So did Golo Mann sum up the outcome of the German Revolution of 1918, an upheaval which profoundly affected Daisy in her personal life. While she and Hans did not lose a throne, *the noble lords,* as Golo Mann called the deposed monarchs, had always been part of Hans's and Daisy's world which now disintegrated overnight; with it, the style of life of this entire class of German high society disappeared, even though Hans did not want to recognize this fact for some time.

* * *

---

1   Golo Mann, *The History of Germany since 1789* (London, 1968), p. 337.

Four weeks after the November Revolution, Daisy wrote an entry into her diary that demonstrated her insight into the cataclysmic events, and their effects on her class and her own life:

December 3, 1918. Partenkirchen.

The country has dismissed its Emperor. Poor man, he had no one brave enough to advise him courageously. I wanted to write him, but ... escaping from revolutionary Belgrade only to meet another revolution in Munich! Oh, if the Emperor had taken off his crown and given it back to the people with the words: 'I shall only bring more trouble to you all by remaining here; I wished you always what was best, and my whole ambition was for my country. ... So, with prayers for all your future ... I leave you!'

He was my friend and exactly knew how I suffered through those horrible years of war; but he has gone; and *Vater*, my dear *Schwiegervater*[2] has also gone. ... I am alone!

Personally, I have nothing left but bitter memories of Germany. I gladly take off my princely crown and retire to a dear green island, or to my hills in France. ... My boys, naturally, will marry Germans, and their wives will not welcome an English mother-in-law.[3]

The sense of belonging nowhere, of having no true home had been part of Daisy's life since the beginning of the war. Now with the war over, the time had come to clear up things between Hans and herself. However, Hans adamantly insisted that Daisy stay away from Silesia. It remains an unanswered question whether his insistence was motivated by political considerations only or for personal reasons as well. At any rate, for months there was no opportunity to spend time together. In June 1918, her brother-in-law Fritz Hochberg had written quite openly to Daisy. Having lived in England until the war, Fritz understood Daisy's state of mind better than most who worried about her. On his Silesian property of Halbau, he anxiously waited for a time when he could return to his beloved Minstead Manor[4].

HALBAU, June 17, 1918

MY DARLING GIRL,
If I could only convince you ... that now is really not the moment to undertake anything. ... You are English, and in Prussian public opinion

---

2   Father-in-law.
3   WLU, pp. 179-80.
4   Located in Hampshire in the New Forest.

England is worse than all the devils in Hell combined. So, whatever you say, Prussia would always sanction anything done against die *Engländerin*.[5] ... Wait your turn, as long as this war lasts it won't come, so patience. ...

Damn your old Hans — he has never been, never will be, the centre of your life. ... When the war is over ... we'll take the next boat and sail for our beloved little island. ... You'll make your main home at Arnewood[6] and come to your German hill house for a yearly trip ... why ... going to Fürstenstein to meet Hans? You'll only quarrel. ... Do leave him alone ... play your cards well.[7]

One Anglophile tried to cheer up the other! Among all the Hochbergs, since Vater's death, Fritz had been Daisy's best friend. Among the Hochberg women, only Daisy's sister-in-law Lulu von Solms-Baruth was a true confidante. However, not even the perceptive Lulu could really comprehend the dreadful conflict of loyalty Daisy was trying to conquer. On November 15, 1918, among the first mail since the Armistice a letter from Silesia arrived in Partenkirchen. But Lulu's well-meant praise only raised new doubts in Daisy's mind whether there was any point in remaining in Germany any longer.

KLITSCHDORF, November 7, 1918.

Bravo! Daisy, well done!
I must say myself I thought *perhaps* you wouldn't mind being made a prisoner by the Entente. I beg your pardon for the thought, or suspicion, and am very glad that you came back; and how right you are, for the sake of your boys — the difference it will make in their lives later on to know that their mother was true. ...

Thank you for your letters; thank God you got out of the Belgrade muddle in time. Bless you,

Yours, LOUISE.[8]

Initially, Daisy felt misunderstood and deeply wounded by Lulu's letter. If even the intelligent Lulu had such strong doubts about Daisy's loyalty and integrity, what could Daisy expect from Silesia's nobility and its ordinary people? Daisy at last understood why Hans displayed such a harsh, heartless attitude towards her wish to return to Fürstenstein. No

---

5   The Englishwoman [Daisy Pless].
6   The old Arnewood Priory near Newlands Manor, part of the estate.
7   WLU, pp. 94-95.
8   WLU, pp. 178-79.

wonder, even though she was thinking about creating a home and a family life for her children as her first obligation, Daisy was drawn to England where the very ill Patsy was desperately waiting for her. With the path to Fürstenstein barred, what was more logical than to follow in the footsteps of her English friends Evelyn Blücher and Muriel Münster,[9] who had managed to return to England immediately after the Armistice!

It took days before Daisy overcame her doubts and fears and resolved to try to get to England. The outcome was a great disappointment – for the time being, Daisy was forced to remain in Germany. The conflict of leaving Germany or staying became the practical and psychological cause for a restless, rootless life; Daisy lost all sense of belonging – to the country of her birth as much as to the country of her marriage – even to her family and to many of her friends. These immediate postwar weeks were the beginning of a life filled with family disagreements and quarrels, never ending money troubles, and frequent experiences of being exploited and deceived. Everything became more painful because of the increasing physical debility, which more and more diminished Daisy's ability to make sound plans and follow through with them.

Daisy's life began to read like a novel! Robbed of all prominence and fame, of wealth and glamour, and more and more restricted in her personal freedom and control over her life, Daisy's attitudes and decisions became sometimes less than rational, often overshadowed by the consequences of her loneliness, isolation, and helplessness. Basically, however, the course of her life was now determined by the external circumstances of revolution, inflation, and political and social upheavals. Daisy's diaries give only a sparse report of her fate.[10]

* * *

It was March 1919 before Daisy received her permit to enter Switzerland as a guest of her friend Nancy Leeds, who was to marry Prince Christopher of Greece in the following year. Daisy saw her journey to Switzer-

---

9   Princess Münster von Derneburg née Lady Muriel Hay.

10   Only the published parts of the diaries have survived from that time. Besides, in certain passages, considerable contradictions including political opinions between the second and the third volumes are apparent, for which their editor Major Chapman-Huston and his carelessness, ignorance and thirst for money must be held accountable. Some letters have survived elsewhere. In addition, in the archives of Castle Pszczyna (Pless) more than 300 pages of documents miraculously survived World War II and its aftermath. They present a shocking, often moving picture of Daisy's life between 1920 and her death in 1943; they are also a mirror of political and social turmoil never before experienced in Germany to that degree.

land as the springboard for her return to England. She had already
written to Lord Balfour asking for his assistance. Spring was beautiful in
Lausanne, but the contents of the letter waiting for her at Nancy Leeds's
villa were shattering:

BRITISH DELEGATION, PARIS, February 25, 1919

MY DEAR PRINCESS OF PLESS,
Since receiving your letter I have been made very unhappy by reflecting
how little I can do to give you any assistance in all your troubles and
difficulties.

Often have I thought of you during these four and a half years of war. ...
The sufferings which the world has gone through in that period are beyond
computation, but perhaps those are most to be pitied who, by the accident
of marriage, have become citizens of a State at war with the country of their
birth.

The worst is that there is no alleviation possible for their position till peace
is declared. Before that happy day arrives they must in law be counted as
belonging to an enemy State and it is not possible, with the best will in the
world, to treat them as still belonging to the land of their fathers. Believe
me I know how much you must have gone through and I would most
willingly help you by every method at my disposal. But Rumbold[11] will have
told you how matters stand and how impossible it is to do more than give
you my very sincere expressions of sympathy.

Yours sincerely,
ARTHUR JAMES BALFOUR.[12]

It did not help Daisy to be told through letters that in England,

some kind friends, I believe, said loudly that I ought to be ashamed to show
my face in England so soon. ... One of the most despicable consequences
of this hateful war was the recognition that even friends whose loyalty one
had never doubted, proved unfaithful and false.[13]

Only in September 1919 did Daisy succeed in reaching England,
grateful to Queen Alexandra and some other friends for their help.
Nobody took notice when she touched the soil of her beloved England
for the first time in five years again. Only the old porter at the dock in

---

11 the British Ambassador to Switzerland.

12 WLU, pp. 296-97.

13 WLU, p. 297.

Southampton brought tears to her eyes when he greeted *Miss Daisy* like a long lost friend.

Neither did anybody wait for her at Waterloo Station. In pouring rain, Daisy travelled through the gray, wet streets of London to the house of Stella Patrick-Campbell. There was nowhere else to stay, and no money to book into an expensive hotel. Daisy was extremely grateful to Stella for offering her shelter so spontaneously. There were worries and bad news all around. Daisy's mother lay very ill in a hospital. Daisy had to expect the worst. Her mother was brave as always; "I watched Patsy as she lay in bed," Stella wrote after visiting her mother-in-law together with Daisy; "her expression of mysterious defiance touched me."[14] A few days later, Daisy's Aunt Min Wyndham died. Nancy Leeds's invitation to Kenwood was a ray of hope at this time. Daisy was only too glad to escape London, where she felt unbearably strange and unwanted. In between, she spent some days with the old Empress Eugenie[15] at Farnborough, and noted with sarcasm that

> apart from my own family, the first homes I was invited to stay after my long, miserable, enforced exile were those of an American and a French-woman![16]

Queen Alexandra wrote in true compassion:

SANDRINGHAM, NORFOLK, September 18, 1919.

MY POOR DEAR DAISY:
I see by the papers that at last you have actually been *allowed* to come back to your beloved home and poor suffering little Mother dear! I am really *so* delighted to hear it as I know *what* you have gone through and suffered during all those five years of awful horrible war and then you were banned from England. I was so sorry I was unable to help last Spring. ... I do hope you found your poor Mother better and ... in your old home! which I hear your brother wants to sell – too bad and horrid! ... Please write and tell me all about *yourself.*

Yours affectionately,
ALEXANDRA.[17]

---

14 See Mrs. Stella Patrick Campbell, op. cit., p. 291.

15 Widow of Emperor Napoleon III of France.

16 WLU, p. 298.

17 WLU, pp. 298-99.

"If I had thought I would find peace in England I was mistaken," wrote a disconsolate Daisy. There was more that upset her. George was not doing well, neither professionally nor in his marriage. As heir to the Cornwallis-West properties, he had to sell Newlands in order to pay his debts, knowing he would never be able to maintain the family estate. Daisy found it hard to forgive her brother for depriving her of the family home. There seemed to be losses everywhere. Shelagh's marriage to the Duke of Westminster finally ended in divorce on June 17, 1919. At least Shelagh was now free to help her mother and in October, she and her mother left for France. Daisy had to stay behind; once more she was reminded of her unprotected legal status. She followed two weeks later, after a sympathetic French physician managed to obtain a visa for her by citing her poor health.

In La Napoule, Daisy found peace. The small colony of English people, that included the Duke of Connaught, received Daisy as in old times. Patsy began to feel better from day to day, and by March 1920, Daisy, wishing to see her children, felt at ease to leave her sister Shelagh, her mother "Patsy", and her maid-companion Dolly Crowther, and return to Germany.

But in June 1920, Shelagh wrote that Patsy felt very poorly and wanted to return to England to die there. Daisy rushed back to France and helped take Patsy home, an effort which proved to be an expedition. Mrs. Cornwallis-West died on July 21, 1920 in the old Arnewood Priory in the New Forest, close to her beloved Newlands Manor.

In her diary, Daisy demonstrated how close to each other she and her mother had always been:

> We shall see no one like her any more. Had she faults and failings? Masses of them, but such endearing, human ones. How she was produced by the early Victorian environment from which she emerged, and which she alternately shocked and delighted, I shall never understand. She was quick in everything: in thought, speech, repartee, temper, sympathy, likes and dislikes; she seldom let judgment wait on reflection, and such was the fineness of her intelligence that she was not very often wrong. A woman who could capture and keep as faithful romantic friends such different men as Mr. Gladstone and King Edward VII was no ordinary person. The poor are by far the best and truest judges of character, and the villagers in and around Ruthin, who knew her in and out, just adored her. They understood her impulsiveness, her wild at times almost foolish, disregard of conventions, because they saw her at close quarters and appreciated her affectionate heart. To them, she was such a great lady, so innately an aristocrat, that she could defy all laws and customs, not only with impunity, but with applause. Only the poorer country people can understand this because, in

their own degree, they themselves demand and exercise a similar freedom. Unlike the middle classes, they put life before mere living.

Like all real aristocrats she had no 'class feeling,' and would be as intimate and fascinating with a washerwoman, a carpenter or a commercial traveller as with King Edward or the German Emperor; no one with Irish blood in them can ever really be a snob![18]

A visit with Shelagh to Bagnolles in August 1920 was to bring rest and improved health for Daisy.

But of course it was too late. Had I been able to return there in the autumn of 1914 as I had intended, I might have been cured. Four years and a quarter of the wear and tear of war, and many months on my hind legs in hospitals and in hospital trains, made, I am afraid, any real hope of recovery almost impossible.[19]

Christmas 1920 was burdened with grave discussions between Hans and Daisy; Daisy left just before New Year 1921, earlier than intended. After her precipitous departure from Fürstenstein, she felt like she was taking flight to the Sanatorium Bühlerhöhe at Baden-Baden. This was the spa where she had celebrated her social triumphs at the side of the Prince of Wales. Now defeated and desperate, Daisy turned to King George V. Her desperate letter gives a sense of how terrible the quarrels must have been at Fürstenstein; the end of the marriage between Hans and Daisy was now a certainty:

Bühlerhöhe bei Baden-Baden January 25, 1921.

Sire.
Your Majesty.
I *beg* Your Majesty to read this and believe that it is serious as I may later ask to put myself if possible under English protection, as an English woman married to a German. Colonel Roddie in Berlin said Let them know this.

The German law, Sire, is helping me, at least it says so, but my husband is behaving vilely. The doctor here says I must sign nothing yet, they are trying to tempt me by promising to buy a villa in France if I agree to a divorce but worded as they wish & I do not understand it; all law reads like Greek. Oh! Sire I only beg that a gentleman may write to Col Roddie in Berlin or to Lord Kilmarnock & say that Your Majesty hearing that an English lady is

---

18 WLU, pp. 303-04.
19 WLU, p. 306.

being put into difficulties and bullied that she may know she is under British Protection.

Oh! Sire I only beg of Your Majesty to believe that those two words 'British Protection' will make the law sit up, and my husband tremble. If I may feel that Col Roddie or Lord Kilmarnock may be with me with the lawyer, and before I sign anything then I shall feel safe.

If I sign a divorce for the sake of a *home* in my villa in France, and a yearly income, shall I be the same in England as long ago if not, then I will not agree, or sign anything.

If it is known by the law and my husband that I am under British Protection fear will come to them, and a new light will come into my life.

I return now to the Hotel Esplanade Berlin.

I only emplore you Sire for the sake of old days to give me a minute's thought, and believe that I have thought many days before writing but nearly all my friends, and my *parents* have gone, & I feel alone, so to touch England's heart now, I touch Your Majesty, and Oh! Sire – help me.

Very humbly in tears,

Your Majesty's true and humble servant.
Princess Daisy Pless.[20]

* * *

In June 1921, more than two and a half years after the end of hostilities, Daisy's official return to Fürstenstein finally took place[21]. It was one of the strangest days Daisy ever experienced in Fürstenstein.

I was formally received by Hans with considerable pomp. I think it was meant to convey to the world of Silesia that I was really quite a harmless person. The night of my arrival there were great festivities and, for a time, both Hans and I hoped and believed that we could settle down together happily after the war. But it was not to be; too much, perhaps, had happened in our personal, our domestic, and our national life to make such hope realizable. Moreover, I knew only too well that I could never again feel at home in Prussia; Bavaria and South Germany was different, never having shown me signs of bitter enmity – but Silesia. ...[22]

---

20 Courtesy, Royal Archives, Windsor Castle.

21 Daisy's earlier brief visits had been very private and unpublicized.

22 WLU, p. 307.

In fall 1921, Daisy returned to Partenkirchen. Reconciled to the impending divorce, Daisy was ready to look at her future by gathering a small household around herself, which next to the servants provided by the Pless Administration in Fürstenstein, included her cousin Ena FitzPatrick. A member of a not very prosperous branch of the FitzPatrick family, Ena had been sent to Germany before the war at the age of sixteen to live with a family that owned an estate with a small manor house in Southwestern Bavaria. As with Daisy, Ena had had to spend the war years in Germany.

The legal proceedings finalizing the divorce took much longer than expected. An enigmatic aspect was the purpose of the protocol that reached Daisy in July 1922 at the Hotel Adlon in Berlin. Prepared in German in Pless, the following protocol was taken to Berlin by C. Herde, the Catholic priest from Nieder Salzbrunn near Fürstenstein:

> I, the Princess Pless, born Mary Therese West, declare herewith, without being placed under duress by anyone, that I regard my marriage to the Prince of Pless as nisi. Grounds are as follows:
>
> In the year 1891, the Prince asked me to marry him. I declined his proposal, as I felt that at the age of eighteen, I was too young and, furthermore, I did not love him. Put under great pressure by my mother who after becoming aware of the Prince's proposal, did not miss any opportunity to bring me together with him, I finally accepted the second marriage proposal by the Prince without having any feelings of love for him. ...
>
> Yielding to the relentless urging by my mother, in fear of remaining quite poor and homeless in view of the very small dowry I could expect, I entered, in the ignorance of youth, into the marriage with the Prince. ... Troubled by feelings of aversion in my heart, I approached the altar in tears. I therefore never considered my marriage as insoluble ... and only the concern for the social conventions in the Germany of that time made me continue this marriage at least for appearances sake. With the all-encompassing social and political changes in Germany, however, I wish to terminate my marriage which has been characterized by a disharmonious relationship from the beginning. The necessary legal proceedings have been put into motion.[23]

Annotated by Father Herde that "in the end, the Princess decided against signing," the Protocol was returned to Pless.

The origin and purpose of this protocol remain obscure. Wording and style go far beyond what Daisy was capable of expressing in German.

---

23 Courtesy National Archives of Poland, Pszczyna Branch (translated from German by the author).

The legal argument underlying the protocol may seem characteristic for a certain type of divorce protocol; it remains doubtful that it was prepared by a divorce lawyer. For its intended purpose, to have Daisy declare herself as the guilty party wanting to terminate the marriage, the arguments seem rather vague. Intriguing is the presence of a country priest like Father Herde at the Hotel Adlon in Berlin, which leads to the impression that Herde had been sent to Berlin by Hans for the purpose of persuading Daisy to sign this protocol which in the end she refused to do.

On October 2, 1922 the final divorce protocol was signed by both parties and became legal, following a proclamation by the court in Berlin on December 4, 1923.

In the end, Hans had been generous, ensuring Daisy a standard of living commensurate with her rank. The settlement included a residence – the villa *Les Marguerites* – in La Napoule at the French Riviera; the purchase and furnishing of a second residence in Munich; costs for hiring a companion, servants, and other personnel; purchase and maintenance of an automobile; and a generous apanage. The maintenance of the style of life Daisy had been used to seemed guaranteed.

What Hans could not provide for was the perpetual protection against the consequences of unforeseeable political events and economic changes. Unexpected by both parties, within one year of the divorce settlement the standard of living Hans had promised Daisy became impossible to maintain. From then on, in a strange sequence of intervals of five to seven years, major developments occurred, which affected the wealth, income, and standard of living not only of Daisy, but of Hans and the entire family as well.

It began with the partition of Upper Silesia between Germany and Poland. Following the plebiscite of March 29, 1921 the districts of Pless and Rybnik with their predominantly Polish population became part of the new Republic of Poland. This change also brought the entire Upper Silesian properties of the Prince of Pless under Polish jurisdiction.[24]

No longer recognizing privileges dating back to the Middle Ages, the Polish government raised the taxation of the Pless properties to ruinous levels. Hans became involved in expensive lawsuits against the

---

24 97 percent of those eligible to vote in the district of Pless participated in the plebiscite. More than 75 percent voted for becoming part of the new Polish state. In the adjoining district of Rybnik, an equally high percentage of citizens exercised their right to vote with 65 per cent in favor of joining Poland. In the entire plebiscite area of Upper Silesia, of 1,215,373 eligible voters 39.5 percent voted for joining the new Polish state while 57.8 percent voted to remain with Germany. 97.2 percent of those eligible exercised their right to vote. From *Schlesien nach der Teilung* (Plankammer des Preussischen Statistischen Landesamtes, Berlin, 1924).

Polish government that were never resolved; they ended with Hitler's invasion of Poland.

Starting in August 1921, inflation destroyed the major part of the wealth of the Prince of Pless. The ongoing rapid devaluation of the German Mark impoverished Daisy and her small household; there were days and weeks when Daisy felt like she was living in abject poverty. There was no cash in the house, and merchants no longer granted credit.

The devastating inflation was followed by Germany's *Golden Twenties,* a short-lived five years of economic recovery that fell victim to the worldwide economic crisis that began in 1929.

In both Germany and Poland, the Pless enterprises no longer created any profits. The debts of the Prince of Pless mounted dramatically. As a drastic savings measure, Hans closed down the household in Fürstenstein and designated Castle Pless as the family's primary residence. Reaching insolvency, the coal mines around Waldenburg and the other Pless enterprises in Germany were put under public trusteeship administered by a board, the *Pless Gremium,* in Berlin. Its chairman controlled even the expenses of Daisy's modest household.

It was to Hans's great disadvantage that he and his two sons Hansel and Lexel had acquired Polish citizenship, before Adolf Hitler came to power. Hitler's Third Reich, with its enmity to Poland, no longer gave the Pless family the support it had enjoyed up to1933 under the old Weimar Republic. At the outbreak of World War II, all Pless properties were sequestered by the Third Reich. This also included the vast properties in Polish Upper Silesia, which was integrated into the Third Reich immediately after its occupation in early September 1939.

During the Hitler years, Daisy's by that time tiny monthly maintenance was affected to a critical degree. As prior to his divorce, Hans had acquired Polish citizenship, Daisy should have by international law retained the right to Polish citizenship as well. This, however, was not recognized by the Polish government. As a consequence of the divorce, Daisy lost her status as a German citizen and received the designation of "Devisenausländerin."[25] Within weeks of Hitler's ascent to power on January 30, 1933, strict currency regulations were introduced by the Third Reich. As Daisy was no longer recognized as German citizen, monthly payments made by the Pless Administration from Pless in Poland, had to be made to the Ministry of Finance in Berlin to be forwarded to Daisy only with the Minister's approval; releasing monies to Daisy often took months.

---

25   "External valuta foreigner."

Six years after the birth of Hitler's Third Reich, Daisy's living situation and financial security became even more precarious when Hitler started World War II with the invasion of Poland on September 1, 1939. By that time, Daisy's progressive deterioration of health due to her chronic illness had made her totally dependent on care provided by others. Adequate funds for medical care and medications were never provided to her by the German state.

For years, Daisy had felt helpless and abandoned. No wonder she was often inclined to make rash decisions, turning from one advisor to the next. No wonder that nearly all attempts to bring control, and at least a measure of security into Daisy's life, were invariably doomed to failure. Often extended by several persons simultaneously, such attempts to help canceled each other out, and Daisy found herself without sufficient disposable income and was forever hounded by creditors and even bailiffs. In the end, she felt betrayed and deceived by Hans. It must be said, though, that she was not quite fair to Hans; since the beginning of the 1930s, Hans had practically lost all control over the use and disposition of his income.

* * *

Too many external circumstances and events again and again affected the generosity and reliability that Hans had promised. After the purchase of the house in Munich was concluded, Daisy agreed to make her home in hotels, sanatoria, or in her villa at La Napoule, until the restorations and changes of the Munich villa were completed. Strangely enough, nobody had thought about the effects of the collapse of the German currency. Within six months of her divorce, Daisy found herself in an extremely precarious situation. Every day, the German Mark lost more of its value. Significantly, as the inflation heated up, so did the battles between Daisy's attorneys in Munich and Berlin and Hans's representatives, that involved, next to the administrations of Pless and Fürstenstein, his attorneys in Berlin and Munich. Later, they were joined by the representatives of the *Pless Gremium*, the German Ministry of Finance, and the government offices controlling foreign valuta in Munich and Breslau.

Against this formidable circle stood the two attorneys in Berlin and Munich who valiantly tried to fight for Daisy's interests.

Finally, Hansel and Lexel also got involved in trying to assist their mother. Unfortunately, each son did so on his own without consulting the other. Daisy became the vicitim of misunderstandings, disagreements, even intrigues between the ever increasing group of government officials and Pless officials, attorneys and advisors of various status, family members, and friends. Their varied endeavours thwarted each other. This struggle continued until Daisy's death. No agreement was ever reached about how to secure a modest, but reliable income for Daisy. The costs of the endless legal battles exceeded by far the pitiful amounts of money Daisy received for her subsistence!

Among several hundred various documents, a dozen letters of Ena FitzPatrick have survived in the archives of Castle Pless. Cries for help on behalf of Daisy and herself, they record in dramatic, at times drastic words the desperate situation of the two women, their embarrassing dependence on the good-will of shopkeepers and other creditors, and the wear and tear on Daisy's and Ena's nerves, as they never knew whether the desperately needed money would be arriving on the expected date, if at all.

Ena's far-from-perfect command of written German gives her messages to Hausmarschall Rittmeister von dem Hagen, the Court Marshal at Castle Fürstenstein, an added effect that unfortunately cannot be brought to life in their English translation:

Burggrafenstrasse 1 Berlin, Nov. 9, 1923

Dear Herr von dem Hagen,
Yesterday, the 8th, I received the money from the bank, 21 780 833 Billion Marks.

Really, Herr von dem Hagen, I cannot comprehend such accounting methods. I find them outrageous! ... This is a ridiculous sum of money, as you know full well that what we owe the sanatorium is much, much more. But this is not the real issue anyway, the [monies sent] were calculated according to the exchange rate of Oct. and not of the 8th of November when one Goldmark is worth 150 000 millions.[26]

I don't know what to do, but if we do not pay to-day, they will throw us out immediately ... and *nowhere* is there anybody willing to take us in without money – I have had it! We have been here at the sanatorium since the 24th without having paid a penny. ... The physician also has to be paid – 130 Goldmark – we have to have his assistance as Her Highness is not doing well at all. Does your Administration have to be so petty and paltry! I am not ashamed to say during my entire war years in Germany when life was really hard for me, I never did so poorly than since I have been dependent on the Pless Administration.

As far as our money is concerned, what you send us is too little and too late, and personally I no longer care whether we end up in the poorhouse in Munich or here in Berlin!

26 Calculated by the gold standard (Goldmark), the German Mark lost its value by the hour during the periods of super inflation.

Please also remember that this is already the 9th and it would not hurt me if I would receive for the month of November my little spending money. Let me tell you, I am normally a very easy-going and patient person, but I cannot keep this up much longer when it is expected that we must live from 'fresh air and love'.

Sincerely,
ENA FITZPATRICK.[27]

Three weeks later, Daisy's attorney urgently turned to his colleague who represented the Pless Administration in Berlin, after Ena's desperate missives to Fürstenstein had not had any effect whatsoever:

Berlin W8, Mohrenstrasse 19
28th of November 1923

Herrn Dr. Walter Schmidt Attorney
Berlin W8, Taubenstrasse 46

Dear Colleague!
In matters of von Pless, I again had a most detailed review with Her Highness the Princess yesterday. Her current situation is more than scandalous. The Princess has to expect any day that the Mother Superior will put her out on the street ... as she cannot afford to give the Princess any more credit. It is an unacceptable imposition on the Princess to have to tolerate all this while the Pless Administration does not move a finger. Even the physician has threatened to terminate his services as his honorarium has never been paid by the Administration.

Even in the smallest and most insignificant matters of daily life there is no money viz. trolley tickets, newspapers, soap etc. I have to stress again – and I have convinced myself again that *in every respect what money is available is being spent in the most prudent manner.*

We have to insist that aside from the still outstanding payments for October and November, the first installment of the December apanage must be paid on time on December 1, as otherwise, there again would be no money available.

All our efforts have only become necessary, because His Highness the Prince has failed to fulfill his most sincerely accepted obligations again and again.

Pünder, Attorney at Law[28]

---

27 Courtesy National Archives of Poland, Pszczyna Branch (translated from German by the author).

28 Ibid.

The conflict around the full and timely payment of Daisy's monthly apanage for which the Pless Administration was held responsible, became even more pronounced after Daisy's move to La Napoule in December 1923. Nobody managed to keep pace with the galloping German inflation. Finally, the German Reichsbank stabilized the country's currency with the introduction of the new *Rentenmark*. Daisy assumed her troubles were behind her, but she had not expected the serious shortage of foreign currency in Germany that continually delayed the conversion of her monthly apanage into French Francs before its transfer to the bank in Cannes. In spring of 1924, the legal battle with the Pless Administration moved to Munich when Daisy retained another attorney and started court proceedings in that city. She asked her attorney to sue not only for the outstanding payments of her apanage, but also for the payment of the 200 000 Marks silver anniversary gift in 1916, which Hans had never paid; and neither had he paid the tax on her apanage as guaranteed in the divorce settlement.

If Daisy was hoping for economic security, she was disappointed again; the introduction of additional attorneys by both sides only postponed the court judgement. In fall of 1924, a new issue arose when the Pless Administration declared Daisy's villa in Munich as "practically ready for occupancy." A new conflict centered on the furnishings of the villa for which, according to the Administration, there were not sufficient objects and materials available in Fürstenstein. Knowing her castle of 600 rooms full of precious furniture and objects from room to room, Daisy was deeply offended. What had been sent to Munich was unacceptable, and Daisy's attorney complained about "the miserable, pitiful condition of the bed and table linen" sent from Fürstenstein. By this time, the changes and improvements of the Munich villa had devoured 154,790 Marks and the Administration in Pless pointedly inquired in Fürstenstein "whether this was to go on in perpetuity."

The problem with the seemingly ill-fated villa in the Ismaningerstrasse was further exacerbated when Daisy and Lexel decided to maintain one household together. Lexel's expensive habits and tastes sent the household costs through the roof. It was impossible to discern who complicated matters more; the at times eccentric Daisy or the happy-go-lucky Lexel. At any rate, all good will and attempts to maintain rational relationships between the warring parties were exhausted to a degree that hurt Daisy most. It did not help that in her desperation, she did not know how to defend herself any more other than by being rigid and ungiving at times to the extreme.

Daisy had lost all pride and enjoyment of owning this actually very attractive and comfortable house located in the Herzogpark, Munich's most prestigious address. In October 1924, she fled to her friend Fanny

Sternberg in Castolowice in Czechoslovakia, where Daisy felt welcome as in old times, and for the first time in what seemed ages, she was happy. However, conflict stubbornly pursued Daisy. Now, when the daily annoyances and money troubles of Munich temporarily disappeared, whatever had troubled the relationship of Daisy and Ena rose to the surface.

A rather distraught Ena turned to Herrn von dem Hagen in Fürstenstein for advice. Daisy, in the meantime, asked Herrn von dem Hagen to engage a Countess Montgelas to succeed Ena as quickly as possible. November found Daisy in Berlin again, in the Hotel Bristol from where she engaged another lawyer in Munich for the purpose of finalizing the furnishing of her villa. Until that matter was settled, she would stay in England with the Countess Montgelas as her companion. Obviously made in desperation, this plan had to be cancelled. The Countess Montgelas was horrified by Daisy's poor state of health and refused to become Daisy's companion, much less to accompany her to England. Torn between pity and loyalty on one side and disgust and anger about Daisy's mood swings on the other, Ena then agreed out of a sense of obligation, and perhaps compassion for Daisy's noticeably declining health, to continue in her role as Daisy's companion. On December 30, 1924, Ena wrote to Herrn von dem Hagen from Solza in Czechoslovakia where Daisy and Ena were spending Christmas and New Year's with Daisy's cousin Olivia Larisch:

> Dear Herr von dem Hagen,
> I received your letter from the 24th instant and I thank you thousand times . . . also because of the money which I was not sure I would ever get and which made me so terribly happy. ... But after thinking about things, I think I should rather forgo this money so that the Princess may have it, so that she can have another lady as her companion and she might not be so alone and lonely in this world. She is so ill and I am very healthy, I trust you understand what I want to say. ...
>
> I was right after all that everything would come to an end very quickly, but I never thought everything would happen that fast.
>
> With my best greetings,
>
> YOUR ENA FITZPATRICK.[29]

Aside from the uncertainties surrounding the financial situation, living with Daisy became more and more demanding physically and psychologically. Now Ena had to fight for appropriate medical care for

---

29 Ibid.

her cousin Daisy. The rapid deterioration of Daisy's health is reflected in the rising cost of her medical care. Several well-known specialists were consulted when Daisy became totally wheelchair-bound. Another attorney was asked to make a compassionate representation to Hans regarding Daisy's medical care, which she considered part of the "appropriate living circumstances" Hans had assured her of in the divorce settlement. The response came in an astonishingly cold and heartless letter from Dr. Schmidt. One must wonder whether Hans had ever seen Dr. Schmidt's reply.

> Berlin W8, Taubenstrasse 46
> December 10th, 1924
> Herrn von dem Hagen
> Office of the House Marshall of the Prince of Pless
> Fürstenstein, Bez. Breslau
>
> Dear Herr von dem Hagen!
> On Monday, we had the visit of Dr. Wangemann, the new attorney of the Princess. The purpose of his visit was to advise us that the Princess was no longer in the position to cover from the apanage the expenses for her medical care which have increased considerably in view of her declining health. ...
>
> I advised Dr. Wangemann that accepting responsibility of the cost of medical care by the Administration was out of the question. ... I made a strong case for the fact that in view of the extremely high costs of medical care, the Princess should and ought to reduce her style of living, as other sick women do as a matter of course. ... The consultation of additional physicians is as costly and economically irresponsible as it is superfluous and useless. ...
>
> Should His Highness the Prince insist on paying part or all of the medical costs incurred I would strongly suggest that this be made out of the 200 000 Mark gift from the year 1916 the payment of which is still under discussion.
>
> With respect,
> W. Schmidt
> Attorney[30]

In this rather nasty document, one cannot help but notice the distinctions made by Dr. Schmidt between Daisy and her husband, between "the Princess" and "His Highness the Prince" and in crudely

---

30 Ibid.

comparing Daisy to "other women" rather than to other "ladies," a salutation even women of the bourgeois middle-class were entitled to.

Throughout the following years, the ruthless Dr. Schmidt acted as the Administration's agent in trying to break Daisy's resistance against moving into the as yet uncompleted Munich villa. On April 29, 1925, Dr. Schmidt suggested that Daisy be given a deadline of ten days to occupy the villa, even though at that time the entire furnishings consisted of two bedsteads; there were no drapes on the windows and the kitchen lacked all utensils. The Fürstenstein Administration re-iterated there were no furnishings to spare that could be sent to Munich. When Daisy petitioned the court for another "judgment by default," Dr. Schmidt urged the Fürstenstein Administration

> to immediately furnish the villa in order to avoid another expensive law suit at any cost. Furnishings should not exceed the bare necessities, merely adequate enough not to give the Princess any reason to refuse moving into the villa![31]

In the same memorandum, Dr. Schmidt recommended to unilaterally reduce Daisy's apanage to 5,000 Mark immediately. Dr. Schmidt had decided on a personal vendetta against Daisy going far beyond the functions he had been retained for by the Pless Administration. While he succeeded in making life terribly difficult and miserable for the emotionally labile Daisy, he did not win. Daisy did not occupy the Munich villa until four years later in summer 1929.

* * *

It is unlikely that Daisy had any inkling of the underlying causes for the stubbornness of the uncooperative Fürstenstein Administration. She was probably unaware of the enormous financial difficulties Hans was facing, because they were generally not made public at this time. This, at least in part, might explain the heartless attitudes assumed by those responsible to represent him in matters concerning his divorced wife. Hans certainly did not demonstrate in his daily lifestyle that his financial situation had drastically changed. The servants delegated by the Fürstenstein Administration to Daisy's household reported the unchanged state of luxury and pomp in Fürstenstein, which only fortified Daisy's attitude to fight for her entitlement, which would give her at least a comfortable, secure life.

---

31 Ibid.

The servants definitely did not exaggerate their descriptions of the lifestyle that still governed the daily life in Fürstenstein. In his memoirs, Lord d'Abernon, the British Ambassador in Berlin, described with absolute astonishment what he observed during a three day visit in Fürstenstein in January 1924 when Germany and her population were still struggling to overcome the consequences of a lost war, followed by a revolution and a still raging inflation that impoverished the majority of the German people.

> The retainers, dependents and servants in the castle number about three hundred, without counting as many more at the Stud and in the gardens. All household details are extraordinarily well organised – magnificent liveries – an English butler, numerous footmen in powder – a chasseur in top boots and uniform who stands behind the Prince's chair, and a police dog, reputed to be very savage, constantly at his heel.

> Personally, I detest display and find it irksome to have two servants perpetually at my door. Magnificence should be reserved for rare – very rare – occasions.

> The general impression of Fürstenstein is that of an old order which changeth not – but which, before long, is likely to disappear. To-day, the world will not tolerate hereditary wealth at this volume accentuated by ostentation and display. Something rather grand in a pompous way will vanish.[32]

It is beyond belief that nothing had changed in Fürstenstein since Daisy's days. The hundreds of personnel still worked in and around the castle; the footmen were still everywhere with their powdered wigs and white knee-stockings. And Louis Hardouin's photographs bear witness to the elaborate parties and balls. No wonder Daisy felt mistreated and deceived!

Nevertheless, the end foreseen by Lord d'Abernon arrived only too soon. There was one more display of pomp and circumstance almost as glamorous as in pre-war times. The memorable day, January 25, 1925, survives in the reminiscences of the Fürstenstein people and in photographs. For a last time, the powdered footmen in their traditional outfits, the uniformed chasseurs, and the maids in their folk costumes were all assembled on the occasion of Hans's wedding to Clotilde de Silva y Gonzales de Candamo of the Spanish House of the Marques de Arcicollar.

Soon after the grand festivities of Hans's wedding, the "dismantling of Fürstenstein," as the former employees call it to this day, began. Most

---

32 See Lord d'Abernon, op. cit., vol.III, pp. 33-34.

of the personnel were dismissed, the household was drastically reduced; it was eventually closed altogether. The "Castle and Park of Fürstenstein" became a tourist attraction open to visitors all week. In the neighbourhood, people said that the Prince of Pless was in big trouble!

In a letter of the House Marshal Herr von dem Hagen to Dr. Schmidt on March 1, 1926, the precarious financial situation is mentioned for the first time in reference to Daisy.

> His Highness is not quite prepared to present to the Court that his own manner of living has undergone colossal restrictions, a fact which stands him in good stead should he plead for a reduction of his obligations towards the Princess.[33]

On June 10, 1926, Herr von dem Hagen wrote to Daisy's attorney requesting the immediate return of the jewelry, which was considered part of the family estate and still in the hands of the Princess. "The policy of nasty pin-pricks" alluded to by Daisy's attorney continued as it had since 1923. Ena FitzPatrick also had her own axe to grind when it came to Fürstenstein; she faithfully represented Daisy in her letters and petitions to Herr von dem Hagen in Fürstenstein, but also did not forget to mention her own predicament. Between February and October 1925, there were weekly letters from Ena in La Napoule to Herr von dem Hagen in Fürstenstein:

> At the moment, the Princess is quite nice to me, for how long, however, one doesn't know, one feels like sitting on a powder keg. ... Still, I keep worrying about the Princess more than about anything else. ...

> You know, Herr von dem Hagen, what is most frightening? Now, that the Princess knows that I want to leave her, she is begging me every day to stay, but I am only too sure, if I say yes, the old trouble will start right away all over again. I have always said and I say it again, it is Ida who is at fault, she has such power over the Princess, and I am totally helpless and cannot defend myself against her. ...

> These 142 Marks are pretty nice, but by no means enough for renting a car for the Princess! It is her unquestioned right to have an automobile available, as she can no longer walk. ...

---

33 Courtesy National Archives of Poland (Pszczyna Branch); translated from German by the author.

Bolky is coming to-morrow, I am so glad, as life is terribly, terribly lonely for me here. ...

Do let me know about the automobile, and I also must ask you that the apanage for May will be here on May 1st. ... We somehow must get by until that day![34]

At the end of October 1925, Ena finally terminated her position as Daisy's companion, to be replaced by Dolly Crowther, who had looked after Daisy's mother for many years. While Ena had always considered her role in Daisy's small household as temporary, Dolly immediately became not only Daisy's faithful companion, but her skillful, loving nurse. As with Mrs. Cornwallis-West, this was a commitment for life for Dolly. Always anticipating Daisy's wishes, and there were many, she remained cheerful and of even temperament at all times no matter what Daisy's mood, and no matter how worrisome the financial problems. Different from the temperamental Ena, who never knew how to hide her anger or her worries from Daisy, Dolly always found a way to gloss over the problems of the household and hide the often desperate financial situation from Daisy. Dolly created an island of peace for Daisy at the villa *Les Marguerites*. Daisy regained much of her old cheerfulness and optimism.

Douglas FitzPatrick was Daisy's cousin, but preferred to identify himself as her nephew: "Although she was my cousin, my father and her mother were brother and sister, there was a tremendous age differential between us."[35] Douglas was the owner of several Rolls Royce automobiles with which he regularly participated in automobile races in England and France. He loved to cross entire countries in his fast cars and was a frequent visitor in La Napoule and in Munich. He told the author how much he admired Daisy's courage and humour, and how her sad state of health never seemed to overshadow the happy atmosphere at *Les Marguerites*:

I spent many holidays at 95 Ismanigerstrasse, my Aunt's Munich residence, and before at La Napoule in the South of France where she had a villa. ...

She became very crippled, and had to be carried to her wheelchair to go anywhere. Sometimes, the wheelchair was by-passed, and she would be carried by me from one room to another. We would play 'The Pless March"[36] on the gramophone, when it was into the dining room. ...

---

34 Ibid.

35 In a letter to the author.

36 "Alte *Kameraden,*" a very popular march, ironically of German origin.

I was driving a big Rolls Royce. The front passenger seat would be removed and a pile of cushions would be put in its place with a back rest which she found much more comfortable and Dolly her faithful Nurse & Companion would make jokes about never thinking Her Highness would sink so low and be seen sitting on the floor!

My Aunt loved these excursions. Later, when I visited her in Munich, a meadow above the Starnberger See was her favourite destination – we called it the *Daisywiese*.[37] [38]

On June 28, 1928, Daisy celebrated her fifty-fifth birthday in an extraordinarily serene mood. Her diary entry reflects not only an acceptance of her fate, but more so, her newly-won courage to continue to live her life as best as possible. All of this had so much impressed her nephew Douglas FitzPatrick.

June 28, 1928. La Napoule. My birthday.
I woke up to find my room full of sunlight, flowers and little presents (the latter given to me by my servants), dogs and canaries. I had visitors coming and going all morning and had very little time to dress; my little maid, Dollie, had made for me a special frock of white georgette with dozens of little frills on the skirt and at the bottom of the wide sleeves. It was really very becoming – at least so they all said when I went to a neighbouring chateau for lunch.

It really was quite touching. My host had all his Russian servants dressed up in most picturesque costumes, and they all played instruments and, as I entered, struck up a lively melody; each guest was presented with a *daisy* and a big bunch of them was given to me; also several little presents and then some speeches, all of which I thought very nice.

Although it was a brilliantly hot afternoon, I gave a small tea-party. ... In the evening we had a quiet little dinner under the palm trees. Miss Coles and General Gourdine's sister came in afterwards to drink my health.

I went to bed very tired at midnight.[39]

The following day, Daisy and her entourage left Cannes on the evening express for Geneva and Munich. The villa at 95 Ismaningerstrasse was finally ready for occupancy:

---

37 "Daisy's meadow".

38 Courtesy Mr. Douglas Fitzpatrick.

39 WLU, pp. 281-82.

July 1, 1928. Munich 7 a.m.
We have just arrived at my future home; everything looks like spring, so cool, fresh and green. What a relief after the dried, pale yellow look of France. I immediately had a delightful bath and went to bed whilst the usual unpacking went on. I felt very refreshed and dressed and had lunch in my garden; one part I specially love – I call it my meadow. It is rough and wild with all sorts of long grasses and daisies growing, and beautifully shady. ... Next spring ... my specially loved meadow will be a mixture of yellow daffodils and blue-bells. I had tea in my hammock in my rose-garden with the fountain playing, and went to bed after an evening of writing letters and a small dinner.[40]

The first night in the new home in Munich seemed a good omen. At least the first summer of her Munich years brought peace and serenity back into Daisy's life.

July 3, 1928. Munich, Tuesday.
It is a lovely hot day, so we are going to take our lunch and motor to Starnbergersee. *Later:* We went out in an electric launch, which was delightful. I, Dolly, the butler and the footman anchored the boat under a tree overhanging the lake and had lunch. We spent all day on the boat, which cost very little money. We gave the boatman his lunch and he was delighted. I hope to do this often this summer, especially when the boys come.[41]

Daisy was now far less isolated than at La Napoule. More and more friends came to visit. Her cousin Olivia came from Solza in Czechoslovakia, and Fritz and May Larisch, who lived in the Munich suburb of Geiselgasteig, simply "dropped in" several times a week. The Wittelsbachs, to which the kings of Bavaria belonged, resumed their old friendship with Daisy.

Princess Pilar comes like a breath of her own Bavarian mountain air. Her mother, Princess Ludwig Ferdinand ... brings not a little of Spain's incomparable charm and olden dignity ... Prince Ludwig Ferdinand, at once a typical Wittelsbacher and a typical Bavarian in his unique mixture of doctor, prince and musician.[42]

Daisy spent one more winter at La Napoule, before Les *Marguerites* was sold for 868,350 Francs on March 8, 1929, to her friend and neighbour, Mr. Henry Clewes, a US citizen and expatriate from New York. It

---

40 WLU, pp. 282-83.

41 WLU, p. 283.

42 WLU, p. 284.

had become impossible for Daisy to maintain both her houses at La Napoule and Munich. Fortunately, the agreement of sale assured Daisy the further use of *Les Marguerites* where all the furnishings remained. However, because of increasing financial restraints imposed on Hans, Daisy's declining health, and her inability to travel long distances without great discomfort, the winter of 1932-33 turned out to be Daisy's last stay at La Napoule. After that, the bizarre fate of *Les Marguerites* is occasionally mentioned in the records of the Pless Administration.

* * *

In October 1928, Daisy relished the triumph of the publication of the first volume of her diaries in London; a rushed German translation of poor quality appeared in the bookstores in the following spring and caused enormous excitement. Once more, the almost forgotten Princess of Pless stood in the limelight, but no longer as the adored or envied personality of the glamorous years of the German Empire. In Germany at least, her revived prominence brought little that was positive for Daisy. A torrent of indignation and hostility swept through the German press and the German aristocracy. Daisy was accused of being self-centered and, worse, of being deceitful and a liar. For the press, the publication of the diaries was an unexpected opportunity to once more – and with more imagination than ever before – analyze Daisy's relationship with Emperor Wilhelm and her activities during the war. While some of her friends, especially among the Bavarian nobility, stood loyally by her side, Daisy lost all sympathy and respect among most members of Germany's aristocracy.

Intrigued by her diaries, Seymour Leslie, journalist and nephew-by-marriage of George Cornwallis-West, visited Daisy in Munich during the fall of 1929. Seymour could only detect weak traces of Daisy's "wonderful, sparkling personality" he had so much admired in former years. Seymour, a chronicler and analyst of the personalities from Moscow to New York, demonstrated much compassion for Daisy when, shortly before his death in June 1979, he explained to the author that

> the Princess of Pless's memoirs have been unfairly derided as full of Edwardian social trivia – but *that* was the atmosphere and climate of her times! In spite of such trivia, they are obviously very intelligent and compassionate. Unfortunately, in all their indignation, her contemporaries ignored the truly interesting and historically significant and valid passages throughout the diaries – a tragedy, last not least for the Princess personally who was thus refused all respect and recognition.[43]

---

43 letter to the author.

In conversation with the author, Daisy's son Hansel did not refrain from criticizing his mother for her indiscretions, but he sincerely deplored that the times were not ready for a politically interested woman like his mother, so passionately engaged in the social and political issues of her day.

If the public response to her diaries pushed Daisy into further isolation, the not insignificant royalties received from the publishers in England and Germany at least temporarily eased her increasingly precarious financial situation. Since her move to Munich, Daisy's apanage had been cut by a further 2000 Marks per month while Daisy's financial obligations kept increasing because of the high fees paid to her physicians and her attorneys. Although Daisy had also lost all control over the expenses of her Munich household, she still received credit from merchants and tradesmen for the purchases of her household and repairs in the house. These were usually arranged by the servants without Daisy's or Dolly's knowledge.

Things became further complicated and complex when Daisy agreed once more to share her household with Lexel. Perhaps too trusting and too impulsive, certainly too young and inexperienced, Lexel created chaos after Daisy asked him to pacify her numerous creditors. Pawning his mother's precious sable and chinchilla furs, and offering her jewel-encrusted crown and all her other jewelry as security, Lexel managed to obtain a considerable credit from a Munich bank which, however, was still insufficient to satisfy all of Daisy's creditors. On April 1, 1933, Daisy declared her son Lexel plenipotentiary, who would assume all her financial obligations.

This step was taken upon Lexel's advice in the hope that this would protect Daisy's apanage from her creditors. Whether that was a useful strategy or not, Hansel was horrified and rushed to Munich when he heard about this arrangement. At the last moment, the seizure of Daisy's entire house and its contents, and her personal possessions could be averted, after one of her creditors had purchased most of her obligations from other creditors and had taken his claim to court.

In this confused situation, the Pless Administration decided to ignore the authority given Lexel by his mother, and from January 1934 Daisy's monthly apanage was transferred to her directly again. The consequence of this not unwelcome arrangement, however, brought Daisy's household into renewed disarray. This was not only a fault of Daisy's poor management of her income, but also of Hans's desperate financial status; the payments to Daisy were 10,000 Marks in arrears. In a submission to Hans, his administrators explained that the expenses of Daisy's household were hardly bearable any longer. As a solution, her temporary relocation to Fürstenstein was urgently recommended.

Early in March 1935, Hansel visited his mother in Munich in order to gently suggest the idea of eventually returning to Fürstenstein. To his surprise, his mother, too tired of the insecurity and confusion at Munich, readily agreed to an immediate move to Fürstenstein. On March 31st, power of attorney was transferred from Lexel to Hansel. Full of hope and excitement, Daisy, who no longer could manage to control a pen, dictated to Dolly the following entry into her diary:

> April 3, 1935. Munich.
> When I finished these pages a few days ago I said nothing sudden, unexpected or wonderful could ever happen to Daisy again. Well, something has. ... I am going back to Fürstenstein – to the home I unwisely and unnecessarily left over twelve years ago. The place where my children belong.
>
> However long estranged, surely it is well that we should all come together in quietness and understanding at last.[44]

With one strike, the Pless Administration succeeded to save hundreds of thousands of Marks. The costs of accommodating Daisy in Fürstenstein instead of the large, expensive villa in Munich had shrunk from thousands of Marks to literally pennies. Daisy no longer had an automobile at her disposal. Her staff consisting of five persons was either dismissed or called back to Fürstenstein. Daisy's personnel consisted now of Dolly Crowther only. One of the cleaning people at the castle was sent twice a week to tidy up Daisy's small apartment. Cooking and shopping became the responsibility of Daisy's companion Dolly. With this arrangement, most of the clauses of the divorce settlement were no longer followed.

Daisy, however, was exceedingly happy to escape the situation in Munich. Fürstenstein looked like home again; ignored was the question of how, during the past ten years, she could have managed to remain in Fürstenstein, which had become home to the second wife of Hans in 1925.

* * *

What was left of the Fürstenstein Daisy abandoned twelve years ago, "forever – and never to return?" What she had once longed for years ago, had become reality, albeit due to the changed circumstances: When she arrived, there was no *golden coach* pulled by six horses, no uniformed *Jäger* awaiting her at the iron park gate; and no powdered footmen at the

---

44   WLU, p. 286.

entrance of the Castle. But on the other side of the narrow entrance of the gatehouse, the families of Fürstenstein surrounded the automobile that had brought Daisy from Breslau. They greeted their Princess with bunches of wild flowers picked around the park, and poems recited by the children. There were far fewer people left, now that Fürstenstein was no longer the home of the Hochberg family, but merely a tourist attraction. They all greeted Daisy in a heartfelt welcome.

With tears in her eyes, Daisy looked up from her wheelchair to the powerful west-façade of her home of past years. The bosquets and bushes in front of it looked well tended, but all the drapes behind the tall windows were drawn, and the building had a strange, abandoned appearance. Daisy had been told that the huge household that had employed hundreds in former times, had finally been closed entirely two years ago. The huge building was no longer heated in winter, and much of the furnishings had been sold or taken to Pless. Only a few hours every day, the huge building would be filled with visitors. Their voices would seemingly bring the castle back to life, but the tourist season had not yet begun, and everything looked deserted.

In the south-wing of the gatehouse, whose origins reached back to the Middle Ages, quarters had been prepared for Daisy and Dolly. The door to her apartment had hardly closed behind Daisy, when one woman who had just welcomed Daisy exclaimed:

> That big castle and its 600 rooms were all hers; now she has to make do with a little apartment that was good enough for the servants![45]

Nevertheless, Daisy felt quite satisfied. She was at peace in the now so quiet world of Fürstenstein. She loved to talk to the people that had remained, especially to their children. Those who remembered *Inse scheene Daisy*[46] were deeply shocked, realizing her beauty had wasted away under the merciless onslaught of illness and total helplessness. They soon learned to admire the dedication of Dolly Crowther, whose continued stay in Fürstenstein was by no means certain. Already on May 3rd, 1935, Hansel had to declare in a letter to the *Deutsche Arbeitsfront*[47] that

---

45 Frau Johanna Fengler.

46 *Our beautiful Daisy* in local dialect

47 The *German Labour Organization* that controlled all matters regarding utilization of manpower; it gave permission to employ household help which, as a rule, was refused to citizens not liked by the government.

the presence of Miss Crowther, my mother's nurse, is absolutely essential, as my mother is almost completely paralyzed and totally helpless.[48]

It did not take long for the Fürstenstein people to notice Dolly's dedication to the Princess and the hard work she accomplished day after day. In the afternoons, the children accompanied Daisy and Dolly on their little outings in the park and filled Daisy's arms with wild flowers picked along the way. Their mothers brought Dolly whom they soon considered one of their own, preserves or a home-cooked meal.

On February 17, 1936, Daisy dictated a letter to Dolly destined for her cousin Douglas FitzPatrick at Sheringham Hall, Norfolk, England:

My dearest Douglas,
Thank you so much for the attractive lucky-pig with the chocolates inside. I only received it a few days ago, it first went to Munich customs & then just a label arrived. The end of January they traced the parcel. I also had to get your address from Ena, who is in the mountains enjoying snow-sports. I hope to return to Munich soon you must come & seè me there. I have been here eleven months, & I feel I want to go back home & to Lexel. ... There is nothing to write about from here. I came really to see my poor old hubby who is not at all well & is now in Berlin. Hansel comes occasionally otherwise Dolly & I are quite alone with the little dogs & Lexel's little Lollypops (monkey). I hope you are well and have 'someone' in your life to amuse you.

All my best thoughts, Douglas dearest & come to Munich whenever you like.
Yours affect'y,
Cousin Daisy.

With best greetings for 1936, Mr. Douglas & beware it is leap year! Dolly[49]

Daisy made no mention of her poor health which alone would have made the return to Munich inadvisable. On June 22, 1935, she had suffered a severe heart attack. Dr. Hauffe had been called from neighbouring Nieder-Salzbrunn. He subsequently wrote to Hansel on August 1.

Her Highness the Princess had completely lost consciousness, her pulse was undetectable, while the heartbeat, although extremely weak could still be felt. ... Her condition was definitely so grave that the worst had to be

48 Courtesy National Archives of Poland (Pszczyna Branch); translated from German by the author.

49 Courtesy Mr. Douglas FitzPatrick.

expected. ... Around July 2 the condition had stabilized approximately at the level present prior to the heart attack ... in its acute phase the heart attack was definitely of a life-threatening nature. Unfortunately, one has to be prepared for a recurrence of such an attack at any time.[50]

Daisy's heart attack had occurred within weeks of her return to Fürstenstein and since that event, Dr. Hauffe remained involved as long as Daisy lived in Fürstenstein. In view of his report to Hansel, it is more likely that Hans had decided to keep his gravely ill former wife company rather than Daisy deciding to remain in Fürstenstein because her "poor old hubby [was] not at all well." It was true that, at this time, Hans was a broken man physically and psychologically. In March 1934, his second marriage had been declared "nisi." Two years later, the early death of his youngest son Bolko had a tremendously debilitating effect on Hans who brooded for months about his son's brief, unhappy, and unsettled life. Photographs of Bolko's burial at Pless show his father following the casket in a wheelchair. Daisy experienced severe heart problems again and, following Dr. Hauffe's urgent advice did not attend her son's funeral.

Financially, Hans's situation had gone from bad to worse because of the tax-suit with the Polish government and the high debt-load of his enterprises in Poland. In Germany, the industrial and commercial enterprises of the Prince of Pless remained under the control of the Pless Gremium in Berlin. It was perhaps for this reason, that Hans decided to bring Daisy from Fürstenstein to Pless. The plan failed; described later by Ena FitzPatrick, her declaration reads like an excerpt of a novel full of intrigue and adventure:

I, the undersigned Edwina Lilly FitzPatrick, declare the following:
In October 1937 my cousin (by marriage) Hans had invited me to Pless. Since 1936 he was living there again with his son Lexel under rather difficult financial situations. It was becoming more and more difficult to transfer money from Poland to Germany, where the rest of the family was living. So Hans and Lexel thought of bringing Mummy Daisy to Pless, where she could live in her old rooms as before the war and under much better circumstances than that little outbuilding in Fürstenstein. Hans asked me if I would drive over to Fürstenstein with a convoy of three cars, a few servants, amongst them his personal valet KUMMER, and supervise, so to speak, the transfer of Daisy and Dolly Crowther with all their luggage to Pless.

---

50 Courtesy National Archives of Poland (Pszczyna Branch); translated from German by the author.

Naturally, I agreed and a few days later I started off with my convoy. Lexel had previously arranged everything with Dolly by telephone.

I arrived in Fürstenstein in the late afternoon and went to Daisy at once, who was delighted at the idea to see dear old Pless and her Lexelboy again. We dined together that evening very cosily and planned to start off for Pless next morning at about 11 a.m.

But next morning I found my door locked from the outside and after a lot of hammering on it to make myself heard, I was told that the Princess had changed her mind and was NOT going to Pless!!! But that I was free to leave with the rest of my retinue.

When I was let out of my room I realised that the house was occupied and surrounded by black-uniformed SS-men.[51] I naturally wanted to go and say goodbye to Daisy, but was told that that was impossible. I was shown a bit of paper on which was written in German 'Ich habe es mir überlegt, ich bleibe doch lieber hier'[52] and signed 'Daisy.'

So there was nothing else left for me to do than to return to Pless again with my convoy. Hans's valet Kummer was FURIOUS and told me that very early this morning Dolly had telephoned Hansel in London and informed him of the change of domicile and a few hours later the house had been surrounded by the Gestapo.

Hans and Lexel were very sad that Mummy Daisy had been prevented from coming to Pless, for neither of them ever saw her again. Hans died in Paris in 1938 and Lexel was Nazi-persecuted and could not go to Germany. I declare that this report is the honest truth which I could swear to if ever it became necessary.

(signed) Ena FitzPatrick.[53]

Although, Ena's signature seems to indicate that her statement had been completed a few years after the event, the story of the failed attempt to bring Daisy and Dolly to Pless remains basically accurate. The former residents of Fürstenstein still remember the shock that gripped everybody when the feared SS surrounded the building in the morning following the day of the arrival of the three heavy automobiles, which had brought Ena and her entourage to Fürstenstein. It will always remain a mystery whether it was Hansel who blocked Daisy's departure for Pless,

---

51 The feared, black-uniformed elite troops of the National Socialist Party.

52 'I have thought about it and have changed my mind; I rather stay here. Daisy.'

53 Courtesy Alexander Graf von Hochberg.

or whether the phone lines from Fürstenstein were monitored and Dolly's conversation with Hansel in London reported to the authorities of the SS who then sprang into action. It appears impossible that Hansel, who was suspect in the eyes of the local authorities anyway, would have contacted the hated SS without consulting with his father in Pless beforehand; and Hans would not have agreed to hold Daisy back in Germany; after all, it had been his idea to bring her to Pless in the first place.

Hans died four months later in Paris and, again, it remains a mystery, whether Daisy's poor health or the decisions of unco-operative authorities – Daisy had no German passport – prevented her from attending her husband's funeral in Pless.

Sadly, Daisy's more than modest and uneventful existence in her little apartment in Fürstenstein became more and more the subject of the whims of the local authorities and the Pless Administration in Waldenburg. Her financial security was plagued by incredible complications and a constant shortage of money which could only be overcome by Dolly's skillful handling of the very modest household and her courageous representation of Daisy's interests and rights with the local authorities. Since the time when Daisy reported to Douglas FitzPatrick that "there is nothing to write about from here," the local authorities including the National Socialist Party and the SS, the Pless Administration in Waldenburg, the Pless Gremium in Berlin, German banks in Breslau, Berlin and Munich and, last but not least, the bailiff at La Napoule were intensely pre-occupied with the expenses of Daisy's tiny household, at what tremendous costs one can only guess; they alone would have assured Daisy a comfortable existence and top medical care.

In 1935, the furnishings and contents of Daisy's villa in La Napoule had been auctioned off because of tax arrears and other unpaid obligations. *Les Marguerites* now came into the complete possession of Mr. Clewes, as the Pless Administration had failed to make tax payments and maintain the villa in an acceptable state. A report in the archives of the former administration in Pless dated June 18, 1936, describes an incredible situation:

> Herr Bommeli, confidant of Her Highness the Princess, was expected to be present when the bailiff would enter the premises of the house. ... However, as Herr Bommeli did not appear, the bailiff found it necessary to proceed in Mr. Bommeli's absence. On his own, he entered the villa and packed those items he considered the personal property of the Princess in various boxes, which ... placed in the garage are ready to be picked up and shipped to Fürstenstein at any time. His advice to the administration in Pless has been totally disregarded. ...

The villa was found in extremely poor condition. ...The electrical wires were hanging like garlands from the ceilings. ... When the main water valve was opened, huge amounts of water immediately run in cascades down the main staircase. ... The central-heating radiators fell of the walls crashing down the steps.[54]

Furnishings still usable were auctioned off; the boxes filled with personal items remained forgotten in the garage where the considerate bailiff had placed them. In 1943 the representative of the German government in Berlin responsible for German properties in France contacted Daisy's attorney Dr. Schwedler in Waldenburg requesting "the settlement of monies due to Mr. Bommeli through the exchange agreement between Germany and the French government in Vichy." In the meantime, Mr. Bommeli had received the boxes containing Daisy's personal possessions that had survived unnoticed in the garage of her former villa since 1935. Fifteen years after World War II, Daisy's cousin Ena FitzPatrick took up residence near La Napoule and received the boxes from Bommeli. Among them, Ena discovered the first volume of Daisy's handwritten diaries.

That the outstanding obligations concerning Daisy's villa in La Napoule were totally ignored only emphasizes the desperate financial situation of the Pless enterprises; all members of the Hochberg family had to face increasing reductions of their income from year to year. As one also might expect, the annual reports of the Pless Administration demonstrate that the defenseless Daisy was the principal victim.

A memorandum dated September 30, 1935, stated that

the payments to Her Highness the Princess were 29,657.45 Marks in arrears and could only be paid to Her Highness, once the situation in [Polish] Eastern Upper Silesia would be settled.[55]

The monies owing – and never paid – to Daisy represented for her a magnificent sum, but there was no hope. A report from the Chancellery of the Prince of Pless in Berlin proved how desperate the situation was during that particular year; a mere 26,000 Marks were available for the entire family. This was a tiny sum compared to what had been paid annually just a few years earlier. The most striking entry in this report is found under the column "Princess of Pless." It noted that Daisy had received "Nothing."

---

54 Courtesy National Archives of Poland (Pszczyna Branch); translated from German by the author.

55 Ibid.

At this point, Hansel turned his attention to the shameful treatment of his mother. Having already assumed personal responsibility for the payments to the rest of the family, he now declared

a moratorium. The attempts of the family members 'to keep their heads above water' will have to continue until either the lifting of the trusteeship or a favourable agreement with the Polish government.[56]

Again, Daisy was hit hardest. In October 1936, Herr Knorn, secretary of the Fürstenstein chancellery, reported with obvious satisfaction that he had fulfilled the order

to achieve a drastic reduction in the expenditures of the household of Her Highness the Princess. In October 1936, the personal expenses of Her Highness the Princess for the month of September were a mere 94.25 Marks.[57]

During 1936, the financial situation of the family seemed to have arrived at its extreme. A review of the annual payments made during the past five years indicated that since 1931, the apanages to all family members had been reduced by eighty per cent. Heroically, Hansel tried to secure a minimum income for each member of the family. On May 24, 1936, he wrote to his father's half-brother Wilhelm in Krucz-Goraj:

My dear Hans-Willusch!
I am afraid I have to advise you of a development which will surely disturb you as much as it did me.

According to a memorandum I received from the President of the Gremium, the payments to the family due for the months of May and June 1936 will be reduced by 50 percent. The Administration in Waldenburg desperately seeks to find a way out of the situation. ...

While in Berlin, I was also advised that as of July 1936, no more payments would be forthcoming to the family.

Despite these disturbing news, I remain yours sincerely,
Hans.[58]

---

56 Ibid.

57 Ibid.

58 Ibid.

No other family member was as vulnerable as Daisy. While the rest of the family managed to raise monies to survive quite decently through sale of personal property, Daisy had nothing left to sell to raise cash to buy even enough food. As Dolly said to a neighbour in Fürstenstein, "We are truly as poor as church mice!" Yet, Dolly would have to face even greater worry. When in May 1937, the Pless Gremium in Berlin resumed modest payments to all family members except Daisy, a shocked Herr von dem Hagen was advised by the Gremium that according to new government regulations, as *foreigner in terms of foreign valuta*, the Princess of Pless was no longer entitled to any payments.

The Pless Administration tried its best to raise some funds through the sale of furniture, in order to cover the costs of daily living and medical attention for Daisy. On August 13, 1937, Daisy's attorney Dr. Schwedler begged the administration for "the amount of 51.60 Mark to pay for the purchase of coal required to heat the apartment of the Princess during the forthcoming winter."[59]

Nothing illustrates Daisy's dramatic situation so dramatically as the letter that the irate, but also courageous Herr von dem Hagen forwarded to the authorities in Berlin:

Schloss Waldenburg, September 2, 1937.
Urgent!
To the
Reichsstelle für Devisenbewirtschaftung[60]
Berlin W 8
Beerenstrasse 43

re: the Princess of Pless

The situation of the gravely ill, 64 year old Princess of Pless has become intolerable! There have been no payments received from Poland. For some time, any other payments have been strictly forbidden by the Office for Foreign Valuta in Breslau; payments or advances by the Administration are equally forbidden.

In order to alleviate the worst of this incredible situation, the Administration has sold all furniture or other possessions not absolutely needed by the Princess; the moneys raised have been completely used up. The most basic needs of daily life, of course, are continuing. Purchases are made by the nurse directly rather than by the Administration. For food, medical care and medicine, expenses have accumulated, but there is no money available

---

59 Ibid.
60 State Office for the Administration of Foreign Valuta.

to pay for them. One cannot expect the merchants to extend further credit; nor can the nurse of the Princess request further credit for food in the full knowledge that she could never pay for it. Should she do so, she would make herself subject to prosecution for fraud (263 StBG)[61]

The Administration of the Prince of Pless anxiously expects the quickly approaching day when the merchants will *no longer extend any credit and the gravely ill patient and her nurse will have nothing to eat, as the Administration will not receive a foreign currency permit,* in order to cover the living expenses of the Princess for which she is legally entitled according to the court judgement in relation to her divorce.

Once more, for reasons of being intimately familiar with the situation for many years just as much as for reasons of *simple decency and humanity,* I must ask you most urgently to direct the Foreign Valuta Office in Breslau to authorize payments as quickly as possible. All required information has been submitted to Breslau.
v.d. Hagen.[62]

* * *

On January 31, 1938, Hans died in Paris at the age of 76 years. The last two decades of his life had been devastating for his personal life, having gone through two divorces and having lost his youngest son under mysterious circumstances. His once enormously successful and profitable industrial enterprises had been brought to the brink of ruin; Hans had lost all control over his enterprises. While it was true that at a time where millions suffered extreme hardship, Hans still lived in comparative comfort, his once legendary wealth had literally melted away within the short span of ten years. Hans was buried in the park of Castle Pless. Daisy did not attend his funeral, for reasons of health and of political restriction as well.

After his father's death, Hansel, now Prince Hans Heinrich XVII of Pless and already a resident of Great Britain, tried unsuccessfully to secure the financial maintenance of his mother. All he could do was leave some of his own money with Dolly when he visited Fürstenstein.

Since 1932, Hansel, who had also obtained Polish citizenship together with his father and his brother Lexel, maintained his official residence in London. After Adolf Hitler terminated Germany's membership in the League of Nations, Hansel had followed the advice of his

---

61 Paragraph 263, German Civil Law.

62 Courtesy National Archives of Poland (Pszczyna Branch); translated by the author.

attorneys who suggested that from London he could pursue his claims against the Polish government with a better chance for success.

In fall of 1938, Hansel visited Fürstenstein again. He did not know that this would be the last time he saw his mother. Convinced that Hitler's policies would soon lead to war, Hansel signed a protocol in the office of one of his attorneys in Breslau, a Dr. Hossmann, who was given the power of attorney to act in the best interests of Hansel's mother, should Hansel be unable to do so himself. Signed by Hansel, Dr. Hossmann, and Daisy's attorney Dr. Schwedler, the protocol further stated that:

> Hans Heinrich XVII Prince of Pless pledges to pay his mother, the Princess Mary Therese von Pless, in accordance with his legal duties of maintenance, the monthly sum of 2,500.00 Marks in advance as well as provide his mother with free housing as before.

> He pledges furthermore, over and above the above-stated sum, to provide his mother with additional funds arising from required medical care. He will also be responsible for the costs of the burial of the Princess Mary Therese von Pless.[63]

Less than a year after signing the protocol, Hansel bought a special edition of THE TIMES at Victoria Station in London and read the announcement of Hitler's invasion of Poland on September 1, 1939. On that first day of World War II, Lexel and Ena fled from Pless to Warsaw. They made little use of Lexel's elegant suite in the Hotel Europejski, but were forced to take refuge in its basement when the Polish capital was bombed by German planes. Before the German armies entered Warsaw, they fled in Ena's *Stöwer* sports-car to Rumania and, from there, by boat to Cairo, and finally to France. While Ena managed to reach England and thus avoid spending another war in hostile Germany – which again became the fate of her cousin Daisy – Lexel returned to Egypt when the German troops invaded France in 1940. In the Middle East, he joined the Polish units which would soon fight at the side of the British Eighth Army. His brother Hansel's fate was much different and very unfair.

When Great Britain mobilized its forces Hansel volunteered for the Scots Guards. Instead of being called up, he was lumped together with the hundreds of German citizens and interned as an enemy alien. More harshly treated than most enemy aliens, Hansel was soon transferred to Brixton Prison where he was kept prisoner for a full three years. Only the intervention of his English relatives, Winston Churchill, and the Duke of Westminster, finally gave him back his freedom. "Your intern-

---

63 Ibid.

ment has been a horrible mistake," the governor of Brixton Prison apologized to Hansel, who immediately following his discharge from Brixton entered the British forces as a volunteer.

No explanation was ever given to him.[64]

In Germany, with the onset of the war, Hansel and Lexel were considered enemies of the people. The London papers had shown a picture of the Prince of Pless wearing a steel helmet and carrying a gas mask during an air raid exercise in his London neighbourhood. In the German press, the description of his appearance was changed to "a British army officer's uniform." At the same time, it became known in Berlin that Lexel had fled Poland and was now living in Paris. This gave the German government sufficient cause to seize all Pless properties. The Pless Gremium in Berlin was dissolved, and the Pless properties in the formerly Polish part of Upper Silesia were placed under the control of the *Treuhandstelle Ost*, which administered all foreign assets on behalf of the German government. The Pless properties in Lower Silesia mainly in and around Waldenburg came under the direct control of the government in Berlin.

* * *

In the early months of the war, Daisy's personal life remained untouched by the war. Fürstenstein had become very quiet, as no more tourists were to be admitted for the duration of the war. Daisy longed for her sons and friends, but was resigned to spend another war far from her English homeland. Dolly shielded Daisy as much as possible from the unpleasantness in their daily life. As an enemy alien, she had to report daily to the mayor of the neighbouring village of Liebichau[65]; to Daisy, she described her daily absences as "getting some fresh air." Neither did she explain to Daisy that after the seizure of the Pless properties in October 1939, the monthly maintenance payments were stopped immediately. Once more, Daisy and Dolly had become totally dependent on the good will of the local merchants and of their neighbours in Fürstenstein. An urgent submission by Dr. Schwedler to the "Administrative Commissioner for the Administration of His Highness the Prince of Pless" remained unanswered.

On November 7, 1939, Daisy dictated a letter to her sister Shelagh — Daisy was now too weak to even place her own signature under the

---

64 Discussion with Lady Mary Ashtown (Mrs. Mary Pless).

65 Since 1945 Lubiechów.

letter written as usual by Dolly. The sadness of her lonely life isolated from her loved ones, and her acceptance of life are touching:

> My darling Shele,
> I have just heard from darling Sol & am asking her to try & get this through to you. I am quite well & as happy as one can be in these sad times; everything goes on as usual except D. takes a three hours walk every morning, in the afternoon she pushes me round the Park, as the trees are so beautiful in these Autumn times. We have had a heavy fall of snow; I have no news from Olivia or any one else & so long to hear of that precious boy of mine & send him all my love & thoughts & although I can't write to you, I think of you, & brother George & my two boys; don't worry about me, as everything is warm & comfy. I hope you are all well. Take care of H. for me. All love, darling Shele.
> Your sister Dany.[66]

Shelagh must have sensed her sister's loneliness that spoke from every line of Daisy's letter, but she probably could not imagine, how desperate and sad her sister's restricted circumstances had become, how very poor her health was, how their lack of money sometimes even left Daisy and Dolly without sufficient food, and that the reason for Dolly's "three hour walk every morning" was the government's order to report daily to the local authorities.

In fall of 1940, rumours began to circulate in Fürstenstein that the German government would soon announce special plans for the future use of the castle. The Princess of Pless would be forced to leave Castle Fürstenstein. Afraid that such an eviction would make Daisy virtually homeless, Dr. Schwedler immediately approached the *Waldenburger Bergwerksgesellschaft WABAG*, which had its offices in Castle Waldenburg. He presented the protocol of July 1939 which declared Daisy's son as the person responsible for her maintenance and free domicile and Dr. Schwedler as the legal agent in his absence. The following day, a happy Dr. Schwedler arrived in Fürstenstein with the announcement that the partly furnished main floor in one of the villas in the park of Castle Waldenburg would be made available for the Princess of Pless, but he had no good news otherwise. His urgent memorandum to Berlin referring to the arrears in the monthly maintenance payments to the Princess of Pless that had reached the incredible amount of 153,000 Marks had not freed any monies for Daisy.

On November 1, 1940, Daisy moved to her last home located almost in the center of the City of Waldenburg. It was a cold, sunny day, but a

---

66 Courtesy Lady Mary Ashtown.

terribly sad occasion for the Fürstenstein people who had asssembled to say good-bye to their Princess. Daisy was deeply moved and could only utter the words "my children, all my dear children" again and again. When their eyes watched Daisy's automobile disappear in the park, the people sensed that a different, unknown, and frightening authority was taking the fate of Fürstenstein in its hands.

Unlike in Fürstenstein, Daisy had no immediate neighbours in Waldenburg. The upper floor of the villa accommodated a high German officer, who kept his distance. Only a family that once had lived in Fürstenstein helped with some chores; their daughter, a music student attending the local conservatory came to play Daisy's favourite Chopin pieces on the grand piano.[67] Once a week, grocery and produce were delivered by a nearby merchant.[68]

Daisy's thoughts were more and more in England. There was no news of any kind about Hansel or Lexel until March 1942 when a postcard arrived from Geneva with the advice that letters and small packages could now be sent to Hansel in care of the *Foreign Relations Department of the International Red Cross* to be forwarded to the *St. John War Organisation* in London. With happiness not experienced for more than two years, Daisy dictated the first of a series of letters addressed to Hansel in England. Somewhere on their way, the letters, handwritten by Dolly, were transposed in typed form onto small, densely filled cards.

Waldenburg (Schles.),
Friedländerstrasse 43
Good Friday, April 3rd, 1942.

My darling Hansel,
I am thinking of you all the time, and do hope you are comfortable and well, and that everyone is kind to you; it is a great pleasure and joy to me, to be able to write to you, this you will understand.

I like very much indeed my new home, you have put me in, such beautiful big sunny rooms, and a lovely view, I have been here for more than a year and a half, quite alone with Dolly, we are both very well and contended. Hansel darling, don't let anything worry you, everything is in perfect order, just as you would wish it to be, it does you great credit and I am proud of

---

67 Mrs. Ena Rost.

68 The young woman delivering goods from the nearby store of the author's uncle, sometimes accompanied by the author's ten year old cousin, reported to the author, how ill and practically immobile Daisy had become; and how embarrassed the "English lady" was when she could not pay the bill. Fortunately the author's uncle was prosperous enough to forgo payments for the goods delivered.

you. Take care of yourself and above all keep well, we are waiting and longing for the day when we shall be with you again. You will get a small parcel often from me through the Red-Cross.

Just to let you know, we never forget you for a single moment, and are always with you in thought. God bless you darling and all my love, and from Dolly too,
Your ever loving Mummie.[69]

Whitsunday
May 24th, 1942.

My darling Hansel,
I wonder if you have got my letter which I wrote on Good Friday and sent through the Red Cross; it was to say how much we both are thinking of you all the time and hope you are comfortable and well.

I like my new Home more each day; there is a big balcony where I sit all day long, and the little Park is looking beautiful just now; there is not much news to write you, as I see no one and have been here one year and eight months, quite alone with Dolly, but we are by no means lonely. The years pass quickly and we just long and wait for the time when we shall be with you again.

I am very well and in five weeks to-day will have my 69th birthday.

Several small parcels the Red Cross have send for me to you; all your birthday and Christmas presents we are keeping for you until we meet again. It would be a joy to get a letter from you if it were possible.

God bless you, Hansel darling, all the love in the world from me and Dolly

Your ever loving Mummie.

P.S. Do you wish me to send you some books, if so, any special ones.[70]

One cannot help but notice how the severity of life in a hostile country and adverse circumstances of absolute loneliness have drawn Daisy and Dolly closer together than ever as they wrote about themselves to Hansel like mother and daughter or as sisters.

---

69   Courtesy Lady Mary Ashtown.
70   Ibid.

Waldenburg (Schles.)Friedländerstrasse 43
July 17, 1942

My darling Hansel,
This is my third letter to you, I hope by now that you have the last two, also
the small parcels sent each month, and the three books, all have been sent
through the Red Cross just to let you know we both think of you every day
and all the day, so intensive are our thoughts for you. We feel that everyone
at least is kind to you, how could any-one be otherwise.

My 69th birthday has passed; the day was rather cold, so in the evening we
had a fire in the Hall, you remember the beautiful oak-fireplace there; we
tried to picture what you were doing, and what an enormous happiness to
us if you had been here too, we long and wait for the day we shall be together
again. Everything is in good order just as you would have wished it to be.

There is no news I can write you, as most of my time is spent in the garden,
and I am very well, a letter from you would be a great joy, if it were possible
to let me have one.

Keep well and your spirits up Hansel darling, God bless you, all the love in
the world from me and Dolly,

Your ever loving though old
Mummie.[71]

Not even one visitor seemed to have called to congratulate Daisy on
her sixty-ninth birthday. But on September 3, 1942, more welcome than
a visitor was the Red Cross card from Hansel, the first news in almost
three years:

To the Foreign Relations Department
Red Cross & St. John War Organization
Warwick House
St. James's S.W. 1 Brixton, 31/7/42.

Sir,
May I ask you to be kind enough and forward the following message to the
Dowager Princess of Pless
Schloss Waldenburg, Silesia, Germany.

Dear Mummy,
What a great joy it was to receive two letters of April 3rd and May 24th from
you and hear that you are well and comfortably installed with dear Dolly in

---

71 Ibid.

your new house. A few days ago I received your parcels. Many thanks. Please continue to write to the same address. No books required. I have plenty to read. Next year I hope I shall be able to be with you on your birthday. I am well.

Fondest love to you and Dolly, your ever loving
Hansel.[72]

Hansel's letter had taken over a month to reach Daisy. Utterly happy, she replied immediately:

September 3rd, 1942

My darling Hansel,
It is with a very happy grateful heart I write you this letter. Today we have both had the greatest joy for more than three years, when your dear letter arrived, and to know at least you are well. One day, I am quite certain, happiness must come to you, for you have had more than your share of anxiety in your still young life. My one great wish is to live long enough to see all your cares and troubles over. I am more than grateful and proud to have such a Son, and think very lovingly of you every day, and above all don't worry. God bless you Hansel darling, we are both longing to see you.

All the love in the world, and from Dolly too,
Your ever loving
Mummi.[73]

Only one of the letters written by Hansel during the following months reached Daisy in Waldenburg. On January 3, 1943, she wrote anxiously:

Christmas has passed, and we both had quite a nice time, ... but our thoughts went out to you, your fourth Christmas away from us. ...

And now the New Year has begun. We drank to your health in champagne, because we consider health the greatest blessing we can wish for you. So this is our New Year's message to you, Good Health and the rest we leave in God's hands and your own, you will always do the right thing, that I know, and although your young life has been so difficult for you, the clouds will roll away and the sun shine on you, and you must get your reward in life in the way that you wish, and not in the way others would have it for you.

---

72 Ibid.
73 Ibid.

I hope you got my Christmas parcel...

My health is much better than six years ago. Do you realise I am seventy in June.

Good bless you and keep you Hansel darling until we meet again. We shall celebrate your birthday on the 2nd of February, and send our loving thoughts across the ether to you.
All my best love ... from Dolly too, it's her birthday today,
Your ever loving Mummy.[74]

Daisy never mentioned her physical frailty and total dependence on Dolly, but her emotional state had indeed much improved since her move to Waldenburg. Dolly shielded her from all political news so that Daisy never became aware how much more horrible World War II was compared to the war of 1914-1918. The front was far away and no bombs had fallen on Waldenburg. People in the western half of Germany referred to Silesia as "Germany's air-raid shelter." Thanks to Dolly's positive nature and her always cheerful mood, Daisy had gained an inner peace and a degree of happiness that helped her much in coping with the terrible physical symptoms of her illness.

In her heart, though, Dolly often felt dejected and depressed. Her daily reporting at the main police station in Waldenburg became a painful task, not to be compared with the long walks she used to take every day from Fürstenstein to the office of the cheerful, friendly mayor in Liebichau.

Daisy's care required super-human strength from Dolly whose stature was rather petite and delicate. Daisy's physical deterioration progressed much more rapidly all of a sudden. The paralysis took hold of her entire body so that helping Daisy take some food every day became a most difficult task for Dolly.

One more message arrived from Hansel, his Christmas greetings, which had taken almost three months to reach his mother. Her reply left Schloss Waldenburg the same day:

March 1st, 1943.
My darling Hansel

I was overjoyed to receive today your Internee Airmail Message of December 8th, but you do not write if you are well or not. ... Have you got also my letters of September 5th and January 3rd ... and October 23rd, I have posted a second parcel on October 31st. ... I am comfortable and very well, Dolly

---

74 Ibid.

too. Your grandmother Mathilde Herzogin von Pless has died on January 15th. My thoughts are always with you. Please write soon again if it is possible. With all love from Dolly and Your ever loving Mummie.[75]

The next news from Waldenburg, for the first time not unduly delayed by the censor, was received by Hansel on July 24, 1943:

13.7.43

Dearest P. Hansl.
It is hard for me to write, and tell you that your darling Mummie changed this sad world for a better one the day after she celebrated her 70th birthday. She was well as usual, and so pleased with all. Directors, secretaries and all the poor people she loved so well were here. Mummie was a little tired on the 29th and in the evening just laid her head on my shoulder and slept. Mummie now rests peacefully since July 3rd in Fürstenstein.

All my loving thoughts go out to you in your solitude. God bless you, Dolly.[76]

* * *

Hansel in London and Lexel in Iraq heard about their mother's death through the BBC news. On July 13, about two weeks after his mother's death, Hansel found his mother's obituary in THE TIMES:

Daisy Princess of Pless – Edwardian Days

Daisy Princess of Pless has died at Fürstenstein, near Breslau. One of the most beautiful women of her time, she was before the last war a brilliant member of Edwardian society and a great hostess in Germany. She did all she could to help Anglo-German relations to remain on an amicable footing.

A detailed description of her youth and her married life with all its vagaries followed, before the obituary turned to Daisy's achievements.

It was not considered 'princely' for the Princess of Pless to go about among the inhabitants of the estates, but after a few years she took the law into her own hands and went where she chose. She fought hard for sanitary improvements in the towns along the rivers of Silesia. Her unfailing consolation was her father-in-law who until his death in 1907 never ceased to support her in her attempts to humanize her surroundings. ... Her greatest happiness derived from her visits to England. ...

75 Ibid.
76 Ibid.

> The South African War revealed to her the jealousy of England which was growing in official Germany. ... The Emperor ... on more than one occasion tried to defend her against her enemies.

> During the 1914-18 war ... her position became extremely difficult. Her efforts to do what she could for British prisoners caused her endless persecution. ... The Emperor invited her to Pless where ... this visit rehabilitated her somewhat. ... A second visit ... showed that the Emperor's influence was already waning. By his order she served on a military hospital train ... but the persecution continued.[77]

The lengthy obituary concludes with a description of Daisy's remaining years. Nothing remotely comparable to the dignified, compassionate obituary in THE TIMES, as a matter-of-fact nothing could be found in the German press. A brief entry in the files of the Pless Administration in Waldenburg mentions

> the publication of death notices in the 'Deutsche Allgemeine Zeitung' in Berlin and the 'Schlesische Zeitung' in Breslau. Death notices to be mailed to friends and acquaintances have not been printed.[78]

Placing a death notice in the Waldenburg daily, *Mittelschlesische Gebirgszeitung* had been explicitly forbidden by the local party leader who did not want any public manifestations of sympathy; his edicts were to no avail, as events would soon prove.

Towards the end of July, Hansel arranged a memorial service for his mother at *St. Mark's* on North Audley Street in London. Neither Hansel nor anyone else attending had any knowledge of the circumstances of his mother's death; not even the exact date of Daisy's death was known. The title page of the program simply stated "Daisy Princess of Pless – died July 1943."

The first detailed letter was mailed immediately after Daisy's funeral by Hansel's aunt, the Countess Olivia Larisch, who was born a FitzPatrick and was Daisy's cousin. Her compassionate, heartfelt letter did not reach Hansel until after the end of the war.

---

77 THE TIMES, July 13, 1943.

78 Courtesy National Archives of Poland (Pszczyna Branch); translated from German by the author.

Dear Hansel!

It is with a heavy heart that I write these lines to you:

Your dear mother passed away calmly on the day following her birthday. I went to stay with your dear mother on her birthday, and found her much better than she had been when I visited her the last time. Your mother was incredibly fresh and overjoyed to see me. I spent happy hours with her and we talked a lot about you and the others who were not present. All the old people came to congratulate her on her birthday. There were masses of flowers and the miners band played for her which gave her great pleasure. She spoke to everyone of them and exchanged reminiscences with the older ones. She smiled like in old times; only once, with tears in her eyes, she said: 'How sad Hansel is not here.' Good and faithful Dolly had prepared telegrams from you and those she loved as well as presents which pleased her very much. The telegrams had to be read out to her over and over again. In the evening she was rather tired and was put to bed earlier than usual; she soon recovered and we drank champaign and proposed her health.

The next morning she complained of great tiredness and it hurt her to eat as the paralysis had affected the throat. She wanted to go back to bed again. She repeatedly said 'I am very ill,' but Dolly comforted me by telling me that she said this often, that her state had sometimes been much worse, but that she had always recovered again. I could return home without anxiety. Before leaving, your mother said to me: 'I shall die, my mother is dead and my father is dead.' I left with a heavy heart, and when I got home at night the sad news was awaiting me that your mother had gone peacefully to sleep on Dolly's shoulder, with a smile on her face, at 7:30 p.m.

Your mother was happy and content in her new home, where she had everything she needed.

I returned immediately as Sissy,[79] because of the grave illness of her mother, could not leave her.

Your mother looked so beautiful and so peaceful. Dolly had placed three roses in her hand which made me think that they were farewell-messages from those whom she loved but could not be present. Only Dolly, old Marie, and I were there when your mother left her house to be taken to the family-vault from where the funeral took place on Saturday, July 3rd.

Two elderly cousins were present, all the higher officials, and many of the old and faithful employees. The chapel was a sea of flowers and profusely decorated with marguerites. The clergyman spoke very movingly. I know how hard it must be for you, dear Hansl, never to be able to see your beloved mother again, and I sympathise with you from the depths of my heart. But

---

79 Hansel's first wife Maria, née Gräfin von Schönborn-Wiesentheid.

it must be a great comfort for you to know that your mother passed away peacefully. Had her life continued, she would have suffered very much as during her last days she could take only liquid food. Dolly is broken-hearted, but very brave. Her future is being provided for in every respect. Olivia.[80]

For the last full day of her life and in her death, Daisy once more became the respected and much-loved Princess of Pless. Her death, as her birthday the day before, was officially ignored by the civil and party authorities of Waldenburg; her funeral was not announced in the local paper; the tens of thousands of Pless employees, except those already retired, were told not to attend services for the Princess of Pless. But the day of Daisy's interment became one last triumph for her; thousands of people attended the interment services, together with all the Fürsten-stein people.

Daisy found her last resting place in the family's mausoleum in the park of Castle Fürstenstein. Her specific wishes for her funeral and last resting place had been buried in the archives of Castle Pless. No-one had any knowledge of her wish to be buried outside the mausoleum, in the peace of her beloved park close to the thousands of rhododendron and azaleas that had been planted according to her wishes. It was a wish that a cruel fate would make true only too soon.

On May 5, 1945, Waldenburg and its environs were occupied by the victorious Red Army. Castle Fürstenstein, which since 1943 had been the object of insane building plans for Adolf Hitler's guest house named *Waldwiese*,[81] had already been devastated; its interior had been drastically altered according to the style of the Third Reich. At the end of the war, the huge building was deserted, unprotected against the plunderers and vandals who swarmed through its halls. Everywhere, people searched and dug feverishly for gold and other treasures. After the war, the castle's castellan Fichte reported:

> Even the family vault (Mausoleum) was plundered, the caskets broken open and their contents thrown about. We managed to inter the Princess outside the mausoleum in the last minute, but her grave was soon dug open again and robbed. Scholz had meant too well and had planted beautiful flowers on her grave very obvious. After the plunderers had left, we re-interred the Princess but levelled the ground so that nobody would recognize her gravesite.

---

80 Courtesy Prince Hans Heinrich XVII von Pless (Hansel).

81 "Forest Meadow."

But the mausoleum was so devastated and its heavy doors so destroyed that they could not be closed again. ... We transported the remains of the other family members to the cemetery in Nieder-Salzbrunn.[82] [83]

Without realizing it, the faithful Fürstensteiners had fulfilled Daisy's last wish and bedded her for her final rest close to the walls of the mausoleum in the shade of the famous two-hundred-years-old linden trees. Those who know, still visit Daisy's grave quietly and unobtrusively, never daring to leave any flowers, because for decades, some people were still searching and digging for the famous chain of pearls the Princess of Pless used to wear in her glamorous years.

In 1959, Harold Nicholson concluded a charming story of reminiscences about Daisy of Pless with the lines:

In a world of snobbery she remained natural. In a world become harsh, her cheerfulness and kindness were a beacon. She had only one final enemy in the world: loneliness. It remains a sad fact that in the end, this one enemy became victorious.[84]

* * * * * *

---

82 Since 1945 Wałbrzych-Szczawienko.

83 Unpublished Report, November 30, 1947.

84 Harold Nicholson in THE TIMES, 1949.

12 | *Epilogue*

T he most thrilling, and perhaps the most worthy form of excitement, is
that which comes from within – created in the soul of man, and not by
any exterior agency. Such excitement is known to all who do good work,
who see it grow out of their labour and their inspiration.[1]

Jennie Churchill

* * *

Jennie Churchill's observation might explain the sources that nourished
her sister-in-law Daisy's "cheerfulness and kindness" and the constant
striving to "humanize her surroundings," which Harold Nicholson so
admired. Another quotation from Jennie's essay "On Personality" also
recalls Daisy to one's memory:

> Whatever the definition, the general idea of personality is one who adheres
> to his own beliefs, rightly or wrongly, and to his own mode of life, without
> fear or respect of his surroundings. ... The great secret of personality is the
> power of giving of oneself – if there is anything to give; without it, the front
> rank can never be reached.[2]

Had she lived at a later stage in history, when politically and socially
engaged women would no longer be considered by men as oddities and
exceptions to the rule, at best as a nuisance and at worst, as a threat,
Daisy would have realized her ideals and ideas with much greater success.
No doubt, she would always have been somewhat of a rebel, but the
greater acceptance and freedom which later generations accorded

---

1   See Eileen Quelch, op. cit., pp. 148-49.
2   Ibid., p. 148.

women, would certainly have permitted Daisy to reach far beyond what she had accomplished in her own times; and her political and social views published in her diaries would have found a more responsive and respectful readership.

In our times, Daisy's humanitarian accomplishments are no longer known. Her political views and pursuits are largely forgotten. Although to this day, the Princess of Pless is frequently mentioned in the historical literature published in Germany, England, or the United States, nearly all references are restricted to the evocation of her legendary beauty and her relationship with the German Emperor. Only here and there, one finds a poignant political or social commentary quoted from Daisy's diaries.

Aside from her chronic illness extending over nearly half her life, her fate of having to spend two wars away from the country of her birth, and to be so undeservedly forgotten as the person she really was, constitutes the ultimate tragedy in Daisy's life. Not even the nature of the illness that devastated her later life was known to her surviving contemporaries and family descendants. Only in 1990 did a former resident of Fürstenstein,[3] who worked as an accountant in the billing office for privately practicing physicians in the Silesian city of Liegnitz mention to the author that early in 1940 she had come across a statement by Daisy's physician Dr. Hauffe confirming his patient's medical condition as "multiple sclerosis".

After the war, Hansel never returned to Germany to live, and remained in London for the rest of his life. He never saw his properties again; after 1945 they were all located in Poland. He spent his energies on developing a system of electronically drying lumber imported from Canada. Calling himself Mr. Henry Pless, in his attitudes and way of life, he represented to the end of his life the best traditions of his class. He described them to a student from the University of Leicester, who was "fascinated by titles."

> Let me assure you that there is nothing fascinating in the titles itself. It is the underlying idea and structure behind it and the conduct of the holder that matters.

> A title is conferred by a Monarch only and by its very nature is inalienable. It is conferred on the recipient and his natural or legitimate heirs. Originally conferred on the first holder for particular courage, loyalty or services to the King and Country it also binds and enjoins each following generation

---

3   Frau Käthe Karuga, who was employed with the Privatärztliche Verrechnungsstelle.

to carry on conscientiously in the same tradition adapted to the particular circumstances of that period.

You may well ask what are these traditions? They are traditions derived from the Catholic Europe of many centuries ago, but still as valid for the Christian world of today as they were then. Their purpose was always, as it is today, to use the words of a contemporary historian, to make Christian men – gentle, generous, humble, valiant and chivalrous. Their ideas: justice, mercy and charity.[4]

As Hans Heinrich XVII, Graf von Hochberg, Freiherr zu Fürstenstein und 4. Fürst von Pless,[5] Hansel died in London on January 26, 1984, seven days before his eighty-fourth birthday.

After years of a restless life, Lexel acquired a large tract of land in a remote area of the Island of Mallorca, which he transformed into a picturesque, charming residence. As Fifth Fürst von Pless,[6] Lexel died at the age of seventy-nine on February 22, 1984. He was buried on his beloved Mallorca.

Hansel's and Lexel's nephew Bolko, only son of their brother Bolko who had died in 1936 at Pless, now lives as Graf Bolko von Hochberg und 6. Fürst von Pless[7] in Munich. His sisters live in London and in Germany.

Daisy's cousin, the indefatigable Ena FitzPatrick, returned to France after the war, where she purchased a property in the hills above the Riviera, not far from Daisy's former villa in La Napoule. Ena died in La Ramatuelle in February 1984 within weeks of Hansel's, and days of Lexel's death. Daisy's cousin Douglas FitzPatrick lived at Sheringham Hall in Norfolk until his death in 1986. Daisy's cousin Countess Olivia Larisch von Moennich died 1971 in the Austrian Steiermark.

The last years of Daisy's brother George were marked by the progressive effects of Parkinson's disease. While never very successful as a businessman, George had always been a proud outdoorsman valuing his health above everything else. His biographer Eileen Quelch closed her biography of George Cornwallis-West with these words:

> Spring was approaching, and he knew that never again would he be able to take his rod to the river. He never could bear waiting. On the first Sunday

---

4   Courtesy Prince Hans Heinrich XVII von Pless.

5   Hans Heinrich XVII, Count of Hochberg, Baron of Fürstenstein and Fourth Prince of Pless.

6   Alexander, Count of Hochberg, Baron of Fürstenstein and Fifth Prince of Pless.

7   Bolko, Count of Hochberg, Baron of Fürstenstein and Sixth Prince of Pless.

in April 1951, while his wife and the nurse were at lunch, he rose from his bed and with superhuman strength got down his revolver from a cupboard, loaded it and took the only way out.[8]

On April 3, 1951, THE TIMES published George's obituary.

Moving as he did in the very centre of Edwardian society (his father was a great-grandson of the second Earl De La Warr and two of his sisters became respectively Princess Henry of Pless and Duchess of Westminster), he was led into an extravagance he could ill afford. An attempt to retrieve his fortunes in business proved unsuccessful. ... It is, however, by his deftly written books of reminiscences of the society he knew so well that he will be best remembered.[9]

As the last member of the Cornwallis-West family, Daisy's sister Shelagh died in 1971.

The saddest fate of all fell to Daisy's faithful companion Dolly Crowther. After Daisy's death, Dolly had remained in Waldenburg to the very end of the war. Just before the Red Army entered the city, she joined the millions of refugees streaming westwards in order to escape the advancing Soviet troops. Dolly perished somewhere in Czechoslovakia in early May 1945. She was buried in an unmarked grave at the roadside not far from the area she had hoped to reach, the part of Germany already occupied by the United States Army.

* * *

No less unexpected was the fate of the manors, castles, and villas where Daisy had spent her life.

Considered safe from air-raids, Castle Fürstenstein was converted in 1943 into temporary quarters of the German railway directorate in Breslau. One year later, Fürstenstein was selected as the future *Wald-wiese*, summer residence and guesthouse of Adolf Hitler. A corps of over thirty architects moved into the castle drawing up plans for a complete renovation of its interior in the style of the Third Reich. This required the near total destruction of almost all rooms except the large ball room and the grand staircase leading to it. In the process, the famous terraces were destroyed, buried under several feet of rubble removed from the interior, and the majestic Castle Square became one vast construction site. This work was carried out by more than two thousand slave labourers

---

8   See Eileen Quelch, op. cit., p. 196.

9   THE TIMES, April 3, 1951.

under the Organisation Todt[10] and over one thousand inmates of the nearby concentration camp Gross Rosen. Accompanied by the rumble of the big guns from the nearby front, the insane project continued in full force until the very last days of the war,

Unexplained remains the senseless destruction of Daisy's *Ma Fantaisie* by the Organisation Todt. Its buildings and gardens were levelled to the ground and only the rhododendrons and azaleas among the birch trees and evergreens on the hillsides above the little lake remain as memories of Daisy's favourite retreat. During the last year of the war, Fürstenstein even lost its six-hundred-year-old venerable name; for the few remaining months of the Third Reich, its official name chosen by Adolf Hitler was *Gästehaus Waldwiese.*[11]

After the armistice of May 8, 1945, the castle, which since 1943 had already been the object of large scale theft, was robbed of its few remaining treasurers. It became the defenceless victim of thousands of plunderers. Its famous archive and its library, which had been transferred to some unknown destination before May 1945, were much later discovered in an old Silesian monastery, and are now part of the Polish National Archives in Breslau, since 1945 Wrocław. In the late 1960s, the restoration of Castle Fürstenstein (since June 1945 named Zamek Książ) and its terraces was started, supported by large sums provided by the Polish government and various industrial enterprises. The huge Baroque East-wing, the monumental West-wing with its Emperor's Hall,[12] the vast terraces, and the park are again the destination of hundreds of thousands of tourists. But missing are the former residents, the owners, and their employees who were moved to Germany after the war when Silesia became part of the reborn Poland. With their reminiscences, they alone could have brought the Fürstenstein of old back to life for the tourists wandering through the castle, across its terraces, and among the rhododendrons and azaleas in the park.

As with many other noble residences in Europe, that lost their purpose and raison-d'être with the death of their owners or, in the case of Fürstenstein, with the owners' enforced departure, Zamek Książ remains to this day a museum requiring enormous amounts of money for

---

10 The National Socialist construction units of the Organisation Todt put millions of slave labourers and concentration camp inmates to work throughout the occupied parts of Europe for the completion of countless gigantic construction projects.

11 Guesthouse Forest Lawn.

12 The huge, several stories high Emperor's Hall had never been finished under the Prince of Pless, but it was "in the last minute" completed by Hitler's architects in the ghastly style of his Chancellery in Berlin

its upkeep. As yet, plans to convert its less historically and architecturally valuable parts into a hotel or convention centre have not come to fruition.

Since democracy returned to Poland in 1990, the City of Wałbrzych, as Waldenburg has been called since 1945, has been the owner of Zamek Książ, a formidable obligation for the city whose coal mines were all closed in the 1990s, necessitating the creation of new industries and jobs for the former 18,000 mine employees and their families.

In contrast to Fürstenstein, the fate of Castle Pless was fortunate. Despite heavy fighting at the beginning and at the end of World War II, in September 1939 and again in April 1945, Castle Pless survived without the slightest damage or loss of its treasures; this was a near miracle, likely the consequence of special orders by the high command of the Soviet Army.

Like Fürstenstein, Castle Pless (called Zamek Pszczyna since 1945) is now a museum, visited by hundreds or thousands of tourists every day. The entire castle has been magnificently restored and the history of its past owners has been brought back to life for today's visitor. The until recently locked, seemingly forgotten private apartments of Daisy are now accessible again. When the author first saw them in 1980, they obviously had never been touched since World War I. The faded photographs of Daisy's parents, her sister Shelagh, and her brother George were still placed on the bedside table in the bedroom where Daisy for the last time in her life spent a night on Sunday, August 15, 1915!

Of all of Daisy's homes, her birthplace Castle Ruthin first lost its function as a family residence. After World War I, the castle served as a reconvalescent home for discharged soldiers. One year after Mrs. Cornwallis-West's death, Castle Ruthin was purchased by the British government and continued its function as a resthome for veterans. In 1961, it was turned into a comfortable hotel.

The financial pressures experienced by George Cornwallis-West also necessitated the sale of Newlands. After World War II, the manor house was divided into freeholds whose residents still valiantly struggle to preserve the famous terraces and the park from turning into a wilderness.

Daisy's villa *Les Marguerites* and its garden are filled with the voices and laughter of happy young people. In the late 1950s, after the death of Daisy's friend and neighbour Henry Clewes, Daisy's former villa was carefully restored with funds provided by the Clewes Foundation and opened as a centre for fine arts students from the United States.

In Waldenburg/Wałbrzych, the Castle continued as the administrative seat of all the former Pless mines until their closure; it now serves as headquarters for different industries. In the park still stands the villa that became Daisy's last home; it is now divided into apartments.

For decades after the war, in a search through any of Daisy's former residences, the visitor would look in vain for a memento or a trace that might be proof of Daisy's past presence. Hotel Ruthin has a few pictures on the walls of the lobby. The current residents of Newlands tell the stories they heard about Daisy and the Cornwallis-Wests, but there are no visible traces of them.

Castle Pless was always an exception. Dozens of paintings on the walls of the castle bear witness to its history and to the Princes of Pless and their families; Daisy is commemorated by at least six paintings; and thousands of documents tell their stories in the castle's archives.

Castle Fürstenstein was so devastated that no traces survived of its past occupants. Through the efforts of its present custodians, however, the past history of today's Zamek Książ, of Daisy and her family, and its ancestors has been brought back to life through pictures, books, and the tales of the visitors guides. In the dense forest east of the castle, one still finds the little lake where Daisy and Hansel caught crayfish in happier times. As the sole site in present-day Silesia, the lake has retained, albeit in Polish as *Jeziorko Daisy*, its former name, reminding today's Polish inhabitants of Fürstenstein and its beautiful Princess Daisy, the now legendary Daisy of Pless.

And in Germany, the variety of the rose "Princess von Pless" is still popular among horticulturists and flower lovers. With white petals coloured pink and yellow in the center, the rose was dedicated to the Princess Daisy of Pless by the horticulturist Peter Lambert of Trier in the year 1911.

* * * * * *

Register of German-Polish/ Czech Place Names

Altwasser	Stary Zdrój
Bad Salzbrunn	Szczawno Zdrój
Breslau	Wrocław
Castolowitz	Castolovice
Daisysee	Jeziorko Daisy
Franzensbad	Frantiskovy Lázne
Freiburg	Świebodzice
Fürstenstein (Castle)	Zamek Książ
Fürstenstein (Alte Burg)	Stary Zamek Książ
Fürstensteiner Grund	Wąwóz Książ
Gleiwitz	Gliwice
Gross Rosen	Rogożnica
Halbau	Iłowa
Hellebach	Pełznica
Hirschberg	Jelenia Góra
Hohenfriedeberg	Dobromierz
Karlsbad	Karlovy Vary
Kattowitz	Katowice
Klitschdorf	Kliczków
Kunzendorf	Mokrzeszów
Laisebach	Pełznica
Langenbielau	Bielawa

Lemberg	Lwów/Lviv (Ukranian)
Liebichau	Lubiechów
Liegnitz	Legnica
Maltsch	Malczyce
Marienbad	Mariánske Lázne
Nieder Salzbrunn	Wałbrzych-Szczawienko
Niederschlesien	Dolny Śląsk
Oberschlesien	Górny Śląsk
Oppeln	Opole
Pardubitz	Pardubice
Peterswaldau	Pieszyce
Pless	Pszczyna
Polsnitz (village)	Pełznica
Polsnitz (river)	Pełznica
Promnitz	Paprocany
Ratibor	Racibórz
Riesengebirge	Karkonosze
Rybnik	Rybnik
Salzbach	Szczawnik
Schädlitz	Siedlice
Schmiedeberg	Kowary
Schlesien	Śląsk
Schwarzengraben	Czarny Potok
Schweidnitz	Świdnica
Teplitz	Teplice
Waldenburg	Wałbrzych

Bibliography

d'Abernon Lord. *An Ambassador of Peace* - Lord d'Abernon's Diaries. London: Hodder & Stoughton, 1929.

Arbeiter-Fürsorge auf den Fürstensteiner Gruben Sr. Durchlaucht des Fürsten von Pless, Waldenburg in Schlesien. Waldenburg: 1904.

Baden, Max von, Prinz. *Erinnerungen und Dokumente.* Stuttgart: Deutsche Verlag-sanstalt, 1927.

Barkley, Richard. *The Empress Frederick.* London: Macmillan, 1956.

Bismarck, Otto Fürst von. *Gedanken und Erinnerungen.* Stuttgart: Deutscher Verlag, 1921.

Blücher, Princess Evelyn. *An English Wife in Berlin.* London: Constable, 1920.

Brooke-Sheperd, Gordon. *Uncle of Europe* - The Social and Diplomatic Life of Edward VII. London: Collin, 1975.

Brozek, Andrzej. Piąty Książe Pszczynskich. Warszawa, 1984.

Bülow, Prince Bernhard von. *Memoirs 1903-1909.* Vol II. Trans. F. A. Voight. London: Putnam, 1931.

Churchill, Winston. *Amid These Storms* - Thoughts and Adventures. New York: Scribners, 1932.

_____. *Great Contemporaries.* London: Butterworth, 1937.

Clary Aldringen, Fürst Alfons. *Geschichten eines alten Österreichers.* Frankfurt: Ullstein, 1978.

Cornwallis-West, George. *Edwardian Hey-Days.* London: Putnam, 1930.

Mrs. George Cornwallis-West (Lady Randolph Churchill). *The Reminiscences of Lady Randolph Churchill.* New York: The Century Company, 1909.

Cowles, Virginia. *Edward VII and His Circle.* London: Hamish Hamilton, 1956.

Daily Graphic, The. London.

Ehrenkrook, Georg von (Herausgeber). *Genealogisches Handbuch der Fürstlichen Häuser.* Limburg: A Starke, 1959.

Field, Leslie. *Bendor – The Golden Duke of Windsor.* London: Weidenfeld & Nicolson, 1983.

Freiburger Bote, Der. Freiburg.

Fulford, Roger (Ed.), *Dearest Mama.* Letters between Queen Victoria and the Crown Princess of Prussia 1861-1864. London: Evans Brothers, 1968.

Gerard, James, W. *My Four Years in Germany.* New York: George R. Doran, 1917.

Graff-Höfgen, Gisela. *Schlesische Spitzen* - Eine Dokumentation über die schlesische Klöppel- und Nadelspitzenherstellung. München: Delp, 1974.

Grundmann, Günther. *Erlebter Jahre Widerschein.* München: Berg-stadtverlag, 1972.

Hudson, Manley O. *The Administration of the Prince of Pless in the Twelfth Year of the International Court of Justice.* Concord, N.H.: The American Journal of International Law, Vol. 28, 1934.

Kaeckenbeeck, Georges. *The International Experiment of Upper Silesia.* London: Oxford University Press, 1942.

Koch, W. John. *Schloss Fürstenstein - Erinnerungen an einen schlesischen Adelssitz - Eine Bilddokumentation.* Würzburg: Bergstadtverlag, 1989.

_____. *Daisy von Pless - Fürstliche Rebellin.* Frankfurt/Main, Berlin: Ullstein, 1990.

Krause, Ernst. *Richard Strauss - The Man and His Work.* Trans. by John Coombs. London: Collets, 1955.

Leslie, Anita. *Edwardians in Love.* London: Hutchison, 1972.

Leslie, Seymour. *The Jerome Connexion.* London: John Murray, 1964.

Lichnowsky, Karl Max Fürst von. *Into the Abyss.* New York: Payson & Clark, 1928.

Ludendorff, Erich. *Meine Kriegserinnerungen.* Berlin: Mittler & Sohn, 1926.

Ludwig, Emil. *Kaiser Wilhelm II.* Trans. E.C. Mayne. London and New York: E.C. Putnam's Sons, 1926.

Magnus, Philip. *King Edward the Seventh.* London: John Murray, 1964.

Mann, Golo. *The History of Germany since 1789.* Trans. by Marian Jackson. London: Chatto & Windus, 1968.

Martin, Ralph G. *Jennie - The Life of Lady Randolph Churchill.* Englewood Cliffs, N.J.: Prentice-Hall, 1969.

Mittelschlesische Gebirgszeitung, Waldenburg.

Monts, Anton Graf. *Erinnerungen und Gedanken des Botschafters Anton Graf Monts.* Ed. by Karl Friedrich Thimme. Berlin: Verlag für Kulturpolitik, 1932.

Müller, Georg Alexander von. *The Kaiser and His Court* - The Diaries, Notebooks and Letters of Admiral Georg Alexander von Müller, Chief of the Naval Cabinet, 1914-1918. Ed. by Walter Görlitz. London: Macdonald & Co., 1961.

Müller-Arends, Hans. *Hindenburg in Waldenburg.* Norden: Waldenburger Heimatbote, 1980.

Neubach, Helmut und Zylla, Waldemar (Herausg.). *Oberschlesien im Überblick.* Dülmen: Oberschlesischer Heimatverlag, 1986.

Nicholson, Harold. *On Daisy Pless.* London: The Times, 1959.

Oberschlesische Volksstimme. Gleiwitz.

Päschke, Carl. *Schloss Fürstenstein in Schlesien* - Ein Schauplatz der Götzendämmerung des Dritten Reiches. Zürich: Neue Zürcher Zeitung, 1954.

Pakula, Hannah. *The Last Romantic* - A Biography of Queen Marie of Roumania. New York: Simon & Schuster, 1984.

Patrick-Campbell, Mrs. Stella. *My Life and some Letters.* Toronto: Ryerson Press, 1926.

Pless, Princess Daisy of. *Daisy Princess of Pless by Herself.* London: John Murray, 1928. German edition *Tanz auf dem Vulkan.* Dresden: Carl Reissner, 1929.

_____. *Better Left Unsaid.* New York: Dutton, 1931.

_____. *What I Left Unsaid.* London: Cassell, 1936.

_____. *The Private Diaries of Daisy Princess of Pless 1873-1914.* Ed. by D. Chapman-Huston. London: John Murray, 1950.

_____. *My Diary 1894-1896.* Unpubl.

Ponsonby, Sir Frederick. *Recollections of Three Reigns.* London: Eyre & Spottiswoode, 1951.

Preussen, Viktoria Louise, Prinzessin von. *Ein Leben als Tochter des Kaisers.* Hannover: Göttinger Verlagsanstalt, 1965.

Quelch, Eileen. *Perfect Darling   The Life and Times of George Cornwallis-West.* London: Cecil & Amelia Wolff, 1965.

Radziwill, Princess Catherine. *Memories of Forty Years.* New York & London: Funk & Wagnall, 1915.

Rose, William John. *The Drama of Upper Silesia.* Brattleborough: Stephan Daye Press, 1935.

Sombart, Werner. *Die deutsche Volkswirtschaft im neunzehnten Jahrhundert und im Anfang des zwanzigsten Jahrhunderts.* Berlin: G. Bondi, 1919.

Spyra, Bronisława. *Państwowe Archiwum Książat Pszczynskich 1287-1945.* Łódz: Wydawnictwo Naukowe, 1973.

Stein, Erwin. *Waldenburg in Schlesien.* Berlin Friedenau: Deutscher Kommunal-verlag, 1925.

Szyperski, Alfons. *Wałbrzych i Jego Zabytki.* Wałbrzych: Towarzystwo Kultury, 1974.

Tirpitz, Alfred von. *Erinnerungen.* Leipzig: Koehler, 1919.

Times, The. London.

Treutler, Alfred von. *Die graue Exzellenz.* Herausg. Karl-Heinz Jansen. Frankfurt: Ullstein, 1971.

Tuchman, Barbara W.. *The Zimmermann Telegram.* New York: Dell, 1958.

Vierhaus, Rudolf (Herausg.). *Am Hofe der Hohenzollern – Aus dem Tagebuch der Baronin Spitzemberg 1865-1914.* Göttingen: Vandenhoek & Ruprecht, 1964.

Warwick, Frances Countess of. *Afterthoughts.* From Martin, Ralph C. *Jennie - The Life of Lady Randolph Churchill.* Englewood Cliffs, N.J.: Prentice-Hall, 1972.

Wilhelm II. *The Kaiser's Memoirs – Wilhelm II, Emperor of Germany - 1888-1918.* Trans. by Thomas Ybarra. New York & London: Harper Brothers, 1922.

Weigelt, Carl. *Die Grafen von Hochberg.* Breslau: Wilhelm Gottlieb Korn, 1896.

Willis, Edward F. *Prince Lichnowsky – Ambassador of Peace.* Berkeley: University of California Press, 1942.

Wood, Martin. *Sargent.* London: T.C. and E.C. Jack, no date.

Young, Harry. *Prince Lichnowsky and the Great War.* University of Georgia Press, 1977.

Zedlitz-Trützschler, Graf Robert. *Zwölf Jahre am deutschen Kaiserhof.* Stuttgart: Deutsche Verlagsanstalt, 1924.

Zivier, Georg. *Festschrift zum 400jährigen Bestehen der Standesherrschaft Fürstenstein.* Kattowitz: 1905.

No author. *Eine Abrechnung mit den Fürstlich Pless'schen Grubenverwaltungen Nied-erschlesiens.* Bochum: Hausmann & Co., 1911.

* * * * * *

Photo Credits

Index